HISTORICAL ROOTS OF THE OLD TESTAMENT (1200–63 BCE)

Society of Biblical Literature

Biblical Encyclopedia

Leo G. Perdue, Biblical Encyclopedia Series Editor
Walter Dietrich, Biblische Enzyklopädie Series Editor

HISTORICAL ROOTS OF THE OLD TESTAMENT (1200–63 BCE)

By

Richard D. Nelson

SBL Press
Atlanta

Copyright © 2014 by SBL Press

All rights reserved. No part of this work may be reproduced or transmitted in any form or by any means, electronic or mechanical, including photocopying and recording, or by means of any information storage or retrieval system, except as may be expressly permitted by the 1976 Copyright Act or in writing from the publisher. Requests for permission should be addressed in writing to the Rights and Permissions Office, SBL Press, 825 Houston Mill Road, Atlanta, GA 30329 USA.

Library of Congress Cataloging-in-Publication Data

Nelson, Richard D. (Richard Donald), 1945–.
  Historical roots of the Old Testament (1200–63 BCE) / by Richard D. Nelson.
      p. cm. — (Society of Biblical Literature Biblical Encyclopedia Series ; Number 13)
  Includes bibliographical references and indexes.
  ISBN 978-1-62837-005-8 (paper binding : alk. paper) — ISBN 978-1-62837-006-5 (electronic format) — ISBN 978-1-62837-007-2 (hardcover binding : alk. paper)
  1. Bible. Old Testament—Sources—Criticism, interpretation, etc. I. Title.
  BS1171.3.N45 2014
  221.6'6—dc23   2014018404

Printed on acid-free, recycled paper conforming to
ANSI/NISO Z39.48-1992 (R1997) and ISO 9706:1994
standards for paper permanence.

Contents

Preface vii
Abbreviations ix

1. The Emergence of Israel (ca. 1200–ca. 1000 BCE) 1
   1.0. Summary 2
   1.1. Breakdown of the Late Bronze Age 3
   1.2. The Setting: Geography and Economics 9
   1.3. The Emergence of Israel 12
   1.4. The Philistines 32
   1.5. Literature of the Period 37

2. State Formation (to ca. 930) 43
   2.0. Summary 44
   2.1. Chiefdom and State 45
   2.2. Saul 49
   2.3. David 53
   2.4. The Vision of a United Kingdom 58
   2.5. Solomon 60
   2.6. Chronology and Archaeology 73
   2.7. Literature of the Period 76

3. The Kingdoms of Israel and Judah (ca. 930–720) 81
   3.0. Summary 82
   3.1. Kings: Sources and Reliability 84
   3.2. Chronology 90
   3.3. Judah and Israel until Omri 96
   3.4. Israel and Judah during the Omri Dynasty 103
   3.5. Israel and Judah during the Jehu Dynasty 116
   3.6. The Downfall of Israel 127

CONTENTS

	3.7.	Archaeology and Epigraphy	136
	3.8.	Literature of the Period	137
4.	Judah in the Assyrian and Babylonian Periods (720–539)............141		
	4.0.	Summary	142
	4.1.	Hezekiah (ca. 726–697)	144
	4.2.	Manasseh (ca. 697–642) and Amon (642–640)	151
	4.3.	Josiah (640–609)	154
	4.4.	Jehoahaz (609) and Jehoiakim (609–598)	161
	4.5.	Jehoiachin (598–597)	162
	4.6.	Zedekiah (597–586)	163
	4.7.	The Babylonian Period	169
	4.8.	Documentary Finds	173
	4.9.	Literature of the Period	175
5.	Yehud and Persia (539–330)..183		
	5.0.	Summary	184
	5.1.	Cyrus II (559–522)	185
	5.2.	The Persian Empire	187
	5.3.	Sources Used in Ezra-Nehemiah	193
	5.4.	The Early Restoration Period: 539–515	196
	5.5.	The Later Restoration Period (515–ca. 430)	203
	5.6.	Jews in Yehud and Egypt from Darius II to Darius III (424–331)	208
	5.7.	Literature of the Period	214
6.	The Hellenistic Period (330–63) 223		
	6.0.	Summary	224
	6.1.	Alexander the Great (336–323)	225
	6.2.	The Successors of Alexander	230
	6.3.	Palestine under the Ptolemies	233
	6.4.	Palestine under the Seleucids	236
	6.5.	The Maccabees	241
	6.6.	The Hasmonean Period	252
	6.7.	Literature of the Period	257

Ancient Sources Index...265
Modern Authors Index...284
Subject Index..286

Preface

It is to John Bright (1908–1995) that I owe my first real exposure to the demanding task of recovering and recounting the historical context of the Old Testament. In 1971 he served as my advisor for a master's-level thesis on the Zion psalms. He was the first to make me fully appreciate that the *map* offered by the Bible by no means represents the actual *territory* of history. His guidance concerning the range and interpretation of primary sources and his insistence on rigorous and logically defensible methodology proved to be invaluable for my later scholarship and teaching. William H. Hallo, in a 1980 summer seminar sponsored by National Endowment for the Humanities, introduced me to the riches of Mesopotamian history and culture and to his *comparative method*, which coordinates source documents and the Bible. With an understanding that both the conclusions and the flaws of this present work are entirely my own, it is dedicated to these two sages.

Abbreviations

ABRL	Anchor Bible Reference Library
ADPV	Abhandlungen des Deutschen Palästina-Vereins
Ag. Ap.	Flavius Josephus, *Against Apion*
ANET	*Ancient Near Eastern Texts Relating to the Old Testament*. Edited by James B. Pritchard. 3rd ed. Princeton: Princeton University Press, 1969.
Ant.	Flavius Josephus, *Antiquities of the Jews*
ASOR	American Schools of Oriental Research
b.	Babylonian Talmud
BBRSup	Bulletin for Biblical Research Supplements
BibOr	Biblica et orientalia
BZAW	Beihefte zur Zeitschrift für die alttestamentliche Wissenschaft
CHANE	Culture and History of the Ancient Near East
COS	*Context of Scripture*. Edited by W. W. Hallo and K. L. Younger. 3 vols. Leiden: Brill, 1997–2002.
BAS	Book of the Acts of Solomon
DH	Deuteronomistic History, Deuteronomistic Historian
ESV	English Standard Version
EV	English version
FAT	Forschungen zum Alten Testament
Hist.	Herodotus, *Histories*
IKL	Israel King List
JKL	Judah King List
J.W.	Flavius Josephus, *Jewish War*
JSJSup	Supplements to the Journal for the Study of Judaism
JSOTSup	Journal for the Study of the Old Testament Supplement Series
LC	Low Chronology
LB	Late Bronze Age

LHB/OTS	Library of Hebrew Bible/Old Testament Studies
LSTS	Library of Second Temple Studies
LXX	Septuagint
m.	Mishnah
MB	Middle Bronze Age
Menaḥ.	Menaḥot
MT	Masoretic Text
NAB	New American Bible
NASB	New American Standard Bible
NIV	New International Version
NJB	New Jerusalem Bible
NJPS	*Tanak: The Holy Scriptures: The New JPS Translation according to the Traditional Hebrew Text*
NRSV	New Revised Standard Version
OBO	Orbis Biblicus et Orientalis
OLA	Orientalia Lovaniensia Analecta
OTL	Old Testament Library
Qidd.	Qiddušin
Roš Haš.	Roš Haššanah
Sanh.	Sanhedrin
SBLABS	Society of Biblical Literature Archaeology and Biblical Studies
SBLSBL	Society of Biblical Literature Studies in Biblical Literature
SBLSymS	Society of Biblical Literature Symposium Series
SemeiaSt	Semeia Studies
SNTSMS	Society for New Testament Study Monograph Series
SOTSMS	Society for Old Testament Study Monograph Series
t.	Tosefta
VTSup	Vetus Testamentum Supplements
y.	Jerusalem Talmud
Yebam.	Yebamot

1. The Emergence of Israel (ca. 1200–ca. 1000 BCE)

Banks, Diane. *Writing the History of Israel* (LHBOTS 438; New York: T&T Clark, 2006). **Barr**, James. *History and Ideology in the Old Testament: Biblical Studies at the End of a Millennium* (New York: Oxford University Press, 2000). **Cohen**, Raymond, and Raymond **Westbrook**, eds. *Amarna Diplomacy: The Beginnings of International Relations* (Baltimore: Johns Hopkins University Press, 2000). **Davies**, Philip R. *The Origins of Biblical Israel* (LHB/OTS 485; New York: T&T Clark, 2007). **Day**, John, ed. *In Search of Pre-exilic Israel: Proceedings of the Oxford Old Testament Seminar* (London: T&T Clark, 2004). **Dever**, William G. *What Did the Biblical Writers Know and When Did They Know It? What Archaeology Can Tell Us about the Reality of Ancient Israel* (Grand Rapids: Eerdmans, 2001). **Dickenson**, Oliver. *The Aegean from Bronze Age to Iron Age: Continuity and Change between the Twelfth and Eight Centuries BC* (New York: Routledge, 2006). **Faust**, Avraham. *Israel's Ethnogenesis: Settlement, Interaction, Expansion and Resistance* (London: Equinox, 2006). **Finkelstein**, Israel, and Amihai **Mazar**. *The Quest for the Historical Israel: Debating Archaeology and the History of Early Israel* (SBLABS 17; Atlanta: Society of Biblical Literature, 2007). **Fritz**, Volkmar. *The Emergence of Israel in the Twelfth and Eleventh Centuries B.C.E.* (Biblical Encyclopedia 2; Atlanta: Society of Biblical Literature, 2011). **Gass**, Erasmus. *Die Moabiter—Geschichte und Kultur eines ostjordanisches Volkes im. 1. Jahrtausend v. Chr* (ADPV 38; Wiesbaden: Harrassowitz, 2009). **Garbani**, Giovanni. *Myth and History in the Bible* (JSOTSup 362; New York: Continuum, 2004). **Grabbe**, Lester L., ed. *Israel in Transition: From Late Bronze II to Iron IIa (ca. 1250–850 B.C.E.)* (2 vols.; LHB/OTS 491, 521; New York: T&T Clark, 2008–2010). **Hess**, Richard S., Gerald A. Klingbeil, and Paul J. Ray Jr., eds. *Critical Issues* *in Early Israelite History* (BBRsup 3; Winona Lake, Ind.: Eisenbrauns, 2008). **Killebrew**, Ann E. *Biblical Peoples and Ethnicity: An Archaeological Study of Egyptians, Canaanites, Philistines, and Early Israel 1300–1100 B.C.E.* (SBLABS 9; Atlanta: Society of Biblical Literature, 2005. **Killebrew**, Ann E., and Gunnar **Lehmann**, eds. *The Philistines and Other Sea Peoples in Text and Archaeology* (SBLABS 15; Atlanta: Society of Biblical Literature, 2013). **King**, Philip, and Lawrence E. **Stager**. *Life in Biblical Israel* (Louisville: Westminster John Knox, 2001). **Liverani**, Mario. *International Relations in the Ancient Near East, 1600–1100 BC* (New York: Palgrave, 2001). **Manassa**, Colleen. *The Great Karnak Inscription of Merneptah: Grand Strategy in the Thirteenth Century B.C.* (Yale Egyptological Studies 5; New Haven: Yale Egyptological Seminar, 2003). **Miller**, Robert D., II. *Chieftains of the Highland Clans: A History of Israel in the Twelfth and Eleventh Centuries B.C.* (Grand Rapids: Eerdmans, 2005). **Mobley**, Gregory. *The Empty Men: The Heroic Tradition of Ancient Israel* (ABRL; New York: Doubleday, 2005). **Nahkai**, Beth Alpert. *Archaeology and the Religions of Canaan and Israel* (ASOR Books 7; Boston: American Schools of Oriental Research, 2001). **Nelson**, Richard D. *Joshua: A Commentary* (OTL; Louisville: Westminster John Knox, 1997). **Oren**, Eliezer D., ed. *The Sea Peoples and Their World: A Reassessment* (Philadelphia: University of Pennsylvania, The University Museum, 2000). **Pfoh**, Emanuel. *The Emergence of Israel in Ancient Palestine: Historical and Anthropological Perspectives* (Oakville, Conn.: Equinox, 2009). **Van De Mieroop**, Marc. *A History of the Ancient Near East ca. 3000–323 B.C.* (Blackwell History of the Ancient World; Oxford: Blackwell, 2004). **Yasur-Landau**, Assaf. *The Philistines and Aegean Migration at the End of the Late Bronze Age* (Cambridge: Cambridge University Press, 2010.

1.0. Summary

The start of the Iron Age in Palestine is conventionally dated to 1200 BCE. During the thirteenth century, the international system of large states and urban centers that had characterized the Late Bronze Age began to break down. A period of chaos, economic decline, and population displacement ensued. Although its origins are unclear, Israel was already a people established in Palestine by the late thirteenth century. A newly established array of small, unwalled settlements in the central highlands appeared in the late thirteenth and early twelfth centuries. These are almost certainly to be associated with Israel's beginnings. These settlements appeared at an earlier time and were more concentrated in the northern hill country (Manasseh, Ephraim) than further south (Judah). At this initial stage, Israel was a loose affiliation of kinship-based clans organized into tribes for the purpose of territorial defense. Military leadership and intertribal cooperation surfaced on an impromptu basis only when needed. The consciousness of any connection among central and northern elements and those to the south (eventually Judah) was weak.

According to Egyptian inscriptional evidence, Philistines from the Aegean settled on the southern coastal area around 1175. The generally accepted ceramic chronology also places the initial phase of their settlement in the first half of twelfth century. The Philistine presence was characterized by Monochrome pottery, locally produced imitations of styles from Cyprus. There is controversy about the pottery chronology, however, and some have advocated an initial settlement date only after 1140. If one does not accept this lower chronology, then a breakdown of Egypt's control of Palestine in about 1140–1130 can be coordinated with a second, expansive phase of Philistine colonization in the second half of the twelfth and early eleventh centuries. This second period is typified by Philistine Bichrome ware. As heirs of former Egyptian hegemony, the better-organized and militarily sophisticated Philistine city-states increasingly sought to dominate Israel. In the latter half of Iron Age I (beginning about 1140), Palestine's urban centers reemerged, for example Hazor, Megiddo, Tell el-Farʿah (north), and Beth-shean.

A lack of consensus within the archaeological community about the chronology of the Iron I and early Iron II periods muddles attempts to correlate epigraphic evidence with information from excavations. Another complication for the historian is that individual archaeologists use varying schemes for these periods. Sometime Iron I is divided into Iron IA and IB. The period from about 1000 to 586 is divided by some into Iron II and Iron III, by others into Iron IIA and IIB, and by others into Iron IIA, IIB, and IIC.

1.1. Breakdown of the Late Bronze Age

1.1.1. Large Interrelated States

In contrast to the upheaval that would characterize the inauguration of the Iron Age, the Late Bronze Age was a period of comparative stability. From about 1500 up until about 1200, a system of major states organized western Asia and the eastern Mediterranean. These states were in contact with each other through trade, warfare, and diplomacy. Trade circled the eastern Mediterranean, branching inland into western Asia. Diplomacy involved the interchange of letters, gifts, wives, and treaties. Egypt controlled Syria-Palestine. The Hittite Empire covered Asia Minor. It had inherited control of the north Syrian states from Mitanni, which had been brought low by Hittite and then Assyrian victories. The Middle Assyrian Empire and Babylonia divided Mesopotamia. The eastern end of this regional system was anchored by Elam. To the west was the Mycenaean world of cities associated by common culture and maritime contact. Although sometimes these large cultural or political regions fought with each other, this configuration offered protection from outside invaders and made relative stability and prosperity possible.

In the crisis of political, social, and economic breakdown that marked the end of LB, events in Egypt affected Palestine directly and immediately. Nevertheless, developments in Asia Minor, Syria, and Mesopotamia set in motion historical forces that would influence life in Palestine for centuries. Dates for ancient western Asian rulers and events before the start of the twelfth century are contested, but many historians follow a Middle Chronology that fixes the fall of Babylon to the Hittite Mursili I (ca. 1620–1590) to 1595. The chronology for New Kingdom Egypt is also a matter of serious debate, especially before Ramesses II.

Egypt. From the mid-seventeenth to the mid-sixteenth centuries, the rulers of the Fifteenth Dynasty in Lower Egypt were Asiatics, many with Northwest Semitic names. Native Egyptians referred to them as Hyksos, "foreign rulers." These Semitic rulers were expelled in about 1550 in favor of the native Eighteenth Dynasty. During the fifteenth century, Egypt and Mitanni competed for control of Syria-Palestine, first engaging in warfare (Thutmose III [ca. 1479–1426]; Amenhotep II [ca. 1426–1400]) and then maintaining peaceful relations. This period of peace resulted from a treaty made by Thutmose IV (ca. 1400–1390) and was maintained later through diplomatic marriages. By the reign of the assertive Seti I (Nineteenth Dynasty; ca. 1290–1279), the Hittites had replaced Mitanni as Egypt's rival in Syria-Palestine.

Babylon. A raid on Babylon about 1595 by the Hittite king Mursili I set the stage for eventual control by foreign Kassites, a situation that lasted through the sixteenth to mid-twelfth centuries. The Second Dynasty of

1. THE EMERGENCE OF ISRAEL (CA. 1200–CA. 1000 BCE)

Isin emerged with the end of Kassite rule in 1155. Its most energetic king, Nebuchadnezzar I (1125–1104), triggered a period of revival.

Mitanni. The same Hittite aggression that provided an opportunity for the Kassites also created space for the establishment of a Mitanni kingdom in northern Mesopotamia and Syria. Hurrians, originally from around Lake Van in Armenia, had migrated into northern Mesopotamia and Syria-Palestine. The campaigns of Mursili I against Aleppo and Babylon allowed these Hurrians to become dominant in a Mitanni confederation that flourished down to about 1330, when it succumbed to Hittite and then Assyrian attacks.

Assyria. Mitanni had reduced Assyria to vassal status. However, Hittite expansion under Suppiluliuma I (ca. 1344–1322) undermined Mitanni and reversed the situation. This opened the way to the expansionistic Middle Assyrian period. Assur-ubalit I (1363–1328) won independence from Babylon. He, Adad-nirari I (1305–1274), and Shalmaneser I (1273–1244) expanded westward into territory formerly controlled by Mitanni. Tukulti-ninurta I (1243–1207) moved northward into territory controlled by the Hittites and sacked Babylon in 1225, further expanding Assyrian hegemony. However, revolt marred the latter part of his reign. He was murdered by one of his sons, and decline set in. Babylon regained its independence. Aramaean tribes began to move into parts of Syria.

Hittites. The Hittite Empire flourished in the fourteenth and thirteenth centuries, reaching its high point when Suppiluliuma I took over the previous dominion of Mitanni. The inevitable conflict with Egypt climaxed when his grandson Muwatalli II (ca. 1295–1272) fought with Ramesses II (ca. 1279–1213) at Qadesh on the Orontes (the latter king's year 5; 1274). Eventually a treaty between Hattusili III (ca. 1267–1237) and Ramesses II (in his year 21; 1259) regularized the border situation and led to a period of stability. The Hittite state fell into internal decline and collapsed as the LB period drew to a close. Former vassal states such as Hamath and Aleppo in northern Syria continued as Neo-Hittite (or Syro-Hittite) states into the first millennium.

1.1.2. Egyptian Domination of Palestine (ca. 1550–1200)

Control of Canaan (the name presumably means "lowland") as a land bridge for trade and military action was important to Egypt. Canaan provided a buffer against northern enemies. The Execration texts (mid-twentieth and late nineteenth centuries; *ANET*, 328–29; *COS* 1.31:50–52) reveal numerous cities in Retenu (Syria-Palestine) within what Egypt conceived of as its sphere of interest. Significantly, only Jerusalem and Shechem are mentioned as highland sites. This pattern of two power centers in the hill country of Palestine would continue in the Amarna letters and then in the two Iron Age kingdoms of Judah and Israel. The colorful Tale of Sinuhe demonstrates the importance of Canaan during Egypt's Middle Kingdom. However, it is clearly fictional and cannot be relied on for an accurate description of the situation there (*ANET*, 18–23; *COS* 1.38:77–82). The forest resources of Lebanon were vital for shipbuilding and construction, something reflected in a literary text reporting the Twentieth Dynasty expedition of Wen-Amon to secure wood for the boat of Amun-Re (about 1100; *ANET*, 25–29; *COS* 1.41:89–93; also see *ANET*, 243). This narrative recounts believable details about the social situation, the practice of prophecy, and the presence of the Sea People Tjeker at Dor.

At the start of Dynasty Eighteen, Ahmose (ca. 1539–1514) expelled the Hyksos (*ANET*, 233–34, 554–55; *COS* 2.1:5–7), conquering the Hyksos fortress city Sharuhen somewhere in southern Palestine (assigned to Simeon, Josh 19:6). Subsequent incursions into Palestine by Thutmose III (1479–1426; *ANET*, 234–41; *COS* 2.2A–C:7–19; see also *COS* 2.3:19–23) and Amenhotep II (ca. 1420–1400) led to conflict first with Mitanni and eventually the Hittites. In reporting the first of his sixteen or seventeen campaigns in Syria-Palestine, Thutmose III boasted about his battle with Canaanite forces at Megiddo. After a seven-month siege he was able to conquer the city itself. A literary tale set in his reign recounts how one Djehuty captured Joppa through a ruse reminiscent of the Trojan horse (*ANET*, 22–23). Reacting to trouble stirred up by Mitanni, Amenhotep II campaigned deep into Syria-Palestine, at one point crossing the Orontes (*ANET*, 245–48; *COS* 2.3:19–23). Thutmose IV (ca. 1400–1390) achieved peace through the first of a series of diplomatic marriages with daughters of the kings of Mitanni (e.g., *COS* 3.92D:239–40). During the reign of Amenhotep III (ca. 1390–1353), all of Canaan seemed securely within the Egyptian sphere of influence. Improved diplomatic relations with Mitanni meant that Egyptian control of Palestine could be achieved through a loose system of dependent city-states governed by kings. In Canaan proper there was only a single governor, based in Gaza, and small Egyptian garrisons in Joppa, Aphek, and Beth-shean. Few cities had walls in LB Palestine, indicating the absence of major threats.

Beginning with the accession of Amenhotep IV (Akhenaten; ca. 1353–1336), internal political and religious upheaval in Egypt led to a foreign policy crisis. While Akhenaten was preoccupied with religious reforms at home, the status quo in Syria, Palestine, and Phoenicia became destabilized. As the Eighteenth Dynasty drew to a close, the Hittites under Suppiluliuma I broke the power of Mitanni and inherited its north Syrian vassals. Egypt lost Qadesh in western Syria and the new kingdom of Amurru to the Hittites. This increased threat from the Hittites created unrest among Egypt's vassals in Canaan. The Amarna letters (*ANET*, 483–90; *COS* 3.92:237–42) reveal the disordered situation. These diplomatic exchanges indicate that the power centers of Canaan were Ashkelon, Lachish, Gath, Gezer, Megiddo, Achshaph, Shimʻon (biblical Shimron; Josh 19:15), Acco, Rehob, and Hazor. These cities were concentrated in the lowlands along the coast, in Jezreel, and in the Jordan Valley. Each local king controlled surrounding areas and their populations. In addition, two hill-country power centers, Jerusalem (under Abdi-Heba) and Shechem (ruled by Labayu), governed larger, more sparsely populated areas. This political configuration would reappear in the kingdoms of Judah and Israel four centuries later.

Under the shadow of menacing Hittite power and in a context of discontented social elements, these local kings competed with each other for the Pharaoh's attention, regularly accusing each other of disloyalty. The small scale of the contest is indicated by suggestions that fifty or one hundred troops would be enough to stabilize a given situation. The heterogeneous population of contemporary Canaan is reflected in the record of earlier campaigns by Amenhotep II: *maryannu* (the chariot warrior class), Canaanites, Habiru/Apiru, Shasu, Syrians, and Nagasuites (*ANET*, 245–47; *COS* 2.3:19–22). Internal unrest centered on the threat presented by antagonistic groups termed Habiru (Egyptian: Apiru). This term designated a social rather than ethnic classification. Habiru were marginalized elements who operated outside the direct control of the city-state kings. In the forested hill country and arid regions, they coexisted with nomadic pastoralists. In the eyes of Pharaoh's vassal kings these Habiru had the potential to foment or catalyze local peasant uprisings, and so the kings repeatedly complained about what they saw as the pharaoh "keeping silent" in the face of crises. The linguistically questionable identification of the generalized social category Habiru with "Hebrew" remains a matter of discussion. In any case this suggestion provides little warrant for detecting the group later designated by Merneptah as Israel in an Amarna age context.

The pharaohs of Dynasty Nineteen were more assertive in Palestine. Seti I (ca. 1290–1279) reestablished Egyptian authority by pacifying troublesome Shasu pastoralists. Reacting to aggression by the kings of Pahil (Pella) and Hamath, he reoccupied Beth-shean and rescued his vassal city of Rehob. Intriguingly, a stela of Seti I from Beth-shean mentions a warlike group of Apiru at Mount Yarmutu, that is Jarmuth, north of Beth-shean in later Issachar (Josh 21:29; *ANET*, 255; *COS* 2.4D:27–28). Seti I was temporarily able to restore Qadesh on the Orontes and Amurru to Egyptian hegemony.

Ramesses II (ca. 1279–1213) reacted when Qadesh allied itself with the Hittites. In his year 5 he claims a major victory there over Muwatalli II (1295–1272), supposedly the result of his personal bravery and astute tactical judgment (*ANET*, 255–58; *COS* 2.5A–B:32–40). The battle of Qadesh was not really the triumph alleged by Ramesses, but at least his army was able to withdraw intact from a dangerous situation. Muwatalli held on to Qadesh and reconquered Amurru. In the end, however, neither side could prevail.

Eventually the growing Assyrian threat to the Hittites, ironically made possible by the Hittites' own weakening of Mitanni power, led to a peace treaty between Ramesses II and Hattusili III (1267–1237). This is extant in both Egyptian and Hittite versions (*ANET*, 199–203). The diplomatic relationship was later reinforced by the marriage of Ramesses II to a Hittite princess. Ongoing Hittite preoccupation with the Assyrian menace allowed Egypt to maintain control of Canaan. To consolidate this, Ramesses II built a string of fortresses near the Egyptian border and Per-Ramses in the delta (*ANET*, 470–71; cf. Exod 1:11). His son Merneptah (ca. 1213–1203) reasserted dominance in Canaan. He was able to fend off attacks from Libyans in an alliance with Sea People raiders and crushed a revolt in Nubia. Egyptian power quickly declined after him, however, and the Nineteenth Dynasty concluded with four short, troubled reigns.

The social and ethnic situation in Canaan was complex. Sources refer to nomadic pastoralist groups under the name Suteans (Akkadian texts) or Shasu (Egyptian texts). Several letters copied as school texts and originating in the Nineteenth and Twentieth Dynasties evidence what native Egyptians considered disconcerting realities about Canaan.

- Anastasi Papyrus I, a satirical letter from the time of Ramesses II, purportedly from an official to a scribe, depicts the land

and people of Syria-Palestine. It describes geography and roads and warns of dangerous nomads (*ANET*, 475–79; *COS* 3.2:9–14).
- Stress and conflict with nomadic groups is also reflected in Anastasi III, notes of an official stationed on the northeastern frontier (*ANET*, 258–59; *COS* 3.3:15).
- Anastasi VI represents a frontier official's report on Shasu seeking entrance into Egypt for economic reasons (*ANET*, 259; *COS* 3.5:16–17).

1.2. The Setting: Geography and Economics

1.2.1. Geography as Destiny

The history of Palestine was shaped by its location as the land bridge between Egypt and lands further north: Syria, Asia Minor, and Mesopotamia. Occupying a narrow strip between the Mediterranean and the Arabian Desert to the east, Palestine is naturally oriented north and south. The territory is circumscribed on the south by the Sinai Desert and to the north by the Lebanon and Anti-Lebanon Mountains. The major north-south route through the land bridge ran inland of the coast to avoid sandy and marshy terrain. Forced even further inland by the Mount Carmel range, the route passed by Megiddo and then split. A northwestern branch followed the coast up to Phoenicia, and a northeastern branch passed via Hazor to Damascus. A minor local route ran along the central ridge of the highlands from Beersheba through Hebron, Jerusalem, and Shechem. A second ancient trade route ran along the plateau east of the Jordan River from the Gulf of Aqabah to Damascus and points north.

Palestine experiences a rapid transition in terrain and climate from west to east. It is segmented into a coastal plain, the central highlands and Galilee, the abrupt depression of the Jordan Valley, and the plateau of the Transjordan. Much of the coastal plain between Mount Carmel and Joppa, anciently termed Sharon, was marshy and forested. Further south, the transitional foothills were known as the Shephelah. Four valleys through the Shephelah lead up eastward into Judah and were strategically important for the defense of Jerusalem. To the north the Aijalon Valley (the ascent of Beth-horon) follows a geologic fault up through Lower and Upper Beth-horon to north of Jerusalem. This approach was defended by

Gezer. South of this approach, a route runs up the Sorek Valley, overlooked by Beth-shemesh. A third route, the Valley of Elah, runs from Gath (Tell es-Safi) via Socoh and Azekah to west of Bethlehem. It was guarded by Khirbet Qeiyafa (perhaps Shaaraim). The southernmost strategic route ascends into the Hebron hills. It was protected in ancient times by Lachish.

The highlands are divided by the fertile east-west Jezreel Valley into Galilee to the north and the central hill country to the south. Galilee consists of rocky terrain, with upper (northern) Galilee being more rugged than lower Galilee, which features fertile valleys. Its northern location meant that Galilee was open to influence and (sometimes) control by Phoenicia and Syria. The Jezreel (Esdraelon) Valley is wide and relatively level, rendering it both a rich agricultural region and a major travel route for trade and invading armies. The presence of the port of Acco at its northwestern end and the overland communication hub of Megiddo provided a gateway that opened the northern hill country (eventually the kingdom of Israel) to the benefits and dangers of international interests and influences.

To the south of Jezreel rise the central highlands, biblically labeled the hill country of Ephraim and then later Samaria, following the Assyrian provincial designation. The most significant city in this region was Shechem, located at the confluence of the central north-south ridge road and routes to the north and west. Shechem lay within the strategic pass between the two summits Gerizim and Ebal. No natural boundary divides the central highlands of Israel from those of Judah. However, the transitional area occupied by the tribe of Benjamin was strategically and economically important to whatever political entity controlled Jerusalem. Southern Benjamin was inherently part of Jerusalem's economic zone, and both northern (via the central ridge route) and western (via the Aijalon Valley) approaches to the metropolis ran through Benjamin.

The Jordan River meanders through a deep valley (Arabah), which is generally fertile in its northern reaches. Farther south the Arabah becomes desert, although a perennial spring makes Jericho a lush place for settlement. Wadi Far'ah provided the main route from the northern part of the valley westward up into the central hill country at Tirzah (Tell el-Far'ah North). Farther south, gorges formed by geological fault lines lead up from Jericho, one directly to Jerusalem.

East of the Great Rift Valley (Jordan Valley) rises a tableland, in recent times designated as Transjordan. Rainfall makes cultivation and stockraising possible until precipitation tapers off to the east into desert. The portion north of the Yarmuk River was called Bashan, and the central portion was designated Gilead. Both territories were considered by Israelites to be part of their patrimony. This created conflict with Ammon, Moab, and especially Damascus. Four waterways cut up the area east of the Jordan. The Yarmuk runs into the Jordan just south of the Sea of Galilee and divides Bashan from Gilead. Farther south, the Jabbok (Wadi Zerqa) drains Gilead. The Arnon (Wadi Mujib) runs into the Dead Sea at about its midpoint. It served as a disputed frontier between Israel and Moab. The Zered (Wadi Hesa) runs into the south end of the Dead Sea and seems to have been considered the border between Moab and Edom. The substantial gorges of each of these watercourses forced the Transjordanian trade route eastward so that it passed through Kir-hareseth, Dibon, Aroer, Heshbon, Rabbath-ammon, Ramoth-gilead, and Ashtaroth.

1.2.2. A Mixed Agrarian Economy

Predominant wind patterns blowing from northwest to southeast generate a gradation in rainfall along the north-south axis. Precipitation that is more abundant causes areas to the north to be more prosperous than those to the south. This drop-off in precipitation sharply increases south of the mountainous saddle of Benjamin territory that formed the frontier between Israel and Judah. As one moves south, Judah becomes increasingly more arid until the Negev (meaning "dry land") begins at Beer-sheba.

There are two seasons, a hot, dry summer and a cooler, wet winter. October early rains soften the ground for plowing, followed by sowing and planting. This stage took about four months. Rain continues during the growing season until the late rains of April and early May. Weeding was the major preoccupation during the growing season. Flax was gathered. The grain harvest began with barley followed by wheat and took about two months. This was followed by threshing and winnowing. Vines were pruned. Then came the harvest of grapes and summer fruits such as dates and figs, and finally olives. The harvest order of barley, wheat, grapes, and olives is described in y. Yebam. 15:2. Basic staples were bread, oil, and wine, supplemented by dates, figs, and legumes (chickpeas and lentils). The high value-to-weight ratio of oil and wine allowed them to be traded beyond the immediate local area. In addition to cultivation, raising sheep and goats added to food security and provided textiles, milk, manure, and meat for communal sacrifices. Oxen were valued as traction animals for pulling plows and threshing sledges.

The agricultural round of a mixed economy, reflected in the festivals of Israel's religious calendar, is illustrated by the tenth-century Gezer Calendar (*ANET*, 320; *COS* 2.85:222). This inscription attempts to coordinate the natural cycle of agricultural activities with lunar months. Because these two ways of experiencing time are fundamentally incommensurable, the text demonstrates interaction between rural thought patterns and an urban need to schedule tax payments and communal labor. A plausible interpretation of this schematic agricultural "to do list" begins with harvesting olives:

- two months of (olive) harvest (October, November)
- two months of planting (December, January)
- two months of late sowing (February, March)
- a month of cutting flax (April)
- a month of harvesting grain (May)
- a month of harvesting and measuring grain (June)
- two months of harvesting grapes (July, August)
- a month of gathering summer fruit (September)

Palestine's broken landscape of plains, highlands, and small watercourse valleys fostered localized economies and restricted conceptual horizons. However, because the northern part of the country was split by the major Jezreel Valley, through which ran the region's major north-south coastal trade route, the north (Israel) was noticeably more open to international cultural and political influences than was the more isolated south (Judah). Overall, the highly varied nature of the landscape meant a correspondingly varied array of agricultural differentiation, a distinct advantage in a time of crisis and a spur to commercial interaction from one part of the country to another.

1.3. The Emergence of Israel

1.3.1. Transition to the Iron Age

The emergence of Israel was part of a much larger regional crisis involving ecological, economic, social, and political disruptions as the relative stability of LB transitioned into the beginning of the Iron Age. This massive economic and cultural shift involved technological change, migration,

1. THE EMERGENCE OF ISRAEL (CA. 1200–CA. 1000 BCE)

and violence. Peoples were on the move. Large-scale migration circled the Mediterranean as restive groups shifted from fringe areas into urbanized territories. The old regional system of large states holding smaller political units in vassal relationships collapsed (see §1.1.1). The Mycenaean world was hammered by a series of city destructions beginning in the last third of the thirteenth century (Pylos and Thebes, for example) and Mycenae itself was abandoned about 1150. Mainland Greece and Crete were seriously depopulated. The stable balance between Egypt and the Hittite Empire disintegrated. The Hittite Empire suddenly collapsed about 1200, leaving behind a constellation of smaller Neo-Hittite states in Syria. One of these was Carchemish, whose rulers bore Hittite royal names. Egypt's Twentieth Dynasty started strong with its second king, Ramesses III (ca. 1186–1155), but lost its control over Palestine under his successors. Assyria halted its annual campaigns for nearly a century after Tukulti-ninurta I (1244–1208). A resurgence of sorts took place under Tiglath-pileser I (1114–1076), who was able to launch a campaign up to Lake Van and another to the Mediterranean. However, most of his energy was taken up with fending off invading Aramaeans or invading their territory in turn. Elamite attacks ended the Kassite Dynasty in Babylon by 1155. Overall, written documentation becomes comparatively rarer for the period 1100–900.

A number of concurrent causation factors for this comprehensive crisis have been proposed, although separating cause from effect can be rather problematic.

(1) The climate became drier. Anatolian dendrochronology shows a period of little rainfall in the first half of the twelfth century. On a larger scale, tree-ring analysis gives evidence of climate change in the northern hemisphere between 1300 and 1000. Sediment cores from Cyprus show a decline in rainfall from about 1200 to 850. Hittite and Ugaritic texts give evidence of famine in Greece and Anatolia. Pharaoh Merneptah sent shiploads of grain to the Hittites. He reports in his Karnak inscription that the Libyans and Sea Peoples who attacked Egypt roamed about and fought to acquire food: "They come to the land of Egypt, to seek the necessities of their mouths." Assyrian documents of the eleventh and first half of the tenth century refer to famine and drought numerous times. In Babylon, grain prices reached ruinously high levels in those years. From the reign of Ramesses III through the rest of the Twentieth Dynasty, the price of wheat in Egypt gradually climbed and remained high until the end of the twelfth century. Artisans working on the royal tombs went on strike numerous times when their allotments of grain were not paid.

(2) Extensive migration may be seen as both a cause and an effect of disruption. Populations were pushed from former settings by factors such as famine, while simultaneously pulled into newly opened opportunities. In addition to the so-called Sea Peoples, twelfth-century population movements included the Aramaeans. This linguistic group achieved power in large parts of western Asia, including Mesopotamia and the Neo-Hittite cities in north Syria. They eventually founded Aramaean states such as Aram-Damascus.

(3) Trade in luxury goods declined as sea and land routes become vulnerable. Imported Mycenaean and Cypriot pottery disappeared throughout the eastern Mediterranean about 1200. A collapse of seaborne trade is suggested by a downturn in the frequency of shipwreck discoveries.

(4) A scarcity of imported copper from Cyprus and tin from Iran forced the adoption of iron. Fashioning iron required simpler tools than bronze did. This meant that itinerant smiths could provide tools and weapons that previously had to be fabricated by palace-based artisans. Even so, both metal technologies existed concurrently. Bronze was superior for armor and vessels; iron could be used for tools and weapons. The development of long double-edged swords with improved grips and short javelins may have reduced the military advantage offered by expensive and technically complex chariots.

(5) The extension of camel domestication for riding and as pack animals led to a shift in trade routes and allowed truly nomadic peoples to make lightning raids from the desert fringes.

(6) Declines in surplus crops subject to taxation weakened centralized governments and undermined the urban redistribution economic systems of palace and temple.

(7) The information technology of the alphabet offered the potential to democratize literacy beyond the highly trained scribal class required to write syllabic cuneiform or Egyptian hieroglyphics. This is evidenced in Palestine by the twelfth-century 'Izbet Ṣarṭah abecedary, apparently a learner's exercise tablet (discussed in *COS* 1.107:362–65).

1.3.2. First Written Mention of Israel

At some point before his year 5 (about 1208), Pharaoh Merneptah engaged in what was essentially Egypt's last imperial move into Canaan. Some years later he commissioned a hymnic inscription (the Merneptah

Stela) celebrating this campaign in the context of his more recent triumphs over the Libyans. In a retrospective closing section of this hymn, he famously mentions victories in Canaan over the cities of Ashkelon, Gezer, and Yanoam (identification uncertain), and over a people called Israel (*ANET*, 376–78; *COS* 2.6:40–41). This is the first historically trustworthy evidence of Israel's presence in Canaan. Merneptah's campaign into Palestine could have taken place as early as year 3 (about 1210). An inscription from Amada from his fourth or fifth year calls him *reducer of Gezer*, and his name occurs on a portable sundial found at Gezer. A memory of Merneptah's activity in Palestine seems to be preserved in the place name Waters of Nephtoah (*mê neptôaḥ*), identified with Lifta in the hill country between Benjamin and Judah (Josh 15:9; 18:15; Papyrus Anastasi III, *ANET*, 258).

Merneptah's inscription is hardly sober fact, but royal propaganda. There are many points of dispute in its interpretation. Nevertheless, it establishes that a group called Israel had a recognized presence in Palestine around 1200 and was important enough for an Egyptian monarch to brag about defeating them. It is significant that Israel is not simply given the standard label Shasu or sand dwellers, stock terms for despised Asiatic folk in Egyptian materials. Instead, Israel is referred to by name as a foe worthy of mention. Israel must have been prominent enough to serve the inscription's propaganda purpose of honoring the king and to be recognized by its intended readership.

Merneptah's assertion "Israel is wasted, his seed is not" is probably an (overstated) claim to have wiped out its progeny, but some scholars construe "seed" as evidence of settled agricultural activity. Given the context, however, "offspring" is the more likely meaning. This emphasis on progeny might indicate some understanding on the part of the Egyptians that Israel thought of itself as a people affiliated by kinship. The determinative (a symbol signifying a word's meaning) that is used to modify *Israel* indicates that Israel was regarded as belonging to a sort of category different from the other three names, which is to say as a people and its territory rather than as a geographic region or political entity. However, one must be careful not to over read this datum in an attempt to extract details of Israel's early social or political organization. To some scholars, the poem's structure seems to incorporate a repetition of Canaan and Hurru (Syria) that encloses the four enemy groups (Ashkelon, Gezer, Yanoam, Israel). However, other scholars detect a ring structure that parallels Canaan with Israel as the two divisions of Palestine, thus locating Israel more precisely in the highlands. The reality is that nothing in the inscription provides any evidence for Israel's location, except that it was somewhere in the territory traditionally targeted by Egyptian expeditions.

Relating this poem to Karnak battle reliefs previously attributed to Ramesses II represents a debated but widely accepted hypothesis. Four of these reliefs depict three towns on mounds, one labeled as Ashkelon, and a scene in the open country that has been thought to represent Israel. If this identification were actually correct, it would be a significant fact that the Israel figures are dressed like Canaanites, not like Shasu nomads. However, the proposal of a relationship between the reliefs and the stela is an extremely tenuous one. First, the attribution of the reliefs to Merneptah rather than Ramesses II is not completely self-evident. Second, the reliefs are physically unrelated to the stela. Third, any identification of a given scene with Gezer or Yanoam (to say nothing of Israel) is completely hypothetical because only Ashkelon is identified. Fourth, the theory fails to account for the multiple other panels of the relief. There are ten in all, and some scenes are missing. Fifth, the hypothesis fails to account for the bulk of the stela text. It is clear that the lines about Ashkelon, Gezer, Yanoam, and Israel are not the main point of the stela, which is properly Merneptah's victory over Libyans. Finally, if a depiction of Israel is actually intended at Karnak, is seems more likely that it would be the one portraying a Shasu group rather than the image of figures dressed like Canaanites, which includes a chariot.

A critical question remains. What is the relationship between Merneptah's Israel and the ethnic and political Israel that sang the Song of Deborah about itself and later gave its name to the northern kingdom? The determinative marking Israel as a people, in contrast to the three cities mentioned, seems to fit with the new unfortified Iron Age I settlements emerging at this time in the northern hill country and exhibiting a partially pastoral background (see §1.3.3.2). It is reasonable to argue backward from the certainties of Iron II to the probabilities of Iron I. There is at least a very general continuity in the location of these settlements with the tribal coalition alluded to in Judg 5 and the kingdom eventually centered at Shechem. However, the precise nature of that continuity remains unclear. Was Merneptah's Israel a distinct people or simply a blanket term used to lump together more than one nonurban group? As will be seen, emergent Israel was undoubtedly a complex amalgamation of groups. It included sedentarized pastoralist nomads, resettled Canaanite farmers, the urban populations of Shechem, Gibeon, Jerusalem, and other cities,

1. THE EMERGENCE OF ISRAEL (CA. 1200–CA. 1000 BCE)

and even perhaps a previously subjugated group displaced from Egypt. In any event, one can at least assert that Merneptah's Israel was one of the population elements that eventually coalesced into historical Israel and that this particular group was important enough to give Israel its name.

1.3.3. Disruption and Adjustment in Palestine

Israel emerged in a political vacuum and in a context of disruption and new opportunities. The evaporation of both Hittite and Egyptian authority meant that no outside power controlled northern or southern Syria or Canaan. After about 1200, the vigorous Seti I, Ramesses II, and Merneptah were succeeded by four nonentities who finished out the Nineteenth Dynasty. At this point, the economic and political interconnection of the LB Canaanite city-states, previously under loose Egyptian oversight, began to break down. New small settlements developed in the highlands, apparently populated by newly settled pastoralists and elements that migrated from areas under the control of Canaanite city-states. One may confidently equate this group with Israel. Nevertheless, the Canaanite city-states continued to exist. A third element, the Philistines, settled in the southern coastal area of Palestine apparently just before or soon after 1175. These Philistines brought with them cultural changes in pottery and dining patterns. In sharp contrast to these changes, the central highlands evidence an overall continuity in material culture spanning the transition from LB II to Iron IA. This indicates that the highland settlers whom we are labeling Israel were not cultural outsiders to Palestine.

History teaches that profound change will be accompanied by violence. Israel's own traditions involved stories of successful conquest (Joshua) and intrepid resistance (Judges). Urban centers were indeed destroyed during this period, but over an extended period (perhaps from around 1200 to 1130). These sites include Lachish, Megiddo, Beth-shean, Hazor, Aphek, Shechem, and Ashdod. However, there is no way to assign responsibility for any one of these events to one or another of the potential candidates: Egyptian armies, Philistine colonists, rival cities, or restive nonurban people such as Israel. There is no reason to think that these destructions were the result of any sort of concerted campaign.

Egyptian hegemony in Palestine ended about 1140–1130 during the Twentieth Dynasty. After a vigorous start with Ramesses III, who fought off an invasion by the Sea Peoples, the other pharaohs of the Twentieth

Dynasty were ineffectual and preoccupied with internal unrest. Few significant Egyptian artifacts appear in Palestine after the time of Ramesses III. The destruction of Megiddo (Stratum VIIA) and subsequent abandonment of the site can be dated to about 1130 or so by a cartouche of Ramesses III and a statue base of Ramesses VI (ca. 1143–1135). The destruction of Lachish Level VI is dated by finds bearing the names of Ramesses III and Ramesses IV (ca. 1155–1148). The retreat of Egyptian dominion opened up opportunities for the Philistines to expand their control and put pressure on Israel. Egypt remained chaotic, politically divided, and weak throughout the succeeding Twenty-First Dynasty (down to 945). Even the new Twenty-Second Dynasty, established at Tanis (945–720), had increasingly to share power with military leaders based in Upper Egypt. As previously mentioned, the Journey of Wen-Amon (*ANET*, 25–29; *COS* 1.41:89–93) is a romantic tale or novella, recounting events from the last part of the Twentieth Dynasty. It witnesses to the decline in Egyptian control of and economic contacts with Palestine. Wen-Amon is an envoy from Pharaoh sent to obtain wood for a new barge for the god Amun-Re. He is robbed by a crewmember, snubbed by the ruler of Dor, forced to wait by the king of Byblos, from whom he was buying the timber, nearly waylaid by a contingent of Tjeker ships, and attacked when forced to land in Cyprus.

The early years of Israel's development would have been untroubled by interference from Mesopotamia as well as by Egypt. Hardly anything is known about the kings of Babylon and Assyria in this period. Several successive dynasties ruled Babylon. The settlement of Chaldeans in southern Mesopotamia between 1100 and 900 created challenges for them. Assyrian kings remained weak and preoccupied with internal affairs until about 900, when Assyria began to push the Aramaeans out of northern Mesopotamia. These Aramaeans had established kingdoms in the area west of the Habur River, the biblical Aram-naharaim (Gen 24:10): Bit-Adini, Bit-Bahyani (Tell Halaf), Bit-Zamani, and Bit-Halupe.

The developing Iron Age in Syria-Palestine became a milieu characterized by two political and cultural patterns: city-states in the Neo-Hittite areas, Phoenicia, and Philistia and ethnic-identity states with larger territories such as Aramaean Damascus, Israel, Judah, Moab, Edom, and Ammon. The destruction of Ugarit and the collapse of the major empires allowed the Phoenician cities to fill the maritime trade vacuum. Large supplies of timber and defensible protected anchorages allowed first Sidon, and then Tyre to dominate trade in the eastern Mediterranean.

1.3.3.1. Canaanites: The Urban Pattern

What one might call the urban pattern in Palestine continued LB precedents. Cities persisted, with populations diversified with respect to occupation and income. Control was centered in a temple, a palace, or both. These cities were associated with a surrounding agricultural population dwelling in rural villages. The agricultural land related to the urban power centers was concentrated in the coastal lowlands and the hills just inland from there, the Jezreel Valley, and the upper and central Jordan Valley. A royal establishment supported elites who maintained the system. These elites consisted of *maryannu* chariot warriors, scribes, priests, and artisans. Unlike the rest of the city population or residents of villages in the countryside, these classes did not support themselves directly by agriculture. The cities also participated in a symbiotic relationship with nomadic pastoralists. Outside of the urban territories, these pastoralists herded sheep and goats and moved seasonally in search of pasture. Their domain was that of the arid areas and forested hills. Their movements, vertically to higher and lower elevations and horizontally out of and then into the agricultural territories, brought them into a social and economic connection with the sedentary population of the agricultural lowlands. This interrelationship between pastoralism and sedentary populations is illustrated by the eighteenth-century Mari documents. Traditions of combat with the "kings of Canaan" (Judg 5:19) with their chariots of iron remained part of Israel's self-conscious identity, even though there is no way of estimating how much actual conflict took place.

1.3.3.2. Israel: The Rural Tribal Pattern

At the start of the Iron Age, changes in economics, politics, and social structure led to the abrupt appearance of a second way of life in the shape of new unwalled villages in the central highlands. Many were totally new sites or resettlements of abandoned locations. In the LB there had been little permanent habitation in this area. Settlement began in the northern hill country of Samaria around Shechem and Shiloh. It was less dense in western and southern parts of the hill country. Later expansion took place on the western ridge of the north hill country and in lower Galilee to the north and west. These communities were generally small, with a population of perhaps 50–150 people. An absence of inequality in housing size or of public buildings for specialized purposes provides evidence for an egalitarian social structure. In contrast to the northern hill country, Judah seems to have remained predominantly pastoral. Settlement in Judah lagged behind that in the highlands of Manasseh, Ephraim, and Benjamin, perhaps because the forests were denser there. Many of these Iron I sites would be eventually be abandoned in a later period of re-urbanization in the late eleventh and early tenth centuries, apparently a consequence of state formation. A similar process happened east of the Jordan in Gilead. A pottery assemblage that continued LB Canaanite culture indicates that the majority of these settlers were indigenous to Palestine.

There are two likely sources for the population of these new hilltop villages: a migration of agricultural populations out of the lowlands and the sedentarization of pastoralists. Political and economic instability seems to have pushed farmers out of their subservient relationship to urban power structure. Perhaps there was pressure resulting from an increase in population and more burdensome local taxation as centralized Egyptian control weakened. At the same time, new agrarian opportunities must have attracted these groups to the highlands. There they could join settling pastoralists in previously unutilized agricultural areas. Increased use of already known agricultural technologies permitted expansion into the central highlands and later into other areas previously unfavorable for agriculture (Benjamin, upper Galilee, and eventually the Negev). Distance from the urban centers and a breakdown in trade patterns encouraged these new settlers to engage in a more secure economy of mixed subsistence agriculture. Population mixing caused by the upheavals associated with the transition to the Iron Age facilitated the spread of technological expertise. Brush removal and deforestation (probably more by fire than by iron tools) cleared new agricultural land (see Josh 17:17–18). Terracing hillsides in order to control erosion and retain water was practiced more extensively. Wadi floors were dammed to preserve water and permit dry farming. On the other hand, the increased use of iron was driven less by supposed advantages and more by availability and cost factors caused by a breakdown in international trade. Flint sickles continued to be employed.

As disruptions caused access to markets for their animals and animal products to diminish, pastoralists also found their old way of life unsustainable. They needed to shift economic strategy. Groups raising sheep and goats could only move a limited distance with their flocks. They had to stay by water. The need for grain and other crops also meant that they had to maintain connections with settled groups. However, the decline of cities resulted in a disruption of the grain supply system on which these

1. THE EMERGENCE OF ISRAEL (CA. 1200–CA. 1000 BCE)

pastoralists depended, so they had to settle down and turn to agriculture. The sedentarization of pastoralists at the start of Iron I was actually a repetition of a long-term pattern. Centuries ago, the crisis at the close of the Early Bronze Age (about 2000) had brought about a move to pastoralism. Then the Middle Bronze Age (2000–1550) was marked by a return to sedentary agriculture. In turn, the crisis at the end of LB encouraged pastoral nomadism until the new situation that developed in Iron I resulted once more in sedentarization.

1.3.4. Israel as an Ethnic Group

The question of the ethnic identity of these new settlers in the central highlands can be answered only by tracing back in time the cultural situation described in the narratives preserved in Judges and Samuel. One can argue back from what is known of later Israel's ethnic distinctiveness to the situation of the earlier Iron I highland settlements. This is reasonable in light of the shared continuity of material culture between these Iron I settlements and the Iron IIB kingdoms of Israel and Judah. Yet it is impossible flatly to equate material culture with ethnicity. Many regional differences between the highlands and the urban lowlands and Philistia were simply consequences of a different location and terrain.

Thus many of the particularities in material culture and agricultural practice associated with the highland settlements are best explained as adaptations to the hill-country environment. Scant rainfall promoted a wider use of plastered cisterns, allowing settlement in places not immediately adjacent to springs or wells. This same lack of precipitation made the intensive labor investment of constructing and maintaining hillside terraces a more attractive production strategy. Stockpiled grain had to be protected in pit silos. Storage of oil and wine took place in distinctive collared rim jars. So-called four-room-house designs would be expected in an agricultural village with domestic animals. These houses generally had a U-shaped plan with one broad room across the back (probably with a loft for sleeping), two long rooms stretching lengthwise to the front, and a central lengthwise open area. Pillars divided the central area from the long rooms. This domicile would hold a nuclear family of parents, unmarried children, and perhaps a couple of slaves. The central area could accommodate domestic animals (cf. the story of Jephthah, Judg 11:31), reflecting a mixed subsistence economy. These residences were similar in size, furnishing evidence of an egalitarian social organization. The absence of public or monumental buildings at these early sites suggests relative social equality. Some settlements were circular in layout, with houses arranged around a large, open space. This arrangement, designed to corral and protect livestock, is indicative of a pastoralist background.

1.3.4.1. Ethnic Markers

However, particular elements of material culture and the distinctive behaviors to which they point can provide information about a group's ethnic identity. These factors serve as ethnic markers that communicate a message of group identity to both those inside and outside the group. One might think of the Amish in North America or the Parsees of India, who avoid objects of material culture (automobiles) and behaviors (cremation) common to their neighbors. The outside groups against which Israel would have asserted its distinctive identity were urban Canaanites and uncircumcised Philistines.

One such behavior appears to be an avoidance of pork consumption. There is a sharp difference between the relatively common occurrence of pig bones in Philistine coastal sites and their absence in Iron Age highland settlements. It is important to note that raising swine had not been uncommon in the highlands as well as the lowlands of Palestine in the LB period. This indicates that the failure to keep pigs in the highland settlements was not entirely a matter of local ecology, although admittedly swine require a lot of water. Pork avoidance would have been a powerful ethnic indicator over against the Philistines, especially for a group with a significant semi-nomadic pastoral heritage of raising sheep and goats in its background.

Secondly, the four room house, although not unique to central Palestine and certainly a result of local ecological conditions and the requirements of a mixed subsistence economy, may also have developed into a cultural marker facilitating and communicating an egalitarian social structure. There is no hierarchy of access in such a domestic design; all rooms are directly accessible from the central space. In addition, this floor plan could have served cultural purity considerations. A ritually impure person had no need to cross through one room to get to another. Similarly, an avoidance of behavior that recognized social hierarchy may also explain the absence of traceable burials or tombs associated with the settlements in question. Perhaps these egalitarian behaviors functioned to distinguish the self-identity of these highland settlers from their urban Canaanite antagonists with their kings and aristocratic military class.

A third possibility is that an avoidance of decorated pottery might have served as an ethnic contrast marker over against the Philistines. As we shall see below, the second stage in Philistine ceramic culture, after an initial Monochrome phase associated with their Aegean heritage, was the use of more highly decorated Bichrome ware later in the Iron I period (perhaps after about 1140). Rather surprisingly, this Bichrome pottery is not found in inland sites of the same period. Some suggest that this means that the standard ceramic chronology needs to be adjusted downward (that is, presently accepted dates should be later; see §1.4.2 below). An alternate suggestion, however, is that an avoidance of such Philistine painted pottery was a conscious or unconscious means of asserting Israel's ethnic exclusivity.

1.3.4.2. Yahweh

In Judg 5:11, 13, Israel (a name bearing the divine element El, compare Ishmael) is termed the "people of Yahweh." It is significant that this god Yahweh was not part of the local Canaanite pantheon. Rather, Yahweh seems to have been a cultural import to Palestine from the south. This is indicated by the Bible's early theophany poetry (Deut 33:2; Judg 5:4–5; Hab 3:3). According to Exod 17:8, 15–16, a shrine called Throne of Yahweh (following MT) was located in Sinai as one of the station points on the exodus itinerary. A home base for Yahweh in the south also synchronizes with the tradition that this god's particular mountain was situated in the Sinai Peninsula, which stands in sharp contrast to the alternative, "Canaanite" concept of Mount Zaphon in the north (Ps 48:3 [EV v. 2]; Isa 14:13). Yahweh is styled the "One of Sinai" in Judg 5:5 (cf. Ps 68:9 [EV v. 8]). Remarkably, there are no Yahweh names among Israel's eponymous ancestors, judges, or even early kings. Moreover, in contrast to Anat (Anathoth), El (Bethel, Peniel), Lady (Baalah, Josh 15:9–10; Bealoth, Josh 15:24) or Baal (Kiriath-baal, Josh 15:60; Baal-tamar, Judg 20:33), there are hardly any toponyms containing a Yahweh element. "Shasu of [the region] Yhw" appear with five other Shasu groups on Egyptian topographical lists of Amenhotep III and Ramesses II. Some have connected this toponym with the god Yahweh, but it is unclear where this place is to be located (perhaps in Edom or Syria).

Judges 5 highlights Yahweh's role as a war god who champions the people in victorious battle. Yahweh is a Divine Warrior, who approaches the battlefield causing earthquake and storm (vv. 4–5) in order to support Israel's poorly armed warriors (vv. 8–9) with superhuman combatants (astral bodies and the River Kishon; vv. 20–21). Similar songs and stories must have encouraged Israel's tribal fighters facing the well-trained troops and chariot forces of the "kings of Canaan" (v. 19) and other threats to Israel's territorial integrity. The custom of designating the enemy and its possessions as *ḥerem*, that is, persons and objects taboo because of their special association with Yahweh, may have reduced tensions over the distribution of booty. Courage and unity would have been maximized by the celebration of successful tricksters like Ehud, Jael, or Samson and tales of wily stratagems like those associated with the massacre of the men of Shechem, the capture of Bethel, or the Day of Midian (Gen 34, Judg 2:22–26; 7:15–23). Divine Warrior and hero traditions continued to play an important ideological role in the monarchy period.

1.3.5. Social Organization

As described above (§§1.3.3.1 and 1.3.3.2), two systems of settlement and land use functioned in different areas of Palestine in the premonarchic period. Urban Canaanite culture operated as a surplus economy. Taxation imposed by a centralized government required farmers to produce a surplus over local needs. A surplus economy requires the production of transportable market crops such as oil and wine. It also generates economic and social inequality because different producers will enjoy different levels of success.

In contrast, the new highland settlements operated as a subsistence economy. As a precaution against the failure of any one crop, it was prudent to grow more than one type of food. Subsistence agriculture requires a relatively low scale of social organization and operates in a context of relative social and economic equality. A staggered planting and harvesting schedule of different crops provides insurance against disaster and maximizes the efficient use of labor. In emerging Israel, agricultural yields would have been supplemented by trade with neighboring pastoralists who raised sheep and goats. Diversified agricultural and pastoral modes of production offered greater security against catastrophe than either approach could on its own. Such a mixed economy would be largely self-sufficient.

Effective social organization and community solidarity were necessary to survive in the highlands. Constructing terraces and digging cisterns required intensive cooperation. Local agricultural specialization caused by variations in rainfall and terrain would lead to interconnections and trade among villages and regions. Growing prosperity would attract enemies and raiders, necessitating arrangements for common defense.

Social scientists describe societies like those that were the precursors of the kingdoms of Israel and Judah as segmentary systems and chiefdoms. As heuristic tools, these classifications have substantial explanatory power in making sense out of the very limited data available. Although all the biblical evidence for Israel's social organization dates from the monarchy period (with the probable exception of Judg 5), those later texts appear to describe realities rooted in the premonarchic period. Many premonarchic social configurations certainly would have continued and remained in force on the local level during the monarchy.

It should not be assumed that there was an inevitable move in complexity or centralization from segmentary society to chiefdom to centralized monarchic state, as though this were some sort of evolutionary process. Chiefdom is not a stage predictably on the way to statehood and kingship, but a realistic way of organizing a population that honors kinship values while achieving a measure of power centralization. The concept of chiefdom will be explored in the next chapter (§2.1.1).

1.3.5.1. Israel as a Segmentary Society

Segmentary societies are based on kinship. Societal relationships consist of an interlocking system of segmentary lineages. Such genealogies describe patterns of descent that take into consideration all the children at each stage of the lineage. In the male-centered kinship system of Israel, this meant that a man was categorized or identified in society not only by his father and grandfather (back to the third or fourth generation) but also by his brothers, paternal uncles, and grandfathers' brothers. These affiliations created a complex and interconnecting network of familial responsibilities involving mutual protection and inheritance. Segmentary kinship associations are likely to be limited in size. Those that prosper and grow will eventually split into separate groups, each tracing its descent back to a different progenitor. Now and again, a leader will arise in times of military crisis. Such a leader will come to power because of particular talents and personal charisma. In the book of Judges these leaders are literally charismatic, because the author attributes their rise to effective leadership as empowered by the spirit of Yahweh (e.g., Judg 6:34). However, leadership in a segmented society is temporary, limited to the duration of the emergency or the life of the leader. Leadership cannot be inherited or passed down to the leader's descendants (in contrast to the office of chief, see §2.1.1).

Real and fictive kinship relationships provided the bedrock of Israel's social organization. Society was composed of kinship groups of various sizes, although the boundaries between these are not always completely clear. As a rule, the larger the kinship unit, the less impact it would have had on daily life. Premonarchic Israel was relatively egalitarian in an economic sense, but also hierarchical and patriarchal within its kinship groups. Kinship affiliation above the nuclear family level exhibited the threefold organization of *bêt-'āb* ("father's house"), clan, and tribe (Josh 7:16–18 and 1 Sam 10:20–21).

On the one hand, linear-descent relationships provided identity and inheritance (2 Sam 19:38 [EV v. 37]; 1 Kgs 21:4). Jephthah's irregular relationship with his half brothers in the *bêt-'āb* of which he was a member causes them to drive him away to protect their inheritance (Judg 11:1–2). On the other hand, a concurrent network of (often fictive) segmented relationships—brothers, uncles, and the like—promoted a sense of obligation horizontally between smaller units. Thus Abimelech could seek support from his mother's *bêt-'āb* (Judg 9:1). Tribes were more likely to cooperate if they thought of themselves as descended from brothers who shared a common ancestor like Jacob, Rachel, or Joseph. Clans also envisioned themselves as sisters or brothers with a common paternity. The closely associated daughter clans of Zelophehad were also understood to be great nieces of other Manasseh clans such as Shechem and Abiezer (Num 26:33; 27:1–11). When the territory of the Jezreel Valley was invaded, Gideon was first able to muster his own clan of Abiezer son of Manasseh (Josh 17:2; Judg 6:34), and other groups only later. In-group affiliation was also promoted by hostility to other groups within Israel. Long-standing intergroup rivalries are preserved in taunting aphorisms such as Judg 8:2 and 12:4—and the insults directed at other tribes in Judg 5.

1.3.5.2. Father's House

The *bêt-'āb* ("father's house") was the basic unit of production and residence. Each *geber* (nuclear family in a single house) was associated by descent with other families into a father's house. Such a *bêt-'āb* consisted of several generations. Included were the wife or wives of the patriarch, sons to whom the paternal inheritance had not yet been granted along with their wives and children, and perhaps some aunts, uncles, cousins, and slaves. These all lived together or very near each other. This close association of three or even four generations made incest rules an imperative necessity (Lev 18:6–18; 20:17-21). Archaeologically, the *bêt-'āb* appears to be reflected in clusters of two or three four-room houses around a common area or compound that served as a locale for shared tasks. Matters of land inheritance were the province of the *bêt-'āb*. Except for the operation of the levirate custom (Gen 38), marriage was exogamous, outside the *bêt-'āb*.

1.3.5.3. Clan

The kinship unit at the local level was the *mišpaḥâ*, a word that biblical translators regularly render as "clan." Clans consisted of several father's houses linked by geography and marriage. The village or clan name was that of a supposedly common, eponymous ancestor. Numbers 26:5-50 and the early chapters of 1 Chronicles provide good illustrations of clan identities. However, whatever biological kinship existed within a clan would actually be more a result of endogamous intermarriage than of linear descent. Clan leadership was exercised by elders and grounded in their age and prestige.

Village or regional names were often also clan names: Tirzah, Shechem, Ephrathah, Shimron, Hezron, Hepher, and so on. Some clans bore feminine (daughter) names. The Samaria ostraca (*ANET*, 321) show that five of the clans represented by sons of Gilead and two represented by Zelophehad's daughters were names of locations. Other place names also indicate clan locations, such as Atroth-beth-Joab ("cattle pen of the house of Joab") or Hazar-Enan ("unwalled town of Enan"). Similarly, Ramathaim-zophim ("elevated place of the Zuphites") was the home of Samuel, who was of the Zuphite clan (1 Sam 1:1). However, other clan names cannot be associated with known locales, for example Zerah (the Judahite clan of Achan, closely affiliated with the Perez clan as its twin, Gen 38:29-30) or the Matrites (Saul). Clan solidarity and identity can be illustrated by a tale that must have been proudly repeated by the Achsah clan. Their eponymous ancestor exhibited the audacity successfully to claim water sources for her descendants (Josh 15:16-19). The Achsah clan was envisioned as related to the Caleb and Othniel groups.

Over time the effects of disparities in fertility and prosperity caused the number and makeup of clans to shift. There could be more than one clan in a village, or a single clan could incorporate neighboring settlements. Clans functioned to provide the cooperation needed to exploit agricultural resources efficiently. They ensured that group labor would be available for intensive projects such as terraces. The safety net provided by the clan encouraged the sharing of resources. Members of a clan shared common fields and pastures. Land ownership was protected by the clan, although the patrimonial land itself was owned individually (compare the situation of Naboth and the prohibition of Deut 27:17). Protection was provided to widows without sons by the operation of the levirate law. Family property or enslaved kinfolk were redeemed by clan relatives (Lev 25:47–49; Num 27:4; Ruth 4:3–6). Blood vengeance also operated on the clan level (2 Sam 14:7). The legal codes of the Hebrew Bible make it clear that clans continued to function into the monarchy period. Clan identity remained important even to certain returnees from Babylon (1 Chr 9:4; Neh 11:4–6; 12:12–21).

That a clan might have a focal sanctuary is implied by Gideon's establishment of an altar and ephod at Ophrah (Judg 6:11, 24; 8:27). Such sanctuaries probably preserved and passed on heroic clan traditions. Sacrifice connected with clan life is indicated by 1 Sam 20:6, 29. Communal sacrifices at holy places served to strengthen family and clan affiliation. The concept of dining together with a divinity would increase social cohesion. Animal sacrifice also served to redistribute food resources and provide a social safety net in order to reduce tensions within a clan. Sacrifice also encouraged the slaughter of herds and flocks and thus reduced the danger arising from a disparity of wealth and overgrazing, both of which would have deleterious social consequences in an egalitarian society with shared pastureland.

The list of the so-called minor judges (Judg 10:1–5; 12:7–15) demonstrates the importance of the founding ancestor for clan self-consciousness. Among these judges, Tola as well as his father Pu(v)ah are clans of Issachar (Gen 46:13; Num 26:23; 1 Chr 7:1–2). Jair son of Manasseh is the eponymous founder of Havvoth-jair, a village kinship cluster in Gilead (Num 32:41; 1 Chr 2:21–23). Elon embodies a clan of Zebulun (Gen 46:14; Num 26:26). Clan hierarchies changed and reorganized over time. Judges 10:1 considers Tola to be a son of Puah, which presents a different genealogical viewpoint from that of Gen 46:13 and Num 26:23. In these latter verses Tola and Pu(v)ah are brothers, two of four sons (that is, clans) of Issachar. The burial place of each clan notable is prominent in the list of minor judges. This suggests that transmission of clan traditions took place at these burial sites.

1.3.5.4. Tribe

The tribe was a fictive kinship association that organized smaller units (clans) through supposed descent from an eponymous common ancestor. Presumably, tribal organization emerged over time as neighboring clans with common interests began to understand themselves to be in a larger kinship relationship. Tribes engaged in collaborative military action in defense of the land (as substantiated by Judg 5) and so were associated with specific territories. Judges 5:17 is an early witness to the importance of territory for tribal identity. Tribal aphorisms and blessings emphasized martial prowess (for Simeon, Levi, Judah, Dan, Gad, and Benjamin in Gen 49; for Ephraim, Manasseh, Gad, and Dan in Deut 33). The Joseph group thought of itself as specially defended by the divinity called Mighty One of Jacob (Gen 49:24).

The practice of gathering at a focal sanctuary engendered a sense of solidarity and territorial ownership. Examples of tribal shrines are Hebron/Mamre for Judah, Tabor for Zebulon and Naphtali (Deut 33:19), and the temple at Dan (Judg 18:19). Both Bethel and Shechem were located close to the border shared by Ephraim and Manasseh. The age of the tradition of a wooden chest (ark) certifying Yahweh's presence is uncertain, but its location at Shiloh suggests that it was originally a cult object for the tribe of Ephraim. Hannah's Ephraimite husband took his family there to sacrifice every year. The effectiveness of tribal self-identity is evidenced by the centuries-long long survival of Benjamin as a group marker, even though its territory was split between the rival kingdoms of Judah and Israel. Benjaminite identity continued to function down into the restoration period (Neh 11) and even beyond (2 Macc 3:4; Rom 11:1).

The Bible preserves a vocabulary of tribal civil and military leadership but gives little information otherwise. Leadership categories included *śar* (Judg 8:14; 9:30), elder, *qāṣîn* (subcommander; Judg 11:6), and the more prestigious military rank of *rō'š* ("head"; Judg 10:18; 11:8). Joshua 13–19 describes an idealistic pattern of borders that filled up the agricultural land and remained relatively fixed over time. However, these detailed borders and the city lists associated with them rest on monarchy period realities. The description of tribal boundaries in Joshua seems to have been an artificial, scribal construction. Nevertheless, it was based on data derived from several sources. Tribal territories could enclose urban or ethnic enclaves (Josh 9:17; 16:9; 17:9).

Some tribes were associated into even larger alliances. In Judg 5, several tribes are mustered for war as the "people of Yahweh" (vv. 11, 13). Tribal genealogies in Genesis reflect understandings of social connections and differential tribal affiliations. Distinctions were drawn between the core Rachel tribes, the six Leah tribes, and the concubine tribes. The Rachel trio of Benjamin, Ephraim, and Manasseh was an alliance older and more basic than the canonical twelve-tribe paradigm. As the house of Joseph, these tribes were linked together by geography and a tradition of descent from Rachel as her son Benjamin and her two grandsons sired by Joseph. Joseph's tomb in Shechem, with its associated altar to El the God of Israel, was probably a focus of pilgrimage and the maintenance of tribal identity (Gen 33:19–20; Josh 24:32). The same may have been true for the tomb of Rachel in Benjamin (1 Sam 10:2). This Joseph affiliation overrides and presumably predates the line of division between the two later kingdoms.

Evidence suggests that organization into tribes and the tribes' association with each other took place inside Palestine. For example, certain tribes were named for their geographic placement: Ephraim (in the southern part of Mount Ephraim), Issachar (bondsman, in a subservient relationship to urban powers in the Jezreel Valley), and Benjamin (southerner, situated south of the other two Rachel tribes). Gilead, listed as a tribe in Judg 5:17, is also a geographical name. Asher may have already been present in Canaan in the time of Ramesses II. Anastasi Papyrus I mentions one Qatsra-yadi, who was chief of the people of Asuru (*ANET*, 477; *COS* 3.2:13).

Fluidity in the names and identity of tribes is evidenced by variant lists (Judg 5; Deut 33; Gen 49). Tribal territories were open to modification. Both the stone of Bohan son of Reuben (Josh 15:6; 18:17) on the Judah-Benjamin boundary and the forest of Ephraim in Transjordan (2 Sam 18:6) indicate some sort of presence for these tribes outside their traditional regions. Towns of Manasseh were located in Issachar and Asher (Josh 17:11). Wadi Kanah marked the boundary between the tribes of Ephraim and Manasseh, but allowed for urban islands of one tribe in the territory of another (Josh 16:8–9; 17:9). Manasseh had branches both west and east of the Jordan.

Caleb and the Kenites seem to have once been independent tribes that were demoted into clans as elements of greater Judah. In contrast, the similar entity Simeon remained on the traditional tribal roster even though it too was completely drawn into Judah. Judah also incorporated the groups

Jerahme-el and Kennaz/Othniel. Gad and Manasseh do not appear in Judg 5; in their place are Gilead and Machir, later considered as clans. Although certain traditions considered Reuben to be the senior tribe, by the early monarchy period it had fallen into insignificance. Gad was clearly occupying Reuben's supposed territory by the time of the ninth-century Mesha Inscription. Reuben's impermanence may have had something to do with the tribe's pastoralist lifestyle (see Judg 5:16).

The Danite migration story (Judg 18–19) is an explanatory etiology for the tribe's concurrent presence in two areas and the origin of the sanctuary at Dan. However, the northward migration of Dan does seem to be a historical fact. Both the Samson traditions and the place name Mahaneh-dan (camp of Dan; Judg 13:25; 18:12) place Dan solidly in the Shephelah between Zorah and Eshtaol, where they would have been under Philistine pressure and unable to expand as their population grew. The city of Dan was indeed formerly called Laish (Judg 18:29), as shown by earlier Egyptian sources (the Execration texts and list of cities conquered by Thutmose III; *ANET*, 242, 329 n. 8). Dan is related to ships in Judg 5:17 in an unexplained way, but there is no reason to connect the tribe to the Denyen/Danaoi among the Sea Peoples.

Folktales in Genesis also preserve traditions about tribal relationships. The story fragment about Reuben's having sex with Jacob's concubine Bilhah sounds like an explanation for the tribe's decline (Gen 35:22; 49:3–4). Shechem, although treated as a genealogically associated clan by Num 26:31, clearly had a rather more complex relationship to the core of Israel, as indicated by the tales told about Dinah (perhaps a clan name) in Gen 34 and about Abimelech in Judg 9.

1.3.5.5. Israel

The overall identity "Israel" as reflected in the Song of Deborah transcended tribal loyalties to some degree. Transtribal loyalties are expressed in the tradition of the patriarchs. All three patriarchs have sanctuary-foundation stories connected to them, although Jacob is more clearly associated with northern sites, Abraham with locations in Judah, and Isaac with the Negev. Burial-site traditions preserved at Machpelah are also evidence of some sort of pan-Israel affiliation. At the same time, a level of intertribal rivalry is suggested by various episodes reported in Judges and was apparently exacerbated by dialectical differences (Judg 12:5–6). The total silence of the Song of Deborah about Judah and Simeon is a clear indication of strained relationships that continued into the monarchy period. Traditions about Saul's conflict with David and the rebellions of Sheba and Absalom (2 Sam 20:1; 1 Kgs 12:16) indicate that any sense of connection between the core central and northern tribes and groups south of Benjamin was tenuous at best. As the monarchy took over their defensive function, tribes seem to have become more geographical regions than functioning kinship groups. In a way, however, the later kingdoms continued to claim an ideology of kinship affiliation through the designations "house of Omri" and "house of David."

1.4. The Philistines

1.4.1. Settlement

The early history of Israel, its self-identity, and the consolidation of its political organization were influenced by the settlement in coastal Canaan of a group of invaders and migrants. These Philistines (Peleset) eventually gave their name to Palestine (Josephus, *Ant.* 1.136; Herodotus, *Hist.* 3.91). The highland settlements that one may identify as Israel began a generation or so before the arrival of the Philistines. They colonized Palestine soon after 1175, although there may have been an earlier wave of settlement.

The prevalent term *Sea Peoples* serves as shorthand in scholarship for a shifting coalition of groups with Aegean and Anatolian roots. The Philistines were one element of a gigantic movement of peoples clockwise around the eastern Mediterranean from the Aegean via Anatolia and Syria to the Egyptian Delta. These population movements left both archaeological and textual evidence of violent upheaval around the Mediterranean. For example, letters between the kings of Ugarit and Alashiya dramatically describe enemy ships and burning towns just before Ugarit itself was destroyed (about 1185). The last king of Ugarit could not answer a plea for help because his ships and troops had been commandeered by the Hittites to fight off an enemy in Lukka. Hattusa, the Hittite capital, was sacked, along with Troy, Miletus, Tarsus, Alalakh, and many other sites.

Notions of a coordinated invasion are misleading, however. Instead, relatively small groups migrated over the period of a generation, sometimes uniting to attack major power centers. Trading expeditions, raiding parties, and the relatively peaceful settlement of migrating families

1. THE EMERGENCE OF ISRAEL (CA. 1200–CA. 1000 BCE)

were also part of the overall picture. The sea routes of this migration moved clockwise: south of Anatolia moving east, then southward along the Levant. Ancient ships would have been too small to transport a mass migration, however, and movement by land must have predominated. Reliefs commissioned by Ramesses III show family groups in Anatolian style oxcarts. The varied ethnic background of the women pictured suggests intermarriage along the migration route. The feathered hats wore by the Peleset, Denyen, and Tjeker/Sikel were widely distributed all around the Aegean.

Biblical tradition was aware of the Mediterranean origin of the Philistines, tracing their homeland to Crete (that is, Caphtor, Gen 10:14; Jer 47:4; Amos 9:7). It also designates a force of royal guards in later Judah as Cherethites and Pelethites (2 Sam 15:18), most likely equivalent to Cretans and Philistines. Cherethites are paralleled directly with Philistines in Ezek 25:15–16 and Zeph 2:5. There was a Negev of the Cherethites (1 Sam 30:14) in the area where Cretans are said to have settled (Deut 2:23).

Some of these groups first appeared as allies of the Libyans faced by Merneptah (about 1208), as described by him at Karnak. This first wave of Aegean people apparently did not include the Philistines per se. Some of Merneptah's opponents can be identified. The Lukka are certainly the Lycians of southern Anatolia. These Lukka had been pirates in the Amarna period and fought with the Hittites against Ramesses II at the battle of Qadesh. Perhaps the Ekwesh can be associated with the Ahhiyawa mentioned often in Hittite texts and as Achaeans in Homer. The Tursha may relate to Tyrsenia (Tyrrhenia) in Italy. The Shekelesh are often associated in scholarship with Sicily and the Sherden with Sardinia, either as their place of origin or as places they eventually settled. These five groups were forerunners of Sea People migrations that confronted Ramesses III in the next generation.

From the Egyptian perspective the true emergency was a second wave of aggressors that arrived about thirty years after Merneptah's successful resistance. Ramesses III faced this crisis in his year 8 (about 1175; there were encounters in years 5 and 12 as well). His inscription at Medinet Habu (*ANET*, 262–63; cf. Papyrus Harris I, *ANET*, 260–62) names the groups he fought and places they attacked before reaching Egypt. This time the Philistines (Peleset) are involved. Other groups were the Denyan (perhaps the Danaoi of the *Iliad*) and the Tjeker (Sicals), who eventually settled at Dor according to Wen-Amon. There was a sea battle at the delta, but probably also a separate land battle that could have fought as far north as Megiddo. The reported size of the coalition was probably inflated by Pharaoh's scribes in order to strengthen his claim of glorious victory.

The most important effect for Palestine was the settlement of the Philistines on its southern coast. This colonization was the result of either Egyptian strategy or impotence. It is possible that Philistine settlement in coastal Canaan actually preceded the reign of Ramesses III. Nevertheless, he claims, concerning several groups including Philistines, "I settled them in strongholds, bound in my name" (*ANET*, 262). Of course this may be a cover story intended for public consumption in order to disguise a development that he was unable to prevent. The Onomasticon of Amenope, an Egyptian list of categorized entities dated to about 1100, gives further evidence for the presence of Philistines in Palestine. It mentions six place names, three of which are Ashkelon, Ashdod, and Gaza in Philistia, and then lists the Sherden, Tjeker, and Peleset. It is a reasonable assumption that these groups inhabited the aforementioned cities.

However, rather than being a unified event, Philistine settlement was likely a gradual, piecemeal phenomenon. This is suggested by the diverse characteristics of the initial occupation phase at each Philistine site. The ground for Philistine settlement had been prepared by Merneptah's destructions of Gezer and Ashkelon. The five Philistine city-states—Gaza, Ashkelon, Gath, Ashdod, and Ekron—replaced the former constellation of LB power centers—Yurza, Ashkelon, Lachish, Gath, and Gezer. Gaza replaced Yurza. Gezer remained outside the Philistine system. Lachish was destroyed in the second half of the twelfth century, perhaps by the Philistines. It experienced a gap in occupation until the start of Iron IIA. The claim by Ramesses III that the Philistines were initially settled in Palestine to advance or protect Egyptian interests correlates with evidence of a Philistine presence at Megiddo, which served as an Egyptian base down through Ramesses VI, and biblical narratives about Philistine garrisons inland (1 Sam 13–14).

1.4.2. Chronology

There is controversy within the archaeological community about the chronology of Iron Age I and the start of Iron II. A controversial Low Chronology (LC), the chief proponent of which has been Israel Finkelstein, has challenged the previously accepted conventional chronology. LC results from a reevaluation of the stratigraphy of Megiddo, the nonappearance of

Philistine Monochrome pottery in sites with Twentieth Dynasty Egyptian pottery, and the striking absence of either Monochrome or Bichrome ware at Lachish VI before its destruction about 1140. Conventional chronology categorizes late Iron Age I pottery (sometimes termed Iron IB) on the basis of finds from the destruction layers that close out sites such as Megiddo VIA, Tell Qasile X, and Tel Masos II. This chronology dates late Iron I from the late twelfth to the very start of the tenth century (about 1150 to 1000). Thus Iron IIA is dated to the tenth century. LC lowers the conventional pottery chronology by fifty to eighty years for these periods. Thus the dates of late Iron I assemblages are lowered down to the tenth century. Iron IIA is brought down from the tenth century to the late tenth and ninth century. Consensus is lacking, but the LC has not yet been generally accepted. Many hope that more rigorous techniques of carbon 14 dating may eventually provide a solution (for further discussion, see §2.6).

With respect to the Philistines, conventional chronology places their first settlement and the start of Monochrome pottery into the first half of the twelfth century (1200 or 1175) with Bichrome developing from it from about 1140 on. The alternate LC pushes this transition down about fifty years. It dates Monochrome pottery to after the end of Egyptian hegemony in Palestine, that is, about 1140, and Bichrome to the eleventh and much of the tenth century. The significant result is that LC dating puts *all* Philistine settlement much later than year 8 of Ramesses III.

It must be said that biblical scholars and historians who are not practicing archaeologists have been more enthusiastic about the LC than professional archaeologists working in Palestine have been. Unfortunately, until the archaeological guild comes to an agreement on this matter, those who practice the craft of history must rely primarily on evidence from other quarters. Thus for now, the historian must depend on the witness of Ramesses III, which points to an initial settlement about 1175. At the same time it should be emphasized that, in any case, the quest for a single settlement date for the Philistines grows out of the dubious notion of a unified migration or invasion. A more gradual, disjointed pattern of settlement is suggested by the varied character of the initial phase at each Philistine site.

1.4.3. Culture

The name Peleset may be related to the Pelasgoi, a group that according to classical sources preceded the Hellenes in Greece. Biblical texts reflect Philistine linguistic influences, which were likely included to add local color to narratives. These "Philistinisms" include the names Goliath, Achish, and his father Maoch (1 Sam 27:2). Loanwords are *ṣeren* (tyrant), *qôbac/kôbac* (helmet; 1 Sam 17:5, 38) and probably *'argaz* ("box"; 1 Sam 6:8, 11, 15).

Philistines settled in numbers sufficient to modify the material culture of the area. This is evidenced most clearly by new forms of pottery that appeared alongside Canaanite types. As mentioned above, distinctive Philistine pottery is represented by a first phase of imported ware that was soon replaced by locally made Philistine Monochrome, similar to styles found in Cyprus. Colonizing potters retained their native Aegean ceramic tradition but produced it locally. Monochrome pottery was followed by a second phase. This Bichrome ware is characterized by black and red designs over a pale slip. Eventually Bichrome developed into Ashdod ware, in which the images of birds and fish become spirals.

Material culture and cultural behavior are associated. Philistines used their locally made imitations of formerly imported Mycenaean and Cypriot ware specifically to support their distinctively Aegean customs of cooking and eating. These pottery types included Aegean flat-base cooking vessels designed to stand on a hearth and wine-drinking sets for mixing wine and water. Philistines cooked Aegean style on a hearth that served as a focus for domestic life, but also used Canaanite bread ovens. Textiles were woven on distinctive looms with spool-shaped (biconical), unperforated loom weights, but spinning whorls followed the Canaanite pattern. The characteristic Philistine house style was the corridor house, in which a passageway separated a service area from a living area containing the hearth. Imported religion appears in the form of cattle shoulder blades with incised edges and Ashdoda figurines that attest to the existence of an Aegean earth goddess cult. These portray an abstract goddess seated on a chair. This female divinity relates to a later Ekron temple inscription from the seventh century that speaks of a ruler Achish (Assyrian Ikausu) and Ptgyh his lady (*COS* 2.42:164). This female deity is clearly the Queen Earth (*Pot[n]ia Ge*) who is addressed in Homeric Epigrams 7. However, biblical references to Philistine worship of the Canaanite god Dagon also suggest a mixed cultural situation concerning religion. Because their characteristic cultural markers appear side by side with signs of continued Canaanite presence, the Philistines seem to have been a military elite of limited size who politically and socially dominated a larger population of indigenous Canaanites.

Philistine settlement led to an increase in raising pigs and cattle and a decrease in tending sheep and goats. This makes sense. Urban farmers cannot move about in order to attend to grazing animals, but require food production to be nearby. Pigs cannot be herded long distances; they eat locally available food. Raising cattle was advantageous because they provided traction for tilling fields that needed to be farmed intensively because of high urban population density. In Iron I and II, finds of pig bones drop off sharply in the highlands in comparison with Philistia and the coastal plain (see §1.3.4.1). This suggests that Israel's pig taboo may have functioned as a marker of ethnic distinctiveness. Circumcision too must have functioned as a strong cultural separator between Israel and Philistia. The Bible strongly emphasizes the absence of circumcision among the Philistines, something that was standard practice in Egypt and throughout western Asia. Indeed, much of what later became characteristic of Israel's distinctive culture may have started as elements of resistance to the intrusive Philistine presence.

Growing tension between the better-organized and armed Philistines and Israel would be expected in border areas. The Bible's picaresque folktales about Samson provide witness to such conflict. It is commonly asserted by biblical historians that the sanctuary at Shiloh was destroyed by the Philistines. This unconfirmed notion is based on traditions of Philistine victories over Israel near Aphek and the witness of Jeremiah (Jer 7:12, 14; 26:6, 9; cf. Ps 78:60). The site (Khirbet Seilun) was indeed destroyed in the mid-eleventh century, but by whom cannot be known. It was largely abandoned for some time.

1.5. Literature of the Period

1.5.1. Songs and Sayings

Components of the Hebrew Bible's poetic and folktale tradition probably had their origin in the prestate period, but there is really no way to be certain how to date any given element. All one can say is that oral traditions must have been recounted and recited already in Israel's early life as a people. Songs and sayings are good candidates for early dating. The Song of the Well (Num 21:17–18) may have been celebratory etiology for the abundant water at Beer in the Arnon Valley. The citation from The Book of the Wars of Yahweh in Num 21:14–15 seems to make a territorial claim.

Taunt songs about nations and tribes would have served to strengthen in-group solidarity (Judg 8:2; 12:4; Num 21:27–30). Tribal sayings such as those incorporated into Gen 49 and Deut 33 would have a similar identity-defining function. A comparable aphorism is cited in the birth narrative of Ishmael (Gen 16:12). These sayings are often based on animal metaphors and puns. Three citations from the Book of Jashar (Josh 10:12–13; The [Song of the] Bow in 2 Sam 1:18–27; and evidently 1 Kgs 8:12–13 LXX) are of a highly varied nature, indicating the existence of some sort of anthology of traditional poetry in the monarchy period.

1.5.2. Sanctuary Etiologies and Graves

A number of sanctuary etiologies are preserved in the patriarchal narratives. They are of course undatable, but a measure of stability in tradition is indicated by their connection to locations where sacrifices were regularly offered. Eventually these narratives would have been recounted by a caste of authorized, onsite priests. Their purpose was to legitimate the holy place in question for potential users and to confirm that their altars were appropriate installations for sacrifice to Yahweh. Legitimacy was provided by a legend recounting a revelation by or appearance of the divinity. Connecting the sanctuary to an eponymous ancestor (Jacob, Abraham) was a way of claiming it for the group, and sacrifice there would be a way of maintaining group identity. Examples are Gen 16:7–14 (Beer-lahai-roi, Ishmael), Gen 28:11–22 and 35:1–7 (Bethel, Jacob), Gen 32:25–33 (EV vv. 24–32] (Penuel, Jacob), and Gen 33:18–20 (Shechem, Jacob). Abraham is connected by folktale fragments to shrines at Shechem, Bethel, and Beer-sheba (Gen 12:6–8; 13:4; 21:33) and by a full-blown narrative to Mamre/Hebron (Gen 18:1–15; cf. 13:18). The antiquity of these sanctuaries is evidenced by names that reflect the name of the god El (El-roy, El Olam, El-Bethel, El-elohe-Israel) rather than Baal or Yahweh. Later monarchy-period etiologies connect the sanctuary at Jerusalem to Moses (by way of the bronze serpent image; Num 21:8–9; 2 Kgs 18:4), Abraham (Gen 14 and 22) and David (2 Sam 24).

The Hebrew Bible provides evidence of pilgrimage to and veneration of the tombs of ancestral heroes. This must have been another mechanism for the preservation and development of traditions. Probably revered tombs were places where stories about worthy forebears were preserved and retold. Joshua's burial site in Ephraim (Josh 24:30), for example, indicates that he was a folk hero belonging to that tribe, even though the book of Joshua puts him in charge of the conquest of territory that is mostly in Benjamin. Stories about Gideon may have been passed on at his tomb in Ophrah (Judg 8:32). The same may have been true for the figure of Samson at his tomb between Zorah and Eshtoah (Judg 16:31) and for Jephthah in Gilead (Judg 12:7). The memory of gravesites and the veneration of tombs would remain a persistent feature of Israel's existence (1 Sam 10:2; 2 Kgs 13:20–21; 23:17–18).

1.5.3. The Song of Deborah

Apart from early poems and oral traditions underlying folktales about ancestors, sanctuaries, and heroes, there seems to be only one possible example of a biblical text from the prestate period. The Song of Deborah (Judg 5) shows strong evidence of an early date. Its poetics are archaic, similar to those from Ugarit, and its frequent obscurity in vocabulary points to probable antiquity. The song's nonstandard tribal catalog, which includes Machir and Gilead, is earlier than the two canonical twelve-tribe lists found elsewhere. Its tribal geography compares in some ways to the description of Saul's kingdom found in 2 Sam 2:9: Gilead, Ashurites (?), Jezreel, Ephraim, Benjamin. This poem may have been preserved and sung at the Tabor sanctuary associated with the tribes Naphtali, Zebulun, and Issachar (Deut 33:18–19; Hos 5:1; cf. the tribal territory description in Josh 19:12, 22, 34). Perhaps it was from there that the victors "marched down" (Judg 5:11, 13-14). At any rate, the later commentary offered by Judg 4 locates the tribal assembly place at Tabor (vv. 6, 12, 14).

The song is hardly contemporary to the events it describes. It looks back to former days, the days of Shamgar and Deborah. Yet it does reflect early, premonarchic concepts and concerns. It knows about aggressive kings ruling Canaanite cities. Yahweh, the Divine Warrior, is located in the south. Judah is not part of the song's horizon. Significant features of the poem are the journey of Yahweh "god of Israel" from his southern locale (vv. 4–5) to help those who are "the people of Yahweh" (vv. 11, 13). The conflict is fought between poorly armed peasants (that is, those who live in open villages) and the kings of Canaan (vv. 7, 11, 19). The Song of Deborah describes tribes who have expectations of each other and some level of transtribal military leadership. Nevertheless, the absent tribes are not condemned as violators of an alliance or covenant, but merely taunted and reprimanded. The poem hints at certain types of economic activity: herding by Reuben and a connection to the sea or seaborne trade on the part of Asher and Dan. Reuben seems to be in a situation earlier than that reflected in the ninth-century Mesha Inscription, by which time Gad inhabited the territory traditionally assigned to them. The absence of any mention of Joseph may suggest that the poem is earlier than the concept of a "house of Joseph" (as in Amos 5:6).

1.5.4. Sources of Joshua and Judges

Except for Judg 5, the materials lying behind Joshua and Judges are not of a sort to provide much useful historical information. The names preserved for various peoples, however, may be a different matter. Study of Homer suggests that historically valid names may be preserved even if the stories in which they appear are not trustworthy. Thus the (W)ilios of the *Iliad* remembers the Wilusa of Hittite sources, and Homer's Achai(w)oi and Danaoi reflect the Ahhiyawa of the Hittites and the Denyen among the Sea People. So one can be reasonably confident that premonarchic Israel not only recounted legends of giant Anakim and ghostly Rephaim but also interacted with real Kenites (probably itinerant metal workers), Avvim (Deut 2:23; Josh 13:3), and Amalekites, even if these latter groups never appear in external sources. Place names also have staying power and can provide unexpected information. Examples are Mahaneh-dan demonstrating Dan's tribal presence west of Judah (Judg 18:12), Waters of Nephtoah recalling Merneptah (*mê neptôaḥ*, Josh 18:15), or Anathoth and Beth-anath (Josh 19:38) referencing the goddess Anat.

The conquest tales of Joshua were told to provide etiologies for the existence of prominent city ruins that dotted the landscape. These conquest narratives sought to claim Israel's land in the face of outside and internal enemies. Cities certainly were destroyed in the early Iron Age, but there is no evidence of a distinctly different culture in the new settlements (in contrast to the Philistine situation). It is best to see the conquest as a literary and ideological construct. Conquest became part of the overall plot movement of Israel's later narrative of its own self-consciousness: patriarchs in Canaan, Egyptian captivity and exodus, then conquest of the land of promise. The conquest of Hormah tradition (Judg 1:17; Num 21:1–3) might be more valuable than most because it runs counter to perspective of an invasion from the east, but the story is still clearly an etiology for the town's name, Destruction. Tales of epic victories over Sihon king of the Amorites and Og king of Bashan, celebrated in the pentateuchal tradition (including the song preserved in Num 21:27–30), also functioned as land claims, in this case to territory east of the Jordan.

Although the book of Judges is certainly a monarchy-period production, its folktales about regional military champions describe a state of affairs that sounds authentic. One can at least argue that Judges bridges the gap from the situation of the Amarna period to the emergence of a monarchy in a believable way. Judges portrays a fluid political situation and social-class turbulence in the highlands. The various tribes have no central organization. The book describes a period of social change that provided opportunities for women (Deborah, Jael) and marginalized male figures such as Abimelech and Jephthah. In the absence of institutionalized leadership, appealing and successful individuals rally loosely affiliated tribes for defense against incursions by outside foes. There are intertribal rivalries over honor. The story of the struggles of Abimelech and Gaal for power in Shechem reflects the expected circumstances of small-scale city-state kingship in relationship to surrounding clans and tribes. Judges remembers the topographic, social, and political distinction between (Canaanite) plains and (Israelite) hill country and the significance of chariots for the kings of the cities. Mention of the Day of Midian in Isa 9:4 indicates that the tradition of Gideon's battle continued to be current in the late eighth century, something also true of the name of Gideon's opponent Oreb (Isa 10:26).

However, the historian cannot move from generalities to specifics. For example, the parallel narrative themes (ad hoc weapon, huge slaughter of Philistines, Lehi) shared by the stories about the similarly named heroes Shamgar (Judg 3:31), Samson (15:14–17), and Shammah (2 Sam 23:11–12) prevents one from treating these tales as genuine historical memories. Individuals can represent groups, so that the hero Ehud in Judg 3 is actually a Benjaminite clan name (1 Chr 7:10), something also true of the minor judges Tola, Elon, and Abdon (Num 26:23, 26; 1 Chr 8:23).

Outside sources from the premonarchic period illuminate individual texts in Judges. Arrowheads of the eleventh century from the Bethlehem area are inscribed "servant of the lioness," referring to a goddess (*COS* 2:84:221–22). This indicates the existence of warrior elites dedicated to a deity and throws light on the figure of Shamgar, "son" of the goddess Anat (Judg 5:6). Biblical tradition (Josh 11:1; Judg 4; Ps 83:10 [EV v. 9]) correctly remembers Jabin as a long-standing dynasty name for the kings of Hazor. Thus Ibni-Addu is king of Hazor in the Mari documents, and the name Ibni recurs among the kings of eighteenth- to sixteenth-century Hazor. Sisera has been thought to be a Luwian or Phoenician name, and Shamgar seems to be a Hurrian one.

1.5.5. The Exodus Tradition

Archaeology demonstrates that early Israel was indigenous to Palestine and did not engage in a campaign of violent conquest. Yet the historian must face the problem that both the exodus and conquest traditions became core elements in Israel's identity and point to an origin for Israel outside of Palestine. The exodus is found in early texts in Amos and Hosea and northern psalms such as Pss 77, 80, and 81. The poem in Exod 15 may be an early monarchy composition, based on its language and apparent reference to Jerusalem. It seems significant that some primary characters associated with Levi bear Egyptian names: Moses, Merari, Phineas, and Hophni. The record of rations for Apiru on Ramesses II state building projects (Leiden Papyrus 348) suggests that it is within the realm of possibility that a subjugated population from Palestine could have experienced the story later told of all Israel.

Nevertheless, it is best to understand the potent notion of an exodus from an anthropological perspective, not a historical one. A story of exodus became the narrative of the annual Passover and Unleavened Bread festivals, replacing older pastoral and agricultural notions. Repeated and accentuated in liturgy, the exodus concept gained so much influence that it served as the organizing center for Israel's self-consciousness. The liberation-from-Egypt motif persisted in supporting Israel's self-identity and in providing a structure for understanding reality because the power of Egypt repeatedly appeared on Israel's conceptual horizon from Shishak to Neco to the Ptolemies. It can be no accident that the supposed biography of Jeroboam I tracks the stories told of Moses. In the exilic period, the tradition of exodus continued to shape self-identity and hope. At least some of the Yahwistic expatriates located in Egypt and Babylon were yearning to return (see Second Isaiah, §4.9.2.6). Moses also would live on as a way of authorizing developing legal traditions in the monarchy period, the exile, and the Persian period.

2. State Formation (to ca. 930)

Becking, Bob. *From David to Gedaliah: The Book of Kings as Story and History* (OBO 228; Fribourg: Academic Press Fribourg; Göttingen: Vandenhoeck & Ruprecht, 2007). **Bodner**, Keith. *David Observed: A King in the Eyes of His Court* (Hebrew Bible Monographs 5; Sheffield: Sheffield Phoenix, 2005). **Cook**, Steven L. *The Social Roots of Biblical Yahwism* (SBLSBL 8; Atlanta: Society of Biblical Literature, 2004). **Dietrich**, Walter, ed. *David und Saul im Widerstreit: Diachronie und Synchronie im Wettstreit: Beiträge zur Auslegung des ersten Samuelbuches* (OBO 206; Göttingen: Vandenhoeck & Ruprecht, 2004). **Dietrich**, Walter. *The Early Monarchy in Israel: The Tenth Century B.C.E.* (trans. Joachim Vette; Biblical Encyclopedia 3; Atlanta: Society of Biblical Literature, 2007). **Ehrlich**, Carl, and Marsha C. **White**, eds. *Saul in Story and Tradition* (FAT 47; Tübingen: Mohr Siebeck, 2006). **Faust**, Avraham. *The Archaeology of Israelite Society in Iron Age II* (Winona Lake, Ind.: Eisenbrauns, 2012). **Finkelstein**, Israel, and Neil A. **Silberman**. *David and Solomon: In Search of the Bible's Sacred Kings and the Roots of the Western Tradition* (New York: Free Press, 2006). **Gilmour**, Rachelle. *Representing the Past: A Literary Analysis of Narrative Historiography in the Book of Samuel* (VTSup 143; Leiden: Brill, 2011). **Grabbe**, Lester L. *Ancient Israel: What Do We Know and How Do We Know It?* (New York: T&T Clark, 2008). **Halpern**, Baruch. *David's Secret Demons: Messiah, Murderer, Traitor, King* (Grand Rapids: Eerdmans, 2001). **Lux**, Rüdiger, ed. *Ideales Königtum: Studien zu David und Salomo* (Leipzig: Evangelische Verlagsanstalt, 2005). **McKenzie**, Steven L. *King David: A Biography* (New York: Oxford University Press, 2000). **Niemann**, H. M. *Herrschaft, Königtum und Staat: Skizzen zur soziokulturellen Entwicklung im monarchischen Israel* (FAT 6; Tübingen: Mohr Siebeck, 1993). **Shalom Brooks**, Simcha. *Saul and the Monarchy: A New*

Look (SOTSMS; Aldershot: Ashgate, 2005). **Torijano**, Pablo A. *Solomon the Esoteric King: From King to Magus, Development of a Tradition* (JSJSup 73; Leiden: Brill, 2002). **Van Seters**, John. *The Biblical Saga of King David* (Winona Lake, Ind.: Eisenbrauns, 2009). **Vaughn**, Andrew G., and Ann E. **Killebrew**. *Jerusalem in Bible and Archaeology: The First Temple Period* (SBLSymS 18; Atlanta: Society of Biblical Literature, 2003).

2.0. Summary

After the end of Egyptian hegemony in Palestine about 1140, the power of the lowland city-states faded. In their place arose kingdoms with ethnic foundations. By about 930 these included the separate kingdoms of Israel, with its capital at Shechem, and Judah in union with the formerly independent city-state Jerusalem. The process of state formation that led to this situation began with the figures of Saul and David, both of whom should probably be considered to have been actual historical individuals. Saul and David were understood by their contemporaries, and certainly by later writers, to be kings. However, in comparison with Solomon and the later sovereigns of Judah and Israel, they were less like kings and more like rulers of kinship-based chiefdoms. The political entities governed by Saul and David were not as firmly structured, centralized, or hierarchical as the full-blown monarchical states that developed after them. It is possible that Saul's regime, centered at Gibeah, and David's authority based in Hebron overlapped chronologically to some extent. Saul was succeeded by his son Ishbaal (Eshbaal in Chronicles, tendentiously Ish-bosheth in Samuel). Ishbaal ruled from Mahanaim east of the Jordan over territory that incorporated Benjamin, Ephraim, the area around the city Jezreel, and Gilead. This territory probably also represents the extent of Saul's jurisdiction.

Credible traditions indicate that David captured Jerusalem and established some sort of shrine (but not a temple) and administrative court there. His successor (and alleged son) Solomon ruled as king over a realm that merged Jerusalem and Judah. It is likely that he engaged in building projects in Jerusalem, including a Yahweh temple, and sought to protect Jerusalem by strengthening sites that defended approaches to the city. He exercised some more limited control or at least influence over cities, tribes, and regions farther north.

2.1. CHIEFDOM AND STATE

The tenth century is a dark period historically in the sense that no extant Babylonian or Assyrian records report on outside affairs. Egypt withdrew from Palestine after Ramesses VI (ca. 1142–1135). The remaining pharaohs of the Twentieth Dynasty (concluding about 1070) and succeeding Egyptian rulers ceased to play a role in Palestinian affairs until about 945. In fact, from the middle of the twelfth century to the middle of the ninth century, Syria-Palestine as a whole was largely free from outside interference and was able to develop its internal political structures independently.

After Israel's emergence, the older Canaanite urban model did not disappear immediately. The result was two cultures sharing Palestine in symbiosis. On the one hand, the city-states remained heirs of LB culture, each centered on a capital city very different in scale from its subsidiary villages. On the other hand, by the last part of the tenth century several nonurban agricultural population groups had emerged into ethnic states. These were Israel with its capital at Shechem, Judah yoked with Jerusalem, and Aramaean states to the north (Damascus, Geshur, and Zoba). Moab, Ammon, and finally Edom emerged as states somewhat later. These states, together with the Philistine cities, eventually divided up Syria-Palestine. Other Aramaean kingdoms stretched north across the Euphrates. On the margins of Palestine lived nomadic groups such as the Ishmaelites to the east, Amalekites south of Judah, and Midianites south of Edom.

These ethnic kingdoms were larger in extent and less densely populated than the older city-states they eventually absorbed. In the beginning, leadership depended on personal ability and notions of shared kinship rather than a centralized, writing-based administration and the concentration of wealth. Group solidarity rested on concepts of a supposed common origin and a shared god. Sources extant behind the present book of Kings indicate that Solomon ruled a polity of some sort as a king. However, many scholars suggest that, insofar as Solomon's purported predecessors Saul and David are to be considered to be actual historical figures, they should not be understood as full-blown kings. Rather they were heads of prestate, kinship-based chiefdom polities in the process of developing into monarchical states.

However, it is important to note that making too sharp a distinction between chiefdom and state is fraught with problems. These two sociological models must be understood as oversimplified constructs. The taxonomy they represent is controversial in present-day anthropological studies, and the two categories have been defined in contradictory and highly nuanced ways. Nevertheless, the general concept of chiefdom as something different from and less complex than a state does have a certain heuristic value. The two categories assist us in coming to terms with what can be known of or surmised about Israel's transition from a segmentary society (see §1.3.5.1) into the political entity ruled by Solomon and the kingdoms of Israel and Judah. The terms *chiefdom* and *state* help bring into focus the dissimilarities among the sorts of governance exercised by Saul, David, and Solomon. However, one should only use these classifications as general categories, while keeping in mind several cautions. These include: (1) Chiefdom and state are not inevitably sequential arrangements, but two alternate ways of organizing a society. Chiefdoms do not automatically develop into states. (2) The modern notion of a territory-based state is an anachronistic category with its roots in postmedieval European developments. (3) The more appropriate (that is to say, emic) category for the governments of ancient western Asia is *kingdom*, which is how they are described in the texts of the period.

2.1.1. Chiefdom

In times of military crisis a leader may arise in a segmentary society. Such a temporary leader achieves power based on talent, success in warfare, and appealing personal qualities. The judges celebrated in the Hebrew Bible seem to have been examples of this sort of transitory leadership. However, under the pressure of economic or military circumstances, such a leader may achieve a higher level of prestige, wealth, and permanency. The individual leader becomes a focus of power that supplements or transcends loyalties owed to one's kinship group. Many anthropologists call this state of affairs a chiefdom. A chief attains status and power by acquiring goods through warfare, exactions, and gifts. He (the male pronoun being apposite) redistributes these goods preferentially to his own affiliated kinship group in order to gain and retain their loyalty. Consequently, these favored groups have a stake in maintaining the chief's authority. Persons related to the chief gain in status and wealth at the expense of other families and clans. The position of chief develops into an office. As such, it exists apart from the person occupying it and carries on past his death. A chief will seek to pass on his position to his son. This tendency is reflected in folktales about Gideon (who refuses the option) and his son Abimelech (who pursues it). Chiefdoms do not exhibit internal specialization in leadership offices. Rather, the chief turns to his own kinship group to serve him on an improvised basis.

The prestige and power exercised by the chief and his kinship group produces a social hierarchy that will likely clash with the values of an egalitarian society based primarily on kinship. Discord over this matter in Israel is reflected in protest texts such as 1 Sam 8:11–18 (the Way of the King), Judg 9:8–15 (Fable of the Trees), the law about kings in Deut 17:14–20, and the so-called antimonarchical texts of 1 Sam 8:1–22; 10:17–27; 12:1–25.

Social theory suggests that, although Israel's development into a kingdom (or kingdoms) was not inevitable, a synergistic cycle of developments would be likely eventually to result in a monarchical state. Originally self-sufficient highland agricultural settlements would grow in population and wealth and need more complex political and administrative arrangements as a result. Chiefdoms would replace the earlier egalitarian pattern of affiliated kinship groups. The chief's supporters could then trade subsistence goods, gathered by the chief from lower status groups, to acquire imported or luxurious prestige goods. Costly spoils gained in warfare would also be distributed to the chief's minions or clients as rewards and inducements. Not only would these goods further increase the status of the chief and his favorites, but they could also be passed down as gifts to those of lower status in order to procure their loyalty or at least acquiescence. In a parallel development, increased prosperity would attract the attention of covetous imperialists (such as Philistines) and raiders (such as Midianites), requiring a more robust military defense, demanding in turn a more centralized command structure. Conversely, pressures exerted by internal population growth would also bring about a desire to trespass into the territory of others.

Biblical authors treated Saul as the failed first king of a kingdom coterminous with the territory that tradition assigned also to David and Solomon (that is, the supposed united kingdom of Israel and Judah). As such, he provided an ideological contrast and foil to David in order to legitimate and glorify the dynasty David founded. However, reading between the lines of what are more likely trustworthy traditions suggests that historians should understand Saul and David as kings perhaps in name, but in reality as chiefs ruling over prestate, kinship-based societies. The stories told about them reflect a transition from chiefdom to statehood.

2.1.2. Statehood

The polity ruled over by Solomon and the later kingdoms of Israel and Judah arose in a context in which kingship and kingdoms were familiar entities. In sociological terms, Israel and Judah were secondary states, reemerging in an area where similar states had existed previously. Neither statehood nor kingship had to be invented in Palestine; statehood would have been a natural direction in which to move.

Social theorists have produced lists of what characterizes a state in contrast to less tightly organized social arrangements. States continue from one generation to the next. States rely on a surplus of goods to support a bureaucratic and military organization and develop systems to collect wealth (taxes, gifts to central temples, tribute, booty) and marshal services (mandatory labor, military conscription). States promote a robust ideology of legitimacy in order to ensure loyalty and compliance. To support this ideology, they exploit religion, erect impressive architecture with a level of magnificence beyond simple functionality, and glorify the ruler's heroism, wisdom, and justice. An ancient state controlled a defined territory, although the marginal borders of its territory were indefinite.

Many features defining a state are things that can show up in the archaeological record. Because states exhibit a hierarchical centralization of political and economic power, a graded hierarchy of settlement sizes can demonstrate concentrations of wealth and influence. Thus states have a large capital city, several somewhat smaller regional urban centers, and still other towns of lesser size. States exhibit a system of differentiated administrative officers and a socially stratified population, some of whom engage in specialized occupations. Such disparities in rank and wealth can be indicated by residential patterns evidencing dissimilar housing size and distinct neighborhoods. States mobilize resources and labor in order to construct public buildings, defensive city walls and gateways, and outlying forts. Fortifications become necessary because increasing wealth draws attacks by envious outsiders. Effective defense of a state's major cities requires complex water systems and central storehouses. Outlying fortresses must be garrisoned by soldiers who need to be supported in part by distributions from the central authority.

In the world of ancient western Asia, statehood inevitably entailed rule by a king, who embodied the requisite high level of centralized supervision and decision making. The Bible is right when it insists that Israel learned kingship from its neighbors (Deut 17:14–15; 1 Sam 8:19–20).

As already indicated, Judah and Israel were not isolated societies, but emerged as secondary states in an environment of long-standing city-state monarchies, which provided models to imitate. Traditions inherited from the pre-Israelite monarchy of Jerusalem seem to have been particularly influential in shaping patterns for the kingdom of Judah (Gen 14:17–24; Pss 2 and 110). We may assume that in Israel and Judah, the kinship ties of family, clan, and tribe were only gradually and never entirely supplemented by the emergence of royal officeholders and patterns of centralized, territorial control. Legal traditions reflected in the Covenant Code and Deuteronomy (cf. also Jer 32:7–9) show that older clan and family structures and newer monarchical systems operated side by side for many generations, particularly on the local level.

In some ways, the previous pattern evidenced by the Amarna letters (see §1.1.2) reemerged in the tenth century. By about 930, the two cities Shechem and Jerusalem once again controlled the central highlands, now resettled by migrating farmers and sedentarized nomads. The result was two kingdoms, Israel and Judah, each having a hybrid character that mixed urban and tribal features. In contrast to Jerusalem, Shechem was more integrated with its surrounding nonurban population, as the traditions behind Gen 34 and Judg 9 witness. One may assume that the swath of urban centers in the Jezreel Valley would initially prevent the domination of Galilee by the Shechem-based kingdom. In Judah a fundamental distinction remained between the capital city and the territory it controlled. Consciousness of this binary polity is evidenced in the survival of the gentilic designation of Jerusalem as the Jebusite and its back-formation Jebus (e.g., Josh 18:28), which reflect an outsider's perspective. The distinction between Jerusalem and Judah persisted as late as the political machinations of the Judahite elite ("the people of the land") in royal politics (involving Athaliah, Azariah, Josiah, Jehoahaz) and the expression "Judah and Jerusalem" in the Prophets and in Ezra. Not much archaeological evidence exists of a tenth-century Jerusalem, but then no traces remain of the LB city-state known from the Amarna letters either.

2.2. SAUL

It is likely that an early consolidation of power took place in Benjamin focused on a military leader named Saul. He and his son tried at least to claim the title of king. An emergent chiefdom or kingdom, appearing in Benjaminite territory and extending into the hill country of Ephraim south of the Jezreel Valley, fits with what is known about early settlement patterns. Areas to the west under Philistine control would certainly have been excluded from Saul's control. There is no way to determine to what degree traditions about Saul reflect actual historical realities. Most likely, the texts that recount those stories originated at a substantially later period. However, the bare historical fact of Saul's name at least and a shadowy outline of his career can be gleaned from elements preserved in later tradition that are likely to be dependable. Trustworthy bits of information occur in the shape of personal names and toponyms embedded in narratives and in rosters or lists used to connect narratives together. Examples of such lists are 1 Sam 14:49–50 and 2 Sam 2:9.

One item of evidence for Saul's historical existence is the tradition of his burial site in Benjamin, in the tomb of Kish at Zelah (2 Sam 21:12–14; cf. Josh 18:28). With Saul were purportedly buried Jonathan and those Saulide family members handed over by David to the vengeance of the Gibeonites. Saul's body was supposedly transferred there from a tomb near a (sacred?) tree in Jabesh-gilead (1 Sam 31:11–13; 2 Sam 2:4). Abner's tomb, unexpectedly located in Hebron (2 Sam 3:32; 4:12), may have been a spot where traditions about Abner and Ishbaal were preserved. Similarly, a narrative about conflict relating to the transition from Ishbaal's rule to that of David was linked to the imposing pool at Gibeon (2 Sam 2:12–32). Saul's persistent geographic connection to Gibeah is certainly significant, particularly when it is designated "Gibeah of Saul" (1 Sam 11:4; 15:34; 2 Sam 21:6; Isa 10:29). Tradition seems to have specifically connected him to a prominent tree there (1 Sam 14:2; 22:6). First Samuel 14:4–5 links Bozez and Seneh, two rocky outcrops in Wadi Suweinit, to an exploit of Jonathan. Saul is said to have built an altar somewhere in the region of the Aijalon Valley (14:35). A monument of some sort at Carmel in Judah was associated with Saul (15:12).

Folk sayings and old poetry provide further indications that Saul was an actual person. First Samuel twice cites a proverbial saying about Saul's ecstatic behavior (1 Sam 10:11–12; 19:24) and twice quotes a popular song linking the rival exploits of Saul and David (1 Sam 18:7; 21:11). Saul and Jonathan's final defeat at Gilboa is memorialized in the (Song of the) Bow from the Book of Jashar (2 Sam 1:19–27). Traditions that cite theophoric names in Saul's immediate family that incorporated the title baal (Ishbaal and Meribbaal, designating either Yahweh or some other deity) along with the Yahweh name Jonathan are not likely to have been late inventions.

His reported two-year reign (1 Sam 13:1) is too short to accommodate the complex stories told about him. For this very reason, the two-year figure is likely to have been derived from an actual written source of some sort (unless it is textually corrupt), although this does not mean that it is correct. Scattered traditions speak of Saul's complex relationship to the partially assimilated foreign enclave of Gibeon in Benjaminite territory. According to 2 Sam 21:1–10, he committed an atrocity against them that was avenged by David. Moreover, the assassins of his successor Ishbaal were from Beeroth, a town of the Gibeonite enclave (Josh 9:17; 2 Sam 4:2–3). First Chronicles 8:29–33 and 9:35–39 make Gibeon the starting point for Saul's genealogy. These verses show that Saul's genealogy through Jonathan's grandson Mica was still being tracked in late preexilic times.

Finally, 2 Sam 2:9 gives what could very well be an authentic description of the extent of Saul's kingdom as inherited by his son Ishbaal and administered by the latter from Mahanaim east of the Jordan. The regions or districts designated as "all Israel" are enumerated as Gilead, the Ashurites, Jezreel (the town and its environs north of the Gilboa ridge; cf. 1 Sam 29:1), Ephraim, and Benjamin. Saul clearly would not have controlled Beth-shean (1 Sam 31:10–12, although archaeology does not support a distinctively Philistine presence there) and apparently not Judah. The curious name Ashurites may refer to elements of the tribe of Asher located in the southern part of the Ephraimite hill country. Rule north of the Jezreel Valley to incorporate the Galilee territory of Asher seems unlikely if Saul did not control the Jezreel Valley cities (Megiddo, Taanach, Beth-shean, and Ibleam; cf. Josh 17:11). The likelihood of Saul's rule over Gilead is strengthened by multiple witnesses of a bond of some sort between Saul and Benjamin with Jabesh-gilead (1 Sam 11; 31:11; 2 Sam 2:4–5; 21:12; cf. Judg 21:8–14 and Obad 1:19).

Saul was celebrated as a Benjaminite folk hero. Resistance on the part of Benjamin to its partial incorporation into the later kingdom of Judah would have been a likely scenario. Such sedition is evidenced by the stories of Shimei's curse (2 Sam 16:5–8) and of the rebellion of Sheba and his Bichrite clan, memorialized by its stock proverbial taunt (2 Sam 20:1; cf. 1 Kgs 12:16). Saul's reputation and popularity were apparently great enough to require later pro-David and pro-Judah tradents and storytellers to spend considerable effort in order to delegitimize him. Saul is variously portrayed as foolish, mad, untrustworthy, and apostate. For example, there is the honey incident of 1 Samuel 14, the unmotivated violence of 1 Sam 18:10–11, the broken promise of 18:17–19, and the employment of a medium as described in 28:6–25. The campaign to vilify Saul also appears in a thinly disguised way in the story of Benjamin's shameful support of an atrocity committed at Saul's traditional power base Gibeah (Judg 19–21).

Yet paradoxically, supporters of the Davidic dynasty also found it necessary to legitimize David' claim to kingship through his connections to Saul. David is portrayed as a mistreated but loyal servant, son-in-law, guardian of royal inviolability (1 Sam 24; 26; also 2 Sam 21:12–14), and partner to a covenant with Saul's heir Jonathan (1 Sam 20:14–17, 42; 23:18; 2 Sam 21:7). David is celebrated as one who honored his oath to Saul (1 Sam 24:21–23 [EV vv. 20–22]). David may also have taken over Saul's wife Ahinoam (1 Sam 14:50; 2 Sam 3:2).

As stated above, the narratives about Saul portray him in terms of being a chief instead of a king. His family is prominent (1 Sam 9:1). He comes to power because of personal attractiveness (9:2; 10:23) and military success (1 Sam 11). He relies on his kinfolk to serve him. Cousin Abner and son Jonathan are military commanders. The stories about Saul are told in a context that expects one of his sons to succeed him. Conflict with the expanding Philistines, who have garrisons in the highlands (1 Sam 10:5; chs. 13–14) and at least temporary influence at Beth-shean (31:10) is exactly what would be expected. Saul's disastrous battle with the Philistines below and on the ridge of Mount Gilboa has strong support in early, poetic tradition (2 Sam 1:20–21).

Beyond this, what is reported about Saul's military exploits and disasters does not rise to the level of historical evidence. Saul is cast into the model of the heroic judges. Speaking as Yahweh in 1 Sam 9:16–17, the Deuteronomistic Historian (DH) presents him as a judge, who "will deliver my people from the hand of the Philistines ... because their cry has come to me." Saul thus continues the effort that Samson and Samuel began (Judg 13:5; 1 Sam 7:7–14). The stirring tale of Saul's decisive reaction as spirit-filled deliverer, called from farm labor like Gideon, to the atrocity of Nahash the Ammonite (reported to be an ally of David; 2 Sam 10:2) also treats him as a judge (1 Sam 11). Saul is described as leading huge armies that incorporate both Israel and Judah (1 Sam 11:8; 15:4). Benjaminite storytellers seeking to glorify him naturally envisaged victories over Israel's traditional enemies: Philistines (1 Sam 13–14; 17), the hated Amalekites (1 Sam 15), Moab, Ammon, and Edom (14:47–48). Conflict with the far-off kings of Zobah (v. 47) sounds completely unlikely. However, if Saul's range of authority did include Gilead, then conflict with Ammon there is at least plausible. The story of Saul's defeat of the Amalekites and subsequent killing of Agag their king (1 Samuel 15) has a clear didactic intention: obey prophetic commands or else. Agag may have been the traditional stock name for kings of Amalek (Num 24:7, 20).

2.3. David

David left behind a wide footprint in tradition but little in the way of historical evidence. Like Saul he was almost certainly a genuine historical figure, but again undoubtedly more like a chief than a full-blown king. Most scholars believe that his role as founder of what became the kingdom of Judah is verified by its designation in the Tel Dan inscription as "house of David" (*COS* 2.39:161–62). This same phrase may also occur near the end of the earlier Mesha Inscription, but the reading remains controversial. David's name is associated with that of Saul in the traditional song preserved in 1 Sam 18:7; 21:11. The name David itself may have been a throne name or title ("beloved one"). One reason for thinking that this was the case is the tradition that one Elhanan from Bethlehem was the slayer of Goliath (2 Sam 21:19). As we shall see, the author of Kings used a source that appears to have had access to a Judahite King List (JKL, see §3.1.2). Since such a JKL was most unlikely to have started with the unheroic Rehoboam, one must assume that it opened with David as dynasty founder and then Solomon.

The kingship of David is portrayed in ways characteristic of the ruler of a chiefdom. His commander Joab and the hero warriors Abishai and Asahel may have been relatives (1 Chr 2:16). The practice of accumulating and distributing goods is indicated by 1 Sam 30:21–25. Narratives imply that David used marriage to expand his circle of relationships, including connections to the family of Saul through Michal and to the clients of the wealthy Calebite pastoralist Nabal by way of Abigail. Ahinoam mother of Amnon may have previously been one of Saul's wives (1 Sam 14:50; 2 Sam 3:2). The genealogical material focused on Hebron (2 Sam 3:2–5) lists multiple wives, and a second catalog of sons indicates that he continued this practice in Jerusalem (5:13–16). One of these marriages may have been the result of a diplomatic arrangement involving the king of Geshur (2 Sam 3:3; cf. 13:37–38; 14:23).

The designation of Jerusalem as "city of David" (2 Samuel; 1 and 2 Kings; Neh 3:15; 12:37; Isa 22:9; 29:1) witnesses to the veracity of the claim that David conquered the city that became the capital of Judah.

Tradition certainly suggests no other candidate for the capture of this previously non-Israelite city. The tale of David's cunning triumph is linked to a feature of the city's water supply (perhaps a natural precursor of Warren's Shaft) and also provides an etiology for an obscure proverb connected to the temple (2 Sam 5:6, 8).

The Jerusalem sanctuary etiology of 2 Samuel 24 asserts the holiness and effectiveness of the Jerusalem sanctuary (cf. 1 Chr 22:1; 2 Chr 3:1) and helps soften predictable puzzlement over the tradition that David did not build a temple. This same function lies behind the pre-Deuteronomistic text of 2 Samuel 7. These two texts offer persuasive evidence that David did not build a temple, in spite of what would normally be expected of a victorious dynasty founder. A feature of the later Jerusalem temple was the ark, the purported saga of which is recounted in the literary composition found in 1 Sam 4–6 and 2 Sam 6. The story concludes with David's bringing the ark to a tent shrine in Jerusalem. This narrative serves as an elaborate etiology for the ark's numinous power and its presence in Jerusalem. The Ark Story probably cannot be used as a source for historical information about David (see §2.7.2). Interest in the ark is also characteristic of the seventh-century DH and of the Jerusalem-centered Zion theology that developed around the time of Hezekiah's escape from Assyrian retaliation in 701 (and later, of course, of the Priestly writer).

Other elements in the tradition about David that may well be trustworthy are narratives linked to toponyms such as Keilah, Horesh, the Rock of Escape, and the hill of Hachilah (1 Sam 23; 26:1, 3). Other localities where tales about David may have been recounted are the Baal-perazim shrine on Mount Perazim south of Jerusalem (2 Sam 5:18–21; Isa 28:21). In the Ark Story, the place Perez-uzzah (2 Sam 6:6–8) may have been a breach (Hebrew *pereṣ*) in the Jerusalem city wall, conceivably associated in some way with the Garden of Uzza (2 Kgs 21:18, 26). The name Achish (king of Gath) is Philistine at least, appearing in two seventh-century witnesses as the name of a king of Ekron. First Samuel 27:1–6 provides an etiology explaining why Ziklag and its environs were a private estate of the kings of Judah. Undoubtedly Absalom's monument near Jerusalem (2 Sam 18:18) provided opportunities for storytelling about him. The place name Atroth-beth-joab (1 Chr 2:54) in the neighborhood of Bethlehem gives some support for the historicity of David's notorious henchman Joab. Traditions about Joab were also tied to the pool in Gibeon and a familiar stone landmark there (2 Sam 2:12–32; 20:4–10). The booty distribution list of 1 Sam 30:27–31 is specific and idiosyncratic enough to be some sort of

2. STATE FORMATION (TO CA. 930)   55

source document cataloging places in the neighborhood of Hebron and Beersheba.

Second Samuel 23:8–39 catalogs a roster of David's elite warriors and accounts of their heroic exploits. First Chronicles 11 repeats a more extensive parallel list. The roster's diverse makeup fits well with the tradition of David's gathering a band of disaffected troublemakers (1 Sam 22:2). The group represents many towns (including northern locations such as Gibeah of the Benjaminites, Pirathon, and Anathoth), David's family members (Abishai, Asahel), and foreigners (from Ammon, Maacah, and Zobah, as well as Uriah the Hittite). Probably this list is a later scribal construct mined from extant heroic tales. The list of Levitical cities and the roster of minor judges are comparable examples of artificial scribal productions (Josh 21; Judg 10:1–5; 12:7–15). A similar text celebrates the fabled exploits of four giant killers (2 Sam 21:15–22). Such traditions extolling David's champions served, of course, to glorify David himself.

For the most part, however, the Hebrew Bible simply recounts folktales of a Habiru-like raider and picaresque hero from Bethlehem who opposed Saul with Philistine support. The materials describing David's rise to power are similar in genre to the fifteenth-century statue of Idrimi king of Alalakh (*ANET*, 557–58; *COS* 1.148:479–80) and just possibly could have their ultimate source in a similar inscription. Like David, Idrimi supposedly experienced flight, joined a Habiru group, attracted refugee supporters, and after seven years seized the throne of Alalakh. However, the plot outlined in Idrimi's inscription is almost certainly fictive. In any case, folkloristic and literary motifs abound in the David tradition. The youngest and least likely of many brothers is chosen by divine designation. A young boy with humble weapons defeats a giant. The hero succeeds in an impossible task to win the hand of the king's daughter. He assembles the equipment he needs, such as an extraordinary sword and intrepid followers. His personal charisma beguiles a worthy woman. Feigned madness (a ruse attributed to Odysseus in classical literature) saves him from a perilous predicament. After many setbacks, through charm, pluck, and piety, the former shepherd boy turns out to be the shepherd of Yahweh's people (the narrative arc from 1 Sam 16:11 to 2 Sam 5:2).

Unsurprisingly, military success over the standard catalog of Israel's enemies was credited to David. He was supposedly victorious over Amalek (1 Sam 30), Philistia, Moab, Zobah and other Aramaean kingdoms, and Edom (2 Sam 8:1–14; cf. 1 Sam 14:47–48 for Saul). Second Samuel 10 reports a major conflict with Hanun king of Ammon and Hadad-ezer of

Zobah, who was leading an Aramaean coalition. This story is used to provide a context for the siege of Rabbah and the episode about Bathsheba and Uriah. A successful conclusion of the siege of Rabbah is said to have allowed David to take over Ammon (2 Sam 12:26–31). It must be noted that the conflicts reported in 2 Sam 10 and 11 are part of the later literary work often called the Court History of David (see §2.7.4) and so cannot be used for historical reconstruction. Moreover, any large-scale regional conflict is unlikely at this early date. Instead, claims of military success were advanced to glorify the memory of David, crediting him with hegemony or influence over a large swath of Syria-Palestine. This ongoing process of venerating David would reach mythic levels in the later Judahite monarchy (Pss 2:8; 72:8).

Biblical literature about David seeks to protect his reputation, presumably against accusations made over the years by inveterate Saulide supporters from Benjamin. One reads that he was explicitly not responsible for the deaths of Saul, Ishbaal, or Abner and publicly mourned each one (2 Sam 1:17–27; 3:28–34; 4:9–12). Ishbaal's misfortune was his own fault (3:6–11; 4:1), as was Michal's fall from favor (6:20–23). David took scrupulous care of Meribbaal and his son Mica (2 Sam 9; 19:25–31] [EV vv. 24–30).

Second Samuel 8:15–18 and 20:23–26 present two variants of a purported roster of David's court officials. If authentic, these lists would indicate a relatively sophisticated level of organization for David's administration. A recorder, secretary, and administrator of forced labor are mentioned. Actually, however, it is likely that these rosters were constructed on the basis of the similar roster preserved for Solomon in 1 Kgs 4:2–6. The Solomonic list evidently derives from a written source used by the author of Kings (see §§2.5.1 and 2.5.2). To fabricate the roster for David, the data of Solomon's list were stripped down and moved chronologically backward one generation. The resulting changes correspond to the situation of David's era and incorporate names found in narratives about David. Following the order of the Solomonic list:

- Azariah son of Zadok was eliminated in favor of his father.
- Instead, Joab, liquidated by Solomon (1 Kgs 2:34), was added at the beginning of the David list.
- The two sons of Shisah were removed, leaving their father behind in the form of the corrupt or variant name Sheva or Seraiah (LXX: Shausha).

- Jehoshaphat son of Ahilud was kept.
- Solomon's commander Beniah son of Jehoiada was given a prehistory as commander of the Cherethites and the Pelethites (2 Sam 15:18; 20:7), because the redactor knew that Joab had been David's general.
- Zadok and Abiathar (the latter only in 2 Sam 20:25) were kept because they are characters in the David stories.
- Azariah and Zabud, sons of Nathan, were eliminated because their father is a character in the David stories.
- Ahishar, Solomon's official over the palace, was eliminated
- Adoniram (Adoram in 2 Sam 20:24 and 1 Kgs 12:18), who administered forced labor for Solomon, was kept in the 2 Sam 20 list (only), because of David's conscription of Ammonite captives (2 Sam 12:31) and perhaps in order to prepare for Adoniram's upcoming role in 1 Kgs 5:28 [EV v. 14] and 12:18.
- 2 Sam 8:17 mentions "Ahimelech son of Abiathar" as priest. This mistakenly reverses the correct sequence "Abiathar son of Ahimelech." Verse 18 remarkably adds David's sons as priests.
- 2 Sam 20:26 adds one Ira the Jairite as David's priest. He would have been a non-Levite from a clan of Manasseh (Num 32:41). Although this perceived anomaly has generated numerous textual variants, this one name at least quite probably rests on a genuine piece of tradition.

To sum up, David probably began his rule over some areas of Judah (Hebron, Ziklag, and the towns and groups south of Hebron listed in 1 Sam 30:27–31). The awkward tradition that at one point he was a Philistine vassal is likely to be authentic. He captured Jerusalem. He made that venerable city his capital, claimed the title of king, and founded a dynasty. He did not build a temple. He had a complex and conflicted relationship with Saul, the Benjaminite ruler. Chronologically, the two figures may have overlapped as rival kings. David may have taken over the territory of Ishbaal's kingdom or at least extended some measure of influence over Benjamin, the hill country of Ephraim, and Gilead. The Philistines would naturally resist the establishment of any effective inland kingdom centered on Jerusalem, so Philistines forays up-country along the city's western approaches could easily have taken place (2 Sam 5:17–25).

2.4. The Vision of a United Kingdom

Historians of ancient Israel have increasing misgivings about the existence of a tenth-century united kingdom. Jerusalem has yielded hardly any archaeological evidence stemming from this period. There is no inscriptional support for a centralized polity in Palestine in the tenth century. The dating of monumental defensive architecture once commonly attributed to the tenth century (Gezer, Megiddo, Hazor), and thus to Solomon, is now under dispute. What is more, the Hebrew Bible describes Solomon's realm as a fabulous empire with a sphere of influence that stretched from the Gulf of Aqaba (1 Kgs 9:26) north into Syria to the Euphrates (1 Kgs 5:1, 4 [EV 4:21, 24]). Today all but the most conservative scholars agree that the notion of a Solomonic Empire of such dimensions is completely implausible.

The concept of a united kingdom of David and Solomon, as described by 2 Samuel and Kings, is a utopian ideal. It embodies a much later national-unity paradigm that had its beginning only in the late eighth or the seventh century. It is significant that no ideology of cooperation between north and south appears anywhere in Judg 2–12. This ideological unity paradigm may be seen in phenomena such as the idiom "from Dan to Beersheba," the adoption of the name Israel into Judahite self-identity (e.g., Isa 8:14), and the secondary computation of reign synchronisms that coordinate the two kingdoms in the book of Kings (see §3.2.2). Perhaps this pan-Israel ideology stemmed originally from the arrival of northern refugees in Judah after the Assyrian conquest of Israel in 720, combined with the expansionistic ambitions of Hezekiah. In that time of crisis, Judah rethought the traditions of its past in order to make itself the true heir of an ideological Israel, a Davidic/Solomonic realm. In this way, Judah, the junior partner in a long and sometimes conflicted relationship with Israel, achieved a refreshed identity. As the Hebrew Bible developed, Judah conceived of itself as the legitimate successor of a glorious united kingdom, while Israel was vilified as a rebellious, break-off nation. David was remembered as the founder not just of a polity designated as "house of David"—the designation for Judah in the Tel Dan stela—but also of a powerful united kingdom inherited by his son Solomon and squandered by his grandson Rehoboam. In a similar way, the ancient shrines of Bethel and Dan were converted into disobedient innovations, illegitimately competing with Jerusalem. The same thing happened to the venerable bull ("golden calf") iconography for Yahweh, the age and legitimacy of which is demonstrated by the so-called bull-site shrine discovered in the northern highlands.

This emergent pan-Israel ideology appears in the Torah. The Judahite patriarch Abraham, whose stories are associated with Hebron, Beer-sheba, and Jerusalem, became the grandfather of the northern ancestral hero Israel/Jacob, who was linked to Bethel, Shechem, and Peniel. In the psalms of the Jerusalem temple, Yahweh is designated "God of Israel" and "Holy One of Israel" (e.g., Pss 68:9, 36 [EV vv. 8, 39]; 59:6 [EV v. 5]; the royal psalms 72:18; 89:19 [EV v. 18]). Significantly, this is also true of the Jerusalem-focused prophet Isaiah (e.g., Isa 12:6; 21:10; 29:23). Yahweh is "God of Jacob" in royal and Zion psalms (Pss 20; 46; 76; 84), and the "floating oracle" of Isa 2:3 and Mic 4:2 designates the temple "the house of the God of Jacob." Many suggest that it was the Aaronic priesthood located originally at Bethel (an association suggested by Judg 20:26–28 and the golden calf incident) that brought these northern elements into the Jerusalem cult.

The concept of a united kingdom served the theological purposes of later writers, especially those of the DH, who was intent on maximizing whatever possibilities were present in available sources in order to promote the ideal of a united kingdom. One of these sources was a prophetic narrative about Ahijah from Shiloh that assumed the split of a single kingdom into two unequal halves (1 Kgs 11:29–39; 12:15). DH characterized the separation as a matter of divine displeasure over Solomon's apostasy and the result of Rehoboam's youthful arrogance. In a more general sense, DH supported this pan-Israelite ideal by writing a history that interleaved and chronologically synchronized the two kingdoms into a single story.

In summary, the story that David was first king over Judah in Hebron, and then later was invited by the leaders of Israel to reign over them, does not provide a sufficient foundation on which to erect a united kingdom of Judah and Israel. Tribal structures and evolving royal administration doubtlessly functioned side by side for an extended period. As will be discussed below (see §§2.5.3 and 2.5.4), Solomon's kingdom seems to have been a clientele state, that is, an admixture of ethnicities, regions, and affiliations each linked directly to the person of the king rather than to each other. His Jerusalem court was associated with northern Israelite entities through associations less structured than direct monarchic rule. Solomon's son Rehoboam could not continue the relationships Solomon had maintained with these various northern groupings. Instead, the Ephraimite leader Jeroboam was able to assemble an ethnic kingdom of uncertain extent in the north. This polity centered on Shechem as its capital. In truth,

Shechem had far better traditional credentials to serve as capital of Israel than the alien city of Jerusalem (Gen 34; Judg 9). This Shechem-based kingdom remained unstable for forty or fifty years until put on a stronger footing by the vigorous and assertive Omri.

Nevertheless, even if there never were a united kingdom, Israel and Judah still shared an undeniable cultural unity stemming from their shared roots in Iron I hill-country settlements and particularly founded on the cult of a shared national god, Yahweh. Shrines or high places to Yahweh were sited throughout the territory of the two kingdoms (notably Beer-sheba, Hebron, Bethel, Gilgal, Shiloh, Tabor, Dan). Yahweh names appear in the early traditions of both north and south. In the north one may point to Joshua, Joash, and Jotham in Judges, and Jonathan. Judah too preserved stories about figures whose names incorporated Yahweh, such as Joab son of Zeruiah and Benaiah son of Jehoiada. Prophets crossed the border to speak messages from Yahweh (Amos). The epic of what it meant to be Yahweh's people existed in parallel versions, a southern Yahwistic and a northern Elohistic account. The ambiguous status of Benjamin, split between the two kingdoms, ensured that the politics of the two kingdoms would always be intertwined. Of course, it was natural that the economically superior and more internationally oriented Israel would dominate the relationship.

2.5. Solomon

Although the once-popular idea of a major Solomonic Empire and a corollary Solomonic enlightenment (a concept particularly associated with Gerhard von Rad) are unsupported by evidence, it is almost certain that Solomon actually existed and ruled as king. He probably built monumental buildings, including a temple in Jerusalem dedicated to Yahweh.

Fragments of evidence for Solomon's existence can be extracted from one of the sources used by Kings, repeatedly cited there as the "Book of the Chronicles of the Kings of Judah" (see §3.1.1). The notices for Rehoboam's accession are dependent on this chronicles source (1 Kgs 14:21, 29). It relates that Rehoboam came to the throne at age forty-one and that his mother Naamah was from Ammon. This strongly suggests that he was the product of a diplomatic marriage of an Ammonite princess to Solomon. This marriage must have been arranged at least forty-two years before Rehoboam's accession, either by Solomon himself or more likely, given the four decades involved, by Solomon's predecessor (ostensibly David). A diplomatic marriage points to the existence of a king and a state of some sort at least one generation and probably two generations before Rehoboam. It may be significant that Nahash the king of Ammon, Saul's adversary, was supposedly David's ally, but that his son Hanun was David's enemy (2 Sam 10). However, this last bit of information is suspicious because it appears in the Court History (see §2.7.4) to justify the war with Ammon and provide background for the Bathsheba episode.

The numbers that describe Solomon's acts and chronology are completely generalized—forty, twenty, seventy—and cannot be given historical weight. Solomon's name may mean "substitute," something that might have given rise to the story of an older brother's death (2 Sam 12:15–23). If it is taken to mean "consolation," it could have helped generate the story of David comforting Bathsheba after the death of her first husband (v. 24). In a tantalizing way, the name Solomon also echoes Shalem, the putative pre-Israelite god of Jerusalem. Solomon's alternate name Jedidiah (beloved by Yahweh) may have been a throne name, perhaps related to the same verbal root lying behind David's name.

Tradition as reflected in the Court History works very hard to convince readers that Solomon was really David's son and legitimate successor. For example, Bathsheba's firstborn has to die because this protects Solomon's legitimacy and claim to the throne. Being born second means that he can be neither Uriah's son nor a product of adultery. Such intense literary effort indicates that there must have been some sort of suspicion about Solomon's origin as David's son. It is not impossible that the supposed biological connection between these two founding royal figures was an artificial political claim, negotiating the relationship between Judah (David) and the urban polity of Jerusalem (Solomon). It may be significant that David and Solomon are never linked with each other in genuinely old material (that is, outside of the Court History, the contributions of DH, and the Hiram story of 1 Kings 5). Second Samuel 5:13–15 may be an exception. However, the designation of Jerusalem as "city of David" (2 Sam 24; 1 Kgs 3:1; 9:24; elsewhere in 2 Samuel and 1 and 2 Kings; Isaiah) provides credible evidence that David indeed conquered the city and passed it on to his successor Solomon. Therefore, the strongest historical bridge between David and Solomon may not be one of parentage but through their successive control of Jerusalem. Solomon would hardly have been the only ancient western Asian figure to claim legitimacy through fictive parentage (Sargon II, probably Tiglath-pileser III, the various rivals of

Darius I)! In any case it was David who gave his name to the subsequent kingdom as house of David.

Citations of materials about Tyre in Josephus derived from Hellenistic historians (*Ant.* 7.66; 8.62; 8.144–149, 8.163; *Ag. Ap.* 1.112–125) are very unlikely to be useful in reconstructing tenth-century history. According to Josephus, Tyrian records specify that the Jerusalem temple was constructed 143 years and 8 months before the foundation of Carthage (thus ca. 957; *Ag. Ap.* 1.108) and that Hiram (Ahiram son of Abibaal) appeared in a Tyre King List (*Ag. Ap.* 1.121–125). It is likely that biblical authors actually learned of the Hiram who supposedly interacted with Solomon (1 Kgs 5:15–32 [EV 5:1–18]; 9:10–14) through contacts with the later Tyrian king Ethbaal (Ittobaal) during the Omride period.

2.5.1. The Book of the Acts of Solomon

Kings implies that it used the Book of the Acts of Solomon (BAS) as a source. The author characterizes the contents of that source as "all that Solomon did and his wisdom" (1 Kgs 11:41). Of course, this citation could have merely been a literary invention by the author of Kings intended to supply Solomon with a source like those cited for later kings or to associate Solomon with the glorious record-keeping achievements of eminent foreign kings. However, the presence of non-Deuteronomistic redactional summaries (3:28; 5:9, 14 [EV 4:29, 34]; 10:4–5, 23–24) makes it likely that BAS was indeed a source document used by DH. BAS appears to have been a literary work with an ideological slant, not an official archive. Nevertheless, there is a strong likelihood that real data taken from some kind of earlier document are embedded in it. Of course, its value as a historical source must be carefully considered on a case-by-case basis. The summary designation "his wisdom" (11:41) suggests it contained folktale material such as 3:4–13, 16–28; 5:9–14 [EV 4:29–34]; and 10:1–10. Yet, as an account of "all that he did," the BAS appears to have incorporated lists of Solomon's officials (4:2–6, 7–19) and building activities (e.g., 9:15–19). Perhaps BAS was a sort of scribal project. Some of the sources it used (such as the correspondence between Hiram and Solomon; 1 Kgs 5:15–23 [EV vv. 1–9]) may have been fabricated model texts copied in scribal education.

Much of what was reported in BAS is unmistakably ideological and cannot be used to reconstruct history: dream theophanies, folktales, laudatory statements about the king's wisdom, King Hiram's services to

Solomon, and a long temple description that appears to reflect much later realities. The Solomon of the BAS rules over all of Israel (1 Kgs 5:27 [EV v. 13]; 8:1–3) as well as over an extensive empire (5:1, 4 [EV 4:21, 24]; 8:65).

BAS is a structured literary work. It is organized by a repetition of the theme of those who "came to Solomon": two prostitutes (1 Kgs 3:16), those from all nations and kings (5:14 [EV 4:34]), Hiram the bronze worker (7:14), and finally the Queen of Sheba (10:1–2). Its description of an idealized past uses common ancient western Asian scribal conventions, such as reports of construction projects, and rhetoric characteristic of ancient royal propaganda. There are extravagant summaries of Solomon's achievements, such as "Judah and Israel were as numerous as the sand by the sea; they ate and drank and were happy" (4:20). Such statements are not far removed from the propaganda claims of Neo-Assyrian kings. Gold is everywhere; the word appears over thirty times associated with Solomon. The Queen of Sheba folktale gathers together in a summary fashion the themes of Solomon's fame: wisdom, international trade, and wealth.

Reports of Solomon's construction of a palace complex would have been an expected feature of any text intended to idealize his glory. The description of Solomon's extraordinary administrative acropolis in 1 Kgs 7:1–12 is again presumably from BAS. It is characterized by obscure and perhaps archaic technical terms. The descriptions focus on the costly splendor of the five buildings, their massive dressed masonry, and their cedar pillars and beams. It is impossible to assess the historical value of this text. It can be said that the scope and nature of what is described is on a scale similar to the acropolis of Samaria built by Omri. On the other hand, the last building on the list (v. 8b) depends on the dubious tradition that Solomon was married to a daughter of Pharaoh (3:1; 9:16, 24). However, some historians feel that such a diplomatic marriage would not have been impossible.

The story of ceding the land of Cabul (1 Kgs 9:11–14) depends on the account of Hiram's supplying building materials for Solomon's projects. It seems to be an etiology of a substantially later border adjustment between Israel and Phoenicia. Descriptions of Solomon's trading activities from BAS (9:26–28; 10:11–12, 14–15, 22, 28–29) are entangled with the legendary motif of his fabulous wealth and cannot be taken at face value.

The building notices in 1 Kgs 9:15–19, with the heading "This is the account of the forced labor," are presumably derived from BAS. They are difficult to evaluate. The question of whether Hazor, Gezer, and Megiddo can be considered evidence of tenth-century centralized planning remains mired in archaeological controversy. However, any ruler of Jerusalem would be interested in fortifying Gezer in order to protect the approach to the city through the Aijalon Valley. Solomon had a representative (see §2.5.3) in the Shaalbim and Beth-shemesh area (4:9) so forced-labor construction in Gezer would be possible even if the story of the city's being a wedding present from some Pharaoh is legendary (3:1; 9:16; for forced labor at Gezer, see Josh 16:10). Solomon could conceivably have engaged in fortification work at the strategically sensitive sites of Megiddo and Hazor if those cities were within the sphere of affiliated groups owing him an obligation for forced labor (for Megiddo, see 1 Kgs 4:12; for Hazor located in Naphtali, see 4:15). First Kings also reports on construction work at Lower Beth-horon and Baalath (9:17–18; for the latter, see Josh 19:44), sites also important to the defense of Jerusalem. Fortification of Tamar in the wilderness (1 Kgs 9:18; some witnesses have Tadmor) would indicate a desire to secure the route south to Ezion-geber on the Aqabah, thus giving some credibility to what is reported in 9:26.

The massively fortified Iron IIA town of Khirbet Qeiyafa (perhaps Shaaraim) offers solid evidence of a strong central administration intent on protecting Jerusalem at this period. This town, situated between Azekah and Socoh, defended Jerusalem from attack from the direction of Gath and Ekron through the Elah Valley. It was built as a new foundation directly on bedrock at the very beginning of Iron IIA and incorporated a casemate wall and a four-chamber gate. Its status as a Judahite site is substantiated by an absence of pig bones. It is difficult to know what to make of the ostracon discovered there. It is written from left-to-right script in an early alphabet consistent with the late eleventh and early tenth century. However, it is unclear if this undeciphered find is even really a text in the normal sense of the word, although several Northwest Semitic roots have supposedly been read.

The Millo (1 Kgs 9:24; 11:27; filled terrace?) of Jerusalem continued to be an architectural feature of the city in later periods (2 Kgs 12:21 [EV 20]; 2 Chr 32:4–5). This Millo is often associated with the massive Stepped Stone Structure uncovered on the east side of the lower city, but could also refer to work done to fill in a saddle to the north of the city of David. The extravagant description of Solomon's temple in 1 Kgs 6–7 is heavily shaped by ideology (gold and cedar abound) and the much later building known to the author of Kings. The historian must discount lavish details reported about layout and decor. The floor plan resembles MB prototypes at Megiddo and Shechem as well as two neighboring ninth-century tripartite temples at Tell Tayinat in Syria. The two freestanding columns are found in an LB temple at Hazor and in a pottery miniature shrine from Tirzah. The reported size of Solomon's temple is larger than any Canaanite or Phoenician temple so far uncovered and is probably an exaggeration.

However, it is completely reasonable to credit Solomon with constructing the first Yahweh temple in Jerusalem. Biblical materials are clear and unanimous that David did not build one, although this is what one would expect a purely idealistic tradition to assert. Nor is there any hint that any king later than Solomon could possibly be a candidate for its construction. Rehoboam already had a temple to ransack for tribute, according to what is probably a reliable notice (1 Kgs 14:26–28). The use of the archaic (that is, non-Babylonian) month names Ziv, Bul, and Ethanim in texts about the temple (6:1, 37, 38; 8:2) may point to an early source. The ark, whatever its previous history, was most likely a feature of Solomon's temple, since something must have indicated the divine presence in the inner room of the building. On the other hand, Judg 18:30–31 suggests that an image of Yahweh would not have been unthinkable at this time. Certainly the possibility that Solomon rebuilt or reused an earlier ("Jebusite") sanctuary instead of initiating an entirely new construction (as hinted by 2 Sam 12:20) cannot be excluded and would be consistent with ancient practice. It is sometimes suggested that 1 Kgs 8:12b–13 (particularly in its LXX form, 3 Kgdms 8:53a) was a temple-building inscription reflecting old religious notions appropriate to the earliest monarchy period.

The Solomon of BAS is Solomon as envisaged by the later royal court of Judah, a legendary figure whose glory subsequent Davidic kings sought to share. Jehoshaphat attempted to enhance his prestige by emulating Solomon's supposed trading prowess (1 Kgs 22:48). The men of Hezekiah collected proverbs attributed to Solomon (Prov 25:1). Judah's theologians would trace the fulfillment of Yahweh's dynastic promise directly through Solomon as David's biological heir (2 Sam 7:12, 14–15; 1 Kgs 2:45; Ps 132:11). According to the Court History, Solomon's ascent to the throne was the product of Yahweh's will (2 Sam 12:25; 17:14). The ideal of a glorious Solomonic realm from Dan to Beersheba (1 Kgs 5:5 [EV 4:25]) would serve the political purposes of Hezekiah and Josiah.

The authors of the Hebrew Bible were not completely positive about Solomon, of course. According to the schema of DH, the latter part of his reign described in 1 Kings 11 was characterized by folly and apostasy. Solomon's diplomatic marriages, which were a sign of his power in earlier tradition (3:1; 9:16), were reinterpreted into an appetite for dangerous foreign women in violation of Deuteronomic law (Deut 7:3-4). The size of his harem was not a mark of glory but the cause of Solomon's apostasy with foreign gods and his construction of shrines to them (1 Kgs 11:7; 2 Kgs 23:13). According to the story told by DH, Yahweh's anger over these wives becomes the theological cause for a division of Solomon's realm. The law of the king in Deut 17:14-20 reflects a similar negative interpretation of Solomon's wives and his horses from Egypt (1 Kgs 10:28).

To bring Jeroboam onto the stage, the author of Kings used a source about three adversaries (1 Kgs 11:14-28, 40). This narrative is shaped by a literary structure intended to vilify Jeroboam. Hadad of Edom flees to Egypt and receives favor there. He has good reason to oppose David's house and returns to cause trouble for Solomon when David dies. Rezon flees his lord the king of Zobah and sets up a kingdom in Damascus. He too becomes an enemy of Solomon with good cause because of David's slaughter of the troops of Zobah (2 Sam 8:3-5). The narrative then moves on to Jeroboam to cast him in a negative light. Like Hadad he is a tool of Egypt, and like Rezon he is a servant disloyal to his legitimate master. However, unlike Hadad and Rezon, in this source Jeroboam has no reasonable cause to oppose Solomon. There is no reason to credit this narrative with historical value.

2.5.2. Solomon's Court Officials (1 Kgs 4:2-6)

The register of Solomon's officials in 1 Kgs 4:2-6 was most likely derived from BAS. Thus it represents a legitimate source with potential historical value. It is comparable to a similar roster of Nebuchadnezzar II (*ANET*, 307-8). In its present context the roster is being used for literary purposes in order to illustrate what it means that Solomon reigned over "all Israel" (4:1). In addition, the list serves the literary purpose of communicating continuity between David and Solomon, because similar lists in 2 Sam 8:16-18 and 20:23-26 appear to offer an earlier stage of royal organization. Finally, the mention of forced labor points forward to 1 Kgs 5:27 [EV v. 13], 9:15-23 and the events of chapters 11-12.

There are strong internal indications of authenticity of the roster itself. First, the name Shisha (1 Kgs 4:3) seems to be an Egyptian word for a royal official or secretary. This foreign title could have been a holdover from the pre-Solomonic administration of Jerusalem. Second, another son of Ahilud besides Jehoshaphat (v. 3) appears in the next list of officials (v. 12). Third, names appear that are not found elsewhere in the Hebrew Bible: Elihoreph (perhaps Egyptian), Zabud (Palmiran: "given"), Ahishar ("my divine brother is righteous"), Abda ("servant"). These are mixed in with the better-known names Benaiah, Zadok, and Nathan. Finally, the historicity of Adoniram/Adoram is buttressed to some extent by the fairly unexpected circumstance that this appears to be a theophoric name meaning "may Hadad be exalted." According to the roster, Solomon's administration was elaborate enough to require (1) three officials dealing with records and written matters, (2) an army commander, (3) a secretary of state supervising deployed envoys or representatives (see §2.5.3), (4) a friend of the king to advise him on public and private affairs, (5) an administrator for the palace and crown property, and (6) an overseer of conscript labor. As indicated above (§2.3), the two lists of David's court officials were apparently derived from this roster (2 Sam 8:15–18; 20:23–26).

2.5.3. Solomon's Agents (1 Kgs 4:7–19)

Almost every study Bible, Bible atlas, and introductory textbook has a map with a title along the lines of "The Administrative Districts of Solomon's Kingdom." These maps provide Roman numeral identifications and boundaries delineating twelve geographic units into which the northern part of the united kingdom was supposedly divided. Although this understanding of the roster preserved by 1 Kgs 4:7–19 is widely accepted, it is a product of overinterpretation and a failure to recognize the difference between a preserved source document and the use made of it by the author who has transmitted it. Calling this a "district list" goes far beyond the evidence. Described more accurately, it is a roster of officials of some sort connected to geographic designations, supplemented with added informational items or glosses, and set into the surrounding account by an interpretive heading (v. 7) redactionally related to 5:17–18 [EV 4:27–28]). A modern European and North American perspective has caused most interpreters to read the roster in terms of a centralized kingdom organized into administrative subdivisions that can be drawn on a map with definite boundaries. This viewpoint appears to be largely uninformed by anthropological models of nonstate, protostate, and emerging state polities.

Bible translations generally reflect this misconception. One reads not merely of neutral officeholders, but of district governors (NIV), prefects

(NJPS), deputies (NASB), administrators (NJB), and even commissaries (NAB). The *Einheitsübersetzung* renders the term as *Statthalter*, that is, "provincial governor." Of course, such interpretive translations are influenced by the redactional heading of the list (4:7): "Solomon had twelve officeholders over all Israel, who provided food for the king and his house. Each had to provide for one month a year." Some translations even carry the preposition "over" from verse 7 into the conclusion of the list in verse 19b, for example:

> And there was one governor who was over the land. (ESV)
> He was the only governor over the district. (NIV)

Yet the preposition in verse 19 is the same as it is in each element of the list proper, "in" and not "over."

Attempts to convert the locations in the roster to districts and map them differ widely. To some degree these differences are caused by uncertainties over site identifications. However, most disagreement is over the extent of verse 12 (so-called Region V) southward into the Jordan Valley and whether the boundary between verse 13 and verse 14 (so-called Regions VI and VII) in Transjordan ran north and south or east and west. The extent of verse 10 (Arubboth and Socoh; so-called Region III) is complicated by its inclusion of the land of Hepher. Joshua 17:2–3 understood in light of clan names from the Samaria ostraca (see §3.5.8) make it clear that the location of Hepher impinges on what is supposed to be Region I (v. 8, hill country of Ephraim). Many but not all such problems disappear once the attempt to map out districts is abandoned.

Viewing this as a list of administrative districts has led historians into far-reaching and unwarranted conclusions. Particularly popular is the notion that this supposed district system reflects Solomon's attempt to undermine tribal structures, especially those of Ephraim (1 Kgs 4:8–10) and Manasseh (vv. 8, 10, 11–12). However, this conclusion assumes that the formalized tribal territories described in Joshua were indeed a premonarchic reality. Scholars also tend to draw connections between the extent of Asher in verse 16 and the Cabul incident (9:10–13), but without any real warrant. The absence (or special place) of Judah in the system is sometimes thought to reflect a specially favored tax status for the tribe. The phrase "in the land" in verse 19b is often equated with Judah (LXX, NRSV).

Some scholars consider this roster to be nothing more than a scribal, fictional composition reflecting the conventional ancient ideology of the wealthy, model king who brings order to the land. They note that the names Ahilud, Ahimaaz (ben Zadok?), and Baana ben Hushai are found in surrounding narrative texts and could have been derived from them. Skeptics also point out that the roster is contextualized by the Deuteronomistic phrase "all Israel" of 1 Kgs 4:7 and develops the topic sentence of verse 1: Solomon was king over all Israel. The subject of palace provisions is simply a continuation of the ongoing literary theme of abundance that concludes with 5:7–8 [EV 4:27–28]. However, this negative viewpoint overlooks the circumstance that the theme of provisioning Solomon's court in verse 7 and the surrounding context is redactional and is not part of the original roster.

It is true that any notion of a month-by-month responsibility for provisioning the royal court from far-off places in Galilee and Transjordan is unrealistic and must represent a literary fiction. This could not have been the original purpose of the roster under discussion. The hypothetical twelve territories possess different climate and topographic features. Each would have produced different sorts of crops and would have had widely varied capacities to support the court. Moreover, overland transport of any but high-value foods (wine and oil) was completely impractical in the ancient world (cf. Deut 14:24–25). The Samaria ostraca (*ANET*, 321) reveal the actual practice of provisioning a royal court. The support system was local, with food being brought in from royal estates and through the structures of nearby clans. The unworkable concept of a monthly rotation of suppliers from distant regions has its origin in the ideological and literary theme of Solomon's wealth, not historical reality.

Nevertheless, this list of officials connected to tribes and city locations still appears to be an authentic survival that is earlier than the text into which it is embedded. It makes no sense as an administrative structure from any later period, yet it seems too idiosyncratic to be a scribal invention. There are several persuasive indications of authenticity:

- The roster has few connections to the textual material surrounding it. For example, the towns of Makaz and Arubboth do not appear in any other Hebrew Bible texts, so there is nowhere from which a creative scribe could have picked them up.

- The absence of personal names in verses 8–11, where only the patronymic appears, suggests either an archival document damaged along one edge or an echo of an administrative practice known from Ugaritic and the Amarna letters. Either possibility is an argument for authenticity.
- There are genuine-sounding particularities and matters of incoherence. For example, two persons are named Baana (vv. 12 and 16). There is also a peculiar overlap between Ben-geber in Gilead (v. 13) and Geber in Gilead (v. 19).
- The division of Benjamin (v. 18) as split between the kingdoms of Judah and Israel is not observed. The geographical extent of the list is not coterminous with the later kingdom of Israel.
- Socoh and Mahanaim are mentioned in Pharaoh Shishak's list (see §3.3.2), possibly along with Arubboth. These towns would have been occupied during the tenth century.
- The absence of Judah cannot be explained on the basis of a literary or ideological explanation and so appears authentic.

Consequently, the underlying text of the list, as opposed to its redactional context, does not seem to be fictional or a reflection of later concerns. In fact, the roster as it stands describes exactly the situation one would expect in a new polity negotiating Israelite tribal and Canaanite city-state realities. No doubt the administrative and scribal structures inherited from pre-Israelite ("Jebusite") Jerusalem must have had the resources to produce and preserve such a document.

What did these officeholders do and how did they relate to their assigned areas and tribes? The roster itself does not indicate that they were governors or were responsible for the delivery of foodstuffs. The title (as noun *nĕṣîb* and *niphal* substantive participle *niṣṣāb*, "one set over") is often translated in similar contexts as "administrator," "governor," or "prefect." First Kings 22:48 (EV v. 47) and Sir 46:18 seem to suggest the meaning "governor," but other examples (1 Kgs 5:30 [EV 5:16]; 9:23; 2 Chr 8:10) imply a position of less importance than a provincial governor. In any case, the title is not found in the list per se, only in its framework (1 Kgs 4:7, 19b; 5:7 [EV 4:27]). It is only 4:7 that positions these persons "over all Israel" and (with 5:7–8 [EV 4:27–28]) associates them with provisioning the royal court. The "over all Israel" formula is redactional and repeated from 4:1. In 1 Kgs 5:7–8 (EV 4:27–28) the viewpoint of the framework erected by 4:7 is continued, and these officeholders are again associated with the delivering of supplies for the palace and fodder for Solomon's horses. In fact, the expression "all those officeholders" in v. 5:7 [EV 4:27] connects directly back to 4:19, and the intervening laudatory material is something of an excursus.

Unlike the preposition "over" in the prefatory 1 Kgs 4:7, the prepositions in the roster itself do not indicate oversight or supervision. The relationship between the named persons and the locations associated with them is handled in three ways. The preposition is "in" (better: "within") for verses 8, 19 (regions), verses 9, 10, 13 (city or city lists), and verses 15, 16, 17, 18 (tribes). There is simply no preposition in verse 11 (region) or verses 12 and 14 (city or city list). Verses 10 and 13 use the preposition "belonged to" in order to indicate supplemental geographic information (v. 13 is an intertextual gloss). When more than one city (vv. 9, 12) is mentioned, the preposition "in" can hardly have been intended to indicate a place of residence or a regional capital, but rather an area of influence. The same would seem to be the case for the tribal designations. The preposition "in" used for geographical entities as diverse as a single city, a list of cities, a geographic region, or a tribe does not communicate oversight, rule, or supervision. In other words, this syntax does not imply an supervisory office like governor, but rather an appointment involving a nonhierarchical relationship to the regions or tribes involved.

Instead of governors, one should think of envoys, representatives, or agents-in-place. (I am indebted to H. M. Niemann for this understanding of the matter. See the bibliography.) These men were reliable sons-in-law (vv. 11, 15), courtiers (vv. 12, 16), and local collaborators who represented Solomon's interests in cites and areas and with tribes, none of which were under his direct control. The list does not describe a system of rule over these northern territories, but instead portrays spheres of royal influence focused on certain towns, regions, and tribes. Earlier tribal structures were certainly still operating. This was not a governance structure so much as a strategy for maximizing royal influence in associated territories and affiliated tribes. The office held by Azariah son of Nathan, designated as "over the officials" in verse 5, does indicate that the royal court coordinated and controlled the activities of these deployed representatives.

Properly understood, the roster reveals a good deal about the extent and nature of Solomon's sphere of influence in the north. Certain regions are designated by tribal names: Naphtali (v. 15), Asher (v. 16; Bealoth probably means "in the highlands"), Issachar (v. 17), Benjamin (v. 18), and perhaps Gilead (v. 19). These reflect five of the ten tribal groupings that appear in the Song of Deborah. Other territories have regional referents (hill country of Ephraim, v. 8; Naphath-dor, v. 11; land of Gilead, v. 19). The others are designated by towns (vv. 9, 10, 12, 13, 14). The first part of the list is patterned as an inner, clockwise circle of regions or areas defined by towns (vv. 8–14). This is followed by an outer grouping of tribes or tribal areas (vv. 15–18). Verse 19a is a region described by a geographic or tribal name. Verse 19b presents a puzzle: "and there was one official who was in the land." Many suggest that this is a reference to Judah, based on the use of the expression "the land" in 9:18. This is the understanding of LXX and NRSV. A textual corruption (through haplography) is also possible since "Judah" is the first word in the following verse 20.

There are contacts with the scheme of tribal territories found in the book of Joshua. First Kings 4:9 overlaps to some extent with the town list for Simeon (Josh 19:41–46). A portion of 1 Kgs 4:12 relates to the wedge of towns not immediately controlled by Manasseh (Josh 17:11–13). Three areas correspond approximately to the Transjordanian tribal allotments described in Josh 13:15–24: Ramoth-gilead (1 Kgs 4:13) with eastern Manasseh, Mahanaim (v. 14) with Gad, and land of Gilead (v. 19; LXX, Gad) with Reuben.

These officeholders, then, were appointed on order to maintain and strengthen Solomon's affiliations and special relationships with various entities in the north.

- The surviving tribal structures of Naphtali, Asher, Issachar, Benjamin, and Gilead
- The Transjordanian strongpoints of Ramoth-gilead and Mahanaim, previously associated with Saul and Ishbaal
- The extensive hill country of Ephraim region that later became the core of Jeroboam's kingdom
- The strategic cities of Dor and the wedge of Taanach/Megiddo/Beth-shean with its influence southward into the Jordan Valley. These latter cities may have retained self-government and did not yet consider themselves or were not considered by others as Israel.

2.5.4. The Solomonic Polity

The situation reflected in 1 Kgs 4:8–19 is precisely what would be expected from a Davidic/Solomonic polity that united Judah with the former city-state of Jerusalem and its supporting agricultural territory. Outside of Jerusalem, what would later become the kingdom of Judah would still have been characterized by tribal and clan structures (that is to say, Simeon, Caleb, Kenez, and Othniel, in addition to tribal Judah). This Jerusalem-centered kingdom was only loosely affiliated with the north, where several distinct tribal and urban organizational patterns were still operating. In the long run, however, climate and geography would lead to a restoration of the earlier situation of the Amarna period. It was only natural that the richer and more densely populated north would eventually coalesce into a unified kingdom with its center at the crossroads city of Shechem.

The extent of what would have been considered the territory specifically belonging to the city of Jerusalem, as opposed to Judah or other elements in Solomon's complex kingdom, cannot be determined. The boundary between Judah and Benjamin given in Joshua (Josh 15:9; 18:16) does not provide enough territory to the south of the city. There are narrative indications of uncertain value that the border of Jerusalem with Benjamin was considered to be Bahurim (2 Sam 3:16; 16:5–8; 17:18), but the location of this place is uncertain. In the Amarna period, Bethlehem had been considered part of Jerusalem's territory.

Rather than being a united monarchy or a small-scale empire, then, Solomon's polity should be understood in terms of clientele state. In such a polity, an assortment of ethnicities, regions, and affiliations are linked directly to the person of the king rather than to each other through a centralized administration.

2.6. Chronology and Archaeology

The incursion of Pharaoh Shishak read in conjunction with 1 Kgs 14:25 fixes the end of Solomon's reign at about 930 (see §3.2.2). In considering chronology, it may be necessary to allow for some overlap between Saul and David since they apparently did not rule over the same territory in succession. The reports that David and Solomon each reigned forty years (2 Sam 5:4; 1 Kgs 2:11; 11:42) can hardly be trusted and actually indicate that no records were available to the biblical authors. The assertion that

David reigned seven years six months in Hebron and thirty-three years in Jerusalem is also unreliable and formulaic (2 Sam 2:11; 5:5). However, it is possible to engage in some rough calculations. Rehoboam was forty-one (the oldest accession age of any king of Judah) when he came to the throne abut 930. This would put his birth about 970. Solomon was supposedly born in Jerusalem after David had begun to reign there (according to the Court History) and must have been at least about fifteen when Rehoboam was born. This means that David would have been ruler in Jerusalem at the latest by about 990 or 985. In the end, however, one must be content to affirm that Saul and David probably governed in the first half of the tenth century and Solomon was reigning by the early second half.

The emergence of statehood is indicated by an abandonment of the small Iron I villages in the highlands and a subsequent period of urbanization beginning in Iron IIA. Almost all the hill-country settlements that had begun in Iron I were destroyed or deserted during the end of Iron I and the beginning of Iron II. A few developed instead into urban centers, Dan, Hazor, and Mizpah, for example. Most of the rural sites of Iron II were new foundations rather than continuations of Iron I settlements. This difference in settlement patterns must be connected with the formation of the two kingdoms. Perhaps security concerns connected with Philistine and other threats first led to an abandonment of villages that would be hard to defend. Subsequently, the two centralized states emerging in Iron II provided enough security to resettle the highlands and at the same time led to greater urbanization. This resettlement process began first in Israel (ninth century) and then in Judah (eighth century).

Unfortunately, disagreement within the discipline about chronology and the interpretation of certain key sites means that archaeology provides the historian with little help in regard to judgments about the magnitude (or even existence) of Solomon's kingdom. The centralized, united, and powerful kingdom described in 1 Kings would certainly have been characterized by centralized planning and large-scale architecture. The conventional view has been to interpret three relatively large cities in the same stratigraphic horizon as evidence of this. Similarities among Hazor X, Megiddo VA–IVB, and Gezer VIII, taken together with the mention of these cities in 1 Kgs 9:15, have been taken to be evidence of Solomon's building activity. All three cities have six-chamber (four-entryway) gates and impressive public architecture. Megiddo and Hazor have casement walls and Gezer either a casemate or a double wall. The scant evidence of domestic architecture at Gezer suggested to the excavators that it was a strong point or outpost defending Jerusalem. Megiddo VA–IVB has two palatial buildings of ashlar masonry. There are issues involving the stratigraphic relationship of various elements such as the date of the gate at Megiddo, which now seems to postdate Solomon and belong to Stratum IVA.

However, the most important controversy has to do with the interpretation of pottery chronology. The generally accepted sequence is as follows: (1) unburnished red slip ware as mid-eleventh to mid-tenth century, (2) hand burnished red slipware as mid- to late tenth century, and (3) wheel-burnished red slip ware as ninth century. Hand-burnished ware is characteristic of Hazor X, Megiddo VA–IVB, and Gezer VIII. The destruction of Gezer is coordinated with this pottery type, and if this destruction can be attributed to Shishak (along with that of Arad XII), a mid- to late tenth-century date is indicated. The capture (but perhaps not destruction) of Megiddo by Shishak is suggested by the discovery of his stela there.

In contrast, the Low Chronology (LC) lowers the dates of Philistine Bichrome (see §1.4.2) and non-Philistine ware correlated to it, so that Megiddo VA/IVB is dated to the mid-ninth century. This lowers the date of the transition between Iron I and IIA to the early ninth century, with Iron IIA concluding with the abandonment of the Jezreel compound at the end of the Omride dynasty (about 840). This means that the LC fixes state formation in Israel to the early ninth century, with Israel being the older of the two kingdoms. The monumental architecture of Megiddo VA–IVB is assigned to Omri and Ahab, not to Solomon. This entails an equivalent redating downward to the Omride period for Gezer VIII and Hazor X. The upshot is that Omri is credited with founding the first kingdom worthy of the name, and that Judah formed into a state only later. There is no room for any tenth-century state ruled by David and Solomon.

The problem seems to be that at present the archaeology of tenth- and ninth-century Palestine lacks secure dating pegs. One dates the close of a period by the destruction or abandonment of a stratum, and archaeologists tend to date destructions by textual evidence. However, there is legitimate controversy over whether one should credit Shishak for any city destructions at all. Moreover, destruction layers can also result from an earthquake or violence caused by internal discord. In the end, the time-scale difference between the conventional chronology and LC is only about fifty to seventy years, and this is not specific enough to provide much help to the historian. Moreover, if Solomon was a less glorious king who ruled less intensely over a less extensive portion of Palestine than the Bible insists, it is unclear that it matters too much to the historian whether the grand construction projects of Gezer, Megiddo, and Hazor are credited to Solomon or to later kings.

It is hardly surprising that remains from tenth-century Jerusalem are scarce, given the city's complex history, explosive growth in later periods, and present situation as a living, urban community. The interpretation of individual excavation results remains a matter of contention. It is increasingly clear, however, that Jerusalem was a fortified urban center with a socially stratified population in the tenth century. The city apparently continued to make use of fortifications originating in MB. Stratified remains on the city's eastern slope indicate that Stratum 14 is to be identified with Iron IIA, that is to say, the tenth century according to conventional chronology. The Stepped Stone Structure is a huge retaining wall, apparently dating from the transition from LB II to Iron I, when it must have supported some sort of monumental architecture. This installation appears to have been partially dismantled in order to allow for the tenth-century construction of an elite residential district on it. The nature and function of what is termed the (apparently Iron I) Large Stone Structure farther up the slope, and apparently associated with the Stepped Stone Structure, remains controversial. The Ophel Inscription, eight letters incised into a large storage jar, indicates some level of literacy at this period, although decipherment has proven to be a challenge.

2.7. Literature of the Period

It is difficult to make a case that any written biblical literature originated in the period of state formation. It is likely that certain orally transmitted sayings, poetry, and folktales can be traced back to the tenth century. Folktales survived because they were tied to locations such as tombs and geographic features. As noted above, traditional sayings are preserved about Saul's ecstatic behavior (1 Sam 10:11–12; 19:24) and the rival exploits of Saul and David (1 Sam 18:7; 21:11). Lists that appear to be old describe the extent of Ishbaal's realm (2 Sam 2:9), Solomon's court officials, and his deployed envoys. Literature of social protest such as the Way of the King (1 Sam 8:11–18) could have arisen at any point in the monarchy, as centralized government became more heavy-handed.

The earlier written sources usually proposed as lying behind the book of Samuel consist of the Ark Story (1 Sam 4:1–7:2; 2 Sam 6:1–9 either continues the story or is a later supplement), the Rise of David (1 Sam 16:14–2

Sam 5:12), and the Court History (2 Sam 9–12 and probably 1 Kgs 1–2). In contrast, other traditions about Samuel and Saul in 1 Sam 7–11, 13–15, are more disordered and do not seem to go back to any earlier unified source. In addition, the author of Kings used BAS (see §2.5.1).

2.7.1. Poetry in 1 and 2 Samuel

Hannah's Song in 1 Sam 2 is a typical psalm of thanksgiving. The author of the final form of Samuel borrowed it to introduce the themes of the book. Along with the poems at the end of the book (2 Sam 22:2–51; 23:1–7), Hannah's Song explores the role of Yahweh in Israel's history as one who performs acts of reversal and transformation. As a god who kills and brings to life and who brings low and also exalts, Yahweh is celebrated as the force behind the deliverance of Israel by Samuel and Saul, Saul's fall and David's rise, and the personal and familial tragedies of David's reign.

Saul and Jonathan's final defeat at Gilboa is memorialized in the (Song of the) Bow quoted from the Book of Jashar (2 Sam 1:19–27). This work was apparently named for the bow of Jonathan (v. 22) and sung as though by David himself ("my brother," "me"). By its very nature the song cannot be dated, but it reflects the traditional story as told in 1 Samuel. It mentions Philistines, Gilboa, and Jonathan's love for David as surpassing the love of women (v. 26; cf. 1 Sam 18:1, 3; 20:17).

2.7.2. The Ark Story

The Ark Story (1 Sam 4:1–7:2; 2 Sam 6:1–9) follows the journey of the ark. The ark is taken from Shiloh and captured by the Philistines. In each Philistine city to which it is moved, the ark causes trouble, insulting the god Dagon, spreading disease, and instigating panic. Repeated mention of Yahweh's "hand" makes it plain that these difficulties are the result of divine displeasure over the way the ark is being treated. Wisely, the Philistines devise a plan that permits the ark to decide for itself where it wishes to go. The ark heads straight up-country into Israel's territory at Beth-shemesh, but even there it continues to bring about calamity. Transported one stage closer to its eventual goal in Jerusalem, it remains quietly at Kiriath-jearim for twenty years. When David tries to take the ark to Jerusalem, a thoughtless misstep forces him to leave it at a house along the way. Soon that household prospers, which David takes as a sign that he should continue to transport the ark, albeit more carefully, to Jerusalem, where Yahweh clearly desires it to end up. This entertaining and sophisticated narrative serves as a justification and etiology for the ark's presence in the Jerusalem temple. It probably does not date from the time of Solomon as a defense for his father's religious policy, as some have suggested, but from the early Judahite monarchy. Perhaps it was intended to counter northern charges that the ark in Jerusalem's temple was not the same ark that tradition situated in the old Shiloh sanctuary or that its transfer to Jerusalem had been an illegitimate move.

2.7.3. The Rise of David

The Rise of David (1 Sam 16:14–2 Sam 5:12) is also a skillful example of literary art. It recounts how Yahweh worked to transfer the kingship from Saul to David. Its theme has often been expressed in the phrase "Saul must decrease and David must increase" (a paraphrase of John 3:30). At the beginning of the story, Yahweh removes the divine spirit from Saul, and the king is tormented by a spirit of depression and distrust instead. David arrives at Saul's court either as a musician or as a heroic giant slayer. David is successful at every turn, praised by the people and beloved even by Saul's daughter and son. Saul's pathological jealousy is inflamed, and acts of increasing desperation testify to his psychological breakdown. He slaughters an entire priestly family and attempts to learn the future by calling up Samuel's ghost. At the same time, David's career trajectory moves upward. Winning military successes, eluding Saul at every turn, protected both by Saul's family and Saul's enemies, David gains riches and wives. David benefits from deaths with which he has nothing to do (Saul, Jonathan, Ishbaal, and Abner). In the end Yahweh establishes him as king. The lowly shepherd boy (1 Sam 16:19) has risen to become shepherd king (2 Sam 5:2). This work was written to legitimate the Davidic dynasty as Yahweh's choice. As an artistically skillful piece of literature, it is unlikely that it could have been composed in the early days of an emergent Davidic/Solomonic state. It must date from a later period of the Judahite monarchy, perhaps composed in order to counter diehard Saulide supporters.

2.7.4. THE COURT HISTORY

The Court History (or Throne Succession Story; 2 Sam 9–20; 1 Kgs 1–2) is the most sophisticated of these three sources. Its point is hardly the glorification of David, Solomon, or the Davidic dynasty. The story wends its way through complex side plots and subplots and is populated by well-developed characters. The work is highly entertaining and displays significant literary artistry and psychological insight. Yahweh's will hides behind the scenes, revealed only by the comments of the narrator. Displeased by David's adultery and murder (2 Sam 11:27), Yahweh raises evil against David from within his own family (12:11), but loves Solomon from the day of his birth (12:24). Yahweh causes bad advice to sound like wisdom (17:14). In the end, Solomon ascends to the throne, but only over the bodies of his rivals and enemies. Given its literary sophistication and theological outlook, this work is likely the latest of the sources utilized in the books of Samuel. Yet at least two themes relate to issues that would have been important in an early monarchic context. First, the continuing hostility of Benjamin and of intransigent supporters of the Saulide monarchy is foregrounded and defused. This is achieved through the ambiguous position of Merib-baal (Mephibosheth) and his guardian Ziba (2 Sam 9; 16:1–4; 19:25–31 [EV vv. 24–30]), the vicious hostility of Shimei (16:5–13; 19:17–24 [EV vv. 16–23]) and his subsequent liquidation (1 Kgs 2:8–9; 36–46), and the failure of the revolt led by the Benjaminite Sheba (2 Sam 20). Second, the work insists that Solomon was David's legitimate biological heir, even at the expense of David's own reputation. This rather desperate measure suggests a pressing need to counter popular doubts and subversive tales about the circumstances of Solomon's birth and the validity of the claim that he was David's son.

3. The Kingdoms of Israel and Judah (ca. 930–720)

Athas, George. *The Tel Dan Inscription: A Reappraisal and a New Interpretation* (JSOTSup 360; Sheffield: Sheffield Academic, 2003). **Daviau**, P. M. et al., eds. *The World of the Arameans* (Sheffield: Sheffield Academic, 2001). **Dever**, William G. *The Lives of Ordinary People in Ancient Israel* (Grand Rapids: Eerdmans, 2012). **Dobbs-Allsopp**, F. W., et al., eds. *Hebrew Inscriptions: Texts from the Biblical Period of the Monarchy with Concordance* (New Haven: Yale University Press, 2005). **Finkelstein**, Israel. *The Forgotten Kingdom: The Archaeology and History of Northern Israel* (Ancient Near East Monographs 5; Atlanta: Society of Biblical Literature, 2013). **Grabbe** Lester L, ed. *Ahab Agonistes: The Rise and Fall of the Omri Dynasty* (LHB/OTS 421; London: T&T Clark, 2007). **Hagelia**, Hallvard. *The Tel Dan Inscription: A Critical Investigation of Recent Research on Its Palaeography and Philology* (Acta Universitatis Upsaliensis 22; Uppsala: Uppsala University Library, 2006). **Hagelia**. *The Dan Debate: The Tel Dan Inscription in Recent Research* (Recent Research in Biblical Studies 4; Sheffield: Sheffield Phoenix, 2009). **Howard**, D. M., Jr., and M. A. **Grisanti**, eds. *Giving the Sense: Understanding and Using Old Testament Historical Texts* (Grand Rapids: Kregel, 2003). **Kofoed**, Jens B. *Text and History: Historiography and the Study of the Biblical Text* (Winona Lake, Ind.: Eisenbrauns, 2005). **Lipinski**, Edward. *The Arameans: Their Ancient History, Culture, Religion* (OLA 100; Leuven: Peeters, 2000). **Matthews**, Victor H. *Studying the Ancient Israelites: A Guide to Sources and Methods* (Grand Rapids: Baker Academic, 2007). **Mazar**, Amihai, ed. *Studies in the Archaeology of the Iron Age in Israel and Jordan* (JSOTSup 331; Sheffield: Sheffield Academic, 2001). **Parpola**, Simo, and Michael **Porter**, eds. *The Helsinki Atlas of the Near East in the Neo-Assyrian Period*

(Helsinki: Casco Bay Assyriological Institute and Neo-Assyrian Text Corpus Project, 2001). **Pury**, Albert de, Thomas **Römer**, and Jean-Daniel **Macchi**, eds. *Israel Constructs Its History: Deuteronomistic Historiography in Recent Research* (JSOTSup 306. Sheffield: Sheffield Academic, 2000). **Robker**, Jonathan M. *The Jehu Revolution: A Royal Tradition of the Northern Kingdom and Its Ramifications* (BZAW 435; Berlin: de Gruyter, 2012). **Routledge**, Bruce. *Moab in the Iron Age: Hegemony, Polity, Archaeology* (Philadelphia: University of Pennsylvania Press, 2004). **Schoors**, Antoon. *The Kingdoms of Israel and Judah in the Eighth and Seventh Centuries B.C.E.* (trans. Michael Lesley; Biblical Encyclopedia 5; Atlanta: Society of Biblical Literature, 2013). **Tadmor**, Hayim, and Shigeo **Yamada**. *The Royal Inscriptions of Tiglath-Pileser III (744–727 BC) and Shalmaneser V (726–722 BC), Kings of Assyria* (Royal Inscriptions of the Neo-Assyrian Period 1; Winona Lake, Ind.: Eisenbrauns, 2011). **Uehlinger**, Christopher, ed. *Images as Media: Sources for the Cultural History of the Near East and the Eastern Mediterranean (1st Millennium BCE)* (OBO 175; Fribourg: Universitätsverlag, 2000). **Wildberger**, Hans. *Isaiah 28–39* (Minneapolis: Fortress, 2002). **Wilson**, Kevin A. *The Campaign of Pharaoh Shoshenq I into Palestine* (FAT 2/9; Tübingen: Mohr Siebeck, 2005). **Yamada**, Shigeo. *The Construction of the Assyrian Empire: A Historical Study of the Inscriptions of Shalmaneser III (859–824 BC) Relating to his Campaigns to the West* (CHANE 3; Leiden: Brill, 2000).

3.0. Summary

Beginning about 930, two monarchic polities developed out of whatever arrangements had earlier governed the peoples of Palestine. The dominant ethnicity was now the people of Yahweh. These were clans and tribes associated with each other through cultural and linguistic similarities, political interactions involving Saul, David, and Solomon, and the worship of a common national god. Judah consisted of tribal Judah (incorporating subsidiary kinship groups such as Simeon and Caleb) in an affiliation of some sort with the ancient city of Jerusalem along with its surrounding economic zone. The kingdom of Judah also included elements of Benjamin. The core of Israel was the hill country of Ephraim centered on Shechem, along with Gilead. Perhaps reacting to these developments, Pharaoh Shishak marched through portions of northern and far southern Palestine

3. THE KINGDOMS OF ISRAEL AND JUDAH (CA. 930–720)

about 925. The two kingdoms would struggle over the line of their shared border for about a generation.

Israel suffered dynastic instability until the rise of Omri, who built Samaria as his capital and was the real founder of the Israelite state. Omri established a long-running dynasty and was able to occupy territory claimed by Moab. From this point on, Judah remained a junior partner in a usually peaceful relationship. Omri's son Ahab was the first king of Israel to face an expansionistic Assyria in the form of the numerous western campaigns of Shalmaneser III. Ahab fought as a major coalition partner in an engagement that stopped an Assyrian advance at Qarqar in 853. Later, King Mesha of Moab successfully regained its territory from Israel, probably in the time of Omri's grandson Jehoram.

Changing international circumstances led to a coup by the usurper Jehu against the Omri dynasty in about 841. The result was the violent death of the kings of both Israel and Judah. However, biblical and outside sources apparently contain divergent accounts of these deaths. The death of Judah's king caused an interruption in the rule of Judah's ruling dynasty, the house of David. It was supposedly restored with the accession of Jehoash, which came about under ambiguous circumstances.

Beginning with the end of the reign of Shalmaneser III in the 820s, Assyria's domination in the west weakened. This circumstance provided the opportunity for the kings of Damascus, successively Hazael and Ben-hadad II, to wage effective warfare against Israel during the reigns of its kings Jehoram and Jehoahaz. However, their successor Jehoash of Israel was able to reverse the tide. Jehoash also came into conflict with Judah's king Amaziah. At the end of the ninth or very beginning of the eighth century, Jehoash paid tribute to Assyria, reestablishing the policy of acquiescence to Assyria followed by his grandfather Jehu.

After the assertive military actions of Adad-nirari III, Assyria again stopped interfering in the west beginning in the 790s. This respite allowed Israel and Judah to enjoy prosperity and independence for about fifty years. The overlapping reigns of Jeroboam II of Israel and Azariah/Uzziah of Judah were characterized by peace, prosperity, and difficult social change. This period of security and good fortune came to an end with the accession of Tiglath-pileser III, who seized the throne of Assyria in 745. Israel's ruling classes were divided over whether to follow a strategy of compliance with Assyria or resist its demands. This disagreement led to internal political unrest. Zechariah, the last king of the Jehu dynasty, was murdered by one Shallum, who in turn was immediately assassinated by Menahem.

Heavy taxation to support Menahem's compliance policy was unpopular. This discontent resulted in his son Pekahiah's facing a military coup. He was replaced by Pekah, who followed a strategy of resistance.

Pekah and Rezin king of Damascus joined together in an alliance to resist Assyria. They put pressure, perhaps military pressure, on Judah's king Ahaz in order to neutralize a potentially dangerous force to their rear. Tiglath-pileser moved west in 734 and then directly against the two renegade kingdoms in 733–732. At some point during this crisis, Ahaz agreed to pay tribute to the Assyrian king. Tiglath-pileser conquered Damascus and Israel and organized all but the portion of Israel in the hill country of Ephraim into imperial provinces. Hoshea, whom Tiglath-pileser had confirmed as Israel's new king, was found to be disloyal. Israel's independence ended when Samaria fell to Assyrian forces, perhaps to Shalmaneser V in 722 or to Sargon II in 720.

3.1. Kings: Sources and Reliability

The sources used by the book of Kings for the names and sequence of the kings of Israel and Judah and the length of their reigns were generally reliable. These data often receive outside confirmation from Assyrian sources. Mesopotamian texts coordinate Shalmaneser III (858–824) with Ahab and Jehu and affirm the usurpation of the throne of Damascus by Hazael (2 Kgs 8:7–15) from its king Adad-idri (misnamed Ben-hadad in Kings). Adad-nirari III (810–783) synchronizes with Jehoash of Samaria. Tiglath-pileser III (744–727) coordinates with Ahaz of Judah, along with Menahem, Pekah, and Hoshea. Sennacherib (704–681) is contemporaneous with Hezekiah. Second Kings puts Merodach-baladan in the right period. The name of Sennacherib's murderer, Arda-Mullissi, is corrupted to Adrammelech in 2 Kgs 19:37. Manasseh overlaps with both Esarhaddon (680–669) and Assurbanipal (668–ca. 627). Kings is also correct about Omri, in a general way about Mesha and his revolt, and the Hazael/Ben-hadad/Rezin royal sequence in Damascus.

3.1.1. Summary Citations

Of course, one must be circumspect about using the book of Kings as a historical source, recognizing that it is promoting definite didactic and ideological objectives. Nevertheless, there is evidence that the book's author used at least two potentially trustworthy sources for the period after Solomon. These are cited as the Book of the Chronicles of the Kings of Judah and the Book of the Chronicles of the Kings of Israel. The phrase translated "chronicles" is literally "the affairs of the time of" and is sometime translated "annals" (NJPS, NRSV). The author of Kings cites these two chronicles documents as a literary strategy in order to validate the reliability of the narrative. The balance of probability is that these were genuine sources, actually or at least potentially accessible to readers. Significantly, with one exception (2 Kgs 21:17, "the sins he committed"), the content summaries offered for these sources are ideologically neutral and do not particularly reflect the theology of the Deuteronomistic author (DH). Since these sources were, supposedly at least, available to readers, one must envision published literary works based on some sort of recorded or remembered data. If the reference to Manasseh's sin (2 Kgs 21:17) is not an interpretive addition by the author of Kings, these works were literary in nature and not official annals or archives. DH used them to construct summary citations that conclude portrayals of the reigns of most of the kings of Judah and Israel: "the rest of the acts of x ... are they not written in the Book of the Chronicles of...?"

There are no summary citations for the brief reigns of Tibni, Ahaziah of Judah, Jehoahaz, or Jehoiachin, and for whatever reason, none for Jehoram of Israel. Significantly there are also no summaries for the final kings of either Israel (Hoshea) or Judah (Zedekiah), suggesting that the cited documents were based on ongoing compilations that ceased with the end of each royal administration. Not surprisingly, neither a summary citation nor any sort of regnal data is given for the interloper Athaliah. She was apparently not part of the accepted list of Judah's rulers.

Most of these summary citations are merely formulaic, but seven include references to the sort of material appearing in the cited source documents. If one had access to these sources, one could expect to read about notable exploits (Baasha, 1 Kgs 16:5), exploits and might (Omri, v. 27), and treachery (Zimri, v. 20). We would learn about Ahab's ivory palace and his fortified towns (22:39), Jehoshaphat's mighty military actions (22:45), and Hezekiah's pool and conduit (2 Kgs 20:20). Beyond these brief statements, Kings does not report anything more about Omri's might, Ahab's architectural use of ivory, or Hezekiah's hydraulic engineering project. Therefore, these citations can hardly be authorial inventions fabricated to lend authority the narrative (as is the case with the citations in 1 and

2 Chronicles). The historian can most likely trust what Kings has extracted from these two sources concerning building projects (1 Kgs 15:23; 22:39; 2 Kgs 20:20), military actions and prowess (1 Kgs 14:19; 15:23; 16:5, 27; 22:45; 2 Kgs 10:34; 13:8, 12; 14:15, 28; 20:20), and coups d'état (1 Kgs 16:20; 2 Kgs 15:15).

3.1.2. Kings Lists and Opening and Closing Formulas

In the ancient world, lists of kings stating the length of their reigns were created and preserved in order to facilitate the dating of legal documents and to make ideological claims about a given dynasty's legitimacy. Behind the summary notices in Kings that open and close the narratives about each king, one may trace the existence of an Israel King List (IKL) and a Judah King List (JKL). These were probably available to the author indirectly through the two cited chronicles documents (see §3.1.1). The IKL and the JKL included at least the names of each king and his length of reign. The existence of separate king lists is indicated by a consistent difference in word order for the length of reign in the opening summaries. For Judah the formula is invariably "x years reigned RN [royal name] in Jerusalem," whereas for Israel the length of reign comes after the verb.

King lists were documents intended to legitimate an orderly succession of rulers. Examples may be found in *ANET* and *COS* (Assyria: *ANET*, 564–66; *COS* 1.135:463–65; Babylon: *ANET*, 271–72; a synchronistic list for both nations: *ANET*, 272–74). From Egypt, there is the Turin Canon, composed in the time of Ramesses II. It includes some brief narrative anecdotes (*COS* 137D:71–73). An example culturally closer to Israel and Judah is a brief Ammonite king list from Tell Siran (ca. 600; *COS* 2.25:139–40). This blessing on a bronze bottle contains a short king list with the purpose of buttressing dynastic legitimacy. The kings are Amminadab, Hissil-el, and Amminadab, all three of whom appear in an Assyrian source.

In addition to data about chronology, the notices that open and close the material on each king preserve information about the king's mother (Judah), age at accession (Judah), city of rule, burial, and the ongoing course of the succession. Since this information is tightly associated with the length-of-reign data, it probably also came from the IKL and the JKL. Once again, two separate lists are suggested by the fact that material about queen mothers and ages at accession are presented only for the kings of Judah. With respect to Israel, the names of the capital cities shift from

Tirzah (1 Kgs 15:25, 33; 16:8, 15, 23) to Samaria (1 Kgs 16:29; 22:51; 2 Kgs 13:1, 10; 15:17, 23, 27; 17:1) just as one would expect. Of course the theological judgments in the opening and closing notices for each king ("did what was evil" and the like) stem from the theological perspective of DH and fall outside the realm of historically useful information.

Recurring references to royal burials seem to have had some cultural importance. The Ugaritic King List was used in a royal mortuary cult (*COS* 1.104:356–57), so repeated references in Kings to the burial of Judah's kings suggest a similar function in a cult memorializing the present king's dead progenitors. The presence or absence of death and burial notices in the regnal formulas was something influenced by the associated narratives. These notices tend to be omitted in cases of violent death. Sometimes they are replaced by a narrative describing the king's demise. Much later, in the Hasmonean or early Roman period, a secondary burial of the reputed bones of Azariah in Jerusalem suggests that the identification of royal tombs continued over a long period. The inscription reads, "The bones of Azariah king of Judah were brought here. Not to be opened."

3.1.3. Other Possible Sources

A selection of texts in Kings that deal with the finances of the Jerusalem sanctuary may go back to a source preserving valuable information about the vicissitudes of temple assets. The main concern of this putative temple treasury source is represented by repeated references to "temple" and "treasure" and a repetition of the verbs "give" and "take." These texts are 1 Kgs 14:26 (Shishak); 15:18 and surrounding information; 2 Kgs 12:19 (EV v. 18) and surrounding information; 14:14; 16:8; 18:15; and 24:13. The reasonably good correspondence between 2 Kgs 18:15 and Assyrian sources concerning the amount of gold tribute paid by Hezekiah corroborates that this piece of biblical data goes back to a trustworthy source. The two witnesses agree on thirty shekels of gold, although the silver tribute is three hundred shekels in Kings but eight hundred according to Sennacherib. Even if Kings (or the chronicles source for Judah) used a temple treasury source, there is no reason to accept its accuracy uncritically, especially in matters such as Solomon's fabulous votive gold shields.

Some sentences in Kings evidence a *waw*-perfect style that may reflect the language of an archival source as mediated by the literary sources used by Kings. Characteristic examples are 1 Kgs 9:24–25 and 2 Kgs 18:4. One can also point to examples of the asyndetic pronoun *he* with the perfect (e.g., 2 Kgs 14:7, 22, 25). Other material in Kings could also derive from archival or inscriptional sources. For example, the report of Menahem's tribute sounds as though it is from a chronicle (2 Kgs 15:19–20) and is confirmed by an Assyrian source. This line of reasoning suggests that we may trust similar data in Kings. However, it may not be possible to distinguish between actual scribal record keeping and an imitation of such records by an author trained in the scribal tradition.

Finally, the judicious historian may with some confidence give cautious weight to items such as the following:

- Events dated by a king's regnal year: 1 Kgs 14:25–28; 2 Kgs 12:7 (EV v. 6); 17:5–6; 18:9–12, 13–15.
- Military reports using the verbs "go up," "besiege," "fight" and "capture" such as 2 Kgs 12:18–19 (EV vv. 17–18); 16:6–9; 24:10–17.
- Reports of conspiracies: 2 Kgs 15:10, 14, 25, 30; 21:23.
- Building reports using the verbs "build" or "make" such as 1 Kgs 7:2–8; 12:25; 15:17, 22; 16:24, 34; 2 Kgs 14:22.
- Registers of items or persons recorded so they can be administered. There are parallels in ancient royal inscriptions (*ANET*, 242–43, 249, 260–61, 278–79).
- Second Kings 25 (and Jer 52) sound as though they are drawn from a contemporary report.

In summary, the existence of written sources means that one can realistically postulate that certain narratives in Kings about battles, building projects, notable acts, and usurpations are trustworthy. The same may be said of basic accession data including age at accession and reign length (but *not* synchronisms, see §3.2.2), personal matters such as illness, and temple-related activities.

In contrast, stories featuring prophets must be handled cautiously. Prophet legends and similar narratives have well-defined ideological purposes. They are intended to glorify the office of the prophet and inculcate trust in the prophetic word. These legends would have been transmitted orally within prophetic circles and by prophetic insiders to others (e.g., 2 Kgs 8:4). Such tales are particularly concentrated in 1 Kgs 13, 14, the story cycle of 1 Kgs 17–2 Kgs 10, and 2 Kgs 18–20. Because the prophet and the prophetic word are the focal points of these narratives, the royal protagonist may sometimes be essentially anonymous, identified as only as "the king of Israel" (see 1 Kgs 20, 22; 2 Kgs 3, 5, 6). In the case of the prophetic stories involving the Syrian Wars (1 Kgs 20, 22; 2 Kgs 6:24–7:20) and the war against Moab (2 Kgs 3:4–27), it is entirely likely that the events reported have been set by the author of Kings into the wrong time period (see §3.4.4).

For the eighth century, apparently authentic elements in prophetic books of Hosea, Amos, Isaiah, and Micah can be used with care as sources of historical information. However, separating out later redaction from authentic prophetic oracles is a difficult and contested process.

3.1.4. Comparative Texts

A consideration of comparative texts of a historical nature is useful in judging the character of potential sources used by Kings and the likelihood that they actually existed. The Weidner Chronicle, perhaps composed about 1150, shares with Kings a schematic pattern and the presumption that events can be explained on the basis of divine causation. This Babylonian document describes how kings who neglected Marduk's cult at the Esagila temple suffered an unpleasant fate (*COS* 1.138:468–70).

Assyrian annals chronicled royal accomplishments year by year with a propagandistic spin. These annals reveal a process of editorial and recensional development from one example to the next. Thus the Monolith Inscription of Shalmaneser III (dated 853–852) covered years 1–6. A second example repeats years 1–6 and then updates matters to year 18. A third example from 828–827 carries events down to year 31, summarizing, modifying, and shortening the earlier texts in the process (*ANET*, 274–301; *COS* 2.113–119:261–306). It should be no surprise, then, that biblical historiographical texts should likewise have a propagandistic purpose and reflect editorial change over time.

A useful comparison can be made with an Assyrian text called the Synchronistic History. This covers a period from the fifteenth century up to Adad-nirari III, reporting on military engagements brought about by Babylonian incursions into Assyrian territory. In a way similar to Kings, it navigates two parallel royal chronologies, those of Assyria and Babylon. This pro-Assyrian work has a theological color, in that the god Assur intervenes to defeat Babylon. Physically, the text is structured into ruled-off panels, one for each king.

The Babylonian Chronicle series represent linked texts that cover events from Nabu-nasir (747–734) to Seleucus II (246–226). These texts report on only selected individual years. There are incised dividing lines and regnal-date formulas at the start and end of reigns. The focus is on kingship, succession, and the fate of divine images (*ANET*, 301–7, partial; *COS* 1.137:467–68, partial).

Although no royal inscriptions have been found for either Judah or Israel, the Mesha and Tel Dan inscriptions provide examples erected by neighboring kings. A limestone stela fragment with one legible word from Samaria suggests that Israel's kings did commission royal inscriptions. The Siloam tunnel inscription was not public, not dated, and mentions no king, so it was probably not official. An eighth-century ostracon from Arad (88) sounds like a copy or draft of a royal inscription: "I became king in ... gather strength and ... king of Egypt" (*COS* 3.43M:85).

3.2. Chronology

The chronology of ancient history rests on dates provided by two total solar eclipses. An eclipse of June 15, 763, is mentioned in the Assyrian Eponym List and fixes the years in that list from 910 to 649: "Bur-Sagale of Guzana, revolt in the city of Assur. In the month Simanu an eclipse of the sun took place." In the Eponym List, each Assyrian year was named for a government official. For partial extracts from this source, see *ANET*, 274; *COS* 1.136:465–66. Assyrian dates are solid and provide a framework for dating events across the ancient Near East. In the Persian period, Herodotus dated the battle of Halys with a total eclipse that took place on May 28, 585 (*Hist.* 1.73–74). In contrast, Egyptian chronology is problematic. Dates for the reigns of Egyptian rulers remain uncertain and disputed until the accession of Psamtik I of the Twenty-Sixth Saite Dynasty.

3.2.1. The Kings of Israel and Judah

The chronology of the kings of Israel and Judah is a notoriously complex problem. Pursuing its intricacies often results in more frustration than useful information. Systems of chronology proposing different dates have their advocates, but none is universally accepted. A common feature of all of these systems is the attempt to make sense of both the reign-length

3. THE KINGDOMS OF ISRAEL AND JUDAH (CA. 930–720)

data and the synchronisms between the two kingdoms. The synchronisms, however, are apparently the product of later authorial activity rather than being data derived from an accurate source (see §3.2.2.). It is more reasonable to trust only the length of reign material in Kings, treating it as data derived from the two chronicles documents (and ultimately from separate Judah and Israel King Lists, see §3.1.2). Using only reign lengths, one can come up with a rough but reasonably useful chronology that can be confirmed and corrected by Assyrian evidence.

Nevertheless, an exasperating number of variables necessitates that this procedure must be done with care and cannot always provide assured results. These variables include the following:

- The likelihood of co-regencies and whether the length of a given king's reign was counted from the start of any such coregency or from the date of his sole rule.
- Whether an accession-year or nonaccession-year system was being used. With an accession-year system, each king begins his reign with an unnumbered *accession year*. Then the succeeding years are numbered after the beginning of the first new year. This is sometimes called *postdating* because the first year of a reign is counted after accession. The alternative is the nonaccession-year system (also termed *antedating*) in which year 1 of a king's reign consists of whatever portion of the year of his accession is left. His second year then starts after the first new year begins. In the nonaccession-year system, the last year of the departing king's reign and the first year of the new king are each counted as part of the total reign length for each king.
- Whether the new year for determining regnal years began in the fall (Tishri) or spring (Nisan).
- The tendency of later redactors and copyists to try to fix data that they saw as problematic. This process of correction is evident in differences between the Hebrew and Greek textual traditions.

The result of these interacting variables means that almost every irregularity can be ingeniously explained by shifting the variables around. As a consequence, competing solutions to most chronological problems in the book of Kings are nonfalsifiable, and anything close to certain resolution is unattainable.

Of course, the reliability of even the reign-length information could be undermined by the possibility that artificial patterns have been introduced. There is definitely at least one redactional element in the total picture. The 480 years from the exodus to the start of temple construction (1 Kgs 6:1) derives from editorial motives that involve both the book of Exodus and the DH as a whole. Moreover, it is possible, if one chooses to do so, to calculate 430 total years of reign lengths for Judah from the date given in 1 Kgs 6:1 for the start of temple construction to the temple destruction at end of Zedekiah's reign (37 years after Solomon's year 4 plus 393 years, treating all regnal years as full years). This figure corresponds to the statement that the people lived in Egypt 430 years (Exod 12:40–41).

Other elements about reported royal tenures have been seen as problematic by some. If Athaliah is not counted, each kingdom has precisely nineteen kings after Solomon. Israel's kings between Jeroboam and Jehoram display a concentric pattern of reign lengths ending in two: 22, 2, 24 (= 12 × 2), 2, 7 days (Zimri), 12, 22, 2, and 12. The reign lengths for Israel from Jehu to Hoshea add up to a suspicious 144 years if one allows for the start of a new year sometime during the short reigns of Zechariah and Shallum. The last four kings of Judah reigned 11 years, then 3 months, then 11 years, and then 3 months. This repetition can be coordinated with outside data, but has seemed questionable to certain scholars.

The possibility of errors in the source materials or by the author of Kings is increased by the presence of similar royal names. Two J(eh)orams and Ahaziahs, one from each kingdom, succeed each other in opposite order just before Jehu's coup. Confusion could also have occurred between the two kings named J(eh)oash. To complicate matters further, it has been suggested that Jehoram of Israel and Jehoram of Judah, whose reigns overlapped according to the structure of Kings, could have been the same person.

3.2.2. Synchronisms

In Kings, royal accessions are also dated by synchronisms with the neighboring kingdom. There are comparative examples of this practice from Mesopotamia (the Synchronistic Chronicle [*ANET*, 272–74] and Synchronistic King List). Although these synchronisms may have been a feature of the sources used by Kings, it is more likely that they were calculated by the author of Kings. In any case they create thorny problems. Does Omri comes to the throne in Asa's year 31 (1 Kgs 16:22–23) or earlier during the reign of Zimri in Asa's year 27 (vv. 15–16)? Most scholars assume that Omri attained the throne in Asa's year 27, with his 12 total regnal years being counted from that point, and that Asa year 31 refers to the later defeat of his rival Tibni, at which point he achieved undisputed rule.

Consider another difficulty. Jehoram of Israel comes to the throne in the year 2 of Jehoram of Judah according to 2 Kgs 1:17. This would make the narrative in 2 Kgs 3 that associates Jehoram of Israel with Jehoshaphat impossible. However, 2 Kgs 3:1 (supported by 1 Kgs 22:51) reports that Jehoram of Israel succeeded to the throne in year 18 of Jehoshaphat. What appears to be a later, redactional solution to this problem is provided by 2 Kgs 8:16 MT, which indicates a coregency of Jehoshaphat and his son Jehoram of Judah. To cite yet another problem, 2 Kgs 8:25 places the accession of Ahaziah of Judah in the twelfth year of the twelve-year reign of Jehoram of Israel, but 9:29 corrects this to the eleventh year in order to allow the two kings Ahaziah and Jehoram of Israel to die simultaneously.

Overall, the LXX has somewhat more consistent data than the MT and must be distrusted precisely on that score. Septuagintal variants appear to be attempts to correct the data given in MT. Although scholars have been able resourcefully to explain every synchronism problem in one way or the other by applying the variables of coregency, accession- and nonaccession-year systems, and fall or spring starts for the new year, the results are for that very reason unpersuasive. The synchronisms are secondary and artificial and should not be used for historical reconstruction.

By overlapping the successive kings in a certain order, the author of Kings created another pattern of synchronism that supplements the numerical synchronisms. Kings reports on the entire reign of one king from accession to death, then turns back to report on the king or kings of the alternate kingdom who came to the throne during the first king's reign. Thus Kings reports on Jeroboam I until his death in 1 Kgs 14:20, then goes back twenty-two years to pick up Rehoboam and report on events of his reign until 14:31. Then Kings reports on Abijam and Asa, each of whom started their reign during that of Jeroboam. The story of Asa continues down to 15:24. Then the author backtracks again to pick up Nadab, Baasha, Elah, Zimri, and Omri, all of whom came to the throne during Asa's reign. Ahab's history begins in 1 Kgs 16:29 and continues to 22:40. Then the narrative returns to the fourth year of Ahab to tell about Jehoshaphat. This pattern continues until Hoshea and Hezekiah. There are some complexities. The story of Athaliah lies completely outside the structure (compare 2 Kgs 10:36 and 12:1). Jehoram of Judah and Ahaziah of Judah are dealt with before the death of Jehoram of Israel is reported. The story of Jehoash of Israel closes twice (13:13 and 14:16).

3.2.3. Length-of-Reign Figures

If one sets aside the synchronisms, one can dead reckon reasonably accurately through history using only the length-of-reign data presumably derived from the IKL and JKL. For the period between the accession of Jeroboam/Rehoboam and the deaths of Jehoram and Ahaziah, the reign lengths make complete sense. The sum of all regnal years between these periods is ninety-eight for Israel and ninety-five for Judah. If both kingdoms used the nonaccession-year system (antedating), one can subtract seven overlap years for Israel's eight kings (none for Zimri, of course) and five overlap years for Judah's six kings. This produces a total elapsed time of ninety-one or ninety years. Jehu's revolt can be fixed by the Assyrian calendar to 842/841. Counting backward from this year, one can be relatively confident that Jeroboam and Rehoboam would have come to the throne, perhaps not exactly simultaneously, about 930. This fits well with the notice that Pharaoh Shishak invaded Palestine in Rehoboam's year 5 (about 925, see §3.3.2).

There is a problem with the period between 853 (Ahab at the battle of Qarqar; Shalmaneser III year 6) and 841 (Jehu's revolt and subsequent tribute in Shalmaneser III year 18). The synchronisms for this period create insoluble problems. However, even when these are ignored, the thirteen years between 853 and 841 are too short a period to allow for (1) a collapse of Ahab's Qarqar alliance with Damascus, (2) the ensuing Syrian wars reported in 1 Kgs 20 and 22, (3) Ahab's death, (4) a partial, two-year reign by Ahaziah, (5) and a twelve-year reign for Jehoram before the usurpation of Jehu. As we shall see, the wars with Syria reported for Ahab probably did not take place during his reign (see §3.4.4). Nevertheless, it is certain that Ahab was king in 853 and Jehu was king in 841. Therefore, if the reign lengths for Ahaziah and Jehoram are indeed correct, either there was a coregency involving Ahab and Jehoram of Israel or Ahab died immediately after Qarqar.

Chronological problems pile up after Jehu, probably the result of undocumented co-regencies and errors. An illustrative example from each

3. THE KINGDOMS OF ISRAEL AND JUDAH (CA. 930–720)

kingdom must suffice to demonstrate these difficulties and their potential solutions.

Pekah. The total reign lengths from Jehu to Hoshea (143 or 144 years), adjusted for seven overlap years, gives 136 or 137 years. This is about 15 or 20 years too long to fit between Jehu's tribute in 841 and the fall of Samaria in 722 (or 720), dates fixed by Assyrian chronology. In order to accommodate other Assyrian evidence (Menahem pays tribute in 740 and 738; Pekah was assassinated in 732), it is usually assumed that Pekah's reported 20 years (2 Kgs 15:27) is an error, perhaps for 2 years.

Azariah/Uzziah. A similar problem appears in Judah, where the sum of all reign lengths from Azariah to Hezekiah produces far too many years. This means that there must have been one or more co-regencies, with the years of coregency being counted as proper years of rule. The synchronisms given in 2 Kgs 14:2 17, 23; and 15:1, 8, simply cannot me made to work unless there was a coregency of Amaziah with his son Azariah. Azariah and his son Jotham (see 2 Kgs 15:5) represent another likely coregency. Although the synchronisms are not trustworthy, postulating two co-regencies in Azariah's fifty-two-year reign, partly as a response to his leprosy, seems plausible. Owing to a lack of trustworthy data, however, the details of these co-regencies cannot be unraveled, although many competing solutions have been offered.

Postulating a nonaccession-year system for both kingdoms works reasonably well. However, Judah seems to have shifted to an accession-year system under Assyrian influence sometime in the last half of the eighth century. This shift had taken place by the time of Hezekiah, if one chooses to believe the synchronisms given in 2 Kgs 18:1, 9–10, which treat Hoshea year 3 as the accession year of Hezekiah.

To summarize, the dates commonly given for the kings of Israel and Judah are only approximations, and various divergent systems have been advanced. Dates cited in popular works and textbooks should be treated with caution until the reigns of Amon and Josiah are reached. In most cases, the present volume will suggest only approximate dates when it does so at all. More positively, however, the very fact of inconsistencies between Judah and Israel can be used to argue that the author of Kings did indeed use two genuine and separate sources of data for regnal years. The regnal-year data cited in Kings (as opposed to the synchronisms) are not artificial or fictional.

3.2.4. Incidental Information

Apart from counting regnal years, the historian may make calculations using data about royal succession in order to uncover incidental historical information. Periods of dynastic instability in Israel are clearly indicated by the brief reigns of Nadab, Elah, and Zimri, and then of Zechariah, Shallum, and Pekahiah. The succession problem caused by the early death of Ahaziah of Judah (age twenty-three) and the usurpation by his mother Athaliah is evidenced by Jehoash's accession at age seven and the birth of his heir when he was only fourteen. He must have married early in order to improve dynastic security. Similarly, the assassination of Amon and uncertainty caused by it is attested to by Josiah's accession at age eight and the birth of his oldest son, Jehoiakim, when he was only fourteen.

It seems suggestive of Hezekiah's assertive foreign policy that he should name his son Manasseh after a northern tribe. It is intriguing that Manasseh became king at age twelve, yet his successor Amon was not born until Manasseh was forty-five. Manasseh was a loyal Assyrian vassal, and this is perhaps illustrated by his fathering Amon by a woman from Jotbah in Assyrian-controlled Galilee. Another indication of Manasseh's vassal status may be the name of his son Amon, apparently linked to the Egyptian capital No-Amon (Thebes). No-Amon fell to Assyria in 664, which would have been about the year of Amon's birth. Amon's early death at age twenty-four supports the report of a coup against him. One of Josiah's wives was from Rumah in Galilee, indicting either an aggressive policy in the north or a continuation of his grandfather's vassalage to Assyria.

3.3. Israel and Judah until Omri

Two neighboring kingdoms with related cultures emerged about 930. Judah developed out of and in continuity with the Solomonic polity that consisted of Jerusalem, along with its surrounding territory, in affiliation with tribal Judah. The kingdom of Judah incorporated portions of Benjamin and kinship groups associated with tribal Judah (Simeon, Caleb, and so forth). The kingdom of Israel centered on Shechem, and its first king was Jeroboam from Ephraim. This configuration of two kingdoms, one centered on Shechem and one on Jerusalem, repeated a pattern going back to the Amarna period. This suggests that the twofold division of Palestine was a natural state of affairs brought about by geographic and geopolitical factors. A self-conscious cultural division between south and north appears in biblical materials as early as the Song of Deborah. First Kings 12:32 points to a plausible difference in harvest festival dates based on the different agricultural situations of north and south.

The approximately coincident if not simultaneous accessions of Rehoboam and Jeroboam about 930 give some credence to the story of revolution and separation within Solomon's area of rule. However, the narrative recounted in 1 Kgs 11–12 has all the marks of a folktale told from a Judahite perspective (return of the exiled champion of the nativist cause, a prince's youthful folly, competing advisors). In any case, Jerusalem, its environs, and greater Judah remained under the control of a Jerusalem-based monarchy. The northern state under Jeroboam coalesced around the heartland of the richer and more populous northern hill country. If the information that Jeroboam's two border sanctuaries were Dan and Bethel can be trusted, his kingdom stretched to its eventual northern extent immediately. Security concerns highlighted by the incursion of Pharaoh Shishak may have helped produce this new state, or conversely, the emergence of a new state in Palestine may have motivated Shishak's action. For about thirty-five years, the two kingdoms jockeyed over their common border that ran through Benjamin. Israel suffered dynastic instability for its first forty-five years or so until the rise of Omri, who should be regarded as the real founder of the northern kingdom.

Israel and Judah developed in distinct ways. Being larger, more open to communication with other states, and possessed of greater resources, Israel was naturally the stronger of the two. Almost all the monumental architecture of this period is situated within the boundaries of Israel: Hazor, Gezer, Megiddo, and Samaria. These construction projects served as concrete statements about royal power and give evidence of a strong centralized authority. Dan is an excellent example of this, with its enlarged gate structure and massive city wall. The religious importance of Dan is witnessed by a high place (dated about 900), objects with cultic significance (such as a bronze/silver scepter or mace head), and a stamped amphora handle: "Yahweh is with me."

At the same time, a significant degree of cultural unity transcended the border between the two states. For example, the four-room house remained prevalent in both areas and reflected a specific social perspective. This floor plan provided privacy and protected ritual purity while permitting an egalitarian direct access to all areas of the house through the central room. Cultural affinity is also suggested by a near absence of pig bones from sites in both Judah and Israel. A common national god was worshiped at Dan, Bethel, Jerusalem, and local shrines throughout Palestine.

3.3.1. Neighboring Nations

By the early to mid-tenth century, several Aramaean kingdoms had emerged in the Beqa Valley (Zobah), northern Transjordan (Geshur, Maacah), and the area controlled by Damascus. According to the tradition recounted in 1 Kgs 11:23–25, one Rezon captured Damascus and became its king during Solomon's reign. A story about temple treasures (1 Kgs 15:18–20) refers to an otherwise unknown Ben-hadad as king of Damascus at the start of the ninth century, whose predecessors seem to have been Hezion and Tabrimmon.

East of the Jordan, Ammon had experienced destruction and a return to a pastoral economy. This was still the case at the end of Iron I, but sites were resettled in the tenth and ninth centuries. Rabbath-Ammon featured an impressive acropolis and was clearly the capital of a centralized state. The mid-ninth-century Amman Citadel Inscription witnesses to an ambitious building scheme (*COS* 2.24:139). King Nahash is connected with Saul in biblical tradition. His son was supposedly Hanun, a contemporary of David (2 Sam 10:1–4). Another son of Nahash was supposedly Shobi (2 Sam 17:27). It is unlikely that these are historically trustworthy references. However, treaty connections between Ammon and Solomon are indicated by the fact that Rehoboam's mother was an Ammonite.

Moab was used as a geographic term in Egyptian texts as early as Ramesses II. It consisted of a less populated southern section between the Arnon and Zered watercourses with a capital at Kir-hareseth and a more densely populated but disputed northern section north of the Arnon (Aroer, Dibon, Medeba, Heshbon). A major trade route (the so-called King's Highway, Num 20:17) ran through Moab on the Kir-hareseth to Aroer to Dibon to Medeba to Heshbon line. This road connected Moab to the spice trade route into Arabia. Trustworthy information about a Moabite kingdom before Kemosh-yatti the father of Mesha is lacking.

Edom occupied territory south of the Wadi Zered and the Dead Sea, running westward along the southern line of Judah's control. This area only shifted from pastoralism to sedentary settlement in the eighth century. There were active copper mines in Wadi Feinan region by the tenth century. The King's Highway ran up eastern Edom. Edom became a state later than either Ammon or Moab. Genesis 36:31–39 sets out a king list of uncertain date for Edom, but Edom in the early Iron Age should probably be classed as a chiefdom rather than a kingdom. Towns did develop—for example, Borzah, on the King's Highway—but none seems to have been the capital of a state. The tradition of one Hadad the adversary of Solomon presumably was preserved in the BAS (1 Kgs 11:14–22). He was supposedly from an Edomite royal family, but the theme of fleeing to Egypt to achieve the favor of Pharaoh sounds suspiciously Israelite in perspective (cf. Joseph and Moses).

3.3.2. Rehoboam

Rehoboam (meaning perhaps "the divine uncle [Yahweh?] has made wide") reigned from about 930 to about 914. His mother was apparently an Ammonite princess, a result of his father's diplomacy. Continuation of rule by Solomon's family from his Jerusalem power base would be an expected development. Those portions of Benjamin that fell within the economic and strategic influence zone of Jerusalem would naturally have been incorporated into the southern state. This absorption took place in spite of Benjamin's long-standing affiliation with the tribes of Ephraim and Manasseh (evidenced by a tribal name—"son of the south"— locating them south of those two tribes). Elements of Benjamin naturally retained a revanchist attachment to their tribal hero Saul. In addition, previously self-contained groups such as Simeon, Caleb, the Kenizzites, and Jerahmeelites were part of Rehoboam's kingdom along with tribal Judah. An enclave of Gibeonite towns (Gibeon, Chephirah, Beeroth, Kiriath-jearim; Josh 9:17; 18:25–28) was also incorporated into Judah.

The line of control between the two kingdoms through Benjamin unsurprisingly remained in dispute. The statements that there was war between Rehoboam and Jeroboam continually and that war continued between Abijam and Jeroboam are completely credible (1 Kgs 14:30; 15:7; also note the summary for Jeroboam: "how he warred," 1 Kgs 14:19). According to 2 Chr 11:5–12, Rehoboam supposedly constructed fortifications to the west, south, and east of Judah.

First Kings 14:25 reports an incursion into Palestine by Pharaoh Shishak (Shoshenq I; ca. 945–924) in Rehoboam year 5. This would have taken place about 925. Since the author of Kings did not really need to mention any date for this event in order to make the etiological point as to why Solomon's fabulous gold shields no longer existed, one may presume that this report and date were derived from a source document and that they should be accepted at face value. The biblical text interprets Shishak's incursion from a Judah-centered perspective and describes it as an attack against Jerusalem. However, the (admittedly incomplete) list of places in Shishak's list indicates that the Negev and the northern part of Palestine were the real target. It seems that Shishak concentrated on Israel and bypassed the less important Judah.

Shishak commissioned a relief at Karnak (the Bubastite Portal) on which he lists toponyms in a context of valor and victory that suggests military conquest (partially reproduced in *ANET*, 242–43, 263–64). The monument gives the date of its erection as Shishak's year 21. Not all the places mentioned were necessarily actually attacked. The campaign may have been more of a show of strength than an actual invasion. Attempts to derive a campaign itinerary out of this list are unconvincing. Shishak's list has been used to coordinate and date city destructions in Palestine and to provide a marker between Iron IIA and Iron IIB. A stela of Shishak found at Megiddo IVB dates that stratum to about 930.

3.3.3. Jeroboam

Israel's first king, reigning from about 930 to about 910, was from Ephraim. His name (meaning perhaps "the divine uncle [Yahweh?] has done justice") may be a throne name taken in conscious opposition to that of Rehoboam. According to 1 Kgs 12:25, Jeroboam built Shechem, undoubtedly as his capital. According to the same verse, he also fortified Penuel east of the Jordan, perhaps to secure against a potential Ammonite threat. "How he warred" in 14:19 presumably refers to his conflicts with Judah.

Kings accuses Jeroboam of founding inappropriate cults at Bethel and Dan. Yet the foundation legends for these sanctuaries date them to the prestate period (Gen 28:11–22; Judg 18:30–31). It is not impossible, however, that these two older sites received special royal attention as border sanctuaries in order to mark the northern and southern parameters of the new kingdom. The parallel in names between Jeroboam's sons Nadab and Abijah (from a prophetic story, 1 Kgs 14:1) and Aaron's two apostate sons (Nadab and Abihu) appears to be evidence of some sort of link between the Aaronic priesthood and Jeroboam's sponsorship of Bethel.

Israel was dynastically unstable until the emergence of Omri. No doubt residual intertribal rivalries played a role in creating dynastic insecurity. If Ben-hadad (I) son of Tabrimmon (1 Kgs 15:18, 20) was actually a historical personage, then pressure from Aramaean Damascus could also have been a factor in Israel's instability. Jeroboam's son Nadab was quickly assassinated and replaced by the usurper Baasha. Baasha's son Elah was promptly caught up in a power struggle involving his chariot officer Zimri ("the conspiracy he made," 16:20), Tibni, and Omri the ultimate victor. In contrast, the succession in Judah went smoothly in this period.

3.3.4. Abijam and Asa (Judah); Baasha (Israel)

Abijam's name apparently incorporates that of the god Yam ("Sea"). In later tradition (1 Kgs 14:1; 1 and 2 Chronicles) it was changed to the more acceptable Abijah. It may be significant that there are no theophoric names directly referencing Yahweh among the kings of either kingdom until Jehoshaphat and Ahaziah of Israel.

First Kings 15:2, 10, seem to indicate that Abijam fathered his son Asa by his own mother Maacah. This is not totally unlikely. Abijam may have taken over Rehoboam's harem in order to strengthen his claim to the throne of Judah at a time when the rules of succession were still fluid (cf. 2 Sam 12:8; 16:22; 1 Kgs 2:22). Alternative explanations for this item of information are that the author of Kings misunderstood the source material and Abijam and Asa were really brothers, or that Maacah continued in the official role of queen mother but was not actually Asa's biological mother. In any case, the survival of this peculiar bit of information indicates that the author of Kings was willing to reproduce source material even if it might seem illogical or offensive. Maacah was eventually deposed as queen mother (1 Kgs 15:13). Even if this verse largely consists of a Deuteronomistic diatribe, this base item of information indicates the early existence of the official role of the queen mother (*gĕbîrâ*; "mighty lady"; 1 Kgs 11:19; 2 Kgs 10:13). The Sarcophagus Inscription of Eshmunazor king of Sidon may provide a parallel to the office of *gĕbîrâ*. Eshmunazor died at age fourteen, and his mother is given shared credit for the military accomplishments of his reign (*ANET*, 662; *COS* 2.57:182–83).

Asa's forty-one-year reign would have spanned the last decade of the tenth century and the first quarter of the ninth century. His medical history (1 Kgs 15:23) sounds a somewhat unexpected note. Since the author of Kings makes nothing theological out of it (in contrast to 2 Chr 16:12), this information was presumably present in the source material. However, if the statement refers to his genitals rather than his feet (cf. Exod 4:25), such a circumstances could have been recorded for its potential effect on the royal succession.

The usurper Baasha was from Issachar, so no doubt tribal jealousies played a role in his rebellion against the Ephraimite Nadab. The economic and political situation of more northern tribal areas would have been quite different from that of the dominant central hill country. Baasha's long reign probably covered the last decade of the tenth century and the first fifteen or so years of the ninth century. Baasha's tribal affiliation indicates that by now Israel had fully incorporated the Jezreel Valley if it had not done so before. Tirzah in Manasseh is reported to have been Baasha's capital and burial site (1 Kgs 15:21, 33). Tirzah remained the capital until middle of Omri's reign.

A siege of Gibbethon (probably Tell Malat) on the Philistine border plays a role in the conspiracy of Baasha against Nadab. A similar encampment against Gibbethon recurs a generation later in the Elah-Zimri-Omri affair. It is unclear why this particular town in the far southwestern corner of the kingdom should have been a focus of Israel's military efforts over a quarter century. This does suggest recurring attempts by Israel to control or limit Philistine influence.

Fighting over the boundary between the kingdoms was begun by Rehoboam and Jeroboam (14:30) and continued under Abijam and Asa (15:7, 16). Reports featuring the verb "build" describe border clashes between Asa and Baasha and the resulting territorial adjustments. Baasha "built" Ramah (15:17), a strategic junction of the central north-south road with a path leading down to the coastal plain through Beth-horon. This move endangered Jerusalem and moved the border down to a point about nine kilometers north of Jerusalem. In response, Asa "built" Geba of Benjamin and Mizpah (15:22, 23; cf. v. 23, the cities that he "built," and Jer 41:9), supposedly with the stones and timber of the Ramah fortifications. A reuse of materials would make more sense with the timber than the stones, of course, so perhaps only a few stones were moved in order to make a symbolic point. Asa's fortifications protected Jerusalem from attack along both the Beth-horon route and the northern approaches. A stable frontier was thus established between Bethel and Mizpah.

Reports about this border dispute are interrupted in 15:16–20 by a narrative of a different character. This tale recounts that, in order to counter the advance of Baasha, Asa appropriated treasure from the temple and royal coffers and sent them to Ben-hadad (I), king of Aram residing in Damascus. This inducement created an alliance between Judah and Ben-hadad, who then advanced into northeast Galilee and forced Baasha to call off his pressure on Judah. Such a series of events would make strategic sense, perhaps, but it sounds suspicious. It seems to be a parallel version of the tribute later paid by Ahaz to the Assyrian Tiglath-pileser (2 Kgs 16:5–9), but moved back in time into Asa's reign. This cut-and-paste operation is evidenced by the striking and suspect verbal parallel between 1 Kgs 15:20 and 2 Kgs 15:29: "captured Ijon, Abel-beth-maacah, Janoah, Kedesh, Hazor, Gilead, and Galilee, all the land of Naphtali" and "conquered Ijon, Dan, Abel-beth-maacah, and all Chinneroth, with all the land of Naphtali." Certainly contact between Judah and distant Damascus seems unlikely at such an early date. This supposed Ben-hadad son of Tabrimmon son of Hezion is not otherwise attested as a king of Damascus. Perhaps he and his actions are nothing more than fabrications reflecting later interactions involving Judah, Israel, and Damascus. Concerning the problem of multiple kings named Ben-hadad, see §3.4.4.

Second Chronicles 14 narrates a fictional invasion of Judah in the days of Asa by one Zerah the Cushite. The content and intention of this tale is completely theological, as the surrounding material shows (14:1–7 [EV vv. 2–8]; 15:1–15).

3.4. Israel and Judah during the Omri Dynasty

In contrast to his predecessors, Omri was able to establish a dynasty that lasted for several generations, from about 885 to 841. He and his son Ahab raised Israel to a level of regional importance. Judah remained in the background and played the role of junior partner during the remainder of the reign of Asa and the reigns of Jehoshaphat and Jehoram of Judah. Omri expanded Israel's control over northern Moab. Ahab faced off Assyria's new expansionism in a successful alliance with Aramaean Damascus.

3.4.1. Elah, Zimri, and Tibni (Israel)

Instability returned to Israel about 885, when Baasha's son Elah was assassinated in a palace coup by the chariot commander Zimri. The casual mention of chariots in this notice is significant as evidence of Israel's increased military sophistication. The name Zimri became a byword for traitor (2 Kgs 9:31). A summary citation of the chronicles document testifies to the historicity of Zimri's conspiracy (1 Kgs 16:20). A counter coup quickly led to the military leader Omri's acclamation while encamped against Gibbethon (the site of Baasha's earlier coup, 15:27) by the troops he commanded. However, it apparently took him several years to defeat another rival claimant, Tibni. It is unclear how long the struggle between Omri and Tibni took. The synchronisms in 16:15 and 23, if taken seriously, suggest that it could have been up to five years. The manner of Tibni's death is unstated and could have been natural.

In addition to what can be asserted on the basis of creditable sources used by Kings, the presentation of Omri's rise to power (1 Kgs 16) reflects numerous literary or folktale motifs. Elah's heedless drunkenness parallels that of Ben-hadad (16:9; 20:16). Zimri dies intentionally in a palace conflagration (16:18). This is reminiscent of the tale told by the Greeks about the rebellious Babylonian king Shamash-shum-ukin, who supposedly threw himself into his burning palace as Babylon fell around him. The parallel stories of the liquidation of the families of their rivals by first Baasha and then Zimri (15:29; 16:12) derive from DH's characteristic desire to demonstrate divine punishment and fulfillment of the prophet word (15:29–30; 16:12–13). This redactional intention also explains the similarity between the prophetic oracles of Ahijah of Shiloh and Jehu son of Hanani (14:11; 16:4).

3.4.2. Omri (Israel)

Omri was able to succeed in establishing a stable dynasty where Jeroboam and Baasha had failed. He reigned for twelve years after he first claimed the throne about 885. Omri remade the kingdom of Israel into a state with a degree of international importance. Micah 6:16 recognizes this, indicating that the statutes of Omri (along with Ahab's deeds) would become a catchphrase for misconduct in later Judah. Israel would be known to the Assyrians as Bit-Omri ("house of Omri"). He allied Israel with Tyre and succeeded in occupying territory controlled by Moab to which Israel had a historic claim.

An alliance with Tyre is evidenced by the marriage of his son Ahab to the royal princess Jezebel (1 Kgs 16:31). Jezebel's father Ethbaal (Ittobaal) is known from the list in the *Phoenician History* of Menander of Ephesus, quoted by Josephus (*Ag. Ap.* 1.123–124; *Ant.* 8.324). This Ithobalos priest of Astarte was a usurper who reigned thirty-two years and was the father of the Baal-ezer, who paid tribute to Shalmaneser III in 841. It is usually thought that the altar and house of Baal said to have been erected by Ahab in Samaria (1 Kgs 16:32) was dedicated to Melqart, the god of Tyre.

Source material reproduced in Kings reports that Omri fortified and built Samaria after six years of rule (16:23–24) as a replacement capital for Tirzah. Supposedly the king purchased the hilltop site from one Shemer. This new foundation was more defensible than Tirzah and, because it was oriented to routes to the north and west, better suited for international contacts. A totally new site also had the advantage of being a purely royal city with no affiliation with local clan or tribal power structures, in contrast to Tirzah, which was considered a clan of Manasseh (Num 26:33; Josh 17:3). Omri's goal was certainly to centralize the nation on a powerful, magnificent capital. The majority of the city was devoted to public purposes. Samaria featured a rectilinear platform intended for an elite district. This large, raised area was supported by substantial retaining walls. The construction featured costly ashlar masonry. Archaeologists attribute two stages of construction to Omri and Ahab respectively. The site has yielded luxury goods of carved ivory (cf. Amos 3:15). Architectural features such as proto-Aeolic capitals for pilasters indicate a high level of wealth. From the Assyrian perspective, Samaria would eventually give its name to the entire region.

We know something of the power that Omri showed (16:27) from the Mesha Inscription (*ANET*, 320–21; *COS* 2.23:137–38). Omri conquered the Medeba plateau of northern Moab, fortifying Ataroth and Jahaz. As the traditional home of the tribe of Gad (according to Mesha) and of Reuben (according to Josh 14:15–21), Israel had a claim to this territory. In order to support its claim, Israel told folktales of a long-ago victory over Sihon king of the Amorites, whose capital was Heshbon (Josh 12:2–3; Judg 11:19–21; 1 Kgs 4:19). This acquisition gave Omri control of the trade route east of the Jordan Valley.

3.4.3. Ahab (Israel) and the Assyrian Menace

Ahab's reign of twenty-two years roughly equates to the second quarter of the ninth century. The material in Kings on Ahab is extensive (1 Kgs

16:29–22:40), second in length only to that about Solomon. However, it consists mostly of literary and theological texts such as prophet legends and reports of the fulfillment of prophetic predictions. Moreover, the wars with Syria that provide the setting for many of those stories (1 Kgs 20, 22) probably are in the wrong place chronologically and actually occurred later (see §3.4.4). Ahab served the author of Kings as a representative villain (16:30). The house of Ahab remains a negative thematic element up through 2 Kgs 21:3, 13.

According to a theologically loaded statement in 1 Kgs 16:31, Ahab married the Sidonian princess Jezebel. Everything else reported about Jezebel is contained in the cycle of Elijah and Elisha prophet legends and is highly colored by prophetic and Deuteronomistic prejudice. Her misdeeds are reported in 1 Kgs 18, 19, and 21, and her gruesome and prophetically predicted punishment is gleefully described in 2 Kgs 9. This latter narrative communicates a popular belief that she was the mother of Ahab's son Jehoram (2 Kgs 9:22). This may have been true because it is likely that sons of a royal princess would have taken precedence in the succession.

Information from Kings about Ahab on which the historian may rely consists of:

- construction of a palace with ivory décor items (1 Kgs 22:39);
- construction of cities (22:39; perhaps including Jericho, 16:34 [absent from the Lucianic LXX]);
- an alliance with Judah, evidenced by a diplomatic marriage of Jehoshaphat's son Jehoram to Athaliah;
- friendly relations with Damascus, evidenced by the alliance that stopped the Assyrians at Qarqar.

Some historians believe that Moab regained its independence during Ahab's reign, but this more likely took place during the reign of Jehoram (see §3.4.6).

Ahab was the first king of Israel to face an expansionistic Assyria. This phase of Assyrian policy began with Assurnasirpal II (883–859) and did not slacken until a period of Assyrian retrenchment between 823–745. Assurnasirpal II campaigned successfully to the immediate north of Assyria and to the east. He crushed a revolt led by the Aramaean state of Bit-Adini and committed vicious atrocities against the ringleaders. To avoid the same fate, Carchemish, Tyre, Sidon, and Byblos promptly paid tribute.

Assyrian foreign policy soon developed into a military juggernaut of annual campaigns, demands for annual tribute, reduction to vassal status, and eventual annexation. Assyrian expansion was driven by massive building projects that required a level of annual tribute so large that it encouraged rebellion. New capitals were built by Assurnasirpal II (Kalhu) and Sargon II (Dur-Sharrukin; Khorsabad). Sennacherib refurbished Nineveh. Dur-Sharrukin, for example, took ten years and thousands of forced laborers and artisans to complete. Sennacherib more than doubled the area of Nineveh, diverting a small river in the process, and constructed a thirty-mile-long canal to bring water into the city. Large-scale deportations were a strategy to provide labor for these building projects and conscripts for units of auxiliary troops. Deportations of defeated populations also reduced the possibility of further rebellions by undermining national identity and social structures.

The Assyrians fielded a professional army supplemented by Assyrian citizens performing mandatory military service. Assyrians not performing a term of service were still part of a militia. Other units were supplied by subject nations. To the traditional infantry and chariot contingents were added cavalry, which served as a mobile force for flanking and shock attacks against infantry. Mounted troops could operate in hilly and forested areas where chariots could not be used effectively. Although still lacking saddles and stirrups, riders could wield bows and spears. The Assyrians were skilled in siege operations, employing sappers, battering rams on wheels, and siege towers allowing archers to shoot at defenders on the walls. Siege ramps were built to allow rams to move up and pry apart weak points.

Psychological terror tactics were an Assyrian specialty. These were cost-effective; sieges were rarely needed. Rebellious cities that did surrender quickly might be spared with only their leaders being tortured and killed. Resistance, however, would mean the torture and mutilation of significant portions of the citizenry. Others residents could expect to be deported to far corners of the empire, a tactic intended to undermine nationalistic or ethnic self-assertion.

Assyrian resurgence continued under the son of Assurnasirpal II, Shalmaneser III (858–824). Shalmaneser was the first Assyrian king to move outside Assyria's traditional sphere of influence into Syria, Babylon, and Iran. He campaigned personally twenty-six times. In 858 Shalmaneser was checked at Lutibu by a north Syrian confederacy involving Bit-Adani and Carchemish. He responded with three campaigns in 857, 856, and 855, leading to the annexation of Bit-Adini as an Assyrian province (2 Kgs 19:12; cf. Amos 1:5). In 854 he led a successful campaign to

Mount Kashiari in southeastern Turkey. Shalmaneser seems to have been motivated largely by a need for booty to pay for projects like a ziggurat at Nimrud and rebuilding the wall of Assur.

Ahab and Israel appeared on Assyria's radar in 853. Shalmaneser found himself confronted by a large coalition force at Qarqar on the Orontes. This south Syrian confederacy included Hadadezer of Damascus, Irhuleni of Hamath, Ahab, and the forces of eight other allies. The campaigns of Shalmaneser are reported in multiple, redactionally interrelated Assyrian inscriptions (*COS* 2.113A–G:261–70). Reading between the lines, it is easy to see that Qarqar was not an Assyrian victory as Shalmaneser claimed, but at best a stalemate that delayed his plans for western conquest. The various inscriptions do not include the common signals of Assyrian success such as pursuit of the foe, the capture of kings, or taking booty. Kings is silent about any military encounter at Qarqar. If Qarqar had been a defeat for Ahab known to DH, the historian surely would have made it into an object lesson underscoring the king's wickedness. According to Assyrian sources, Ahab fielded ten thousand infantry and two thousand chariots at Qarqar. Although this number may be an exaggeration intended to magnify the strength of the opposing alliance, even half this many chariots would be a powerful force. Ahab reportedly supplied more chariots than any other coalition partner did and contributed the second most powerful total force to the effort. The ability to field a large army so far from home proves that Israel was now a strong centralized kingdom with an effective taxation system. Shalmaneser refers to Ahab as king of *Israel*. Later, the designation "house of Omri" (Bit-Omri) would be increasingly used by Assyrians.

Although the next three operations of Shalmaneser were fought closer to home (852–850), trouble in south Syria set in motion successive campaigns there in 849, 848, and 845. Shalmaneser was finally able to subdue the area when the anti-Assyrian alliance collapsed. This collapse resulted from the appropriation of the throne of Damascus by the usurper Hazael from Hadadezer (about 845) and the usurpation of Israel's kingship by Jehu, who submitted as Assyrian vassal in 841.

3.4.4. Historical Problems Relating to Aram-Damascus

Two major problems complicate attempts to untangle the relationship between the Aramaean kingdom of Damascus and Israel in the ninth and early eighth centuries. First, Kings creates confusion by reporting about three kings of Damascus named Ben-hadad. This total is at least one Ben-hadad more than can be fitted into the extrabiblical evidence.

Ben-hadad son of Tabrimmon is reported to be a contemporary of Asa and Baasha (1 Kgs 15:18–20). He is conventionally labeled Ben-hadad I.

Another Ben-hadad is named as the adversary of Ahab in the conflicts reported in 1 Kgs 20. This Ben-hadad also appears as the adversary of Jehoram (Israel) in the prophet stories of 2 Kgs 6:24–7:20. Similarly, the prophet legend in 2 Kgs 8:7–15 reports Hazael's murder of his royal master, but misidentifies the victim as Ben-hadad. Assyrian sources (*COS* 2:113C, D, G:266–68, 270) attest that the predecessor of Hazael was really named Hadadezer (Assyrian: Adad-idri). This is the same Hadadezer who was Ahab's ally at Qarqar. Some try to preserve the accuracy of Kings by making the strained assumption that the otherwise unattested Ben-hadad of 1 Kgs 20 and 2 Kgs 6 and 8 was simply another name for the well-attested Hadadezer, predecessor of Hazael. The more reasonable solution is that the author of Kings made a mistake. Kings recounted stories about the wars fought between Israel and Ben-hadad son of Hazael several decades too early. By erroneously placing these wars in the reigns of Ahab and Jehoram (1 Kgs 20, 22; 2 Kgs 6), the contemporary to Ahab and Jehoram was misidentified as Ben-hadad when he was really Hadadezer. Most likely there never was a Ben-hadad contemporary to Ahab and Jehoram (Israel). He is an artifact of the compositional process that fashioned the book of Kings. Perhaps Ben-hadad was simply the default name for any Syrian king in prophetic traditions.

Finally, there is the contemporary of Jehoash of Israel, the Ben-hadad who was son of the usurper Hazael (13:3, 24–25). He is the only Ben-hadad known from extrabiblical documents. He is mentioned in the Zakkur Inscription as Bar-Hadad son of Hazael king of Aram (*ANET*, 655–56; *COS* 2.35:155). It was once common to identify this Ben-hadad with the "Bir-hadad … king of Aram" who erected the Melqart Stela (*ANET*, 655; *COS* 2.33:152–53), but this is now widely disputed. Nevertheless, there can be no doubt that it was first Hazael and then his son Ben-hadad who repeatedly attacked Israel after the reign of Ahab. The designation Ben-hadad II could be applied to this king.

The wars fought by Damascus against Israel present a second but connected problem. It is widely accepted by historians that the prophetic stories in 1 Kgs 20 and 22 describing warfare between Damascus and Israel cannot have taken place in the reign of Ahab, who was an ally of Hadadezer of Damascus. A quick and unmotivated shift on Ahab's part away from the alliance with Hadadezer to a state of war would have been entirely unlikely as long as the Assyrian threat required the two to remain allies. These wars are described only in prophet stories, the purpose of which was to glorify the prophetic office and word. They were used by the author of Kings to flesh out the negative portrayal of Ahab. When these stories name the enemy king, he is Ben-hadad, but as discussed above, Ahab's contemporary was Hadadezer. It is significant that, although Ahab's name is scattered about in 1 Kgs 20 and 22, the more common expression in those chapters is a generic "king of Israel." The name Ben-hadad is also introduced as the adversary of Jehoram (Israel) in the siege of Samaria described in 2 Kgs 6:24–7:20, but only in 6:24. Moreover, Ben-hadad's royal adversary in this section is never called Jehoram. He is only a nonspecific, anonymous "king of Israel."

The historian cannot treat the royal names provided in the Elijah-Elisha cycle of prophetic narratives (the base text of 1 Kgs 17–2 Kgs 10) as historically trustworthy information. None of the Syrian Wars referenced in those stories took place in the reign of Ahab, and this is probably the case with the reign of his son Jehoram as well. Insofar as the mention of Ben-hadad in 1 Kgs 20; 22; 2 Kgs 6:24–7:20 has any historical value, the wars these texts describe involved the later Ben-hadad II, son of Hazael. All accounts reporting conflict between Israel and Syria fit best into the successive reigns of Hazael (involving perhaps Jehoram, then Jehu and Jehoahaz) and of his son Ben-hahad II (involving Jehoash). The slightly scrambled account of these wars in 2 Kgs 13:3–5, 7, 22–25, is basically correct. Hazael oppressed Israel from the start of his reign about 845 and continued to do so through the reigns of Jehu and his son Jehoahaz. Ben-hadad II continued his father Hazael's policy until Jehoash was able to turn the situation around and defeat him.

3.4.5. Jehoshaphat (Judah)

Jehoshaphat reigned twenty-five years during the second quarter of the ninth century. According to the source used by Kings, Jehoshaphat demonstrated power and waged war (1 Kgs 22:46 [EV v. 45]). Edom was dominated by Judah (22:48 [EV v. 47]; cf. 2 Kgs 8:20, 22). Jehoshaphat made peace with Israel according to 1 Kgs 22:45 [EV v. 44]. This latter note corresponds with 1 Kgs 22:1–36, which describes war with Syria, and 2 Kgs 3, which reports war with Moab, both fought in alliance with Judah's

3. THE KINGDOMS OF ISRAEL AND JUDAH (CA. 930–720)

northern counterpart. These two narratives, however, are prophet legends and may not be trustworthy from a historical point of view. Reports about Jehoshaphat's trading ships and his refusal to cooperate with Ahaziah of Israel (22:49-50 [EV vv. 48–49]) sound like remnants of a folktale that echoes in some way Solomon's exploits described in 1 Kgs 9:26–28; 10:22. Jehoshaphat's supposed elimination of the *qĕdēšîm* (22:47 [EV v. 46]; traditionally "male temple prostitutes," better: "consecrated cult functionaries") is most likely not from any source material but repeats a favorite ideological theme of DH (1 Kgs 14:24; 15:12; 2 Kgs 23:7).

Second Chronicles 17–20 recasts the reign of Jehoshaphat into a series of inspirational and cautionary tales. Chapter 20 recounts a fictional invasion of Judah during the reign of Jehoshaphat by Moab and its allies at the instigation of Aram. The author of Chronicles uses this tale to launch a highly theological object lesson about prayer, faith, and marvelous deliverance.

3.4.6. AHAZIAH AND JEHORAM (ISRAEL)

Ahab was succeeded by his son Ahaziah, whose short reign was followed by that of his brother Jehoram (the obvious relationship is made explicit in 2 Kgs 1:17 LXX). No mention is made of conspiracy or war, so Ahaziah's death must have been the result of something untoward. According to the Elijah-Elisha cycle, Ahaziah fell through a window lattice and was fatally injured (2 Kgs 1:2), evidencing at least a popular awareness that his reign had been brief.

Jehoram and Joram are interchangeable variants used in the Hebrew Bible for the sons of Ahab and Jehoshaphat. It is likely that all of the eight-year reign of Jehoram of Judah overlapped with the twelve-year reign of Jehoram of Israel. Second Kings 9:14–28 reports that Jehoram of Israel was killed in Jehu's coup along with Ahaziah the son of Jehoram of Judah. The Tel Dan inscription seems to tell a different story (see §3.4.8). These deaths took place in 842 or 841 because Jehu paid Assyrian tribute in 841. Calculating from this date and allowing for the date of Ahab's battle of Qarqar, the reign of Jehoram (Israel) has to be squeezed into ca. 852–841.

In 2 Kgs 3:4–27 the Elisha collection of prophet legends describes a campaign by Jehoram of Israel and Jehoshaphat against Mesha, king of Moab. It is uncertain whether the figure of Jehoram was always part of the tale. In contrast, Jehoshaphat's name is used numerous times and is directly tied into the narrative by the oracle of verse 14. Jehoram is named only in verse 6. The anonymous designation "the king of Israel" is used elsewhere. The ideological point of this prophet legend is the power of Yahweh's prophetic word and the immoral nature of Moab as typified by human sacrifice. Its details should not be used to reconstruct history. In contrast, the propagandistic Mesha Inscription offers useful historical data about Moab's struggles with Israel. Attempts to coordinate 1 Kgs 3 with the Mesha Inscription must take into account the literary and ideological nature of both texts.

Mesha king of Moab erected an inscription (*ANET*, 320–21; *COS* 2.23:137–38) describing in alternate sections his building activities (lines 1–4, 21b–27, 30–31a) and his military accomplishments (lines 5–21a, 28–29, 31b–end). The inscription appears to be reviewing incidents that took place some years in the past. Mesha does not necessarily describe events in chronological order. The text exhibits theological concerns about the god Kemosh and literary artistry (a *waw*-consecutive narrative in lines 5–21a; envelope structures in lines 4 and 7 ["looked down"] and lines 10 and 13 ["men lived ... made men live"]).

The inscription alludes to two generations of Israel's expansion and control, first under Omri (in parallel with Mesha's father Kemosh-yatti, who reigned thirty years) and then for half of the reign of Omri's "son," totaling forty years (line 8). If this "son" were Ahab, Mesha's successful rebellion would fall halfway into Ahab's twenty-year reign. However, the expression "son" most likely alludes to a successor of Omri who was weaker than Ahab was. This would be Jehoram, Omri's *grand*son. Mesha's calculations match the data preserved in Kings reasonably well if Jehoram is meant. When overlaps attributable to a nonaccession-year system are taken into consideration, the total years of reign for Omri, Ahab, and Ahaziah, along with half of Jehoram's twelve-year tenure, is close to forty years. Obviously the stela would have been inscribed after Jehoram's death in order to make this calculation. Kings itself reports that Moab rebelled only after the death of Ahab (2 Kgs 1:1; 3:5). Certainly, a successful Moabite rebellion before that time seems unlikely, given Ahab's military strength at Qarqar.

The territory north of the Wadi Arnon was in dispute between Israel and Moab. Mesha says that Omri had subjugated Moab and occupied the land of Medeba in the reign of Mesha's father. After about forty years Mesha rebelled successfully against Jehoram. There are several ways to interpret the subsequent course of events as reported by Mesha. One might reconstruct the story line as follows. Jehoram built Jahaz and occupied it as part of a campaign from the north against Moab (lines 18b–19). Jahaz would have been south and east of the main area of current Israelite control. Ataroth, ancient home of Gad, had been built earlier by an unspecified king of Israel. In contrast, Dibon and Aroer seem to have always remained in Moabite hands and did not have to be recaptured by Mesha. The god Kemosh drove the king of Israel away, and Jahaz was recaptured. Then Mesha advanced farther north and took Ataroth and Nebo. He slaughtered the populations of Jahaz and Ataroth. He incorporated Jahaz into the realm of his capital Dibon and resettled Ataroth with his own people. The sacred paraphernalia of Yahweh were commandeered from Nebo. For a while Nebo may have remained under Israelite control, but it had definitely become part of Moab by the end of the eighth century (Isa 15:2; Jer 48:1, 22). Mesha also moved against Horonan farther to the south (lines 31–32; most likely Horonaim).

In passing, Mesha reveals that elements of the tribe of Gad had once lived at Ataroth, which agrees with Num 32:34. His unrestrained slaughter of the civilian population of Nebo shows that the Israelite custom of devoting enemy noncombatants to destruction (*ḥerem*) sometimes actually took place. Kemosh was conceived of as a warrior god like Yahweh, ordering attacks at the break of dawn though oracles and delivering his people from their oppressors. It is significant that Mesha recognizes Yahweh as Israel's national god.

One cannot coordinate Mesha's report with the story told in 2 Kgs 3. The events described are completely different. Mesha describes an Israelite attack from the north by way of Jahaz. The prophet legend, in contrast, reports that Jehoram, Jehoshaphat, and the king of Edom moved against Moab from the south and unsuccessfully besieged Mesha in the southern city of Kir-hareseth. Although it is possible that Jehoram had launched an earlier, failed campaign before the events reported by Mesha, it is more likely that the prophet legend simply lacks historical value. Nevertheless, both the Mesha Inscription and 2 Kgs 3 share the common ideology of a national god who fights and protects his nation and his favored dynasty.

Jehoram could have been involved in warfare with the usurper Hazael at Ramoth-gilead as reported in 2 Kgs 8:28–29. The regime change from Hadadezer to Hazael probably took place a few years before the rebellion of Jehu, perhaps about 845, the date of Shalmaneser III's last campaign in the west. Israel was no doubt in a covenant relationship with Hadadezer, its partner at Qarqar, guaranteed by treaty oaths. Hadadezer's murder by

Hazael destroyed that alliance, and Jehoram may have felt bound by his covenant oaths to move against Hazael. The natural outcome of the rupture would be warfare focused on the Gilead frontier. Conflict between Jehoram and Damascus might also provide the historical background to the prophet legends recounted in 2 Kgs 6:24–7:20, but their context is more likely the Jehu dynasty (see §3.4.4). Perhaps it was the dissolution of Israel's alliance with Damascus that allowed Mesha king of Moab to break free.

3.4.7. Jehoram and Ahaziah (Judah)

Jehoram, the son and successor of Jehoshaphat, reigned eight years during the tenure of the king of Israel bearing the same name. Suggestions that the two Jehorams were the same person ignore the information given by their respective accession notices, which are the most trustworthy data available. The MT of 2 Kgs 8:16 includes the textually uncertain "Jehoshaphat being king of Judah" in order to suggest a coregency with Jehoshaphat. This gloss was apparently introduced in order to solve a problem in the synchronism chronology caused by comparing 2 Kgs 3:1 with 8:17. Jehoram was married by his father to Athaliah the daughter of Ahab, undoubtedly in order to bolster an alliance between the two kingdoms (8:18; "daughter of Omri" in v. 26 should be taken to mean granddaughter; cf. Gen 32:1 [EV 31:55]).

Jehoram reportedly engaged in unsuccessful military action against rebellious Edom (2 Kgs 8:20–22a) and, surprisingly, against Libnah, a city of Judah in the Shephelah (8:22b; Josh 15:42). Second Chronicles 21:10 predictably explains that this was because of the king's apostasy. Yet a local rebellion could have been triggered by nativist objections to Jehoram's marriage connection to the royal house of Israel or by a perception of weakness caused by to his defeat by Edom. When rule over Damascus shifted from Hadadezer to Hazael, the resulting change in the balance of power could have made a successful revolt by Edom possible and led to discontent in Libnah.

Ahaziah was a son of Jehoram and of Athaliah. His synchronism with Jehoram of Israel in 8:25 (twelfth year) is corrected by 9:29 (eleventh year) in order to take into account the simultaneous deaths of the two kings. Second Kings reports that Ahaziah fought in alliance with Jehoram of Israel against Hazael at Ramoth-gilead (8:28). This report seems to have been introduced for purely literary purposes and is probably not from the chronicle source used by Kings. Instead, the Ramoth-gilead campaign is used to set the scene for the following prophetic story about Jehu's coup (2 Kgs 9–10). Describing a joint expedition enables Jehoram to be wounded and convalesce at Jezreel. This in turn provides a reasonable background for Ahaziah's sympathetic visit to his relative. His visit provides a narrative opportunity for the intensely dramatic double royal assassination by Jehu. At the same time, this same military action at Ramoth-gilead provides the literary context for the prophetic anointing of the new king Jehu. Second Kings 9 and 10 are saturated by Deuteronomistic theology and prophetic ideology. The Tel Dan stela suggests that the biblical account of the deaths of Jehoram and Ahaziah is either untrue or more complicated than presented.

3.4.8. The Deaths of Jehoram (Israel) and Ahaziah (Judah)

The biblical story is clear enough. Jehu the usurper kills Jehoram and Ahaziah in a confrontation at Jezreel (2 Kgs 9:14–28). At the intersection between the Way of the Sea and the road south to Israel's core hill country, Jezreel was a strategic military site and a royal administrative center. That some act of violence connected with the dynasty of Jehu was thought to have taken place there is indicated by Hos 1:4 ("the blood of Jezreel").

However, the Tel Dan Inscription provides another perspective. Epigraphically, the inscription is dated from about 850 to the beginning of eighth century. It seems to have been erected by an Aramaean king in order to commemorate a victory. Hazael is the best choice as its author, although his son Ben-hadad is also a possibility. The reference to the previous, deceased king as "my father" does not literally fit Hazael's situation as a usurper, but could be a propagandistic fabrication in the interests of legitimacy. The inscription raises many issues (see *COS* 2.39:161–62, esp. nn. 1, 9, 10), not the least of which is the relationship between two fragments that clearly join and a third fragment that does not join. Nevertheless, the restoration of the names Jehoram and Ahaziah is highly likely: "[Jeho]ram son of [Ahab] king of Israel and kill[ed Ahaz]iah son of [Jehoram kin]g of the House of David." The Syrian king boasts: "I killed two kings" (read as dual). The prevalent interpretation of the inscription attributes the deaths of Jehoram and Ahaziah directly to Hazael rather than to Jehu.

Yet the inscription is open to other interpretations. It might be a piece of untruthful political propaganda by Hazael claiming credit for Jehu's act. Or perhaps Jehu was acting as an ally of Hazael, and Hazael is taking credit for his partner's action. The subject of "I killed" might even be the god Hadad, claiming credit for the death of the two kings at the hands of Jehu. It has even been suggested that Jehu may have been the author of the inscription, although glorification of the god Hadad by an Israelite king seems unlikely.

If restored correctly, the inscription proves a synchronism between Jehoram and Ahaziah. It shows that in the second half of ninth century, an Aramaean king knew of two kings and two states, "Israel" and "house of David." The expression "house of David" shows that there was a commonly held belief that the dynasty of Judah had been founded by David and that this opinion was current less than a century after the start of the succession of Judah's kings subsequent to Solomon. The stela apparently witnesses to an expansion on the part of the Omri dynasty into the territory of the predecessor of the Aramaean king who erected it and its author's victory over Israel, a victory that resulted in the deaths of Jehoram and Ahaziah. This king captured Israelite territory that included Dan and erected his victory stela there. Such a victory by Damascus over Jehoram and Ahaziah could be related to the military operation against Hazael alluded to in 2 Kgs 8:28–29 and the successful operations by Hazael against Israelite territory described in 10:32–33.

3.5. Israel and Judah during the Jehu Dynasty

3.5.1. Jehu (Israel)

The latest date for Jehu's accession would be 841, when he paid tribute to Shalmaneser III, so his twenty-eight-year reign would have lasted until about 814. Rather surprisingly, the chronicles document for Israel used by Kings alludes to his power (2 Kgs 10:34), but is silent about his conspiracy (contrast 1 Kgs 16:20; 2 Kgs 15:15). This may be another indication that the narrative of Jehu's murder of the two kings and seizure of the throne may not be completely accurate. The prophetic narratives about Jehu are structured so that the violent events predicated in 1 Kgs 19:15–17 would be accomplished by the actions taken in by Hazael and Jehu in 2 Kgs 8:7–15 and 9:14–10:27. If these prophetic materials and Deuteronomistic ideological statements are set aside, very little about Jehu remains. He was defeated by Hazael, which resulted in a loss of territory, and established a dynasty that lasted a century (10:32–36). Assyrian sources provide more information about him.

Following Qarqar, Shalmaneser III campaigned in Syria in 849, 848, and 845, but was blocked by coalitions led by Hadadezer. After this alliance fell apart, Hazael, who had by then usurped the throne of Hadadezer, had to stand alone against Shalmaneser III in 841. He was defeated in battle but withdrew to Damascus. In that same year, the usurper Jehu appears as king of Israel, paying tribute to Shalmaneser at Ba'ilirasi (Mount Carmel?). Probable motives for Jehu's overthrow of the Omride dynasty include setbacks suffered by Jehoram of Israel in Moab, Hazael's military pressure on Israel, and especially the radically different international situation caused by Hazael's usurpation. Now that Israel's alliance with Damascus had collapsed, Jehu must have thought it politic to respond to insistent Assyrian pressure by paying them tribute. Hosea 10:14 refers to atrocities committed by Shalmaneser III against Beth-arbel (possibly in Transjordan), which perhaps took place about this time.

Thus Jehu reversed the long-standing Omride policy of resisting the Assyrians. His accession was probably supported by political elements in Israel that opposed this resistance strategy. Such a policy would have been viewed by many as increasingly dangerous at a time when Assyrian aggressiveness was increasing. Jehu's submission to Assyria must also have been seen as a way of fending off aggression from Damascus. Vacillation between policies of resistance and acquiescence to Assyria now become a standard feature of Israel's internal politics.

The effects of Jehu's acquiescence policy were disastrous, at least in the short term. Israel was now an ally of Hazael's enemy Assyria and as such continued to be the target of his military campaigns. The summary statement for Jehu in 2 Kgs 10:32–33 speaks of massive defeats at the hand of Hazael throughout Transjordan as far south as the Arnon River. Amos 1:3–5 remembers war crimes by Damascus in Gilead, perhaps by Hazael.

Hazael's successes may be credited to Assyrian developments. Shalmaneser III made a second, unsuccessful attempt to capture Damascus in his year 21 (838). After this, Hazael was free of Assyrian pressure and thus able to defeat Jehu and his son Jehoahaz. Hazael's military achievements are verified by three inscriptions on pieces of booty he acquired (*COS* 2.40:162–63). Assyria's domination in the west continued to weaken in the last years of the reign of Shalmaneser III. A few years before his death, his oldest son led a rebellion against him. A younger son, Shamshi-adad V (823–811), was able to put down the revolt with Babylonian assistance in

822, but control in the west was lost. Hazael and then Ben-hadad could continue to harass Israel without fear of interference.

Several Assyrian texts (three annals and two summary inscriptions), including the famous Black Obelisk, must be studied together to get an accurate picture of the situation (*COS* 2.113C–G:261–70; *ANET*, 280). These texts provide outside confirmation of the death of Hadadezer and the usurpation of Hazael. Hazael is belittled as son of a nobody (*COS* 2.113G). The Assyrians recognized Jehu, the man of Bit-Omri, as the legitimate ruler of Israel. Highlighting Jehu as an exemplar of a loyal vassal, the Black Obelisk indicates that Jehu remained so at least down to the date of this inscription (828–827). The famous picture of Jehu bowing while giving tribute is half of a visual *merismus* in which he exemplifies a larger number of western vassals. His portrait balances the illustration of Sua of Gilzanu, who represents eastern vassals. The image should not be understood as a representation of any single occasion (such as 841) but as a celebration of loyal tribute payment. In fact Jehu's tribute of 841 is not mentioned in the version of the annals on this monument.

3.5.2. Athaliah (Judah)

Another effect of Jehu's coup and the death of Ahaziah was the disintegration of the alliance between Israel and Judah that had been sealed with the marriage of Ahaziah's mother, Athaliah, to Jehoram of Judah. According to the chronicles document for Judah, Jehoash ascended the throne at age seven (2 Kgs 12:1 [EV 11:21]), a trustworthy indication that extraordinary circumstances were involved in the succession. Athaliah presumably had served as queen mother for her son Ahaziah. The office of royal mother served as an institutional guarantee of her son's dynastic legitimacy. Based on the accession age of Jehoash, Athaliah reigned (see the verb in 11:3) for six or seven years. However, neither she nor the years of her rule were included in the JKL, since Kings presents no regnal introduction or summary conclusion for her. She was Ahab's daughter (8:18, 26), although not necessarily by Jezebel.

In this extraordinary situation, Athaliah must have been able to use the office of the king's mother as a claim to represent the continuity of royal administration. Her foreign policy would obviously be opposed to Jehu and his Assyrian vassalage and, based on what is claimed in the Tel Dan Inscription, also to Hazael. This means that Athaliah would have been completely isolated. Her assassination may have been an attempt to reestablish good relations with the kingdom of Israel. The subsequent coup against Jehoash indicates that this was a period of unprecedented dynastic instability. It can be no accident that the chronicles source used by Kings became much more specific about the geographic origins of royal mothers following Athaliah.

The biblical story of her usurpation and death is highly literary and ideological. In 2 Kgs 10 Jehu had arranged for the massacre of Ahab's heirs and Ahaziah's kinfolk. This was a common-enough practice (cf. 1 Kgs 15:29; 16:11). However, in this case the narrative is replete with literary elements: seventy family members (cf. Judg 9:5 and *COS* 2.37:158), paronomasia with "heads," forty-two kinfolk of Ahaziah (six times seven, cf. 2 Kgs 2.24), and fulfillment of the word of Yahweh (2 Kgs 10:6–8, 10, 17). Athaliah follows suit by eliminating "all the seed of the kingship" (11:1). A lone infant heir to the throne, one of her grandsons, is dramatically saved from cold-blooded slaughter and hidden by his aunt right under Athaliah's nose. The shields of King David are brought onstage to serve as background props for her assassination. The new king takes the customary stance by the pillar. Athaliah's death is followed by a covenant with Yahweh and anti-Baal mob action. Then the city was quiet (11:10, 14, 17–18, 20). The participation of mercenaries from Caria in southwestern Asia Minor as a royal or temple guard could be taken as an indication of a high level of sophistication for the Judahite royal establishment. However, this might be a reference to an elite native unit called the Rams instead (11:19).

Athaliah's control of Judah is surely factual. There would be no reason otherwise to tell a story that so endangers the genealogical legitimacy of the Davidic dynasty. Clearly her interregnum was so widely known that it required a counterstory designed to defend the dynasty and explain the break in succession. Why, the potential reader might wonder, would this enigmatic boy, purportedly the son of Ahaziah and Zibiah from Beersheba, have appeared so suddenly out of the blue to be set on the throne by the temple establishment? The answer: He had been rescued from death and hidden in the secret recesses of the temple by his aunt, whose family connection guaranteed his legitimacy.

Perhaps the reality about Athaliah is more benign. If we choose to discount the tale of her murderous actions against her own son's kinfolk as the propaganda of the winning side, she may actually have served as something like a regent for her uncrowned grandson. Apart from guilt by association, there is no indication that she had anything to do with the house of Baal (2 Kgs 11:18) or any other religious apostasy.

3.5.3. Jehoash (Judah)

It is unclear whether the forty-year reign of Jehoash was intended to include Athaliah's period of rule, but the synchronism calculation of 2 Kgs 12:2 (EV v. 1) assumes that it did not. He was roughly the contemporary of Jehu and Jehoahaz. Most of the narrative about him has to do with information connected to the administration of the temple, which was probably taken from a source that related the vicissitudes of the temple treasury (see §3.1.3). The one exception is the trustworthy report of his assassination taken from the chronicles document for Judah (12:21–22 [EV vv. 20–21]). Jehoash fell victim to a conspiracy by two named officials. The assassination site was in the house of the Millo, probably an administrative center or royal residence, see Judg 9:6, 20). The conclusion to this incident is reported in 2 Kgs 14:5, providing the occasion for a Deuteronomistic comment. It is impossible to determine what political (or personal?) motives lay behind this attempted coup. Tensions would have been high if Hazael really had occupied Gath (12:18–19 [EV vv. 17–18], because this compromised the defense of Jerusalem. Jehoash's son Amaziah, who liquidated the conspirators, went on to pursue a disastrous policy of military challenge to Israel (13:12), so perhaps the conspirators were opposed to such a strategy.

Temple repair was an important royal virtue and played a legitimating role in the inscriptions of kings, including usurpers. Although the story of Jehoash's temple repairs provides a remarkably detailed etiology for certain later administrative practices, it also incorporates a date, which would seem to indicate that it was taken from an archival source of some kind (2 Kgs 12:5 [EV v. 6]). The author of Kings went on to use this report as a template for describing a similar temple restoration project by Josiah that led to the discovery of the law book (22:4–7, 9).

Imprecisely associated with the preceding narrative ("at that time," 2 Kgs 12:18 [EV v. 17]) is a report that Hazael, after seizing Gath, prepared to march against Jerusalem. He was supposedly bought off by Jehoash, who had to plunder temple treasures to do so (vv. 18–19 [EV 17–18]). However, an attack by Hazael so far south and west of his usual theater of operations in the northern part of Transjordan seems highly improbable.

The report about raiding the temple treasury appears to be a literary construct, exhibiting suspicious narrative parallels to stories told about Asa (1 Kgs 15:18), Ahaz (2 Kgs 16:8), and especially Hezekiah (18:13–15).

Second Chronicles 24:23–24 asserts that Jehoash was wounded in a battle with Hazael, but this is simply an example of the Chronicler's ideology. It provides an appropriate punishment for Jehoash's murder of the son of Jehoiada the priest.

3.5.4. Jehoahaz (Israel)

Calculating from Jehu's tribute payment in 841, Jehoahaz would have reigned ca. 814–798. The material about him consists almost entirely of theological judgments asserting that royal sin caused repeated defeats by Hazael and his son Ben-hadad and resulting military weakness. The Asherah pole mentioned in 2 Kgs 13:6 is a theological construct created by DH, alluding back to Ahab (1 Kgs 16:33) and forward to Hezekiah, Manasseh, and Josiah (2 Kgs 18:4; 21:3; 23:4, 6, 15). The preceding discourse on sin is formatted on the basis of the structural pattern of Judges (2 Kgs 13:2–5: doing evil in Yahweh's sight, divine anger, oppression by the king of Aram, entreaty to Yahweh, Yahweh appoints a deliverer). This unnamed "deliverer" (cf. Judg 2:18; 3:9, 15) is commonly understood to be Adad-nirari III (810–783), whose successes against Damascus in 796 relieved Israel of pressure from that quarter. This proposal demands an unreasonably high level of geopolitical knowledge and interest on the part of the author and intended readers. It is more reasonable to follow the lead of 2 Kgs 13:22–23, 25; 14:25–27. These verses suggest that the answer to Jehoahaz's prayer was first embodied in his son Jehoash, and in the long run by Jeroboam II. The author schematizes the overall situation: Jehoahaz was oppressed by Hazael and then by Ben-hadad. Subsequently, Jehoash defeated Ben-hadad (13:3, 22, 24–25). As discussed above (§3.4.4), the conflicts described in 1 Kgs 20, 22 (involving Ahab), and 2 Kgs 6:24–7:20 (with Jehoram) fit better into the reigns of Jehu, Jehoahaz, and Jehoash.

3.5.5. Jehoash (Israel)

Calculating from a reign of circa 841–814 on the part of Jehu, Jehoash would have reigned ca. 798–783. During his tenure, Assyria reasserted itself under Adad-nirari III. The Assyrian king waged successful campaigns against Damascus and Palshtu in 805 and continued to fight in the west in following years. His most decisive campaign was that of 796, which marked the end of Damascus as a serious military force. According to the Zakkur Inscription (*ANET*, 655–56; *COS* 2.35:155), Zakkur king of Hamath was besieged in his capital by a coalition of kings led by Bar-Hadad son of Hazael king of Aram. This siege was apparently broken by Adad-nirari III in 796. Ben-hadad was forced to pay tribute to Adad-nirari after this defeat (*ANET*, 282; *COS* 2.114E:274–75). Jehoash of Israel also paid tribute to Adad-nirari sometime between 805 and 796 (Rimah Stela, *COS* 2:114F:275–76), reinstating or continuing the acquiescence policy of his grandfather Jehu. Taken together, these events allowed Israel to gain independence from Damascus. Jehoash was apparently able to defeat Ben-Hadad several times and regain cities that had been lost by Jehoahaz. That the number of Jehoash's victories was specifically three (13:25), however, derives from a prophet legend about Elisha (13:14–19).

Security on his northern and western borders permitted Jehoash to turn his attention southward to Judah. The bare fact of conflict between Amaziah and Jehoash is reported in the chronicles document for Israel (13:12; 14:15). This trustworthy but minimal report is elaborated in the story told in 14:8–14.

3.5.6. Amaziah (Judah)

Amaziah appears primarily as a contemporary and antagonist of Jehoash of Israel. Independent of this role, he is reported to have eliminated his father's assassins and waged a successful campaign into the heart of Edom (14:5, 7; cf. v. 10). This allowed his son Azariah to build Elath, indicating a resumption of trade through the Red Sea (v. 22; cf. 16:6).

There was definitely military conflict between Amaziah and Jehoash of Israel (13:12; 14:15). The narrative set forth in 14:8–14 may have come from a source describing the vicissitudes of the temple treasury (v. 14). Admittedly, the report is introduced by the common literary motifs of a foolish challenge and an unheeded cautionary fable about pride. The story seeks to place blame on Amaziah. Nevertheless, such a humiliating report of defeat, the capture of Amaziah, the seizure of treasure and hostages, and the demolition of a section of Jerusalem's wall would hardly have been recounted by Judahite source unless it were substantially true. Nothing further is made in a literary or theological way of Amaziah's capture or the hostages, so again this information seems to have been derived from a source. Such specific details about the demolished portion of Jerusalem's wall also sound authentic. An encounter at Beth-shemesh in the northern Shephelah would be completely understandable, given its strategic location guarding the approach to Jerusalem from the coast.

Amaziah reigned twenty-nine years. Given his disastrous record, it is not too surprising that he was assassinated by conspirators at age fifty-three after fleeing to Lachish (14:18–19). The "people of Judah" (as opposed to the power structures of Jerusalem; cf. 23:2) arranged for the succession of his sixteen-year-old son Azariah, who had been born the year of Amaziah's accession when Amaziah was twenty-five years old. Two royal assassinations in a row (Jehoash and Amaziah) are evidence for the intense external pressure from Israel that Judah experienced during the reign of its aggressive king Jehoash. The information that Azariah reigned fifteen years after the death of Jehoash (14:17) is secondary and was calculated on the basis of the synchronisms of 14:1, 23. As mentioned above (§3.2.2), one must postulate repeated co-regencies in Judah during this period.

3.5.7. Jeroboam II (Israel) and Azariah/Uzziah (Judah)

Israel's subservience to Assyria would be brief. Adad-nirari's hold on the west loosened. He was forced to campaign closer to home and experienced pressure from Urartu. Assyrian weakness continued under Adad-nirari's sons, Shalmaneser IV (782–773), Assur-dan III (772–755) and Assur-nirari V (754–745). The Eponym Chronicle indicates that no campaigns were fought in 768, 764, 757, or 756. It mentions plagues in 765 and 759 and internal revolts between 763 and 759. Assyrian power reached its nadir under Assur-nirari V, which is the period of the Sefire Treaty with Arpad (*ANET*, 532–33). Because of Assyrian weakness, Israel and Judah were able to enjoy prosperity and independence for about fifty years until the accession of Tiglath-pileser III in 745. For this reason, the overlapping reigns of Jeroboam II and Azariah/Uzziah were a time of peace and prosperity for some elements of the population, but also a time of challenging social change.

Kings has little to say about the forty-one-year reign of Jeroboam. His (throne?) name may be a policy statement, indicating his intention to restore Israel to the glory of its founding king. The chronicles document for Israel described his might and his warfare and included a notice that he recovered Damascus and Hamath for Israel (2 Kgs 14:28). Setting aside the puzzling appearance of Judah in this verse as an erroneous gloss, this presumably reliable notice indicates that Jeroboam gained some level of influence over the two major Aramaean states on his northern border. Amos 6:13–14 provides an independent witness to other victories east of the Jordan at Karnaim and Lo-debar. In spite of general Assyrian weakness, a campaign in 773 against Damascus by a general of Shalmaneser IV was able to extract tribute from its ruler Hadiyani (Pazarcik Stela, COS 2.116:283–84; in Hebrew this would be Hezion). This event may have given Jeroboam an opportunity to restore and solidify Israel's border in the north.

The author of Kings expanded theologically on the bare information in 2 Kgs 14:28 with references to Yahweh's word, the prophet Jonah, and Yahweh's compassion for and commitment to Israel (vv. 25–27). Presumably the author knew of a more extensive prophet story featuring an interaction between Jeroboam and this Jonah from a town in lower Galilee, but merely alludes to it in verse 25. Jeroboam is portrayed as a tool of Yahweh's favor, continuing the theological theme of 2 Kgs 13:5, 23. This is likely a tacit explanation for Jeroboam's exceptionally long reign, even though he is judged to have done evil.

The Hamath of 14:28, apparently taken from the source document, is treated in verse 25 as Lebo-hamath by the author of Kings. This locale is stated to be the northern anchor for Israel's restored border all the way down to the Dead Sea. Lebo-hamath is generally thought to be Lebweh in the valley between the Lebanon and Anti-Lebanon Mountains near the headwaters of the Orontes. In the DH, Lebo-hamath functions as an ideological border, marking the supposed northern extent of Solomon's kingdom (1 Kgs 8:65). This was also the ideal northern extent of restored Israel as envisioned in Ezekiel (47:15, 20; 48:1).

Given the nationalistic policies and accomplishments of Jeroboam son of Jehoash, some have suggested that the royal cultic installations at the border shrines of Bethel and Dan, attributed in 1 Kgs 12 to the first Jeroboam, really were established by the second one (Hos 13:2; Amos 7:13). The social conflict of this period is reflected in Amos and Hosea, both of whom voiced threats against the royal establishment (Hos 1:4–5; Amos 7:1–9).

Azariah of Judah enjoyed similar successes and prosperity during his fifty-two-year reign. He was sixty-eight when he died. The synchronism of

2 Kgs 15:1 contradicts other data in chapters 14 and 15. Some suggest that the notices of his father's captivity and period of survival after Jehoash's death (14:13, 17) provide evidence for a fifteen-year coregency at the beginning of his reign. A second coregency of Azariah with his son Jotham at the end of his reign is also likely, resulting from the isolating skin disease reported in 15:5. Azariah's leprosy and separate residence is an item about which the author offers no theological comment and so is certainly from the source document. The alternate name Uzziah (four time in chapter 15; references in prophetic books) was probably his throne name. It is very unlikely that Azariah is the Azriyau mentioned in the annals of Tiglath-pileser III (*COS* 2.117A:285 n. 10).

According to a notice attached to the regnal formula for his father, Azariah rebuilt Elath, thus opening up trade possibilities through the Red Sea (14:22). Since this implies undisputed control over the Negev and the route leading farther south, Azariah seems to have exploited his father's subjugation of Edom (14:7). Second Chronicles 26 expands on Azariah's achievements and creates a moral tale out of his illness.

3.5.8. Social and Economic Hardship

Oracles preserved in the books of Amos and Hosea reflect economic and social disparities that reached a climactic level during the reigns of Jeroboam II and Azariah. Various long-term developments over the course of the monarchy period led to a relentless reduction of the economic status of small landowning farmers. A tax-gathering monarchy, urbanization, and a transition from a barter economy to one that included the use of weighed-out portions of silver led over time to an unhealthy concentration of wealth in the hands of the elite. However, it remains difficult to judge how much actual impoverishment existed. Prophetic criticism was sharp (e.g., Hos 12:8–9 [EV vv. 7–8]; Amos 5:10–13; 6:4–7; 8:4–6; and later Isa 5:8–10; Mic 2:2). However, the intensity of this prophetic critique was also driven by the particular ideology of the prophets and their audiences and cannot be taken entirely at face value.

Urban expansion reached its peak in the eighth century. Differences in the relative size of cities indicate a hierarchy of power. Each kingdom had a capital significantly larger than its other cities (Jerusalem, Samaria). Israel had several regional power centers represented by cities of smaller size; for example, Dan, Gezer, Shimron, Hazor, Dor, Ibleam, Tirzah, and Megiddo.

Judah displayed a similar pattern on a smaller scale, with Lachish being the most prominent second-level city. Urbanization promoted vocational specialization and a concentration of wealth caused by taxation and trade. Archaeological analyses demonstrate that Judah continued to lag behind Israel in urbanization and the centralization of power. Some scholars suggest that this means that Judah had a less complex and sharp pattern of social and economic stratification than Israel.

The process that led to this social disparity is clear enough in general terms. Production surpluses set in motion barter trade and specialization. The skillful, lucky, and influential were able to accumulate capital and real estate. This in turn meant that loans could be made to distressed farmers. Default on these loans and resulting debt slavery further increased the social gap between rich and poor. The resulting alienation of traditional land ownership led to the formation of large private estates, sometimes specializing in high-value items such as oil and wine. Some peasants would still own their land but lived a marginal existence. They were in constant danger of descending into the ranks of impoverished daily wage laborers, debt slaves, or sojourners. This sojourner class was made up of those who had to leave their home area in order to find work on other farms (compare Deuteronomy's "your sojourner" and "the sojourner within your gates"). Royal government intensified the whole process with demands for taxation and forced labor.

The rural Judahite aristocracy was termed "the people of the land" (*'am hā'āreṣ*). These free landowners tended to be politically active. A second elite group consisted of an urban aristocracy made up of royal officials and important priests. Titles presented in biblical texts and epigraphic evidence show the range of positions that could be held: administrator over the house, scribe, recorder, servant of the king, military commander, and *sar* of the city. The influential and far-reaching family of Shaphan provides a late-monarchy example of the urban elite.

Economic and social change and the demands of royal government stressed older systems of loyalty-based family and clan affiliation. Differences between laws set forth in Deuteronomy in the Neo-Assyrian period and those of the older, more traditional Covenant Code illustrate changes that were required as society moved away from kinship-based systems of loyalty.

Light on this period is provided by the Samaria ostraca (*ANET*, 321), dated to the reigns of Jehoash of Israel and Jeroboam II. These records, found in what seems to have been an administrative building, provide evidence for the districts and clan eponyms in the area around Samaria. Theophoric personal names contain both Baal and Yahweh elements, and some names are of Egyptian origin. These ostraca appear to be delivery memoranda for items sent from royal farms located around the capital. That these foodstuffs were the products of royal estates (and not tax receipts) is indicated by small amounts involved and the limited distribution of names. These products were apparently intended to support members of the royal court in a system similar to that described as operating between Meribbaal and Ziba (2 Sam 9:9–11).

3.6. The Downfall of Israel

The security and prosperity of Israel came to an end with the accession of Tiglath-pileser III (744–727). He seized the throne from the ineffective Assur-nirari V and began a new phase of Assyrian expansion. Tiglath-pileser must be considered the real founder of the Neo-Assyrian Empire. He defeated Urartu, reduced Babylon to vassalage, and conquered Damascus. His successes were continued by Shalmaneser V, Sargon II, and Sennacherib. Assyria's revived ascendency would last for some sixty years (744–681).

Tiglath-pileser reigned in Babylon under the name Pulu and so is called Pul in the Bible. He campaigned in the west in 743, 738, and 734–732. He perfected a threefold sequence of steps against recalcitrant states that in the end led to complete Assyrian control. These successive stages are illustrated by the fate of several kingdoms including Israel and consisted of the following:

- Collection of voluntary tribute and status as a satellite state (Damascus and Israel in 738, Judah in 734);
- Reduction to vassal status and replacement of the delinquent king with a more acquiescent puppet king (the rump state of Israel [Samaria] in 732);
- Reduction to provincial status under control of a governor (Damascus, Megiddo, and Gilead in 732; Israel [Samaria] in 722 or 720).

Tiglath-pileser's expansionistic policy was designed to create a buffer of vassal states to protect against Egypt and Arab groups. These included

Judah, Moab, Edom, and the Philistine cities. For this reason Judah was a more strategically valuable as a vassal buffer state than Israel was. Israel would eventually be dismembered and reduced into several Assyrian provinces. Damascus would suffer the same fate.

3.6.1. Zechariah and Shallum (Israel)

Upon the death of Jeroboam, the formerly stable situation in Israel was replaced by internal political unrest driven by Assyrian-inspired insecurity. In quick succession Zechariah the last king of the Jehu dynasty was murdered by Shallum, who in turn was assassinated by Menahem. The desperation of Israel's situation is evidenced by reported war crimes committed by Menahem in his sack of Tiphsah and neighboring territory (2 Kgs 15:16).

Israel's ruling classes split over the choice of a compliance policy or a resistance policy. The tribute required by compliance was economically devastating, but resistance was perilous. Zechariah, the fourth king of the Jehu dynasty, was likely identified with that dynasty's customary willingness to accommodate to Assyrian demands. Both Jehu and Jehoash had paid tribute. Shallum's short-lived conspiracy (Kgs 15:15) thus must have represented groups advocating a resistance policy. Menahem's countercoup was clearly a victory for the compliance party, and his son Pekahiah continued in this direction. The rebellion of Pekah brought the resistance-policy faction back into power, with disastrous results. Hosea's accusation, "they made kings but not through me" (Hos 8:4), describes this pattern with deadly accuracy.

The text of 2 Kgs 15:10 is problematic: Shallum killed Zechariah either in public or at Ibleam. Menahem moved against Shallum at Samaria from the old capital of Tirzah.

3.6.2. Menahem and Pekahiah (Israel)

Menahem followed a strategy of loyal nonresistance. He paid tribute at least twice to Tiglath-pileser, in 740 (in all probability) and 738 (more certainly) (*ANET*, 283; *COS* 2:117A–B:284–87). The year 740 corresponds to Tiglath-pileser's capture of Arpad and 738 to his capture of Hamath. Rezin of Damascus and Hiram of Tyre also paid tribute in 738. Second

3. THE KINGDOMS OF ISRAEL AND JUDAH (CA. 930–720)

Kings 15:19–20 indicates that Menahem paid tribute in order to turn away an active threat from Assyria ("came against the land.... turned back"), which does not correspond to anything in extant Assyrian records. Kings also reports that it was paid to confirm his hold on royal power. In order to raise this sum, Menahem had to resort to heavy taxation. The text of 15:20 is usually understood to mean that he exacted fifty shekels apiece from each of sixty thousand to seventy-two thousand taxpayers to achieve a thousand talents. This number seems too high to represent the men of substance in Israel. Perhaps some of the total came from monies already deposited in the treasury. Even so, a payout of a thousand talents of silver (thirty-four metric tons) would be a major financial burden and would certainly strengthen the hand of the resistance party. As a result, Menahem's son Pekahiah was quickly eliminated by Pekah.

The wording of 15:14 ("went up") suggests a military attack, which implies that Menahem was a military officer. The circumstances of Menahem's sack of Tiphsah (textual variant: Tappuah) when it failed to surrender to him and his terroristic war crime against its population (v. 16) are left unstated. However, this event indicates that he faced substantial opposition, perhaps already from an insurgency led by Pekah. The difficult "from Tirzah" in this verse may be a badly placed indication of the starting point of his attack. Ripping open pregnant women was a stereotypical atrocity (2 Kgs 8:12; Amos 1:13).

3.6.3. Pekah

Menahem's son Pekahiah was quickly killed in a coup and replaced by Pekah, perhaps his adjutant. A unit of soldiers from Gilead participated in the assassination, which took place in the royal palace. This circumstance may indicate that regional differences played a role in the support of Pekah and his policy. Pekah pursued an aggressive (and likely more popular) resistance strategy in alliance with Rezin of Damascus. The Gilead region probably felt a natural affinity with Damascus and probably thought of itself as less open to Assyrian attack than areas west of the Jordan. The role of Argob and Arieh in 2 Kgs 15:25 is ambiguous. They may have courtiers of Pekahiah slain with him, coconspirators who assisted Pekah, or two locales from which troops came to assist the Gileadite contingent. Argob is a region in Bashan, and Arieh may be a misreading of Havvoth-jair.

Pekah could not have reigned as sole king of Israel for the twenty years claimed for him (15:27). Menahem paid tribute in 740 and 738 (Tiglath-pileser year 6 and 8), and Pekah's successor Hoshea paid in 731 (Tiglath-pileser year 15). Twenty years could be a propagandistic claim of an earlier accession or an indication that Pekah had earlier established a rival kingdom in Gilead (perhaps with Rezin's support) that overlapped with Menahem's reign in Samaria.

Pekah's reign definitely included the dramatic events of 734–732 that fundamentally transformed the state of affairs in Syria-Palestine. When this crisis was over in 732, Rezin had been killed and Tiglath-pileser had reduced the territory of Damascus to a province. The same thing happened to Karnaim. Former Israelite territory was formed into the provinces of Gilead and Megiddo. Israel had a new king, Hoshea, who paid tribute to Tiglath-pileser in 731. The events of 734–732 can be outlined in a general way, but the details and precise order of what happened remain obscure. Three witnesses must be taken into account: Assyrian records, the source material used by Kings, and prophetic material in Isaiah. Each witness must be weighed according to its perspective and genre.

Tiglath-pileser concluded a series of campaigns in the west (743–740, 738) with his defeat of Hamath and Calneh in 738, remembered in Amos 6:2 and Isa 10:9. This success led various rulers, including Menahem of Israel and Rezin (Ratsiyan) of Damascus, to pay voluntary tribute in that year. The Assyrian king next focused on areas to the northeast of his empire, where he campaigned in 737 and 736, and on Urartu in a 735 campaign. This change of focus apparently provided Rezin with what he saw as an opportunity to form an anti-Assyrian alliance with Israel, the Phoenicians, the Philistines, and certain Arab groups.

From this point on, fragmentary and problematic Assyrian sources present a confused picture of events. The annals and summary inscriptions show evidence of redaction over time (*ANET*, 282–83; *COS* 2.117A–G:284–92). The Eponym Chronicle for 734–732 (*COS* 1.136:466) records one campaign against Philistia and two against Damascus. Tiglath-pileser advanced against Philistia in 734 as far as Gaza. With this outflanking movement, he was able to seize the coastal route south, thus cutting off any possibility of Egyptian interference. The king of Gaza had fled to Egypt, but returned and submitted as a vassal. Ekron, Ashdod, and Ashkelon also submitted as voluntary vassal states. This incursion represented a direct threat to the status quo of Syria and inland Palestine. If they had not already done so, Pekah and Rezin of Damascus united in response to

3. THE KINGDOMS OF ISRAEL AND JUDAH (CA. 930–720)

this danger. The response of Ahaz of Judah to this Assyrian move (and perhaps to a threat from Israel and Damascus) was to pay tribute in 734 or shortly thereafter.

In 733 and 732 Tiglath-pileser moved against Damascus and Israel. The defeat of Rezin and his Arab allies forced Rezin to retreat to Damascus, where he was besieged, "shut up like a bird in a cage," for forty-five days (for this expression, compare Sennacherib and Hezekiah; §4.1.3). Tiglath-pileser devastated the territory of Damascus. The actual fall of the city of Damascus and the execution of Rezin in 732 are reported only in the Bible (2 Kgs 16:9), but these events cannot be doubted. An intriguing personal note is provided by a dedicatory inscription memorializing one of Tiglath-pileser's loyal vassals who perished in the Damascus campaign (Panamuwa Inscription, *COS* 2.37:158–60). Some of the population of the Damascus kingdom was deported, and it was reduced to provincial status.

Tiglath-pileser also devastated portions of Israel. His forces operated in Galilee and Gilead. He reports taking captives from some of its cities, including Hannathon and Jotbah in lower Galilee. He plundered the country, carrying off livestock. Yet Israel's capital Samaria was spared, apparently because of the timely accession of a new king, Hoshea, along with a strategic unwillingness to invest effort in an unnecessary siege. Assyrian sources can be interpreted to credit the death of Pekah either to elements in Israel or to Tiglath-pileser himself. Hoshea was accepted (or installed) as king by the Assyrians. However, Israel lost much of its most productive territory, which was organized into provinces of the Assyrian Empire. The Jezreel and Beth-shean Valleys together with Galilee became a province controlled from Megiddo, and a second province encompassed Gilead. The administrative status of the coastal area south of Mount Carmel (Dor) is uncertain. In 731 (probably) Hoshea sent tribute to Tiglath-pileser while he was in southern Babylon. Israel was now reduced to the vassal state of Samaria consisting of a much diminished territory limited to the hill country of Ephraim and Israel's share of Benjamin.

Elements of the biblical accounts can be coordinated with these Assyrian records. In its material on Pekah, Kings reports a campaign of capture and deportation by Tiglath-pileser involving "Ijon, Abel-beth-maacah, Janoah, Kedesh, Hazor, Gilead, and Galilee, all the land of Naphtali" (2 Kgs 15:29; the probable source for 1 Kgs 15:20). This list sounds like a campaign itinerary through Israel from its northern border to Hazor, then east into Transjordan, then back to the west against Galilee. From the biblical perspective (2 Kgs 15:30) Hoshea came to the throne through an internal coup. From the Assyrian perspective Tiglath-pileser was the decisive actor. In any case, Hoshea's strategy of compliance bought a decade of limited independence for what was left of Israel.

3.6.4. Jotham and Ahaz (Judah)

Both the synchronism system (2 Kgs 15:32; 16:1) and the organizing structure of Kings puts Jotham's reign completely within that of Pekah. The chronology issue is complicated by Jotham's coregency with his father, Azariah, which included palace administration and governance of the elite "people of the land" outside Jerusalem (15:5). A second coregency for Jotham with his son Ahaz is also likely. Coregency explains why Hoshea is said to have ascended the throne of Israel in both Jotham year 20 and Ahaz year 12 (2 Kgs 15:30; 17:1; cf. 15:32-33; 16:1). According to Kings, Pekah and Rezin moved against Judah already in the time of Jotham ("Yahweh began to send"; 15:37). A temple construction project is credited to Jotham (v. 35). Second Chronicles 27:1-6 supplies additional fictional exploits and successes to present Jotham in a favorable light in contrast to his father.

The regnal introduction for Ahaz is concerned with accusations of religious impropriety expressed in Deuteronomistic language (2 Kgs 16:3-4). Ahaz's new altar and his architectural changes to the temple described in verses 10-17 are usually interpreted negatively as concessions to Assyrian sensibilities (v. 18b). Yet the both the narrative itself and the tone of the Deuteronomistic author are neutral. In fact, these royal initiatives can be viewed positively as an improved altar, removal of images now thought to be inappropriate (cf. the images described 1 Kgs 7:27-39, 44), and a proper reduction of the king's role in temple affairs. One hint of the serious crisis that Ahaz faced is the statement that he passed his son though fire (2 Kgs 16:3). This was probably a divination technique rather than a human sacrifice.

The books of Kings and Isaiah narrate the circumstances of the crisis of 734-732 from the perspective of Judah. The biblical viewpoint is that a desperate Ahaz requested aid from Tiglath-pileser and did so because of an actual invasion by Pekah and Rezin ("came up to wage war on Jerusalem and besieged Ahaz"; 2 Kgs 16:5-8; Isa 7:1 reflects related wording). However, whether their hostility actually reached the level of outright war (as suggested by the standard scholarly formula Syro-Ephraimite War) is uncertain. Ahaz is undeniably listed with other kings of the west who paid tribute to Tiglath-pileser, but no direct indication of a date is given, although the date of the relevant inscription is 729. The Assyrians give his name as Jehoahaz, with its theophoric prefix.

The comparatively sparse presentation of 2 Kgs 16:5–9 speaks of an invasion and stalemated siege of Jerusalem. No reason for this act or previous negotiations with Pekah and Rezin are mentioned. Kings also reports that Rezin took Elath from Judah, which led to its occupation by Edom (v. 6). Ahaz reacts to the situation by sending a message of submission to the Assyrian king along with a gift. The king of Assyria attacks and captures Damascus, deports its population to the unknown location Kir, and executes Rezin. Kings had already reported on the fate of Israel in 15:29. Thus the rather insular Judahite perspective is that it was Ahaz's request that led to Tiglath-pileser's capture of Damascus and killing of Rezin. It is possible, however, that Ahaz instead submitted and paid tribute only after the Assyrians had appeared on the scene. If Ahaz was actually offered a chance by Rezin and Pekah to join their alliance against Assyria, his refusal to do so can be explained on the basis of shrewd geopolitical insight. It is also possible that he was respecting oaths that had been taken in Yahweh's name as part of an earlier treaty relationship with Menahem and Pekahiah.

Isaiah 7:1–17 narrates a parallel but distinctive and much more dramatic and theological story about Ahaz and the Assyrian crisis. This narrative is representative of a certain genre of prophetic stories that involve an encounter between prophet and king or other public figure and center on the prophetic word (e.g., 2 Kgs 13:14–19 or Amos 7:10–17). Such stories are obviously less helpful for reconstructing history than items taken from the sources used by Kings. In the Isaiah presentation, the enemy kings attempt an attack, and the royal party and Ahaz are afraid. The prophet is directed by Yahweh to deliver to Ahaz an oracle of salvation calling for faith and confidence. The first part of the oracle (Isa 7:6) reveals the enemies' motivation through quoted speech. They intend to conquer Jerusalem and install one son of Tabeal (better: Ben-tabel), about whom nothing is known. Isaiah offers further reassurance by foretelling the impending birth of a sign child who will portend a quick and positive outcome for Judah when the Assyrians arrive. In Isaiah, the opposite of fear is faith (7:4, 9; 8:6), but what faith means as far as governmental policy is concerned is never specified. Nothing is said in Isaiah about any submission of Ahaz to Assyria or any gift to the king of Assyria. Isaiah gives Ahaz no direct advice about foreign policy. Nowhere in this narrative are Ahaz's actions with regard to Assyria explicitly or implicitly interpreted as a lack of faith in Yahweh. Isaiah's oracle against Damascus and Ephraim in 17:1–3 also appears to date from this period.

Second Chronicles 28 retells and supplements the material in Kings in order to detail Ahaz's wickedness more specifically. Ahaz is described as a devotee of Baal. Separate attacks by Damascus and Israel were divine punishments, and the Edomites and Philistines also invaded and took territory. The king's new altar explicitly becomes an opportunity for apostasy.

Tiglath-pileser subdued rebellion in Babylonia in 729 and 728, and took on himself the traditional religious role of the Babylonian king. Merodach-baladan of Bit-Yakin, the king of the Sea-Land, avoided the fate of other rebels by submitting before the Assyrians could attack.

3.6.5. Hoshea and the Final Days of Israel

Our understanding of the events surrounding the fall of Samaria is deficient because of a paucity of Assyrian evidence and confusion in the biblical reports. The end game for Israel is described in 2 Kgs 17:3–6; 18:9–11. According to 17:3, Hoshea paid tribute as a vassal to Shalmaneser V (727–722) after a hostile approach by him. However, the actual situation may be that the accession of Shalmaneser V presented Hoshea with a perceived opportunity for his otherwise unexplained rebellion described in verse 4. According to this notice, Hoshea had been in seditious contact with So king of Egypt and withheld the annual tribute he had paid in the past. Hoshea would have found it challenging to meet Assyrian tribute demands. Israel's contacts with its former territories to the west, in the agriculturally productive Jezreel Valley, and in the Transjordan had been decisively altered. What was left of Israel must therefore have been in a dire position economically.

The unknown name So may refer to Osorkon IV, a ruler of Tanis often considered the last king of the Twenty-Second Dynasty (ca. 730–715) or to the city of Sais, capital of the overlapping Twenty-Fourth Dynasty. According to 2 Kgs 17:4, Hoshea was captured and imprisoned, perhaps when he appeared before Shalmaneser to plead for forgiveness. This was followed by a three-year siege of Samaria by Shalmaneser that began in Hoshea year 7 (= Hezekiah year 4) and was over in Hoshea year 9 (= Hezekiah year 6). Kings reports a deportation of Israelites to Mesopotamia and western Iran and their replacement with alien settlers (17:6, 24; 18:11).

Although the biblical story seems clear enough, nonbiblical records complicate attempts to reconstruct the fall of Samaria. According to a source used by Josephus, in 725 Shalmaneser had begun what turned out to be a five-year siege of Tyre (*Ant.* 9.283–287, citing Menander). This event may perhaps be coordinated with Hoshea's rebellion and Shalmaneser's move against Samaria. The notice in the Babylonian Chronicle for the year Shalmaneser came to the throne (*COS* 1.137:467–68) lists as his sole notable accomplishment that he shattered Samaria. He died in 722, and that would be the year of his victory against Samaria. His successor was Sargon II (721–705).

Sargon's annals and other inscriptions of historical importance are accessible in *ANET*, 284–88, and *COS* 2.118A–J:293–300. Sargon reported that in his year 2 (720) he moved successfully against Hamath, Damascus, and Samaria. He claimed victory over Samaria in that year, describing the spoil and over twenty-seven thousand captives he had taken. Sargon also asserts that he rebuilt Samaria and resettled it with other peoples. He incorporated a unit of two hundred chariots manned by Israelite troops into his army. Israel was assimilated into the Assyrian Empire as a tribute-paying province with an appointed governor. However, Sargon does not seem to have greatly devastated the city of Samaria since there is no archaeological evidence of destruction. It is difficult to know what to make of Sargon's claim to have subdued "Judah which lies far away" (*ANET*, 287; *COS* 2.118I:298).

There are several possible ways to untangle the confusion as to whether Samaria fell to Shalmaneser in 722 or to Sargon in 720.

(1) Kings has conflated the accomplishments of Shalmaneser and Sargon. The author seems to have had imperfect and limited knowledge and is interested in making an ideological point. Unsurprisingly, there is no citation from the chronicles document for Israel for Hoshea. Kings mentions Shalmaneser only twice (17:3; 18:9), never Sargon, and otherwise uses the generic phrase "king of Assyria."

(2) Sargon, whose succession was irregular and who immediately faced rebellions, sought legitimacy by falsely claiming credit for some of his predecessor's accomplishments. This included Shalmaneser's capture of Samaria that immediately preceded his death in 722.

(3) There were two separate Assyrian campaigns and two victories over Samaria, first by Shalmaneser in 722 and then by Sargon in 720 after a second rebellion.

(4) Sargon completed Shalmaneser's work. Shalmaneser invaded the territory of Samaria and captured Hoshea but did not actually take the

city itself. The siege of the city continued through the transition from one Assyrian king to the other and was completed in Sargon's second year.

Israel's national identity was undermined by Assyria's policy of deportation. Some Samarian deportees were settled in the upper Euphrates area, some in distant Media, and some constituted chariot teams for the Assyrian army. The Nimrud Ivories, with Aramaic and Hebrew inscriptions, apparently represent booty from the fall of Samaria (*COS* 2.88:224). Epigraphic evidence of Assyrian administration at Samaria, Hazor, and Gezer exists. It is significant that names such as Menahem appear at Calah and Hosea at Nineveh. In 690 the governor of Samaria acted as eponym. Archaeology, both in surface surveys and in excavations, indicates a radical drop in the population of Galilee. It seems that in the case of Galilee anyway, the deported local population was not replaced by outsiders. There is strong evidence that northern refugees from this debacle moved south into Jerusalem, expanding its population and boundaries and bringing northern literature and traditions.

3.7. Archaeology and Epigraphy

Several epigraphic finds throw light on the situation of Israel and Judah in the period covered by this chapter. The Aramaic inscription of Deir 'Alla is a literary text about the seer or prophet Balaam, dated perhaps about 760. It consists of black text with red section headings written on a plaster wall. Its genre is something close to biblical prophetic texts. Although it is written in Aramaic and mentions only non-Israelite gods, it was found in Gilead. This shows the impact of Aramaean cultural influence in the area. It mentions the god Shagar, who is reflected in a linguistic expression found in Deut 7:13; 28:4, 18, 51.

Texts from the eighth century at Khirbet-el-Qôm (*COS* 2.52:179) and Kuntillet 'Ajrud (*COS* 2.47A–D:171–73) provide background for theological notions about Yahweh from that period. A temple, dated to Iron IIA by its excavators, was uncovered at Tel Motza (Khirbet Beit Mizzah, probably the Mozah of Josh 18:26), west of Jerusalem in Benjamin. It features an entrance facing east, what is apparently an altar, and nearby cache of vessels, chalices, and small figurines of humans and horses.

The epigraphic evidence includes intriguing personal names. A jar handle is inscribed "belonging to Ahab." One from Tel Rehov reads "belonging to the cupbearer Nimshi," perhaps indicating that Jehu's father had been a member of the royal court. Jeroboam II appears on a seal from Megiddo, engraved into precious stone with an image of a lion: "belonging to Shema, servant of Jeroboam." An unprovenanced seal impression with a sun disk and two uraei reads "belonging to Ashna servant of Ahaz." Two seals belonged to courtiers of Azariah (Uzziyaw). (For these last three finds, see COS 2.70R:200.) A seal in the Moussaieff collection of unprovenanced finds reads "belonging to Ahaz [son of] Jotham king of Judah."

3.8. Literature of the Period

The royal courts of Israel and Judah required literate bureaucracies to administer public affairs, and various epigraphic finds indicate their activities (Samaria ostraca, early Arad letters, use of Egyptian hieratic numerals on weights [COS 2.81:209], seals and seal impressions of royal officials). The three literary documents used by the author of Kings (BAS and the chronicles documents for Israel and Judah) must have depended on such recordkeeping and propaganda production by an official scribal class.

3.8.1. Covenant Code

The Covenant Code (Exod 20:22–23:33) is the oldest legal collection in the Hebrew Bible and can reasonably be dated to this period. It is certainly earlier than Deuteronomy, which updates many of its provisions. Topics include religion (images, altars, religious calendar), various personal and property offenses, and duties to the poor and marginalized. The setting is that of settled agriculture communities governed by local elders, without the interference of a king or centralized authority (22:27 [EV v. 28] does mention a leader or chieftain). There is no trace of urban or commercial life. These circumstances seem to fit the earlier kingship period better than that of the later, more centralized Judean monarchy. Topics, procedures, and a casuistic ("if … then" case law) format parallel those characteristic of other ancient west Asian law codes. The Covenant Code was inserted into the Sinai and conquest narratives and redactionally linked to them by 20:22 and 23:20–33.

3.8.2. Prophetic Legends and Oracles

Prophets and prophetic circles were active in the ninth and eighth centuries. As can be seen in the books of Amos, Hosea, Micah, and Isaiah, the followers of respected prophets preserved, edited, and supplemented the poetic oracles of the figures they venerated. These circles, the "sons of the prophets," also carried on a tradition of recounting prophetic narratives. Such stories were originally passed on by word of mouth in order to magnify the office of prophet and the power of the prophetic word. Properly assigned the form-critical label "legend," these stories present prophets as exemplary figures to be respected (2 Kgs 8:1–6), obeyed (1 Kgs 17:10–16; 2 Kgs 5:10–14), and even feared (2 Kgs 1:9–15; 2:23–24).

The author of Kings used legends about Ahijah (1 Kgs 11:29–39; 14:1–18), Shemaiah, (1 Kgs 12:21–24), Micaiah (1 Kgs 22:1–28), and anonymous prophets (1 Kgs 20:13–43). The narrative about two unnamed prophets and the altar of Bethel (1 Kgs 13) was probably passed on as a grave tradition (see 2 Kgs 23:16–18). Material about Isaiah makes up an extensive and relatively independent section of Kings (2 Kgs 18:13–20:19). Stories about Elijah and Elisha constitute nearly all of 1 Kgs 17:1–2 Kgs 8:15 and were most likely incorporated from a single written source. This legend cycle is held together by the transfer of Elijah's mantle (2 Kgs 2:13–14) and Elisha's completion of Elijah's mission (1 Kgs 19:15–17). Prophetic legends and folktales cannot be used as historical sources, except in an indirect way insofar as they reveal religious and social history.

Amos (in the reign of Jeroboam II) and Hosea (between about 750 and 725) condemned the rulers and upper classes of the kingdom of Israel. The oracles of judgment they spoke can be isolated from the books that bear their names, albeit with some uncertainty. The authentic oracles of these two prophets open a window on the devastating social effects of the economic changes of the eighth century. Increased production of the cash crops of wine and oil undermined the mixed, subsistence-agricultural patterns that had formerly provided small farmers with security in bad times. A breakdown in the venerable social safety net of village and clan life led inevitably to peasants losing their land and falling into debt slavery. This happened when they could not pay off loans they had been forced to agree to in order to survive. Abetted by a village courts system that was easily corrupted by bribes and influence, more and more land fell into the hands of absentee property owners.

3.8.3. Yahwist and Elohist Materials

For a century or more, biblical scholars almost universally postulated the existence of two connected documents lying behind the pre-Priestly form of Genesis–Numbers. Distinct Elohist (E) and Yahwist (J) sources were supposed to have told the story of Israel's national origins from their respective northern and southern perspectives. This earlier consensus has broken down. Space prevents even the briefest discussion of the numerous fragment and supplement theories that have arisen in recent decades to explain the present shape of the Pentateuch. Nevertheless, it can hardly be denied that distinct differences in presentation exist between certain connected streams of texts involving the patriarchs and exodus and that some of these differences can be explained on the basis of geography. It also remains true that consistent forms of expression and theological outlook can sometimes be used to categorize narrative doublets into two pre-Priestly groupings. The revision of Yahwist and Elohist source texts from Exodus and Numbers in Deuteronomy 1–3 demonstrate that at least some of them are demonstrably pre-Deuteronomistic.

4. Judah in the Assyrian and Babylonian Periods (720–539)

Albertz, Rainer. *Israel in Exile: The History and Literature of the Sixth Century B.C.E.* (SBLSBL 3; Atlanta: Society of Biblical Literature, 2003). Barrick, W. Boyd. *The King and the Cemeteries: Toward a New Understanding of Josiah's Reform* (VTSup 88; Leiden: Brill, 2002). Dubovský, Peter. *Hezekiah and the Assyrian Spies: Reconstruction of the Neo-Assyrian Intelligence Services and Its Significance for 2 Kings 18–19* (BibOr 49; Rome: Pontifical Biblical Institute, 2006). Eph'al, Israel. *The City Besieged: Siege and Its Manifestations in the Ancient Near East* (CHANE 36; Leiden: Brill, 2009). Grabbe, Lester L., ed. *Good Kings and Bad Kings: The Kingdom of Judah in the Seventh Century B.C.E.* (LHB/OTS 393; London: T&T Clark, 2005). Grabbe, ed. *Like a Bird in a Cage: The Invasion of Sennacherib in 701 BCE* (JSOTSup 363; Sheffield: Sheffield Academic, 2003). Kalimi, Isaac, and Seth Richardson, eds. *Sennacherib at the Gates of Jerusalem* (CHANE 71; Leiden: Brill, 2013). Kelle, Brad E., and Megan Bishop Moore, eds. *Israel's Prophets and Israel's Past: Essays on the Relationship of Prophetic Texts and Israelite History in Honor of John H. Hayes* (London: T&T Clark, 2006). Kim, Uriah Y. *Decolonizing Josiah: Toward a Postcolonial Reading of the Deuteronomistic History* (Sheffield: Sheffield Phoenix, 2005). Lipschits, Oded. *The Fall and Rise of Jerusalem: Judah under Babylonian Rule* (Winona Lake, Ind.: Eisenbrauns, 2005). Lipschits, and Joseph Blenkinsopp, eds. *Judah and the Judeans in the Neo-Babylonian Period* (Winona Lake, Ind.: Eisenbrauns, 2003). Middlemas, Jill. *The Templeless Age: An Introduction to the History, Literature, and Theology of the Exile* (Louisville: Westminster John Knox, 2007). Middlemas. *The Troubles of Templeless Judah* (Oxford: Oxford University Press, 2005). Morkot, Robert G. *The Black Pharaohs: Egypt's Nubian Rulers* (London: Rubicon, 2000).

Mykytiuk, Lawrence J. *Identifying Biblical Persons in Northwest Semitic Inscriptions of 1200–539 B.C.E.* (SBL Academia Biblica 12; Atlanta: Society of Biblical Literature, 2004). **Smith**, Mark S. *The Early History of God: Yahweh and the Other Deities in Ancient Israel* (2nd ed.; Grand Rapids: Eerdmans, 200)2. **Sweeney**, Marvin A. *King Josiah of Judah: The Lost Messiah of Israel* (Oxford: Oxford University Press, 2001). **Vanderhooft**, David S. *The Later Babylonian Empire and Babylon in the Latter Prophets* (Harvard Semitic Museum Monographs 59; Atlanta: Scholars Press, 2000). **Zevit**, Ziony. *The Religions of Ancient Israel: A Synthesis of Parallactic Approaches* (London: Continuum, 2001).

4.0. Summary

The submission of Ahaz to Tiglath-pileser inaugurated a long period of deference to Assyria that lasted up to the end of the Assyrian Empire. Although the first half of Hezekiah's reign was characterized by an emerging policy of resistance, this was brought decisively to an end by the campaign of Sennacherib in 701. Sennacherib's ensuing punitive measures included a significant loss of Judahite territory in the Shephelah. Hezekiah's successor Manasseh followed a deferential compliance policy that made possible a period of political stability and prosperity. Even though Judah's territory had been reduced by Sennacherib, the size of Jerusalem increased. Immigrants from the former kingdom of Israel made up much of this population increase. Soon after Manasseh's death, a coup triggered by internal dissatisfaction with his compliance policy failed. His grandson Josiah was eventually able to make use of opportunities presented by increasing Assyrian weakness to chart a more independent course. However, he apparently remained an Assyrian vassal, formally at least.

For Assyria, the seventh century was one of growing challenges from various quarters. To meet these threats, Assyria needed its vassals to supply its armies, but the consequent need for heavy taxation also made those vassals more willing to take the risk of rebellion. In addition, Assyria's highly centralized power structure meant that its kings had to be talented and politically astute, something that could not always be counted on. As a result, Assyria experienced an undercurrent of dynastic instability, as evidenced, for example, by the Vassal Treaties of Esarhaddon. These were imposed on Assyria's vassals to ensure the peaceful succession of Assurbanipal. Things fell apart rapidly for Assyria near the end of the reign of Assurbanipal. His sons Assur-etel-ilani and Sin-shar-ishkun contended with each other for the throne, and Assyrian power continued to disintegrate. The native Babylonian Nabopolassar seized power in Babylon in 626. Along with his Median allies, Nabopolassar sought to finish off Assyria. To prevent Babylon from gaining hegemony over all of western Asia, Egypt acted as Assyria's ally. Sin-shar-ishkun died in the sack of Nineveh in 612. Assur-uballit II (611–ca. 608) became king, presiding briefly over what was left of Assyrian power.

The enigmatic death of Josiah in 609 at the hands of Pharaoh Neco brought to an end the religious reform he had instituted. In an anti-Egyptian move, Josiah was succeeded immediately by Jehoahaz, who was not Josiah's oldest son. However, when Neco was returning home from his failed attempt to bolster the Assyrian cause, he replaced Jehoahaz with the legitimate heir Jehoiakim. Neco's subsequent defeat at Carchemish in 605 marked the end of Egypt's attempts to block Babylonian hegemony. As a result of Carchemish, Jehoiakim smoothly switched his loyalty from Egypt to Babylon. Nebuchadnezzar II, who now ruled Babylon, experienced some kind of setback against Egypt in 601, apparently giving Jehoiakim the confidence to withhold tribute from Babylon. Nebuchadnezzar responded by attacking Judah in late 598. Jehoiakim died, leaving his son Jehoiachin to face the consequences. The Babylonians captured Jerusalem in 597, deposed Jehoiachin, deported some of its population, and installed Jehoiachin's uncle Zedekiah as king. Jehoiachin was not executed, but confined in Babylon, where he soon became a focus of nationalistic aspirations.

Perhaps counting on support from Egypt, Zedekiah broke faith with Nebuchadnezzar, who instituted a siege of Jerusalem in 588. After eighteen months, Zedekiah was captured, and the city was taken in 586. Zedekiah and his sons were executed. Jerusalem and its temple were burned, and portions of the population were deported. Although the land was not totally depopulated, economic life took a sharp downturn. Deportees from Judah were settled in Babylon, Nippur, and along the Chebar Canal. Many came to terms with their lives as expatriates and settled into a reasonably secure existence. Nebuchadnezzar appointed one Gedaliah as governor of what had been the kingdom of Judah. Gedaliah was assassinated in an unsuccessful pro-Davidic uprising. The last king of the Neo-Babylonian Empire was Nabonidus, whose policies affronted elements of Babylon's power structure. This paved the way for Cyrus the Great to occupy Babylon in 539 after a series of remarkable victories.

4.1. Hezekiah (ca. 726–697)

The biblical presentation of the reign of Hezekiah consists of several different sorts of material. Some statements are clearly drawn from the chronicles source for Judah, such as Hezekiah's campaign against Philistia and his construction of a conduit and pool (18:8; 20:20). In addition, Kings includes Deuteronomistic judgments about a religious reform program, a credible note about the serpent icon Nehushtan (18:4–6), and notice of Hezekiah's submission to Sennacherib and abstraction of tribute money from the temple treasury (18:14–16). If one were to read only this far, the course of events would be simple: Hezekiah revolted, Sennacherib attacked and captured many towns, and Hezekiah submitted before any serious action against Jerusalem could be taken.

However, at this point in 2 Kings there then follows a complex, interrelated series of narratives written from a prophetic perspective and involving the figure of Isaiah. These prophetically oriented narratives consist first of an extended dramatic scene set at the walls of besieged Jerusalem. This scene features two long speeches in 18:17–37, with verse 22 linking the speeches into the larger Deuteronomistic context. These speeches then provide the context for Hezekiah's consultation of Isaiah and the oracle that resulted (19:1–7). Next a threatening letter from the king of Assyria leads to Hezekiah's prayer and a complex prophetic response by Isaiah (vv. 8–34). The accuracy of Isaiah's prophetic word is immediately confirmed by the destruction of Sennacherib's besieging army, his return home, and his assassination (vv. 35–37). Then follow prophetic stories concerning Hezekiah's sickness (20:1–11) and his folly with the envoys of Merodachbaladan (vv. 12–19). Sorting through this compilation of material in an attempt to reconstruct historical events has proved to be a challenging task. This section of Kings is repeated in Isa 36–39.

There are chronological problems with Hezekiah's reign. His age at accession (twenty-five) does not fit the information that Ahaz came to the throne at age twenty and reigned sixteen years. This would make Ahaz the father of Hezekiah at age eleven. Clearly, postulating a coregency of Ahaz and Jotham is in order. Second Kings 18:9–10 synchronizes the fall of Samaria to Shalmaneser V (722; ruled 726–722) with Hezekiah year 6 and Hoshea year 9. This correlation would put Hezekiah's accession in 727 or 726, perhaps after a coregency with Ahaz. If one calculates backward from the date of Josiah's death in 609, Hezekiah's reign would also be about 726–697. Second Kings 18:13, however, equates Sennacherib's invasion in

701 with Hezekiah year 14, only eight years later than the fall of Samaria as opposed to the expected twenty-one years. If accepted, this latter piece of data would put Hezekiah's accession much earlier, in 716 or 715. However, this statement seems to be an erroneous conclusion adopted from narrative of Hezekiah's illness (20:6). The author of 18:13 wished to account for the fifteen extra years of life awarded to Hezekiah, which the author supposed to be after 701. Subtracting this figure from Hezekiah's twenty-nine-year reign led to the mistaken conclusion that 701 was his fourteenth year.

4.1.1. Hezekiah and Sargon II

After a precarious start, Sargon II (721–705) moved to bolster his reign in 720, fighting indecisive battles to the south with Elam and the Chaldean Merodach-baladan (Mardik-apla-iddina II, ruler of Babylon 721–710), who had seized the throne of Babylon with Elamite support. Elamite resistance forced Sargon to turn back. In that same year, 720, Sargon moved against a western rebellion, defeating the Aramaean Yaubidi at Qarqar. He either captured Samaria as part of that campaign or simply stabilized the situation there and took credit for an earlier victory by Shalmaneser V in 722 (see §3.6.5). Sargon then moved down the Philistine coast and eventually captured Gaza. He left reliefs recording this operation in his palace at Khorsabad. Some scholars suggest that Zech 9:1–5 refers to this campaign, but the usual date suggested for this text would exclude this possibility. Rebellious Carchemish was defeated in 717 and incorporated into the empire. Sargon settled Arab groups in Samaria (*ANET*, 286; *COS* 2.118A:293), defeated Pharaoh Osorkon IV (ca. 730–715), and established a colony of Assyrians on the brook of Egypt. A successful campaign against Urartu in 714 allowed Sargon to turn his attention once more to Babylon in 710. Although Merodach-baladan was able to escape, Sargon became ruler of Babylon at the New Year festival in 709. He reportedly deported 108,000 Aramaean and Chaldean inhabitants of Babylonia.

It is unclear when Hezekiah began his movement toward a more resistant policy in his relations with Assyria. Sargon II carried out three campaigns in Syria-Palestine, in part to put down rebellions (720 [Hamath], 716, and 712 [Ashdod]). It does not seem that Judah was the target of any of these operations. The last of these campaigns was in response to a rebellion in 714–712 by the usurper Iamani of Ashdod and other Assyrian vassals. They were no doubt encouraged by the resurgence of Egyptian power under Piankhy (Piye; 740–713), effectively the founder of the Twenty-Fifth Dynasty. The Nubian pharaohs were naturally interested in Judah's continued existence as a buffer state against Assyrian imperialism and would have also wanted to control the trade routes along which copper and tin moved, as well as the wood Egypt needed for construction. According to Isaiah 20, Hezekiah may have been invited to participate in this conspiracy, but wisely chose not to. The foreign-nation oracles of Isa 14:28–32 and 18:1–19:15 may also allude to temptations to join in a resistance to Assyria at this time. The result of Ashdod's rebellion was its reduction into an imperial province. Between 710–705 Sargon was fully occupied in the south and with Babylon. The reported embassy of Merodach-baladan to Hezekiah (2 Kgs 20:12–19) could have taken place during this period and not after 701, as the sequence of events presented by Kings would suggest. It would make sense for this astute troublemaker to try to stir up discontent among Assyria's vassals. However, the story is highly etiological and comes from a prophetic source that may not be historically trustworthy.

4.1.2. Hezekiah and Sennacherib

Sargon was killed in battle in 705 at Tabal in Cappadocia. He was replaced by his son Sennacherib (704–681), who quickly faced rebellion in Babylon. For some reason, Sennacherib had not been previously installed as ruler of Babylon as Sargon, Shalmaneser V, and Tiglath-pileser had been. The old nemesis of the Assyrians, Merodach-baladan took advantage of this and had himself proclaimed king of Babylon once again. He was backed by Elam and Chaldean tribes. Sennacherib defeated him in 703, but he escaped again. Merodach-baladan along with the Egyptian pharaoh Shabaka (712–698) had been stirring up trouble in the west. According to 2 Kgs 18:7–8, Hezekiah now made his move: "He rebelled against the king of Assyria.… He struck the Philistines as far as Gaza and its territory." This area was under Assyrian protection, so Hezekiah's attack constituted an unequivocal act of rebellion. Others joined in. Ekron deposed its pro-Assyrian king Padi and handed him over to Hezekiah, who kept him captive. The rebellious king of Ashkelon occupied Joppa. Sidon and Tyre refused to pay tribute.

Archaeology shows that Hezekiah had prepared for his break with Assyria. The large numbers of *lmlk* jar stamps found at Lachish can be associated with his stockpiling of supplies there. The inscription means either "belonging to the king" or "[to be sent] to the king." These jar stamps have also been found at other sites against which one would reasonably expect Sennacherib to move. They relate chronologically to the 701 destruction of Lachish. These jars were produced at some single location and connected in some way to the royal economy of wine or oil distribution. There are two types, a winged scarab and a winged sun disk, and both were apparently used at the same time. The place names stamped on them (Hebron, Socoh, Ziph, and the unknown *mmsht*) represent locations in the Judah hill country and Shephelah, perhaps agricultural collection centers under state supervision (*COS* 2.77:202–3).

The Siloam tunnel with its inscription is a second piece of evidence for Hezekiah's preparations (*ANET*, 321; *COS* 2.28:145–46). The text was engraved in an elegant script with word dividers and was placed at the entrance to the tunnel. The upper portion was smoothed and left blank, as though unfinished. Although the function of this inscription is puzzling (it is not a royal building inscription, for example), it supports the accuracy of 2 Kgs 20:20. The tunnel itself was dug from both ends at once, apparently following seepage through cracks in the rock. Once the two work parties drew close enough, listening to the sound of the other team allowed them to meet about in the center. It should be noted, however, that the biblical verse does not unambiguously refer to a tunnel but to a *conduit*. Isaiah 22:8b–11 also refers to preparations to strengthen the city's wall and secure its water supply, although the date of these projects cannot be established. The thick Broad Wall of Jerusalem, built across the north of the western expansion district (Mishneh), could also relate to preparations for Sennacherib's invasion. Hezekiah would certainly have felt he could depend on the long-standing, massive fortification of Lachish and the fortified outpost of Ramat Rahel just south of Jerusalem. A significantly large number of *lmlk*-stamped jar handles were found at Ramat Rahel. It is possible that 2 Chr 32:3–6, 28, also offers trustworthy information on Hezekiah's preparations.

In his third campaign, conducted in his year 4 (701), Sennacherib moved against Hezekiah's allies first. Although Sennacherib had this campaign recorded in his annals (*ANET*, 287–88; *COS* 2:119B:302–3), the sequence of events and their relation to each other remain unclear. Several different reconstructions are possible. Sennacherib defeated Sidon and Tyre, forcing the king who ruled these cities to flee to Cyprus. Tyre's mainland possessions were given to Sidon, and a pro-Assyrian king was installed in Sidon. After forcing out the king of Sidon, Sennacherib received tribute from the rulers of Ashdod, Ammon, Moab, Edom, and other places, at Acco. A subsequent move down the coast seems to have been intended to cut off any possibility of Egyptian aid reaching Hezekiah. Sennacherib deported the rebellious king of Ashkelon in connection with capturing Joppa and its territory. The people of Ekron, which had earlier handed their pro-Assyrian king Padi over to Hezekiah, had sought Egyptian help. Sennacherib encountered Egyptian forces at Eltekeh (in the coastal area, see Josh 19:44) and claims to have defeated them, but once again, the position of this episode in the sequence of events remains unclear. The Assyrian king defeated Ekron and punished its rebels. He was able to pressure Hezekiah into releasing the loyal Padi and restored him to his throne as a tributary vassal.

With Philistia under Assyrian control and the threat of Egypt blocked, the invasion route into Judah was open. Sennacherib moved against fortresses and cities outside of Jerusalem, eventually capturing and looting forty-six of them. Micah 1:10–16 is usually thought to incorporate a roster of some of these places south and west of Jerusalem, including Gath and Lachish. According to the Azekah Inscription usually attributed to him (*COS* 2.119D:304–5), Sennacherib conquered that strategic Judahite town. According to 2 Kgs 19:8, he attacked Libnah. But Sennacherib's greatest accomplishment was the reduction of the heavily fortified city of Lachish, which he justifiably celebrated in a series of dramatic palace reliefs. The destruction of Lachish Stratum III is thus dated to 701. Excavation there uncovered the massive siege ramp at the city's southwest corner and a huge counter-ramp constructed inside the walls. Arrowheads and stones from slings indicate savage fighting, as do mass burials of men, women, and children (thirteen hundred skeletons). The Lachish reliefs show prisoners going into exile carrying baggage.

The biblical text raises a problem with its mention of Tirhaka (Taharqa) king of Cush (Nubia), who supposedly came to the aid of Judah (2 Kgs 19:9). Since this person did not rule as pharaoh until ten years after these events (690–664), he was hardly a king at this point, but such confusion would be understandable. More seriously, various lines of evidence indicate that Taharqa would have been much too young in 701 to be leading troops and was apparently still in Nubia at that time. Most likely the name of the better-known Tirhaka replaced the more obscure Pharaoh Shabaka (712–698) in popular memory.

Herodotus (*Hist.* 2.141) reports a defeat of Sennacherib by an Egyptian force at Pelusium that supposedly resulted when field mice disabled the bows and shields of the Assyrian army by gnawing at them the night before the conflict. Some have connected this tale with Sennacherib's maneuvers on the Egyptian border (2 Kgs 19:9). Josephus mentions the Herodotus account and then goes on to cite Berossus, apparently to the effect that that disease struck down an Assyrian army led by Rabshakeh outside Jerusalem, killing 185,000 men (*Ant.* 10.18–23). However, it is most likely that the actual Berossus quotation has dropped out of the manuscript tradition and that, in the text that follows the gap, Josephus is simply repeating the story of 2 Kgs 19:35–36. The pro-Egyptian and Hellenocentric perspective of Herodotus pervades the tale he tells. However, Herodotus does witness to the existence of a popular story telling about a divine judgment against Sennacherib through nonhuman intervention, one that led to the wholesale defeat of his army. Linking Herodotus's mice with an annihilation of the Assyrian forces by bubonic plague, however, requires several leaps in reasoning and accepting Josephus's claim of a pestilence (*Ant.* 10.21).

The old hypothesis of an otherwise undocumented second attack by Sennacherib (about 688) is unnecessary. It rests in part on reading the sequence of narratives in 2 Kgs 18–19 as recording events in chronological order rather than as the result of redactional activity.

4.1.3. Jerusalem in 701

Attempts to reconstruct what happened outside Jerusalem in 701 present the historian with a classic exercise of comparing and weighing biblical and nonbiblical evidence. Second Kings 18:1–16 and 20:20–21 provide the core historiographical elements in the presentation of Hezekiah. The other texts are from prophetic materials and must be treated with greater caution. With regard to Sennacherib's threat to Jerusalem, the biblical narrative combines two prophetic stories (18:17–19:9a + 36–37 and 19:9b–35) with more trustworthy statements that appear to come from a source document (18:13–16). Biblical and Assyrian sources agree on three things: Sennacherib captured fortified cities (18:13), Jerusalem was not captured, and Hezekiah paid tribute (18:14–16). The question of a siege is unclear. The Assyrian sources report that Hezekiah was restricted by a surrounding earthwork to Jerusalem "like a bird in a cage," but mentions no other typical element of a siege. The Bible reports the presence of an enemy army outside the walls (18:17; 19:35), but explicitly says in an oracle of Isaiah that no siege ramp was raised (19:32).

The prophetic material extols the accuracy of Isaiah's prophetic word in 19:21–28, 32–34, by asserting that Sennacherib withdrew owing to supernatural intervention (19:35–36). This description has much in common with portrayals of divine slaughter in Exod 12:29–30 and 2 Sam 24:16. Probably Sennacherib reasoned that simply accepting Hezekiah's submission and payment of tribute was the most cost-effective way to deal with Judah's rebellion. Certainly Sennacherib's attainment of the submission of Sidon and Ashkelon, numerous other conquests, and his success in keeping Egypt out of the picture must have put him in a strong bargaining position. Sennacherib permitted the Judahite tribute to be sent to him, which may indicate an abrupt departure on his part. Whatever actually happened, however, Sennacherib's failure to prosecute the war to final victory had a striking impact on popular religious opinion. The contrast between the seemingly providential survival of Jerusalem and the horrific fate visited on Lachish just forty miles away could not have been stronger. The belief that Jerusalem was under the guaranteed protection of Yahweh became a popular creed (Pss 46; 48; 76; Jer 7). Oracles preserved in Isaiah promise the salvation of Jerusalem in similarly dramatic language (e.g., Isa 10:16–19, 33; 30:30–33).

The Rabshakeh (*rab shaqe*, "cupbearer"), credited in the prophetic material with carrying on the negotiations, was an Assyrian royal official who often led diplomatic missions. Sennacherib's assassination did not actually happen until 681, but otherwise the biblical report in 2 Kgs 19:37 is basically accurate, although Assurbanipal seems to suggest he was smashed to death by images of protective deities rather than cut down by the sword (*ANET*, 288). The name of the assassin Arda-Mulissi was corrupted to Adrammelech in the biblical report. The prophetic sources preserved other bits of accurate information. The name in the Royal Steward Epitaph (*COS* 2.54:180), restored as *Shebnah*, seems to establish the historicity of Hezekiah's steward ("who was over the house"; 2 Kgs 18:18; 19:2; Isa 22:15–19). There are unprovenanced seal impressions for "Jehozarah son of Hilkiah servant of Hezekiah" and "Eliakim son of Hilkiah" (2 Kgs 18:18).

The effects of Hezekiah's revolt were serious. Judah lost a slice of territory in the west to Ashdod, Ekron, and Gaza. A portion of Judah's population was exiled. Hezekiah had to pay a special exaction of booty and experienced an increase in his regular tribute. Nonetheless, for the rest of his reign Sennacherib had to turn his attention back to Mesopotamia. In fact, he may have been unwilling to invest in a difficult siege of Jerusalem because of developments in Babylon, where Merodach-baladan seems to have been inciting the Chaldeans yet again. In 700 Sennacherib invaded Babylon and installed his own son Assur-nadin-shumi as king. This was only the first of several campaigns required by insurgencies on the part of Elam, the Sea-Land, the Aramaeans of Bit-Yakin, and Chaldeans (in 694, 690–689). Finally, Sennacherib plundered Babylon, burned it, and tried to efface it. His youngest son Esarhaddon was named ruler of Babylonia. In 681 Sennacherib was killed in a temple by some of his other sons who were angry over the preference shown to their younger brother Esarhaddon. Esarhaddon (680–669) quickly forced them to flee to Urartu. He rebuilt and enlarged Babylon, a project that consumed his entire reign.

4.2. Manasseh (ca. 697–642) and Amon (642–640)

Manasseh came to the throne at age twelve, perhaps as a coregent. This circumstance seems to point to some otherwise unexplained crisis in Hezekiah's reign. Perhaps Manasseh's name, reflecting that of a northern Israelite tribe, indicates something about Hezekiah's nationalistic policies. He enjoyed a long reign, which one must take as accurate, given that he was later demonized as an apostate. He was a loyal vassal to Esarhaddon (680–669). No doubt the debacle of his father's rebellion impressed upon him the folly of a resistance policy. Manasseh is listed among other vassal kings who provided forced labor for Esarhaddon to construct his palace in Nineveh in 677–676 (*ANET*, 291). He later provided support to the military campaign of Assurbanipal against Egypt (*ANET*, 294). Another indication of Manasseh's compliance policies may be found in the name of his successor Amon. *Amon* could be connected to the city No-Amon (Thebes), which fell to Assurbanipal in 664. This would be about the year of Amon's birth. On the other hand, the name does occur elsewhere in the Hebrew Bible and can be taken to mean "faithful."

The chronicles source about Manasseh may have described the sin he committed (21:17), but the detailed reports given in verses 3–16 consist almost entirely of Deuteronomistic vilification. If there were indeed elements of Assyrianization in his religious policy, say in the form of accepting astral deities (2 Kgs 21:3, 5; cf. 23:11–12), they would have been voluntary acculturations to dominant Assyrian culture. Equine figurines from Jerusalem and Lachish bearing disks on their heads suggest veneration of the sun, although it should be remembered that solar images were sometimes used to describe Yahweh (2 Sam 23:4; Mal 4:2). It is difficult to assess the historical value of an unprovenanced seal bearing the inscription "belonging to Manasseh son of the king" with a star and a crescent moon representing astral deities.

Jerusalem grew significantly, and new areas were enclosed: the Mishneh ("second quarter") on the western hill and the Maktesh ("hollow") in the central valley (Zeph 1:10–11). Jerusalem may have expanded to three times its previous size. Although it is hard to date Jerusalem's expansion on its western hill or the Broad Wall constructed to protect this expansion district, the reign of Manasseh must have been a period of increasing settlement. Jerusalem was now the only real city left in the kingdom. Much of this population increase can be attributed to immigration from former territories of the kingdom of Israel and areas of the Shephelah lost to Judah.

Manasseh's long reign overlapped with that of Esarhaddon (680–669) and much of Assurbanipal's (668–ca. 627). Viewing matters from the perspective of Assyria, the seventh century proved to be an increasingly challenging time. Urartu had been decisively defeated by Sargon II in 714, but Elam and Babylon continued to be problematic neighbors, although Sennacherib was able to sack Babylon in 689. Scythians and Cimmerians threatened the edges of the empire, and Arabs caused problems east of Syria-Palestine. Esarhaddon faced an invasion by Scythians in 679 that triggered a revolt of his vassals in Asia Minor. He was able to suppress these rebellions and push the invaders westward into Phrygia. In 677 he reacted to a rebellion by Sidon and plundered the city. Nonetheless, the king of Tyre revolted with encouragement from Pharaoh Taharqa of the Nubian Twenty-Fifth Dynasty, probably in 676. At this time Esarhaddon was sending cavalry into Iran in order to weaken the growing power of the Medes and secure peace with Elam.

Egypt remained both a tempting target for Assyria and a source of trouble. In 675 Esarhaddon was ready to deal with the troublesome Taharqa. His first invasion was halted by a sandstorm, but the next year he began a siege of Tyre and then moved south to capture some strong points in the delta. Esarhaddon invaded Egypt again in 671 and captured Memphis. He installed new rulers, including a certain Neco, eventually to be founder of the Twenty-Sixth Saite Dynasty as Neco I (672–664). Two years later, however, Taharqa was back from his refuge in the south and recaptured Memphis. Esarhaddon was returning to Egypt in order to deal with this crisis when he died. The succession went smoothly. Assurbanipal became king of Assyria, and his brother Shamash-shin-ukin ruled Babylon. This trouble-free transition of power was possible because Esarhaddon had appointed these two sons as his successors. The Vassal Treaties of Esarhaddon (672), agreed to by vassals such as Manasseh, safeguarded the succession of Assurbanipal (*ANET*, 534–41). The language of this treaty had a direct effect on the composition of Deuteronomy. Ezra 4:2 indicates that some alien group in the early Persian period believed they had been settled in Palestine by Esarhaddon (and possibly by Assurbanipal according to one interpretation of v. 10).

In 667 under Assurbanipal, a force of Assyrians and allies invaded Egypt, defeated Taharqa again, and recaptured Memphis. In 664–663, Assurbanipal reacted to an onslaught by Twenty-Fifth-Dynasty pharaoh Tantamani (664–656), the replacement for Taharqa who had died in 664. The Assyrian king moved into Egypt again, besieging and capturing the southern city of Thebes (No-Amon, Hebrew No') in 664. The capture and destruction of this ancient religious center was a major event. He appointed Psamtik I (Psammetichus, 664–610), the son of Neco I, as ruler of the delta area. This Twenty-Sixth Saite Dynasty would preside over a restoration of Egyptian culture. In 653 the king of Elam attacked Mesopotamia. While Esarhaddon was busy dealing successfully with this crisis, Psamtik expelled Assyrian garrisons from Egypt between 653 and 651 with the support of mercenaries from Gyges of Lydia. These troops included Greek and Aegean naval forces. Psamtik also besieged Ashdod and captured it after twenty-nine years (Herodotus, *Hist.* 2.157; cf. Jer 25:20).

Assurbanipal could not respond effectively because of a rebellion in 652 by his brother Shamash-shum-ukin, ruler of Babylon. It required a costly campaign for Assurbanipal to defeat his mutinous brother, climaxing in an act of self-immolation by Shamash-shum-ukin in his burning palace in 648. Elam had supported this rebellion and continued to be restive. Assurbanipal punished Elam by an invasion between 647 and 645 that culminated in a brutal campaign of destruction against Susa. Ironically, the elimination of Elam would open the way for the Medes to exploit new opportunities in the area. Campaigning between 641 and 639, Assurbanipal pacified Arab groups. Assurbanipal may have died in 631 rather than 627. Dates at the very end of the Assyrian period are uncertain owing to the absence of eponym lists after 649.

Amon was born when Manasseh was forty-five years old and so is unlikely to have been his first son. Amon's short two-year reign and the succession of his son Josiah as a child provides confirmation of the coup and countercoup reported in 2 Kgs 21:23–24. Most likely, Amon was assassinated by a nationalist faction that wished to reverse Manasseh's policy of compliance with Assyria, no doubt encouraged by expanding Egyptian influence under Psamtik. The uprising against his assassins was staged by the "people of the land," suggesting that this conservative group sought a continuation of Manasseh's compliance policy. The events of 701 had demonstrated that this rural landowner group would be especially vulnerable in the event of another Assyrian attack. Amon had fathered Josiah at age sixteen, perhaps indicating some concerns involving the succession.

4.3. Josiah (640–609)

Josiah came to the throne at age eight. He was presumably at first controlled by his supporters, the propertied rural class (people of the land), who wished to continue Manasseh's compliance policies. An understandable concern to guarantee the succession led Josiah to father Jehoiakim at age fourteen.

Egypt and Assyria shared a long-standing alliance throughout the reigns of Psamtik I and Assurbanipal, although Psamtik followed an increasingly independent policy as Assyrian influence waned. There is a gap in Mesopotamian records between the annals for Assurbanipal that break off about 639 (*ANET*, 294–301) and the Babylonian Chronicle, which picks up with 626 (*ANET*, 305–7; *COS* 1:137:467–68). There was a struggle for the throne of Assyria during the latter part of Assurbanipal's reign as his twin sons, Assur-etel-ilani (627–623) and Sin-shar-ishkun (622–612), vied with each other. Assurbanipal spent his final years in Harran. After Assurbanipal and his appointee to the throne of Babylon, Kandalanu (647–627), both died, Assyrian power continued to disintegrate. Assur-etel-ilani and Sin-shar-ishkun continued their dispute over succession until the former's death in 623. After a year when there was no recognized king in Babylon, Nabopolassar (626–605), governor of the Sea-Land, seized power in Babylon from 626 on, apparently representing a native Babylonian dynasty. He spearheaded opposition to Assyria along with the Medes as his allies. Nabopolassar's invasion of Assyria strengthened the alliance between Egypt and Assyria.

Judah seems to have been a junior partner in this coalition and still an Assyrian vassal, at least nominally. Since Egypt and Assyria were allies at this time, a friendly relationship between Judah, as an Assyrian vassal, and Egypt must also have existed. The hypothesis of an Egypt-Judah-Assyria alliance throws light on both Josiah's encounter with Neco II in 609 and

Neco's subsequent sponsorship of Jehoiakim to replace Jehoahaz (2 Kgs 23:34; cf. Isa 19:23-26).

The continuing challenges faced by Assyria, followed by open warfare between it and Babylon, permitted Josiah to follow a more independent policy than his grandfather had. There was probably no expansion of Judahite jurisdiction in a formal sense into the Assyrian province of Samaria, except in the territory of Benjamin (see below). There would have been no real power vacuum as Assyria withdrew from Palestine, since Assyria's ally Egypt would still have been concerned about stability on its northern border. However, an ability on the part of Josiah to take action against cultic installations in Bethel and elsewhere (1 Kgs 13:2, 30-32; 2 Kgs 23:15-19) is entirely possible, especially if Josiah could operate at least nominally as an Assyrian vassal.

The district list for the kingdom of Judah in the book of Joshua (15:21-63; 18:21-28) is to be dated to Josiah's reign. The Benjaminite district described in 18:21-24 shows a border shift reflecting Judah's expanded administrative control. The portion of Benjamin up to the Bethel-Ophrah line that had formerly been part of the kingdom of Israel was now incorporated into Josiah's kingdom. The "in the wilderness" district (15:61-62) correlates with evidence of expanded settlement in the Judean desert at this time. Josiah (or his grandfather Manasseh) reoccupied Lachish and Libnah in the Shephelah, cities presumably lost to Judah after 701 (Josh 15:39, 42; 2 Kgs 23:31; 24:18).

Whether Josiah expanded his control even further west in order to incorporate Mesad Hashavyahu (Yavneh-yam) on the Mediterranean is a debated question. A Hebrew ostracon discovered in that fortress would seem to indicate this, but the occurrence of Greek pottery there points to the presence of Greek mercenaries, most likely in the employ of Egypt. However, postulating an ongoing Egypt-Judah-Assyria alliance would explain both sets of finds. The ostracon in question is a petition from a farm laborer, written by a scribe, to a local governor (*sar*). The letter provides social background for the cloak law of the Covenant Code and Deuteronomy (Exod 22:25-26 [EV vv. 26-27]; Deut 24:12-13; *ANET*, 568; *COS* 3:41:77-78).

4.3.1. Josiah's Reform

Much discussion revolves around the religious reforms reported for Josiah's year 18 (622/621; 2 Kgs 22:3). Questions continue to be raised about the historicity of the book-finding legend in chapter 22 and its relationship to Deuteronomy and the DH. On the one hand, such stories were a stock literary motif in the ancient world. On the other hand, the use of this literary format is no decisive argument against the historicity of what it reports. After all, Mesopotamian kings regularly publicized their restoration accomplishments on the basis of real foundation inscriptions actually discovered (or at least the objects of staged discoveries). It is hardly surprising that 2 Chronicles supplements the story with an earlier turn to proper religion by Josiah in his eighth year, without any report of specific reforming actions. Chronicles wants to magnify Josiah's piety "while he was yet a boy" (2 Chr 34:3a). Chronicles then goes on to narrate royal reforms instituted in Josiah's year 12, again before the discovery of the book of the law (34:3b–7), when the king would have been of an age to make his own decisions.

The context for the discovery of the book of the law is a renovation of the temple, the narrative for which was adapted by the author from the story of Jehoash's reform in 2 Kgs 12:9–15. Repairing dilapidated temples was a standard public relations activity undertaken by ancient kings, and there is no reason to think that Josiah would not be interested in such a project. The careful reader will note, however, that the biblical text in Kings does not directly or explicitly relate the finding of the book to the reconstruction project. It is found in the temple according to Hilkiah, but nothing is said about the circumstances. It is almost universally accepted that this book is intended to be some early form of Deuteronomy.

The original report of Josiah's reform in chapter 23 probably consisted only of a bare list of action verbs and their direct objects ("he burned ... deposed ... broke down ... brought out ... defiled," etc.), which seems to have come from a written source of some sort. Much of the content of Josiah's reform in its present shape consists of parallels to earlier parts of Kings and even to the book of Joshua. The best explanation for this circumstance is that DH had the reforms of Josiah in mind when composing earlier sections of Kings. Second Kings 23:4–12 undoes the apostasy of Manasseh item by item (cf. 21:3–7). The high places (usually understood to be raised platforms used for sacrifice) that have been a persistent concern of the author of Kings are decommissioned. Second Kings 23:13 cancels deviations that go back to Solomon (1 Kgs 11:7), and 2 Kgs 23:15–20 refer to the sins instituted by Jeroboam I. These include "all the houses of the high that were in the cities of Samaria" (v. 19, echoing 1 Kgs 13:32). A reformed Passover is said to restore the observance to the situation of

Josh 5:10–12, celebrated as commanded by Deut 16:5–7. Other items of apostasy do not occur in such precise fashion earlier in Kings (23:5, 7, 11), indicating the use of a source document: burning incense to astral deities, houses of sanctified male cult personnel, women weaving hangings for Asherah, horses dedicated to the sun, and the chariots of the sun.

4.3.2. Cult Centralization

The most radical reform reported for Josiah was a policy of consolidating all sacrifice in Jerusalem. Cult centralization grew out of an intersection of nationalistic politics, economic dynamics, ambition to concentrate royal power, and a reduction in the size of Judah. The roots of Josiah's centralization policy are likely to be found in the crisis of Hezekiah's rebellion in 701. To meet the Assyrian threat, Hezekiah required more concentrated political and economic structures than had previously operated in Judah. Then, following the debacle of the Assyrian invasion, Judah's significant loss of territory, and the devastation of most of its second- and third-rank cities would have naturally led to an increase in the economic and religious significance of Jerusalem. At the same time, shrinkage in royal tax revenues produced by this loss of territory increased the apparent advantages of consolidating and controlling the economic engine of sacrifice in the capital city. As political policy, centralization would have been a strategy for control and supervision favorable to the economic and political interests of the king, the royal court, and priests of the central sanctuary. Consolidating sacrifices at one place was simply a functional parallel to gathering taxes into a central treasury.

The devastation of Sennacherib's invasion ruined many local sanctuaries, and the loss of Judahite territory to the west may have cut off access to others. As a result, there would have been a natural increase in religious traffic to Jerusalem. Sacrifices formerly taken to other shrines would be offered there instead. At the same time, a smaller Judah could more easily bear the logistic burdens that centralization entailed. Centralization also increased the prestige and governmental supervision of the royal sanctuary at Jerusalem. At a single location, authorities could more easily monitor ritual behavior and public expressions of potentially disloyal religious opinion (one thinks of Amos and Jeremiah). Judah's kings would have especially wanted to increase the prestige of their own royal shrine over that of its rival Bethel, which continued to be a focal point for sacrifice and devotion even after the end of the kingdom of Israel (2 Kgs 17:27–28). Moreover, the prestige of Jerusalem must have skyrocketed after the events of 701, which were seen as evidence of Yahweh's election and special protection of the city.

It is reasonable to hypothesize that the ideal of centralization was preserved and transmitted from the time of Hezekiah to that of Josiah by a reform movement that produced the book of the law discovered by Josiah's officials (that is, the core of Deuteronomy). Apparently, a clandestine reform movement took root among the powerful, aristocratic scribal and priestly families of Jerusalem, whose position was threatened by Manasseh's religious and political policies. The existence of this resistance movement, both inside and outside the royal court, is demonstrated by the assassination of Manasseh's son Amon by his court officials and the subsequent installation of the pliable child Josiah by the people of the land. The boy king Josiah was molded by the opinions of those who served as his regents. When the time was ripe, he would be ready to co-opt religious opinion for political advantage. Reform and centralization supported Judah's claim to be the authentic heir of Israel's legacy over against rival groups in the northern Assyrian provinces of Samaria, Gilead, and Megiddo. Centralization also provided the social unification and economic strength Josiah would need to profit from the new opportunities presented by increasing Assyrian weakness and the emergence of new configurations of power.

A single place for sacrifice also would counter divisive popular notions of multiple Yahwehs associated with individual shrines. People venerated the "god of Dan" and the deities of Samaria and Beer-sheba (Amos 8:14), as well as the "Yahweh of Teman" and the "Yahweh of Samaria" (Kuntillet ʿAjrud inscriptions; *COS* 2.47A–C:171–72). In the end, cult centralization advanced the emerging concept of monotheism advocated by the nascent Deuteronomistic movement by replacing a plurality of shrines with a single central place of authorized sacrifice supervised by approved cultic personnel who were under the control of the royal establishment (note the repetition of the concept "the king commanded the priest"; 1 Kgs 16:15–16; 2 Kgs 22:12; 23:4).

Sometimes archaeological data concerning altars and shrines are advanced to support the historicity of Josiah's centralization reform. Shrines were indeed destroyed and not rebuilt, but all seem to have met their end before the seventh century. Examples include Arad, Lachish, Megiddo, Taanach, and Shechem. Successive Assyrian campaigns are probably to blame for the decommissioning of these cultic sites.

Josiah's reform measures were mostly directed against practices involving the worship of Yahweh rather than of other gods. The pillar/tree symbol of Asherah was closely associated with Yahweh. Yahweh was conceptually identified with the sun (2 Sam 23:4; Mal 4:2). The *lmlk* jar stamps feature two-winged emblems and four-winged sun beetles, both apparently borrowed from Egyptian solar iconography. The Taanach cult stand exhibits what is commonly interpreted as an aniconic symbol of Yahweh (an empty window) and, on a lower register, a horse topped by a winged sun emblem. This also supports solar associations for Yahweh.

4.3.3. Josiah's Death

Josiah's untimely death was as significant as his reforms in shaping the future course of events. By the last third of his reign, the situation of Assyria had dramatically deteriorated. For a decade Nabopolassar and the Assyrian army had fought back and forth, with Egypt providing military support to Assyria. In 615 Nabopolassar failed in an attempt to capture the city of Assur. However, while the Assyrian army pursued him southward, the Medes under Cyaxares (ca. 625–585) were able to invade Assyria and capture Assur, which fell in 614. Nabopolassar and Cyaxares sealed an alliance outside the ruins of the city. According to Greek historians, the alliance was secured by marriage between Cyaxares's daughter Amytis and Nabopolassar's son, Nebuchadnezzar II. The latter's Akkadian name was Nabu-kudurri-usur, which produced the biblical variant Nebuchad*r*ezzar found in Ezekiel and much of Jeremiah.

Fighting in concert, Nabopolassar and the Medes sacked Nineveh in 612 after a three-month siege against Sin-shar-ishkun. The book of Nahum celebrates this event with unrestrained glee. Sin-shar-ishkun was killed when Nineveh fell and was succeeded by Assur-uballit II (611–ca. 608), who was based in Harran. Nabopolassar spent the next year consolidating his hold on Mesopotamia. He marched around Assyria unopposed in 612 and 611 (Babylonian Chronicle; *ANET*, 305). Then in 610 the Medes and Babylonians captured Harran.

Pharaoh Neco II (610–595) had sought to control portions of the Assyrian legacy as Babylon rose to power. So in 609 he moved up through Palestine in order to support the battered remnants of the Assyrian army, joining them at Carchemish. On his way north, Neco and Josiah met up at the strong point of Megiddo. Exactly what took place there remains a mystery. "Josiah went to meet him, and Neco killed him at Megiddo when he saw him" (2 Kgs 23:29). Based on how the Chronicler read this scene, it has traditionally been assumed that Josiah died in battle. Second Chronicles 35:20–27 claims that Josiah was trying to block Neco's advance. Much of this report, however, is similar to the story of the death of Ahab (1 Kgs 22:30–37). Clearly the Chronicler is attempting to explain Josiah's shocking end by turning Neco into a spokesman for God, whose warning Josiah ignores (2 Chr 35:21–22). None of this should be given historical weight.

Historians sometimes associate the events surrounding Josiah's death with what Herodotus has to say about Neco (*Hist.* 2.159): "He also engaged in a pitched battle at Magdolos with the Syrians, and conquered them; and after this he took Kadytis [Qadesh? Gaza?], which is a great city of Syria." Whether this location is actually Megiddo is debatable.

Various hypotheses have been advanced. Some of these lie behind the interpretive translations offered by many modern versions:

(1) Was Josiah trying to block Neco's advance in order to undermine the increasingly desperate Assyrian cause? This would seem to be the height of folly and would have had to result from a reckless loathing for Assyria on par with that of the prophet Nahum. Actually, there is no indication that Josiah had ever abandoned his formal vassalage to Assyria.

(2) Does the syntax of Kings indicate a misunderstanding that Neco was marching up *against* the king of Assyria and not to his aid? The preposition is admittedly ambiguous, but can mean "toward" as well as "against." The charge of recklessness on Josiah's part would still stand. Why risk everything in a quixotic move to protect a weak and distant Assyria? Of course, we know from the Babylonian Chronicle that Neco and Assyria were on the same side in opposition to the Babylonians and the Medes.

(3) Was Josiah trying to defend Megiddo against the Egyptians in order to protect territory in the north into which he had recently expanded? As already indicated, there is really no evidence that Josiah controlled or sought to control extensive portions of the former northern kingdom.

In fact, full weight must be given to the reality that no battle is mentioned. If, as suggested above (§4.3), Josiah and Neco were allies at this point, perhaps treachery or a perception of treachery on one side or the other was involved. Conceivably Neco executed Josiah for breaching a treaty agreement with Egypt. Alternatively, perhaps Neco deceitfully arranged for a summit meeting with an inconvenient ally at Megiddo and treacherously liquidated him. Megiddo, previously an Assyrian provincial capital, was much more likely to have been in Egyptian hands than under

Josiah's control. Neco may have been unwilling to leave his escape route back to Egypt under control of an independently minded ally who might change sides at any time.

In Nabopolassar year 16 (609), the Babylonians and Medes marched against Harran and forced the Assyrians and their Egyptian allies to abandon the city and cross back over the Euphrates. In June 609, Neco and Assur-uballit recrossed the Euphrates and tried to recapture Harran, but had to withdraw in August. This failed operation apparently resulted in the death of the last Assyrian king. The Medes and Babylonians proceeded to divide up the Assyrian Empire between them.

4.4. Jehoahaz (609) and Jehoiakim (609–598)

The people of the land group who had installed Josiah three decades ago reacted to Neco's liquidation of Josiah by enthroning Jehoahaz (Shallum). In so doing, they bypassed Jehoiakim (Eliakim), an older son of Josiah. This unusual move must be understood an act taken in opposition to a faction in Judah that favored Egypt. Jehoahaz's mother was Hamutal from Libnah in the Shephelah. She was also the mother of Judah's last king, Zedekiah. Three months later, on his way back from Harran, Neco deposed Jehoahaz. Neco replaced him with Jehoiakim, who presumably could be counted on to comply with the policies of his father's killer. Jehoahaz was held captive by Neco at Riblah in northern Syria and eventually died in Egypt (2 Kgs 23:33–34; cf. Jer 22:10–12).

Jehoiakim was the legitimate heir, older by a couple of years than his deposed half brother. His mother, Zebidah, was from Rumah, possibly in Galilee (perhaps Khirbet Rumeh).

His connection to a notable Galilean family might explain some of the hostility between him and the Judahite landowning class. Neco exacted a substantial tribute from Jehoiakim, who raised it by assessing it from his political enemies, the same people of the land who had sought to bypass him (2 Kgs 23:35). The strength of this vassal alliance is illustrated by Egypt's later willingness to turn over the troublesome prophet Uriah to Jehoiakim, who then put him to death (Jer 26:23). The palace discovered at Ramat Rahel may provide the reference point for Jeremiah's diatribe against the building activities of Jehoiakim (Jer 22:13–19).

The international situation was soon transformed. Nebuchadnezzar, crown prince of Babylon, launched a joint Babylonian and Median attack on the Egyptian and Assyrian base at Carchemish and defeated them. This battle of Carchemish took place in 605, Jehoiakim year 4 and Nabopolassar year 21 (Jer 46:2). The death of Nabopolassar forced Nebuchadnezzar to rush back to Babylon. He reigned from 604 until 562. Herodotus celebrates him as the rebuilder of Babylon (*Hist.* 1.178–186). The battle of Carchemish provides the context for the oracle preserved in Jer 46:3–12.

As a result of Carchemish, Jehoiakim switched his loyalty from Egypt to Babylon. Perhaps he did this immediately after the battle. Quoting Berossus, Josephus reports that Judeans were exiled to Babylon after Carchemish (*Ant.* 10.222; *Ag. Ap.* 1.137–138). More likely Jehoiakim's switch took place after Nebuchadnezzar devastated Ashkelon in December 604 or a year later during Nebuchadnezzar's western campaign in 603. Second Kings 24:1 reports that Jehoiakim's submission to Nebuchadnezzar lasted three years, perhaps encompassing the years 603, 602, and 601. Nebuchadnezzar experienced a failed or at least indecisive military adventure against Egypt in 601. This episode apparently gave Jehoiakim the confidence to withhold tribute from Babylon. This conflict between Babylon and Egypt in 601 may be the battle to which Herodotus refers (*Hist.* 2.159) when he reports that Neco fought at Magdolos (a fortress named Migdol, perhaps near the Egyptian frontier) and then conquered Kadytis (taken to be Gaza). However, for another interpretation, see §4.3.3. Jeremiah 47:1 seems to allude to this capture of Gaza, and Jer 46:13–28 could refer to the same campaign

Any of several of Nebuchadnezzar's incursions into the west, including his move against Jerusalem in 597, could have provided the context for a letter from one Adon king of Ekron (presumably) that calls on a pharaoh (Neco II, it would seem) for military support as Nebuchadnezzar advances against the coastal city-states and has reached Aphek (*COS* 3.54:132–34).

Nebuchadnezzar would not fully respond to the disloyalty of Jehoiakim until late 598. In 600 Nebuchadnezzar did not campaign in the west. Then he found himself occupied with Arabs in 599. So Nebuchadnezzar's first step was to have his local allies harass Jerusalem in the interim before he could arrive (2 Kgs 24:2).

4.5. Jehoiachin (598–597)

The Babylonian army finally marched out in Kislev of Nebuchadnezzar year 7 (mid-December 598 to mid-January 597). Jehoiakim apparently died at about the same time. His eighteen-year-old son Jehoiachin (Jeconiah) became king and had to face the consequences of his father's defiance. There is some uncertainly about the circumstances of Jehoiakim's death. Second Kings 24:6 says he "slept with his fathers," suggesting a peaceful demise. Jeremiah's oracles, however, predicted for him a death mourned by no one and a disrespectful treatment of his body, and these statements were allowed to remain unrevised (Jer 22:18-19; 36:30). Perhaps Jeremiah was simply wrong, and his followers felt too much respect for his oracles to correct them. After Jehoiakim there are no more citations by the author of Kings from the chronicles of the Judah source document, 2 Kgs 24:5 being the last one. However, the source presumably continued to provide introductory regnal data for the last two kings (vv. 8, 18).

According to 2 Kgs 24:7, the king of Egypt (still Neco II) did not move into Palestine to support Jehoiachin but had been bottled up by the territorial gains of Nebuchadnezzar down to the Egyptian border. Nebuchadnezzar himself arrived after the siege of Jerusalem had begun (vv. 10-11). Jehoiachin surrendered relatively quickly (v. 12), thereby saving Jerusalem and its population from destruction. His capitulation may have taken place just before or after the actual fall of the city. In any case, Jerusalem was secured on March 15/16 (2 Adar), 597 (near the end of Nebuchadnezzar year 7; *ANET*, 564; *COS* 1:137:468). Jeremiah speaks of a deportation in that year of about three thousand persons (Jer 52:28). About a month later, in year 8, Jehoiachin and members of his court were deported to Babylon, along with eight thousand to ten thousand other skilled and elite persons (2 Kgs 24:14, 16). He had reigned three months.

4.6. Zedekiah (597-586)

Nebuchadnezzar replaced Jehoiachin with his uncle Zedekiah (Mattaniah). Zedekiah was only a few years older than Jehoiachin. He was a full brother of Jehoahaz and thus representative of the faction of the royal family that opposed Egypt and could be expected to follow a policy of compliance with respect to Babylon. Nevertheless, Nebuchadnezzar kept Jehoiachin under some sort of confinement in Babylon, presumably as a backup king in case Zedekiah became too independent. Influential elements in Judah continued to consider Jehoiachin the legitimate king, and dates were sometimes recorded according to his exile (2 Kgs 25:27; Ezekiel). Jar handles (from

Tell Beit Mirsim, Beth-shemesh, Ramat Rahel) stamped with the seal of "Eliakim servant of Yaukin" (Jehoiachin) are no longer thought to refer to King Jehoiachin or his estates.

Nebuchadnezzar faced troubles with Elam in 595 and revolt in Babylon in 594. As a result, he was forced to execute many of his troops. The last entry in the Babylonian Chronicle reports a western campaign in Kislev of his year 11 (Dec 594/Jan 593). According to Jeremiah, Zedekiah—motivated by Nebuchadnezzar's difficulties—held a regional summit with Edom, Moab, Ammon, Tyre, and Sidon. The purpose was to strategize about resistance (Jer 27:3). This most likely took place in 593 (Jer 28:1, Zedekiah year 4; discounting Jer 27:1 MT). Jeremiah and his followers supported a compliance policy. Other political and prophetic elements supported resistance (Jer 27–29). Jeremiah 51:59 speaks of a visit by Zedekiah to Babylon in his year 4 (593). Perhaps he was being called to account because of his sponsorship of that rebellious conference.

Zedekiah's restiveness may have been connected to the recent accession of the assertive Pharaoh Psamtik II (Psammetichus; 595–589). After victories in Nubia, Psamtik made a triumphal tour into Palestine in about 591. This must have stirred up local aspirations to throw off Babylonian hegemony. This event was described by a grandson of the priest Pediese, who accompanied him. Psamtik II sent mercenaries, including Jews, to the south of Egypt, and they left graffiti at Abu Simbel. Psamtik soon died and was succeeded by the equally aggressive Hophra (Apries; 589–570).

The date for the onset of Zedekiah's fateful rebellion is uncertain. Its first consequence was an eighteen-month siege of Jerusalem that began in Zedekiah year 9 (588). The Lachish letters (*ANET*, 321–22; *COS* 3.42:78–81) provide tantalizing glimpses of incidents and affairs in the period just before the start or during the early stages of the Babylonian invasion. They are addressed by one Hoshiah, seemingly an outpost commander, to Jaush (Yaosh), who was apparently in charge of Lachish. Letter 3 refers in part to military negotiation of some sort with Egypt. Letter 4 speaks of the observation of watch signals from Lachish, but notes that those from Azekah cannot be seen (cf. Jer 34:7). Perhaps this is an inquiry about a smoke-signal test run according to a predetermined arrangement or perhaps only a statement of the fact that Azekah was not close enough for its signals to be seen. The popular interpretation—we can *no longer* see Azekah—as though Azekah has fallen to the enemy but Lachish still holds out, is overly romantic. Letter 6 reflects a problem of low morale incited by thoughtless or defeatist statements (cf. Jer 38:4).

4.6.1. The Siege and Capture of Jerusalem

The second siege of Jerusalem took much longer and caused more suffering than the first. From Jeremiah we learn of sharply contested differences of opinion within the city, as well as a cynical ploy by the slave-owning class, who liberated and then re-enslaved their slaves (Jer 34:8–16, 21). This took place when Lachish and Azekah were the only cities beside Jerusalem still holding out (v. 7). The pseudo-reform was aborted when the siege was temporarily lifted (Jer 37:3–10), owing to an expedition by Pharaoh Apries (589–570; Hophra in Jer 44:30). Apries's struggle with Tyre and Sidon, described by Herodotus (*Hist.* 2.161), may have taken place at this time. Apries retreated when Nebuchadnezzar approached, abandoning Jerusalem to its fate.

Kings carefully dates the events of Judah's final days, apparently relying on a dispassionate and neutral chronistic account, which may have been produced by scribes in the local administration established by the Babylonians. The book of Jeremiah provides a more dramatic account from the perspective of the prophet's followers. Famine was the greatest horror faced by those in a besieged city. Starvation set in motion desperate acts of inhumanity (Deut 28:53–57; 2 Kgs 6:25–29; Jer 19:9; Lam 2:20; 4:3–10). According to 2 Kgs 25:3, food ran out for the refugee people of the land, that is, the rural populace who were taking shelter within the city. At this point the enemy broke through the city wall. Zedekiah and elements of his army managed to escape under cover of darkness through a gate near the palace and slipped through the enemy cordon. The fleeing group was intercepted and dispersed near Jericho, and the king was captured. He was taken to Nebuchadnezzar, who was then at Riblah in Hamath. Perhaps in accordance with penalties predetermined by in a treaty to which Zedekiah had agreed and violated (Ezek 17:13–18), his sons were killed and he was blinded and deported. About a month later, a Babylonian official, Nebuzaradan (Nabu-zer-iddina, known from *ANET*, 307), burned the temple, the palace, and other structures in the city; tore down at least portions of the city wall; and deported much of the population. This deportation included some who had previously submitted to the Babylonians. Nebuzaradan also escorted a party of priestly, governmental, and military officials, including elements of the people of the land to Riblah. Nebuchadnezzar had them executed.

Jeremiah 39:1–10 retells part of the story of the city's fall in a somewhat abbreviated version of 2 Kgs 25:1–12, but also adds a few credible details.

According to Jer 39:3, a panel of Babylonian officials entered the city after the wall had been breached and held some kind of public session or juridical proceeding in the middle gate. It was this ominous gathering that provided the motive for Zedekiah's flight (v. 4). The Masoretic punctuation of verse 3 is incorrect, but when properly divided the verse mentions two other persons who appear as officials of Nebuchadnezzar in Babylonian sources. These are Nergal-sharzer (Nergal-sar-usur, the king's brother-in-law) and Nebo-sarsekim (Nabu-sharrussu-ukin; cf. NIV). The Jeremiah version of events adds a second detail. Second Kings 25:12 reports that Nebuzaradan did not exile the poor but left them behind to work the land. Jeremiah 39:10 states that this strategy entailed a policy of land redistribution. The poor were given the land they were to cultivate: "Some of the poor who owned nothing ... he gave them vineyards and fields."

Archaeology provides dramatic evidence of the siege and destruction of Jerusalem. Layers of charred debris are widespread. Neo-Babylonian arrowheads have been found. Building stones were broken and scattered, and debris thrown down over the wall. Analysis of fecal matter in toilets has indicated to researchers the effects of stress caused by starvation.

Details concerning statistics and dates of the deportations from Judah are not easy to untangle. Jeremiah 52:28–30 gives the dates of three expulsions as Nebuchadnezzar years 7, 11, and 23, but the first two dates cannot be easily matched with what Kings reports or suggests. Quite probably there were more than three deportations. Most likely they occurred in Nebuchadnezzar year 7 (before the city's first fall in 597; Jer 52:28), year 8 (after its fall; 2 Kgs 24:14–16), year 18 (during the siege but before the city's second fall; Jer 52:29), year 19 (586; 2 Kgs 25:11; Jer 52:12–16), and year 23 (582; Jer 52:30). Statements of dubious value in 2 Chr 36:6–7 and Dan 1:1–4 report a deportation during the reign of Jehoiakim.

Figures for the numbers deported also vary. Jeremiah's numbers sound precise for the three deportations recorded in Jer 52:28–30: 3,023, 832, and 745. Second Kings gives an accounting only for the first expulsion that it reports (24:14–16; 8,000 or 10,000, perhaps to be taken together as 18,000). According to some scholars, the total of those exiled was probably about 20,000 over the fifteen-year period in question. An unknown number of other Judahites undoubtedly perished as a result of the conflict, and others like Jeremiah fled to Egypt (2 Kgs 25:26; Manetho, frg. 68, 69). Prayer inscriptions from a cave at Khirbet Beit Lei in the Shephelah expressing concern for the highlands of Judah have commonly been interpreted as the work of refugees from Nebuchadnezzar's depredations (*COS*

2.53:180–81). Some historians have connected the deportation of 582 with Josephus's description of a Babylonian campaign to the west and a subjugation of Ammon and Moab in that year (*Ant.* 10.181–182). Judahite expatriates in Babylonia were resettled in agricultural redevelopment projects. The nature of their life is reflected in Jeremiah's advisory letter to them (Jer 29:4–7).

4.6.2. Dating the Capture of Jerusalem: 587 or 586?

There is no dispute that the second capture of Jerusalem took place in the summer month of Tammuz (2 Kgs 25:3; Jer 52:6). There is enormous uncertainty, though, as to whether the year was 586 or 587. Both dates appear in textbooks and introductory literature. This ambiguity arises from statements in the Babylonian Chronicle, the Bible's confusing (and perhaps contradictory) data, and the question of whether Judah was using a calendar starting in Tishri (fall) or one starting in Nisan (spring). Second Kings 22:3 and 23:23 put both the discovery of the law book and Josiah's newly reformed Passover (falling in the middle of Nisan) in his year 18. This points to a Tishri (fall) start for the year. However, the dramatic scene portrayed in Jer 36:22 indicates that Judah in its final years must have commenced its new year with Nisan, so that winter and the need for domestic heating would occur in the ninth month. Apparently Judah shifted to the Mesopotamian practice sometime in the last years of its existence. To further complicate matters, the possibility that different intercalation procedures (the insertion of a thirteenth leap month into some years) were used in Babylon and Judah cannot be excluded. A rabbinic source declares that in this early period the intercalation pattern in Judah was not fixed, but based on observation (t. Sanh. 2:2). Attempts to date the second fall of Jerusalem depend on conclusions drawn about the city's first fall in 597.

The argument for 587 requires a Nisan (spring) start of the new year and runs as follows. The Babylonian Chronicles report the capture of Jehoiachin and the start of Zedekiah's reign. Both events happened sometime after the fall of the city on 2 Adar (March 16) 597. The Babylonian Chronicle suggests that Zedekiah was appointed immediately, that is, before the start of a spring new year and thus still during Nebuchadnezzar year 7. Jeremiah 52:28 records that a deportation also took place in Nebuchadnezzar year 7. Nebuchadnezzar would hardly want to delay matters, especially if he needed to get back for a 1 Nisan 597 New Year ceremony in

Babylon to begin his year 8. So the small remnant of year 7 that remained between the early part of Adar and 1 Nisan 597 was Zedekiah's accession year. His first full year of reign would be Nebuchadnezzar year 8, that is to say, 597/596. His eleventh year, the year Jerusalem fell for a second time, would thus be 587/586. This would place the end of his reign and the capture of Jerusalem in the summer of 587. Jeremiah 52:29 records a deportation in Nebuchadnezzar year 18, again in 587/586. One may also calculate by counting backward from the release of Jehoiachin in what is assumed to be the accession year of Amel-Marduk (Evil-merodach), which the Babylonian Chronicle dates as 562/561. Thus Jehoiachin was released just before the new year on 25 or 27 Adar 561 in the thirty-seventh year of his captivity (2 Kgs 25:27; Jer 52:31). This would place the first year of his captivity from Nisan 598 to Adar 597, which supports the 587 date for the fall of Jerusalem. However, this argument requires that one understand the expression in 2 Kgs 25:27 to refer to an *accession year* and not *the first full year of reign*, which is hardly a certain conclusion.

The case for a 586 date begins with 2 Kgs 24:12, which says that Jehoiachin gave himself up in Nebuchadnezzar year 8 (597/596), thus after the fall of the city and *after* 1 Nisan 597 (cf. 2 Chr 36:10, "at the return of the year"). One can then assume that Zedekiah became king after 1 Nisan 597 as well. Consequently, Zedekiah's accession year would be Nebuchadnezzar year 8 (597/596), his first full year 596/595, and his year 11, 586/585. This agrees with Jer 32:1-2, which equates Zedekiah year 10 with Nebuchadnezzar year 18. The beginning of the final siege according to 2 Kgs 25:1 (Jer 39:1; 52:4) was on 10 Tebet of Zedekiah year 9 (Nebuchadnezzar year 17), that is to say, in winter 588/587. The city fell in Zedekiah year 11 (Nebuchadnezzar year 19; 586/585). Second Kings 25:8 and Jer 52:12 date the temple destruction to the seventh or tenth day of the fifth month (Ab) in Nebuchadnezzar year 19, that is to say, in summer 586. The breach in the wall a month earlier took place in the same year (586) on the ninth day of the fourth month (Tammuz) according to Jer 39:2; 52:6-7 (the month is not specified in 2 Kgs 25:3). The deportation of 832 people in Nebuchadnezzar year 18 (587/586; Jer 52:29) seems to have been a group captured during the siege and deported earlier, not the main deportation reported in 2 Kgs 25:11.

In the less likely event that Judah started its year in the autumn with Tishri, a 586 date is indicated no matter what. Zedekiah's year 1 would overlap with Nebuchadnezzar 8 and 9. Then his year 11 would overlap Nebuchadnezzar 18 and 19, with summer falling in year 19, that is, 586.

Ezekiel 33:21 states that the messenger bringing news to Babylon of Jerusalem's fall in Zedekiah year 11 arrived "in the twelfth year of our exile," apparently December 586 or January 585. This supports the 586 date for the city's capture. One cannot be sure how long his trip would have taken, but Ezra took four months. It is important to remember that the numeral indicating the year of deportation will be one year higher than the year of Zedekiah's reign because no accession year is applicable. Ezekiel 24:1–2 indicates that the siege of Jerusalem began on the fifth day of the tenth month of an unspecified year 9. According to Ezekiel's usual dating practice, this would be the ninth year of the exile or Jehoiachin's ninth year of reign. However, we can be sure that the siege began in *Zedekiah's* year 9 instead, so the date in Ezek 24:1–2 does not square with the way things are calculated in Ezek 33:21.

To summarize: Jerusalem was first captured in the 597 portion of Nebuchadnezzar year 7, which was Jehoiachin's accession year. Nebuchadnezzar year 8 (597/596) was the first year of Jehoiachin's captivity and Zedekiah's accession year. Jerusalem's final catastrophe took place in summer 586, which coordinates with unambiguous, source-based statement of 2 Kgs 25:9 that it took place in Nebuchadnezzar year 19, which was Zedekiah's year 11. The siege began in Tebet 587 in Nebuchadnezzar year 17 and Zedekiah year 9.

4.7. The Babylonian Period

Judah had been a relatively independent and stable monarchy for three and a half centuries. After the fall of Jerusalem, the nation underwent a demographic and economic collapse, except in central Benjamin. There was massive destruction in Judah south of Jerusalem, but Benjamin was apparently largely untouched. The archaeological picture testifies to extensive destruction in Jerusalem, Ramat Rahel, Lachish, Gezer, and Hebron. In contrast, there was continuity of settlement in Benjamin, at Gibeon, Bethel, and Mizpah, for example. The Shephelah was lost. The Edomites took the defeat of Judah as an opportunity to continue their expansion into southern Judah. This incursion had begun even before the fall of Judah, as witnessed by Arad Ostraca 24 and 40 (*COS* 3.43K–L:84–85). Judahite reaction to this loss of ancestral land was venomous and long lasting (Ps 137:7; Obadiah; Mal 1:3–4).

In order to ensure some degree of stability, the Babylonians appointed one Gedaliah from the elite Jerusalem family of Shaphan. The book of Jeremiah shows that members of this family had been proponents of a policy of compliance with Babylon. Gedaliah's base of operations was Mizpah in Benjamin. This choice for an administrative capital matches with the increased importance of Benjamin after the catastrophe that devastated Jerusalem and Judah. Judges 20–21 attests to the importance of Mizpah, and Neh 3:7, 15, 19, indicates that its prominence continued down into the restoration period. Perhaps the "house of Yahweh" mentioned in Jer 41:5 was actually in Mizpah (cf. Judg 20:1). The large number of jars found at Mizpah with $m(w)ṣh$ stamp impressions suggests that the town was an administrative storage center. Mozah was a town in Benjamin (Josh 18:26). The onyx seal of "Jaazaniah servant of the king" found at Mizpah (cf. 2 Kgs 25:23) raises questions about Gedaliah's actual position. He was governor according to 2 Kgs 25:23. Did he or the Babylonians style him as king? If so, this would help explain the subsequent action by the pro-Davidic Ishmael.

Baalis (Baʻalyišaʻ) king of Ammon instigated the assassination of Gedaliah by Ishmael son of Nethaniah, a highly placed member of the royal family (2 Kgs 25:25; Jer 40:13–41:10). This may have taken place only a few months after the fall of Jerusalem ("in the seventh month"). However, the year is not given, so Gedaliah's tenure may actually have lasted several years. If so, his death might have led to the otherwise unexplained deportation of 582 (Jer 52:30). It is probable that Gedaliah's opponents were nationalists and royalists, possibly opposed to his resettlement policies (Jer 40:7–12). Most likely his attempt to repopulate vacant agricultural land was seen as undercutting prior property rights or claims, particularly those of the landlord class. As a member of the Davidic family, Ishmael may have been trying to stake a claim to the throne for himself. This would explain his aborted kidnapping of the king's daughters (Jer 41:10). Confronted by a rescue mission, the assassin fled to Ammon (v. 15). Fear of Babylonian reprisals for the Gedaliah debacle motivated some of Judah's population to migrate to Egypt (Jer 41:17–43:7).

Deportees from Judah were settled in Babylon, Nippur, and along the Chebar Canal. This great canal branched off the Euphrates near Babylon, circled through Nippur, and rejoined it near Warka. Exiles were settled for purposes of economic redevelopment. This is indicated by the names of some of their settlement sites, namely Tel Abib ("ruin with ears of grain"), Tel-melah, and Tel-harsha (Ezra 2:59; Neh 7:61; Ezek 3:15). The element *tel* indicates a ruin mound from an earlier period. From Ezekiel one learns that elders played a decisive role in community affairs. Yahwistic prophets were active in the exile community. Examples in addition to Ezekiel are the optimistic prophets Ahab and Zedekiah, who were condemned by Jeremiah (29:21-23). The exile proved to be a period of remarkable literary activity and theological ferment among Babylonian Jews.

Years were reckoned according to the reign of Jehoiachin, at least by the author of Ezekiel. Clearly, even during the reign of Zedekiah some in Judah continued to view Jehoiachin as the legitimate king. For example, the prophet Hananiah predicted the quick return of Jehoiachin (Jer 28:3-4). Jeremiah was of the opposite opinion and forecast that none of Jehoiachin's descendants would sit on the throne (22:28-30). Babylonian records from the year 592 indicate that at that time the Babylonian government was supplying Jehoiachin and his five sons with food rations. In these records he is still called "king of Judah" (*ANET*, 308). Apparently he was in prison or under house arrest, at least by the time he was released and granted privileges by Amel-Marduk in 561 or 560. Jehoiachin would have been about fifty-five at the time. It was customary to grant release to prisoners as a public relations gesture at the start of a new reign. Jehoiachin was installed with other captive kings as guests at the palace table. In addition to being a sign of favor, of course, this was also a way of monitoring Jehoiachin's behavior (cf. 2 Sam 9:10-13).

Suggestions that the territory of Judah had been emptied of its inhabitants are overstatements. They result from an uncritical acceptance of the viewpoint of the later returnees, who considered themselves as the only true inheritors of Judahite (Jewish) identity. Nebuzaradan left vinedressers and tillers of the soil in land (2 Kgs 25:12), because he would have desired the continuation of a robust agricultural economy in order to produce taxes and export products such as grapes and olives. Religious life also continued. As part of his insurgency, Ishmael killed a contingent of pilgrims from Shechem, Shiloh, and Samaria on their way to present grain offerings and incense to a temple of Yahweh. This may indicate the continuation of a sacrificial cult at the site of the destroyed Jerusalem shrine or an active temple functioning at Mizpah or Bethel.

After the destruction of Jerusalem, Nebuchadnezzar besieged Tyre for thirteen years (usually dated 585-572). This ended when Tyre submitted to Babylonian authority and the recalcitrant Itto-baal III was replaced by the vassal king Baal II (*Ant.* 10.228; *Ag. Ap.* 1.156). Ezekiel 29:17-18, dated to 571, refers to the end of this siege. For the last decade of his reign,

Nebuchadnezzar remained firmly in control of the western portions of his empire. He moved inconclusively against Egypt in 568 (*ANET*, 308; perhaps Ezek 29:19-21). Before his death he subdued the tribes of northwestern Arabia.

Nebuchadnezzar was succeeded by his son Amel-Marduk (561-560; biblical Evil-merodach), who released Jehoiachin late in Adar in 561 or 560. In quick succession, Amel-Marduk was assassinated (according to Berossus) and followed by Neriglissar (559-556). After leading one western campaign, Neriglissar in turn died mysteriously and was succeeded by his minor son Labashi-Marduk, who reigned two or three months in 556. A coup of some sort led to the accession of the usurper Nabonidus (555-539). A son-in-law of Nebuchadnezzar, he was from Harran in northern Mesopotamia. Nabonidus had captured Harran from Astyges king of Media, who was engaged in a long struggle with Cyrus the Great. Nabonidus advanced the cult of the moon-god Sin. He restored that god's temple at Harran, where his mother, Adad-guppi, served as high priestess (*ANET*, 560-62; *COS* 1.147:477-78). Adad-guppi, who died at age 104, must have been a remarkable personality. A fictional autobiography, highlighting her devotion to Sin and his temple, has been preserved. Nabonidus also restored religious sites in Ur, one of the cities of Sin, and installed his daughter as priestess of the moon-god there.

Around 549, Nabonidus retreated to the town of Teiman in the Arabian dessert, leaving the important religious duties in Babylon to his son and regent Bel-shar-usur. He is the Belshazzar of the book of Daniel, where, however, he is identified as king and incorrectly described as son of Nebuchadnezzar. Nabonidus may have had other reasons for his move to Teiman, since it allowed him to control the trade routes into Arabia. For example, an inscription of Nabonidus from Khirbet es-Sil (Edomite Sela) evidences Babylonian territorial claims in the southwest.

Nabonidus is pilloried in most sources, where he is viewed from pro-Marduk and Persian perspectives. For example, the Verse Account of Nabonidus (*ANET*, 312-14) is a vilification intended to support the cause of Cyrus (see also *ANET*, 562-63). Economic difficulties, famine, and pestilence were popularly blamed on his lack of devotion to Marduk and his failure to show up for the foundational New Year ceremony of the Babylonian cult. Nabonidus eventually did return to Babylon, in 542. Meanwhile Cyrus was winning repeated victories in Media and Asia Minor, and the Neo-Babylonian Empire had only a few years left. While it lasted, however, culture flourished. Babylon was rebuilt in magnificent style. Ancient texts were studied and recopied. Astronomy reached a high level of sophistication. Eclipses were recorded, and the movements of heavenly bodies could be predicted.

4.8. Documentary Finds

A number of epigraphic finds throw light on the period covered in this chapter. Unfortunately, one must account for the very real possibility of counterfeits among those that are unprovenanced. Serious doubts have been raised in connection with the Three Shekel Temple Gift (by Jehoash or Josiah; COS 2.50:174–75) and the Widow's Plea (COS 3.44:86–87), while others defend their authenticity.

The Census Ostracon from Tel ʿIra (late eighth to first half of the seventh century) and the Ophel Ostracon (late seventh century; COS 3.86:203–4) reveal how a census or muster would have been recorded. Royal economics are illustrated by ostraca from Tell Qasile, one reading "1100 [jars?] of oil, of the king" and another "30 shekels of gold of Ophir for Beth-horon." Weights inscribed with Egyptian hieratic numbers witness to Egyptian economic influence and the practices a professional scribal class (eighth–seventh centuries; COS 2.81:210). Religious affairs in Judah are illuminated by the Jerusalem Pomegranate (possibly a forgery; COS 2.48:173), the Creator of the Earth Ostracon (COS 2.49:174), and the Ketef Hinnom Amulets, which repeat a blessing close to that of Num 6:24–26 (COS 2.83:221).

The Arad ostraca cannot be dated with enough precision to do more than provide general background (ANET, 568–69; COS 3.43:81–85 (both partial). A group of eighteen relate to the last years of Judah's existence. They witness to a centralized royal administration (Arad 18; 24; 88) and Judah's trouble with encroaching Edomites (Arad 24; 40). Some record rations for Kittim, probably Greek mercenaries from Egypt or supported by Egypt.

The fakery problem is a major factor in the evaluation of unprovenanced seals and bullae, that is, seal impressions (COS 2.70:197–201 for a selection). A cache of fire-hardened bullae was uncovered in situ in a house in Jerusalem, but many others have been purchased from the antiquities market. The impressive collection known as the Burnt Archive is without provenance, but thought to be genuine by many scholars. Notable seal impressions include the following:

- A bulla from Lachish reads "Gedaliah [Gedalyahu] who is over the house," but there is no particular reason to connect this with the Gedaliah appointed by the Babylonians.
- Two unprovenanced bullae made by the same seal read "Berechiah [Berehyahu] son of Neriah the scribe." If genuine, which is very much in dispute, this would certainly be Jeremiah's secretary Baruch (Jer 36:32).
- A seal impression discovered in Jordan of "Milkom-or servant of Baalyasha" is likely to be that of an official of the king of Ammon (Jer 40:14).
- Two bullae found at an excavation in Jerusalem contain the names of figures mentioned as Jeremiah's opponents in Jer 38:1: "Gedaliah son of Pashur" and "Jucal [Yehukual] son of Shelemiah."

Other seals and bullae whose provenance is unknown would (if genuine) indicate that other persons who appear in the biblical narratives describing the final period of Judah's existence were genuine historical figures. Examples are Jerahmeel son of the king (Jer 36:26), Elishama servant of the king (Jer 36:12), Gemariah son of Shaphan (Jer 36:10, 12), and Seraiah son of Neriah the scribe (Jer 51.59). Names that might be connected to the earlier Josiah period include Hilkiah the priest, Asaiah servant of the king (2 Kgs 22:12, 14; COS 2:79:204), and Azaliah son of Meshullam (cf. 2 Kgs 22:3).

More generally, seals and bullae corroborate administrative titles that correspond to biblical usage, for example, "governor of the city," Gedaliah "over the house [palace]" or Pelaiah "over forced labor." The office titled "son of the king" is attached to one Elishama and (apparently) his grandson Ishmael. In regard to religious affairs, an unprovenanced seal inscribed in eighth century script reads "[belonging to Ze]kariah priest of Dor," and on the back "belonging to Zadok son of Micah." This suggests the existence of a Yahweh sanctuary at Dor. Perhaps most significantly, bullae bear witness to the existence of a large number of papyrus documents, indicating an active scribal culture in Judah. This increases the probability that written sources and archives were available to the biblical authors. From the perspective of the history of biblical religion, it is significant that seals became almost completely aniconic from the seventh century on.

4.9. Literature of the Period

4.9.1. The Assyrian Period

4.9.1.1. Deuteronomy

Deuteronomy takes the form of a speech given by Moses to Israel, speaking just before the conquest of the land. The core of Deuteronomy is an Assyrian-period production. Traditional legal materials, such as the Covenant Code, formed the basis for a document fashioned on the model of Assyrian loyalty treaties. The Vassal Treaties of Esarhaddon (672) were intended to safeguard the succession of his son Assurbanipal. These had a direct effect on the ideology and language of Deuteronomy (*ANET*, 534–41). The process that led to the creation of Deuteronomy could have begun in the reign of Manasseh. Opposition to his vassal policies may have caused the formation of a group intent on religious and social reform. The wide-ranging themes and outlooks of the book suggest that Deuteronomy was composed by dissident Jerusalem scribal circles in collaboration with the rural landowners of Judah, elements of the priesthood, and persons schooled in wisdom. The core of Deuteronomy may have been composed during the reign of Manasseh and the early years of the reign of Josiah. In Josiah's reign, this dissident reform theology appeared publicly as the book of the law of Moses and became the basis for a major reform by Josiah. Later additions took into account new historical situations and literary contexts. Chapters 1–3 and 31 connect Deuteronomy to the larger composition of the DH. The addition of the Song of Moses (chapter 32) offered a prophetic theology of history, and the Blessing of Moses (chapter 33) emphasized Deuteronomy's nature as Moses' final testament.

Deuteronomy is characterized by theological creativity that reused traditional concepts in innovative ways. For example, the concept of a covenant relationship with Yahweh, an element of the preaching of Hosea (6:7; 8:1), was developed into a grand unifying theme and presented through the format of the Assyrian loyalty treaty. Deuteronomy transformed old laws into new social programs (e.g., Deut 14:22–29; 15:1–11). The doctrine of Yahweh's unity and complete incomparability (6:4) led to Deuteronomy's radical call for cult centralization.

4.9.1.2. Deuteronomistic History

The concept of a Deuteronomistic History (DH) describes a unity of outlook and composition that holds together Deuteronomy and the Former Prophets. DH is an extended account of Israel's life in the land as viewed from the perspective of the theology of Deuteronomy. The absence of Deuteronomistic language from large expanses of the text of Joshua through 2 Kings indicates that the historian used sources to assemble the work. The sources used in 1 and 2 Kings have been discussed above (see §§3.1.1, 3.1.2, and 3.1.3). Many revisions to the original hypothesis that a single, exilic DH composed the work soon after the release of Jehoiachin have been proposed.

Two competing approaches dominate the discussion. What has been called the "layer model" proposes that two supplementary redactions took place after the foundational work of an exilic historian (DtrG). One of these exhibits an interest in prophecy (DtrP). A second, nomistic (DtrN) revision emphasizes obedience to law in order to protect the distinctive identity of the exiles. In contrast, what may be called the "block model" insists that the work of a preexilic historian (Dtr1) was later carried forward and revised by an exilic editor (Dtr2). Dtr1 is usually dated during or shortly after Josiah's reign as a document intended to provide support for his policies. Alternative forms of the theory point to Hezekiah's reform as the date of initial composition. The block model contends that an earlier, optimistic history was converted in the Babylonian period into a reflection on defeat and exile. More recently, a three-stage process spanning the pre-exilic and exilic periods has been suggested. A primary Assyrian-period stage consisted of a disconnected library of shorter scrolls. A second stage linked these individual documents into a Deuteronomistic History reflecting on the crisis of defeat and exile. A third stage continued the editorial process into the Persian period.

Recently some have claimed that the books that make up the DH, particularly 1 and 2 Kings, are very late and cannot be shown to be pre-Hellenistic. This extraordinary assertion is largely based on the undeniable fact of the late date of the extant biblical texts. With respect to the book of Kings, this notion can be disproved with little difficulty:

- A direct line of cultural and ethnic connection runs from Iron Age Palestine to the extant manuscripts. The ancient world of

Egypt and Mesopotamia made a standard practice of recopying earlier texts of a canonical nature.
- Kings does not exhibit serious anachronisms, late place names, or large amounts of information that can be falsified. In fact, the reverse is true. Many correspondences exist between Kings and outside sources, not the least impressive of which is the ability to put foreign rulers in correct sequence.
- The Assyrian names in Kings mirror Assyrian forms, not later Babylonian or Aramaic versions.
- By the Hellenistic period, Jews shared their traditions and texts over a wide geographic area from Egypt to Babylon. It is inconceivable that relatively recent texts or traditions could have been accepted as authoritative by these dispersed Jewish communities or imposed upon them by a central authority.
- The book of Kings is written in Standard Biblical Hebrew, which has demonstrable connections to pre-Persian-period epigraphic materials and is unmistakably different from the Late Biblical Hebrew of works such as Chronicles.
- Kings and the other historical books of the DH show complex diachronic developments that must have required a good deal of time to accumulate before the LXX translation process for these books began (ca. 200).

4.9.1.3. Micah

The effect of prophetic traditions from one generation to the next is illustrated by the circumstance that Jeremiah's contemporaries remembered Micah's oracle of judgment against Jerusalem (Mic 3:12) and used it to evaluate Jeremiah's own threats (Jer 26:18). Micah's oracles are embedded in the present form of the book that bears his name. They criticize the leadership of both Samaria and Jerusalem for social and economic injustices. In contrast to Isaiah, Micah represented the viewpoint of rural Judah rather than that of Jerusalem. His own hometown of Moresheth(-gath) was one of the doomed towns of the Shephelah listed in Mic 1:10–16. This list is often reconstructed into an itinerary for Sennacherib's invasion path in 701. Whatever the truth of this may be, the rural areas of western Judah bore the brunt of the devastation that Jerusalem escaped.

4.9.1.4. Isaiah

Material about Isaiah forms the core of the complex book that bears his name. Like other monarchy-period prophets, his oracles condemned the social situation of his day. Other oracles of salvation and judgment along with several narratives reflect the shifting relationships between Judah and Assyria in the reigns of Ahaz and Hezekiah. Isaiah took seriously the ideology that Jerusalem was under Yahweh's special protection. The king of Judah had a duty to trust this divine promise and refrain from fear or disbelief. Isaiah shared this concept with the so-called Zion psalms of the temple liturgy.

4.9.1.5. Zephaniah

The prophetic activity of Zephaniah dates to the early years of Josiah, before that king's reform began in 621. Against the background of the policies of Manasseh, the prophet announces God's judgment on the nation's leadership. Like Amos (5:18–20), he uses the Day of Yahweh tradition that had its roots in temple liturgy and descriptions of the victories of Yahweh as Divine Warrior. The coming Day of Yahweh threatened punishment on Judah as well as on its enemies.

4.9.1.6. Nahum

Nahum expresses fierce joy over the impending fall of Nineveh in 612. The Assyrian conquest of Thebes in 663 is used as a comparative parallel to Nineveh's vulnerability (3:8). Israel's Divine Warrior theme (e.g., Judg 5, Zion psalms, Hab 3) is used to assert that Yahweh's power is supreme in unfolding world events and that the punishment of Assyria is is just.

4.9.2. The Babylonian Period

4.9.2.1. Habakkuk

The Chaldeans, that is, Judah's Babylonian enemy in the last days of its independence, provide the historical background for Habakkuk. They are an active threat, so most scholars date the core material to the reign of Jehoiakim sometime before the calamity of 597. The prophet's stubbornly repeated complaint is that Yahweh, who is supposedly a righteous God, is doing nothing about the catastrophes the people are suffering. In 2:6–20, a taunt song derides a nonspecific wicked tyrant who embodies the offenses committed by Babylon. The prophet's psalm-like prayer in chapter 3 expresses trust in Yahweh's ultimate benevolence.

4.9.2.2. Jeremiah

The book of Jeremiah is a complex compositional production containing oracles and biographical narratives that date from the reign of Josiah through the events of 586 and beyond. These diverse materials, relating in a variety of ways to the historical Jeremiah, are supplemented by Deuteronomistic interpretations of his message. The materials may be divided into four periods: 627–622 (chs. 1–6), 609–597 (chs. 7–20, 25–26, 36), 597–586 (chs. 21–24, 27–29, 37–39), and 586 and afterward (chs. 40–44). The book is a source for much valuable information about courses of events and the internal politics of Judah during the nation's final years. Jeremiah himself was representative of the power group and elite families in Jerusalem that opposed the resistance strategy employed by Jehoiakim and Zedekiah in turn. Jeremiah's temple sermon (chapters 7 and 26) reveals the seductive importance that the theology of Jerusalem's supposed inviolability had on those who advocated such a resistance strategy. The prophet's so-called laments (e.g., 8:18–9:1; 12:1–13; 20:7–18) appear to provide autobiographic insights into his personal struggles.

4.9.2.3. Lamentations

This artistically structured collection of five poems grieves over the physical and social destruction of Jerusalem in 586 and the deportation of its prominent citizens. The poems provide vivid insight into the horrendous suffering experienced by its citizens. They also reveal the psychic dislocation of those who experienced the destruction of their city and temple, deportations, and the reversal or unraveling of traditions of election and providence that gave meaning and structure to life. They are similar to the genre of Mesopotamian city-laments (*ANET*, 455–63, 611–19; *COS* 1.166:535–39). Lamentations was meant for those who have survived and who must come to terms with their loss, work through their grief and anger, and carry on. These poems were probably sung in public mourning observances (Zech 7:1–7, 8:19).

4.9.2.4. Ezekiel

The book of Ezekiel may derive from the hand of the prophet himself. It offers the perspective of a priest who had been deported with the initial group of exiles who settled in Babylon after 597. Dates are provided consistently throughout by means of thirteen chronological notices. Beginning in 593, the reader encounters Zedekiah's stirrings of rebellion. A date set forth in 24:1–2 marks the beginning of the Babylonian siege. The news of Jerusalem's definitive end arrives in the community of exiles in 585 (33:21–22). This event marks a turning point in the prophet's message from one of doom to one of hope. An oracle dated to 571 (29:17) reflects on the successful outcome of Nebuchadnezzar's siege of Tyre and predicts an effective attack by Babylon on Egypt (which took place in 568, but without a clear result; *ANET*, 308). Ezekiel displays an early stage of the notion that the exiles in Babylon represented the true heirs of Judah and its tradition, something that would have a decisive effect on events when exiles who shared that conviction returned to Judah to take control of its religious and political life.

4.9.2.5. Obadiah

Obadiah reveals the antagonistic reaction to Edomite occupation of ancestral Judahite land after the Babylonian conquest (Ps 137:7; Lam 4:21–22). Edom will be brought down with defeat, but the exiles of Israel and Jerusalem will regain Canaan and the Negev. Intertextual relationships between Obadiah and other prophetic books throw light on the editorial processes that created the prophetic canon. These allusions include Obad 5–7 and Jer 49:9–10; Obad 1–4 and Jer 49:14–16; Obad 4 and Amos 9:2; and Obad 19 and Amos 9:12.

4.9.2.6. Second Isaiah

The anonymous prophet whose poetry constitutes chapters 40–56 of the book of Isaiah was active in the last years of the Babylonian Empire. Jews living in Babylon made up the original target audience. The prophet refers to Cyrus by name and presupposes that news of his stunning victories have reached Babylon's Jews (Isa 44:28; 45:1–8). This dates the composition to between 550 and 539. The prophet relies on the spirit and oracles of Isaiah of Jerusalem to reassure exiled expatriates that Yahweh is soon to intervene in world affairs. Cyrus is an anointed divine instrument to bring about a second exodus back to their ancestral land. Second Isaiah expresses a radical monotheism that insists that Yahweh is the only God and intends to be recognized as such universally (45:7; 49:26; 52:6). The wording in places reflects the language of Psalms. It is clear from reading Second Isaiah that some elements of the exile continued to esteem remembered words of the preexilic prophets and still found meaning in the traditions of creation, the exodus, Zion, and David. They resisted the alien religious culture to which they were being exposed, in part, by promoting a radical and universal monotheism and the hope of a return home.

4.9.2.7. The Priestly Writing

A large share of the narratives and laws found in Genesis through Numbers originated from the perspective of Priestly lore and legal tradition (designated as P). There is no consensus about how this Priestly matter relates to Yahwistic and Elohistic materials that date from the monarchy period (see §3.8.3), whether there are diachronic layers in the larger whole, or how the priestly material relates to the final editing process that resulted in the Pentateuch. It is certain that P preserves earlier, preexilic traditions, but the date of the composition of its basic redactional shape remains unresolved. Most likely the Priestly writing was compiled in the Babylonian period as a way of preserving Priestly traditions and knowledge in the crisis of exile. The lore it preserved had been passed on through the living institutions of temple and ritual, but now had to be written down in order to safeguard Jewish identity in an alien environment. The postexilic temple of Zerubbabel, from which the ark was absent, does not really come into view. Instead the Priestly writing visualizes the landless wilderness period, the ark, and an idealized tabernacle. The theological horizon of P is far-reaching and erudite, encompassing creation, election, covenant, and ritual. As one would expect from material composed by exiles, it is concerned with legitimacy, orderliness, identity, and purity. As a challenge to Jews living outside the homeland, the Priestly writing ends before the conquest. Israel is poised on the verge of a new life of worship and obedience. The question of the identity of the law of Moses promulgated by Ezra (Neh 8) and its relationship to P or the Pentateuch remains a matter of dispute.

4.9.3. Psalms

Psalms asserting the same Zion theology that is reflected in Isaiah, such as Pss 2, 46, 48, 68, 76, 78, and 132, had their origin in Judah's monarchy period, although the notions they represent would continue to influence the faith of following generations. The same is true of what are called royal psalms that celebrate the divine election of the Davidic dynasty (Pss 2; 45; 72; 110). Both categories of temple music must have been performed in the preexilic Judahite temple cult. Some psalms display archaic features that suggest they were composed relatively early (Pss 18; 29; 68). The collection and formation of the Psalter itself should be dated to the Second Temple (Persian) period (see §5.7.6).

5. YEHUD AND PERSIA (539–330)

Albertz, Rainer, and Bob **Becking**, eds. *Yahwism after the Exile: Perspectives on Israelite Religion in the Persian Era* (Studies in Theology and Religion 5; Assen: Royal Van Gorcum, 2003). **Allen**, Lindsay. *The Persian Empire: A History* (London: British Museum Press, 2005). **Berquist**, Jon L. *Approaching Yehud: New Approaches to the Study of the Persian Period* (SemeiaSt 50; Atlanta: Society of Biblical Literature, 2007). **Briant**, Pierre. *From Cyrus to Alexander: A History of the Persian Empire* (Winona Lake, Ind.: Eisenbrauns, 2002). **Curtis**, John. *The World of Ancient Persia* (London: British Museum Press, 2005). **De Souza**, Philip. *The Greek and Persian Wars, 499–386 B.C.* (New York: Routledge, 2003). **Edelman**, Diana. *The Origins of the Second Temple: Persian Imperial Policy and the Rebuilding of Jerusalem* (London: Equinox, 2005). **Fried**, L. S. *The Priest and the Great King: Temple Palace Relations in the Persian Empire* (Winona Lake, Ind.: Eisenbrauns, 2004). **Gerstenberger**, Erhard, S. *Israel in the Persian Period: The Fifth and Fourth Centuries B.C.E.* (Biblical Encyclopedia 8; Atlanta: Society of Biblical Literature, 2011). **Grabbe**, Lester L. *Judaic Religion in the Second Temple Period: Belief and Practice from the Exile to Yavneh* (New York: Routledge, 2000). **Grabbe**. *Yehud: A History of the Persian Province of Judah* (vol. 1 of *A History of the Jews and Judaism in the Second Temple Period*; LSTS 47; London: T&T Clark, 2004). **Japhet**, Sarah. *From the Rivers of Babylon to the Highlands of Judah: Collected Studies on the Restoration Period* (Winona Lake, Ind.: Eisenbrauns, 2006). **Kartreit**, Magnar. *The Origin of the Samaritans* (VTSup 128; Leiden: Brill, 2009). **Lipschits**, Oded, and Manfred **Oeming**, eds. *Judah and the Judeans in the Persian Period* (Winona Lake, Ind.: Eisenbrauns, 2006). **Lipschits**, Oded, Gary N. **Knoppers**, and Rainer **Albertz**, eds. *Judah and the Judeans in the Fourth Century B.C.E.* (Winona Lake, Ind.: Eisenbrauns, 2007). **Schaper**,

Joachim. *Priester und Leviten im achämenidischen Juda: Studien zur Kult- und Sozialgeschichte Israels in persischer Zeit* (FAT 31; Tübingen: Mohr Siebeck, 2000). **Schniedewind**, W. M. *How the Bible Became a Book: The Textualization of Ancient Israel* (Cambridge: Cambridge University Press, 2004). **VanderKam**, James C. *From Joshua to Caiaphas: High Priests after the Exile* (Minneapolis: Fortress, 2004).

5.0. Summary

In contrast to the Assyrian and Neo-Babylonian period, there is a shortage of historical records from the Persian period. The sources we do have tend to be Greek (Herodotus; Xenophon, *Anabasis*; Ctesias, *Persica*) and thus weighted toward Western events and influenced by xenophobic Greek attitudes toward their long-standing enemy. The Bible basically ignores the two periods between the completion of the temple and the careers of Ezra and Nehemiah (515–458) and between the conclusion of Nehemiah's second term as governor and the successors of Alexander (ca. 430 and 330).

When Cyrus established the Persian Empire, he joined together the territories of the previous Mesopotamia-based empires that included Syria-Palestine, the Median Empire to the east, and the Lydian realm in Asia Minor to the west. His successor Cambyses would expand this patrimony by incorporating Egypt, and Darius I added areas farther east and on the European mainland. This unprecedented configuration of power would last for two hundred years, until the successors of Alexander divided it up. The empire was held together by a satrapy structure that promoted strong administration integrated with centralized imperial policy, but was still able to incorporate local differences. The powerful satraps were restrained by other officials who reported directly to the king and intelligence forwarded by watchful agents of the royal court. It was characterized by effective communications, a degree of tolerance for local religious and legal custom, and a threat of military action against rebellious elements. Imperial policy balanced conciliatory gestures with calculated brutality.

When the gates of Babylon opened to Cyrus, Jews living in Palestine, Egypt, and Babylon had had fifty or sixty years to come to terms with their loss of nationhood, temple, and homeland. Those outside Palestine mostly acclimated to their lives as second- or third-generation alien communities and would eventually grow into substantial and mostly successful expatriate populations. Peasants who had remained in Samaria and Judah worked the land and honored Yahweh. One group living in Babylon, however, saw its mission as returning to the homeland and city of their forebears and rebuilding. Straggling back over decades, these returnees imposed their vision of genealogical purity, orthodox worship, and codified law on whatever elements of the local population they were willing to accept as community members. At least at the beginning, there was understandable conflict with worshipers of Yahweh in Samaria and Transjordan. Yet by the end of the fifth century, we find the governors of Yehud and Samaria agreeing to a common response to Egyptian Jews who had asked for permission to rebuild their temple.

The two-hundred-year-old Persian Empire collapsed rapidly before the onslaught of the Macedonian king Alexander, who changed the balance of power in Persia's long-standing struggle with the Greeks.

5.1. Cyrus II (559–522)

Cyrus II (the Great), scion of the Achaemenid dynasty of Persia, was great-grandson of Teispes (ca. 650–620), who was supposedly son of the eponymous (and possibly fictional) Achaemenes (Hakhamanish). Cyrus began his career as king of Anshan, the traditional title of the Persian rulers of an area in Elam. This southeastern portion of the Zagros Mountains is today the Iranian province of Fars. Cyrus was a vassal of Cyaxares, king of the Medes (ca. 625–585). Cyrus's trajectory as empire builder entailed the sequential conquest of three major powers: the Medes, Lydia, and Babylon. In 585, the battle of Halys between Lydia and Cyaxares king of the Medes had been broken off because of a total solar eclipse. This event led to an alliance between the warring parties. Astyages (585–ca. 550) succeeded his father, Cyaxares, in that same year and continued the Median alliance with Lydia and Babylon. He married his daughter Amytis to Nebuchadnezzar in 585 in order to formalize the alliance. Median territory incorporated Cappadocia, Armenia, areas west of the Tigris, Persia south of Media itself, and then stretched west into Bactria.

The Nabonidus Chronicle is an important source for the rise of Cyrus (*ANET*, 305–7). In 553, Cyrus rebelled against Astyages. After three years of fighting, Astyages's troops mutinied during the battle of Pasargadae (550). Apparently the Median troops handed their king over to Cyrus.

Cyrus completed his conquest of the Median Empire with his capture of Ecbatana in 549. He was able to integrate the Median forces and their leadership into his own system of warfare and rule. He first moved against Bactria and the Oxus River area before turning to Asia Minor. In 547 he marched up to Urartu and killed its king. Croesus of Lydia (560–ca. 546) had expanded the small empire inherited from his father by bringing all the Greek cities of Asia Minor under his control. Supposedly encouraged by the ever-ambiguous oracle of Delphi, Croesus moved against Cyrus. The conquest by Cyrus of the Lydian realm involved an indecisive battle at the Halys River and climaxed with a sack of the Lydian capital Sardis, perhaps in 546.

Following major battles at the Diyala River and at Opis on the Tigris in 539, Cyrus entered Babylon without any battle (according to his own witness) in October of that year. Greek sources, however, describe a degree of Babylonian opposition before the city was breached (Herodotus, *Hist.* 1.188–191; Xenophon, *Cyropaedia* 7.5.7–32, 58). Cyrus's entry was supposedly achieved by diverting the flow of the Euphrates. What probably happened was that his general Gubaru (Gobryas) had been sent ahead and entered the city in early October. Nabonidus retreated and was captured. After negotiations with Babylon's leaders, Cyrus himself staged a triumphal entry about three weeks later, on October 29. The story that Gobryas was a traitorous, disgruntled Babylonian official seems to be a fictional embroidery by Xenophon. Gobryas was made governor of Babylon, but soon died. The images of the gods that had been taken from their home cities by Nabonidus were returned home.

A major factor in the quick collapse of Babylonian resistance was the outrage felt by the city's religious establishment at the indifference shown to the god Marduk by Nabonidus. The Verse Account of Nabonidus reflects this attitude, depicting Babylon's last king in an unfavorable light as unjust and irreligious (*ANET*, 312–14). However, Nabonidus may have had strategic and commercial reasons for the long sojourn in northwestern Arabia that prevented his participation in the annual *akitu* festival (see §4.7). Cyrus died in 530 in a battle in northeastern Iran against central Asian nomads. He was buried in Pasargadae, where his tomb may still be seen.

In the Cyrus Cylinder (*ANET*, 315–16; *COS* 2.124:314–16) Cyrus claims the divine sanction of Marduk for his actions as deliverer of Babylon. This piece of propaganda is a building inscription for his renovation of Marduk's temple, so naturally Marduk is credited with Cyrus's victory. With this claim, Cyrus is repeating Babylonian royal traditions. He vilifies

Nabonidus for impious crimes against Marduk. He declares that his army treated the population peacefully, and that they in turn welcomed him with joy. He boasts of his policy of returning the images of gods to their home cities and the population of nations to their native lands.

The presumably fictive decree cited in Ezra 1:1–5 (2 Chr 36:22–23) at least shows an awareness of Cyrus's policy in this respect and echoes the themes of the Cyrus Cylinder. Even though Ezra 1:1–5 is not a genuine imperial decree, the return from Babylonia by the minority of the deportees who did so must have been encouraged and permitted by Persian policy. Persia would have supported this and similar moves in order to increase tax revenues from economically distressed areas. Moreover, Cyrus would certainly want to strengthen Palestine as a buffer against Egypt, still ruled by Pharaoh Amasis (570–526), a former ally of Croesus. Palestine was also the route through which Persian armies would eventually march against Egypt. There is probably some level of authenticity to the document quoted in Ezra 6:3–5. This record refers to an earlier decree by Cyrus (with the docket title "concerning the house of God in Jerusalem"). However, the wording quoted says nothing whatsoever about a return of exiles to Jerusalem. Certainly any claim that there was an empire-wide policy concerning the repatriation of deported peoples goes beyond the evidence.

5.2. The Persian Empire

The Persian Empire exhibited important strengths that contributed to its two-hundred-year duration. These strengths included a powerful and flexible military. Foot soldiers were highly maneuverable, armed with both spear and bow, carrying a light wicker shield, and lightly armored. Persian cavalry, armed with bows and spears, outclassed its opposition. Both elements of the army were well trained and highly mobile. The Ten Thousand Immortals represented the elite core of the infantry and, along with a similar group of cavalrymen, owed sworn loyalty directly to the person of the king. In addition to the former Elamite capital Susa and the former capital of the Medes, Ecbatana, Cyrus built an impressive royal center at Pasargadae in Persia proper.

The satrap system offered a centralized polity that was still able to incorporate local differences. Satraps operated on a structure of rewards and multiple parallel lines of direct reporting to the king. For example, the commanders of the local garrisons were directly responsible to the king, not to the satrap. In addition, the *Eyes and Ears of the King* were officials who conducted surprise audits and investigations of local operations. A system of royal roads linked the empire together. One of these was the Royal Road built by Darius that crossed rivers and passed through mountains to join Sardis in the west to Susa in Elam. The Persians set up guard posts to keep roads safe and to monitor who was on the move. Way stations provided fresh horses to couriers who carried royal messages. They were supposedly able to travel from Susa to Sardis in seven days, a journey that took ninety days on foot.

Commerce was also furthered through an introduction of royal coinage to supplement the Lydian coinage earlier promoted by Croesus. The gold *daric* became the standard in the Near East and the Greek world until the time of Alexander. Darius completed a canal begun originally by Neco II connecting the Red Sea to the Nile Delta. New technologies in irrigation increased the acreage of productive land. Increasing international contact meant that rice from India was being grown in Mesopotamia and pistachios from Asia Minor were planted in Syria.

The use of imperial Aramaic supplied a unifying force to the empire. At the same time, the shift from cuneiform on clay tablets to writing on perishable papyrus is a major reason for the frustrating dearth of documentary evidence from the period. The Persian government was efficient at extracting taxes and tribute from its citizens, so much so that Alexander's later release of gold from the Persian treasury caused dangerous monetary inflation. The Persians were strongly influenced by Elamite culture, and Elamite remained an important imperial language.

There were also noteworthy weaknesses in the imperial system. The size and ethnic diversity of the empire led to rebellions. The well-trained and highly motivated Persian army was gradually supplemented by diverse contingents of less reliable subject peoples. A more systemic problem was a pattern of inner-dynastic competition. Primogeniture among a king's sons was not a strongly recognized principle. Choice was supposedly the prerogative of the god Ahura Mazda, a concept that naturally resulted in numerous palace intrigues. For example, Darius was not the direct successor to Cyrus's son Cambyses. As a result, he had to face down many local pretenders. Most seriously, a dangerous troublemaker claimed to be Bardiya the brother of Cambyses. In fact, modern historians tend to suspect that this figure really was the brother of Cambyses and that Darius was the actual usurper (see §5.4.1). The successions of Darius II, Artaxerxes II, Artaxerxes III, and Darius III were all marred by controversy and bloodshed.

5.2.1. Jews in the Province of Yehud

In Palestine during the close of the Babylonian period, there had been a modest recovery inland and a more robust revival along the coast. In the Persian period, the independent kingdom of Sidon controlled its section of the Mediterranean coast. According to the Periplous of Skylax (sixth century?), Sidon also controlled the Palestinian coast from Dor down to Joppa. Inscriptions of Tabnit, king of Sidon and priest of Ashtoreth (*COS* 2.56:181–82; *ANET*, 662) and his son (*COS* 2.57:182–83) bring to light the dynastic succession of Sidon in the second quarter of the fifth century. Tyre controlled the coast in its neighborhood, as well as Acco and Ashkelon. The inscription of Yehawmilk of Byblos indicates that this city also was self-governing in the fifth or fourth century (*COS* 2.32:151–52; *ANET*, 656).

The territory of Yehud can be determined from the settlement list repeated in Ezra 2 and Neh 7 and the distribution of coins and seals. The province ran from Bethel down to the area near Idumean Hebron and westward from the Jordan River and Dead Sea up to, but excluding, the Shephelah. The Shephelah lowlands may have been under the control of Dor or Sidon. The inclusion of returnees from Bethel, Ai, and Jericho indicate that portions of Yehud lay outside the borders of the former kingdom of Judah. The great majority settled in Jerusalem, which is to be expected since the deported families had originally been well-to-do or oriented to the royal palace and temple. The population of Yehud thus consisted of a volatile mixture of the descendants of peasants left behind by the Babylonians to keep the land under cultivation and an elite class of returnees. These latter were convinced they were the true heirs to the religion and culture of Judah and prided themselves on their pure genealogies. They reinforced their special status by insisting that the Yahwistic population of Samaria was really a mongrelized immigrant group (cf. 2 Kgs 17:24–33). At the same time, these elites, including priests, found it advantageous to marry members of foreign families and spouses with dubious pedigrees. Such marriages connect them politically and economically to outside interests that could benefit them. Conflict was inevitable.

According to the roster in Neh 3, the province Yehud was divided into at least five districts (Jerusalem, Beth-haccherem, Mizpah, Beth-zur, and Keilah). Jews were also present in the Benjaminite area around Lod and Ono (Neh 11:35), apparently not part of the actual territory of Yehud. The population lived in small, unwalled villages, with Jerusalem being the only urban center. Jerusalem was much smaller than it had been in the late monarchic period. The city encompassed only the eastern hill, at a line higher up the slope than before, along with the temple site to the north. Galilee enjoyed some resettlement, but archaeological remains there connect more strongly culturally to the Phoenician coast than to Samaria or Judah.

Persian strong points were scattered around the area. These included Tel el-Hesi, Ramat Rahel south of Jerusalem, En-gedi, and Lachish (the site of the so-called Persian Residency). Persian-era seal stamps provide insight into the administrative situation. Three-fourths of the $m(w)ṣh$ stamp impressions were found at Mizpah, indicating that its status as an administrative center continued into the Persian era. Others examples were uncovered in the territory of Benjamin. This place name should be identified with Benjaminite Motsah (Josh 18:26). For other Persian-era seals and stamps bearing the names of "Elnathan the governor" and one belonging to a son of Sanballat the governor of Samaria, see COS 2.78B, D:203–4.

These new setters had a strong ideology of legitimacy determined by genealogy (Ezra 2:59). Formerly the term "people of the land" had referred to the class of landowners based outside Jerusalem who had often been involved when the royal succession was in crisis. This now became a pejorative designation used by the returnees to describe the local Yahwistic population that had not been taken to Babylon (Ezra 4:4).

Aramaic, the language of international communication and trade, began to replace Hebrew during the Persian era (cf. Neh 13:24), but the timing and progression of this transition remains a matter of dispute. Imperial Aramaic reflected set standards of a professional scribal tradition. Both Hebrew and Aramaic appear on coins and seals from the period, but the use of Hebrew on these objects was likely a way of asserting ideological claims. Aramaic dominates other inscriptional finds. Aramaic script began to be used to write Hebrew. Jewish Aramaic texts related to Palestine include the Elephantine and Wadi ed-Daliyeh papyri. On the other hand, the biblical literature that was written in the Persian period (Ezra-Nehemiah, Chronicles) was composed in Hebrew. The significance of Neh 8:7–8, which describes Levites giving the sense of Ezra's reading of the law, does not seem to relate to translation from Hebrew into Aramaic (cf. the Levites' role in vv. 9 and 11). However, some modern versions interpret the scene in this way. Hebrew would enjoy an ideological renaissance in the fourth and third centuries when Persian control ended, as demonstrated by the composition of Sirach in Hebrew. Nevertheless, the shift to Aramaic as the region's everyday language was unstoppable.

Like Yehud, Samaria was a Persian province within the satrapy Beyond the River. For the most part, it enjoyed better agricultural resources than Yehud. The northern and western parts were the most densely populated. Settlements were small, and Shechem and Samaria are the only cities showing evidence of Persian-period settlement. Although recent excavations are reported to have revealed evidence for a Samaritan temple on Mt. Gerizim from the mid-fifth century, confirmation of this interpretation is still awaited. The irreversible breakdown in relations between the Yahwists of Samaria and those of Yehud, however, happened only in the Hellenistic period.

5.2.2. Jews in Mesopotamia

The Babylonians had settled some Jews in order to reclaim abandoned areas, as evidenced with names compounded with *tel*, "ruin": Tel Abib (Ezek 3:15), Tel-Melah, Tel-Harsha (Ezra 2:59). They enjoyed a limited state of self-government, indicated by references to the elders of Judah or Israel in Ezekiel. Years were reckoned according to the reign or exile of Jehoiachin, at least by the author of Ezekiel. In Mesopotamia, Babylonian cultural influence on the Jews is indicated by their use of Babylonian personal names (compare Sheshbazzar or Zerubbabel). What become the standard month names in the Jewish calendar, such as Nisan and Adar, were a matter of Babylonian influence (y. Roš Haš. 1:56d). These names are used only by biblical books from the postexilic period (Ezra-Nehemiah, Esther, and Zechariah).

A collection of 730 tablets preserves the business archives of a family of merchant bankers, the Murashu of Nippur. These date from 455 to 403. They reveal a clan of prosperous Jews who owned real estate. Other archival texts mention Jews in eastern Syria during the Neo-Babylonian period (ca. 604–601). A group of commercial documents from 498 (the time of Darius I) refers to Al Yahudu (city of Judah) in the area of Sippar. Following a well-attested practice in Babylon, this place seems to have been named for the original home of its settlers. A recently revealed collection of approximately one hundred tablets covers a period from Nebuchadnezzar year 33 (ca. 572) to Xerxes year 13 (ca. 473). Written by professional Babylonian scribes in Akkadian cuneiform, these tablets sometimes also include notes in Aramaic alphabetic script. The tablets in this collection seem to have been discovered in the neighborhood of ancient Borsippa. They describe commercial and legal activities of a population, many of whom bore Hebrew and Yahwistic names. Some were involved in military service as archers. They witness to a significant level of economic integration and adoption of local legal practices by the descendants of Jewish deportees. However, postexilic biblical materials also indicate that Babylonian Jews emphasized the cultural markers of Sabbath, circumcision, and purity regulations. This focus served as a strategy to limit assimilation with the dominant culture, at least among those deportees who eventually returned to Yehud.

In influence of Zoroastrian religion on emerging Jewish thought is a controversial matter. The extent of its official role in the Persian Empire remains uncertain. In his inscriptions, Darius refers to the will and order of Ahura Mazda. Zoroastrianism seems to have been the personal religion of the ruling Acheamenids from the time of Darius forward. Dating various elements in the Avestas is a difficult matter, although the Gathas (hymns) are the oldest material. Clearly a new form of the older Ahura Mazda religion was emerging in this period, but how much of this was accepted by imperial structures remains unclear. It seems significant that neither Herodotus nor Xenophon makes any references to Zoroaster. Nevertheless, distinctive elements of Zoroastrian thought did appear in Second Temple Judaism. These include a cosmic battle for world order, resurrection (although this is challenged by some scholars), an eschatology of fire and final judgment, supernatural entities analogous to Satan (Angra Mainyu), angels (Amesha Spenta) and demons (*daewas*), ethical dualism, and an emphasis on purity. It is probable, however, that the main impact of Zoroastrian thought on evolving Judaism was actually felt later, in the Hellenistic and Romans periods. Moreover, later developments in Zoroastrian religion may have been influenced by third- and fourth-century Christianity.

5.2.3. Jews in Egypt and Transjordan

Jews emigrated to Egypt after the Babylonian victory. Already in Isa 11:11, the prophet envisions a return of groups from Egypt, who may have fled Palestine after the crises of 722 and 701. The events reported in Jer 42:1–43:7 are likely characteristic of many who went south to join earlier Jewish residents in Egypt whose origin is undocumented. We know of probable Jewish garrisons in Midgol in the Delta, Memphis, Tahpanhes, and Patros (Jer 44:1). Letter of Aristeas 1.13 reports that Judean troops were used by Psamtik I (or possibly II) in an attack on Cush. One such Jewish garrison appears in the documents from Elephantine, claiming that its temple had been founded before the arrival of Cambyses.

Jews in contact with Jerusalem also lived east of the Jordan. By the time of Nehemiah, the Tobiad family, whose genealogical credentials were supposedly suspect (Ezra 2:59–60), seems to have had their power center in the territory of Ammon (Neh 2:19 : "Tobiah the Ammonite servant"). This Tobiah joined his fellow Yahwist Sanballat governor of Samaria (whose two sons bore Yahwistic names) in opposing Nehemiah's policies. He had to be evicted from a temple apartment when Nehemiah returned for his second term as governor. At a later time, the Zenon papyri and the Tobiad Romance used by Josephus show that these Tobiads grew into a wealthy and influential Jewish clan in Ammon (see §§6.3.1 and 6.3.2).

5.3. Sources Used in Ezra-Nehemiah

The chief source for the history of the restoration period (539–ca. 425) is Ezra-Nehemiah. Unfortunately, this book is confused in places and untrustworthy in others, particularly in its attempts to associate the missions of Ezra and Nehemiah. The book quotes several purported source documents. Some seem to be fictive, while others appear authentic. The trustworthy ones include inventory lists (Ezra 1:9–11; 8:26–27) and rosters (8:1–14; 10:18–43; Neh 3:1–32; 9:38–10:27; 11:3–24, 25–26; 12:1–26). The list of returnees in Ezra 2:1–70 and repeated in Neh 7:7–72a is most likely a repurposed census or tax roll (for parallels from Alakah, see COS 3.125–126:276–77). In addition, several documents and letters in Ezra purport to be official documents. These are characterized by the designation of Yahweh as "God of heaven" (as in Ezra 1:2; 5:11–12; 6:9–10; 7:12, 21–24).

5.3.1. Ezra 1:2–4

The Cyrus edict (Ezra 1:2–4) is generally regarded as fictive, but still reflective of Cyrus's policy. The memorandum cited in Ezra 6:3–5 covers some of the same ground and may be substantially authentic. If Cyrus's attention really did focus on the obscure situation of Jerusalem and its temple so early in his reign, it is likely that some group of influential Jews brought this matter to the attention of his government. Perhaps Cyrus's actions can be seen as a reward for pro-Persian attitudes on the part of such Jews, attitudes consistent with those of the author of Second Isaiah. Already in the poetry of Second Isaiah, the rebuilding of Jerusalem and the refounding of the temple had been deeds hoped for from Cyrus (Isa 44:28). Such a petition from an influential group of Jews could have provided some of the language for Cyrus's document: "its height sixty cubits and its width sixty cubits, three courses of great stones and one course of timber" (echoing 1 Kgs 6:2, 36).

5.3.2. Ezra 4:6–23

Ezra 4:6–23 gathers together three communications that reflect situations different from the context into which they have been slotted. The narrative context is supplied by Ezra 3:8–13, which describes a first start made by Zerubbabel on rebuilding the temple. This is dated in the second year of the return (537). Ezra 4:1–5 then provides an explanation for the ensuing delay in temple construction from 537 to 520. However, what follows in Ezra 4:6–23 has nothing to do with building the temple. Instead it reports on opposition to the construction of fortifications in Jerusalem, which took place at a substantially later date. Verse 6 vaguely describes accusations against the Jews made to Xerxes I in his accession year (485); this event is simply dropped and not described further. After this, in v. 7 a group of officials is described as writing to his successor Artaxerxes I. Then another explanatory preface in Aramaic (vv. 8–11) introduces an Aramaic letter to Artaxerxes addressed to him by the officials and people of Samaria (vv. 12–16). This letter accuses those reconstructing Jerusalem of planning a rebellion. It cites as evidence the city's long history of insurrection. The king is urged to research the historical record in the royal archives. It is probable that this letter is genuine and is connected to understandable worries about imperial security in light of the Egyptian revolt at the start of the reign of Artaxerxes or the subsequent revolt of Megabyzus, the satrap of Beyond the River in 448. The king's answer is reproduced in vv. 17–22. A search of the annals has revealed that Jerusalem was once the residence of mighty kings who controlled the whole area of Beyond the River and has been a center of repeated sedition. Work on building the city is to stop. Verse 23 describes how the recipients of the king's reply used force to halt construction. Finally v. 24a takes the reader back in time again to the year 537 and the topic of v. 5, that is, the delayed restoration of the temple. Verse 24b then fast-forwards seventeen years to year 2 of Darius (520).

5.3.3. Ezra 5:6–17; 6:3–5; and 6:6-12

In Ezra 5:3–5, Tattenai governor of Beyond the River and others are reported as questioning those building the temple concerning authorization for the project. Tattenai is attested in a nonbiblical source from Darius year 20 (502), but we do not know what his status may have been in year 2. A letter describing their encounter with the Jewish elders, supposedly written by Tattenai to Darius, is reproduced in vv. 6–17. This letter quotes the response that had been given by the Jewish leaders when questioned (vv. 11–16). In their reply, the Jewish elders reviewed the history of Solomon's building the temple and the disaster of 586. They asserted that Cyrus had authorized reconstruction and told of the return of the temple vessels and the foundation laid by Sheshbazzar. Tattenai and the other writers request that a search be made in the royal archives.

Ezra 6:3–5 purports to be a memorandum uncovered in Ecbatana as a result of this investigation. The memorandum describes a decree of Cyrus authorizing temple rebuilding, supporting the project with state funds, and describing some details of its construction. This memorandum is followed in vv. 6–12 by a decree of Darius that permitted the project to go ahead. Sacrifices are to be offered for the Persian king and his family. In this supposed authorization document, Darius rather suspiciously sounds like a good Deuteronomist in v. 12: "the God who has established his name there" (cf. Deut 12:11).

5.3.4. Ezra 7:12–26

Ezra 7:12–26 represents Artaxerxes's letter of commission (*firman*) in Aramaic to Ezra, and seems authentic. Ezra is to investigate the extent to which the law of "your God" is being observed, to enforce obedience to it, and to facilitate state support of the Jerusalem temple cult. A strong indication of authenticity is the random word "finished" inserted into v. 12.

This is apparently either a clerical notation that the matter has been dealt with or scribal shorthand to fill out the standard verbiage in the greeting (cf. NJPS, "to Ezra the priest, scholar in the law of the God of heaven, and so forth"). Mention of the king's seven counselors in v. 14 is another sign of authenticity. The existence of these officials is known from Greek sources. Again, however, elements seem to have been added to the text in the transmission process, such as the standardized list of temple clergy (vv. 13, 24) and the huge amounts of money supposedly appropriated from state funds to support a small, provincial temple (v. 22; about three metric tons of silver). Within the letter is an edict addressed to provincial treasurers to disburse funds for this purpose to Ezra (vv. 21–24) and providing a tax concession to temple personnel.

Putting these fictive and legitimate documents (along with Ezra 4:1–5) together in chronological order, they report on these alleged events:

- An initial start of temple construction in 537 as authorized by Cyrus (1:2–4; 3:8–13; 6:3–5).
- Opposition of the people of the land who bribe officials. Construction stops (4:4–5).
- Second start of the temple in 520. This is questioned by Tattenai and others (5:3–17), but subsequently authorized by Darius (6:1–12).
- Unspecified accusation against Judah and Jerusalem written to Xerxes (4:6).
- Opposition to some fortification project in Jerusalem in a letter to Artaxerxes I (4:7–23). Construction on this project is stopped.
- Commissioning of Ezra to perform his mission, also during the reign of Artaxerxes in 458 (7:12–26)

5.4. The Early Restoration Period: 539–515

Sheshbazzar is titled prince of Judah and was supposedly governor (Ezra 1:8; 5:14). Evaluating the respective careers of Sheshbazzar and Zerubbabel depends in part on whether there was a genealogical connection of Sheshbazzar to Jehoiachin. Zerubbabel was undoubtedly Jehoiachin's grandson via Shealtiel (1 Chr 3:17–18; Haggai and Zechariah). An alternate tradition names Zerubbabel's father as Pedaiah (1 Chr 3:19). The real question is whether Sheshbazzar was the same person as Shenazzar, the fourth son of Jehoiachin. Although often asserted by scholarship, this identification is completely uncertain. Sheshbazzar is the equivalent of the Akkadian Shamash-apla-usur. However, the Greek textual tradition of Shenazzar's name (Sanabassaros) suggests that Shenazzar's Akkadian name was Sin-ab-usur. This indicates that Sheshbazzar and Shenazzar were different people. In spite of his role with the temple vessels and the founding of the temple, Sheshbazzar may even have been a Persian rather than a returning Jew.

Moreover, Sheshbazzar is significantly absent from Ezra 2:1–4:5. He only appears in material reporting on the time of Cyrus (Ezra 1:8, 11; 5:14, 16). Although both he and Zerubbabel are said to have begun the foundation of the temple (3:8; 5:16), these appear to be two different acts confused by the author of Ezra-Nehemiah. Apparently an initial (and aborted) foundation event took place in the second year of return (537) under the direction of Sheshbazzar. A second restart and a refounding ceremony under the leadership of Zerubbabel took place in 520 (on September 21 and December 18 according to Hag 1:14–15; 2:18). When the reader of Ezra-Nehemiah puts together Ezra 3:2, 8 and 5:14, 16, the leadership roles of Zerubbabel and Sheshbazzar appear to overlap. This impression, however, seems to be the result of either authorial confusion or an editorial strategy intended to enhance the reputation of Zerubbabel by associating him with temple rebuilding from the very start. This trajectory in the developing tradition was continued when 1 Esd 6:18 added Zerubbabel to Ezra 5:14. Zerubbabel may have been involved in the first foundation event in 537, but this remains uncertain. In any case, Zerubbabel and Sheshbazzar never appear together in the text of Ezra-Nehemiah.

One can reconstruct the sequence of events as follows:

(1) In 539 a group of returnees came back under the authorization of Cyrus. They brought with them the captured temple vessels that had been put into the charge of one Sheshbazzar (Ezra 1:6, 11; 5:14), a supposed inventory of which is preserved in 1:9–11. These vessels were of tremendous ideological importance (e.g., 2 Kgs 25:14; Isa 52:11; Jer 27:16–22), equivalent to the statues of the other gods that Cyrus returned to their home temples. In Tishri 538 an altar was built on the old temple site. It was used for a celebration of the Feast of Booths (Ezra 3:2–4).

(2) In the second year of the return (537), a foundation ceremony of some sort took place under the leadership of Sheshbazzar, in which Zerubbabel may have also been involved (3:8–13; 5:16). The verb usually

translated "lay a foundation" means "found, establish," and does not necessarily refer to construction activity. The tears of the elderly at the sight of "the founding of this house" (v. 12 NJPS) indicates, however, that the size or diminished grandeur of the temple was evident. Construction was stopped because of local and external opposition and, probably, a scarcity of resources in the pioneer community.

(3) After a long delay, another ceremonial founding was instigated by Zerubbabel in 520. The prophets Haggai and Zechariah were instrumental in motivating this second round of construction. In Ezra 5:1 and 6:14 they appear in *inclusio* verses that enclose the building process. Whatever may have happened in 537 under Sheshbazzar, these prophets' near eschatological expectations about the temple (and Zerubbabel) indicate that the foundation ceremony of Zerubbabel was seen as the primary event from an ideological perspective (Zech 4:7, 9–10).

5.4.1. Cambyses (529–522) and Darius I (521–486)

Events in Yehud in 520 seem to be related to what was unfolding on the bigger stage of the Persian Empire. Cambyses (529–522) had begun as coregent with his father, Cyrus. He conquered Egypt in 525. The staging point for his campaign was Acco (Strabo, *Geography* 16.2.25), and he was supported by Arabs along the way (Herodotus, *Hist.* 3.7–9). Pharaoh Amasis died at this time and was replaced by Psamtik III (Psammetichus; 526–525). Cambyses marched toward Egypt. Arab allies provided some troops, and he was accompanied by a heavy naval presence furnished by Phoenician and Ionian Greek vassals. In 525 he defeated Psamtik in the eastern Delta at Pelusium. He then successfully besieged Memphis and captured Psamtik. Cambyses became pharaoh, inaugurating the Twenty-Seventh Dynasty of Persian pharaohs, which ran up through Darius II. He remained in Egypt, campaigning with limited success up the Nile, toward the oasis of Amun, and against the Libyans (Herodotus, *Hist.* 3.1–38). According to an autobiographical inscription of the former Egyptian naval commander and physician Udjahorresnet, Cambyses behaved like a proper pharaoh in religious matters. He visited the temple of Neith in Sais, where he arranged for offerings and restored its ritual and personnel. This would have been a politically motivated act, however, because this sanctuary had been the dynastic center for the 140-year-old Twenty-Sixth Saite Dynasty that Cambyses had just replaced. In contrast, Herodotus claims that Cambyses exhumed the mummy of Amasis and desecrated it.

Darius I (521–486) was not the direct successor to Cyrus's son Cambyses, but descended from a collateral branch of the royal family. He defended his irregular accession to the throne in the Behistun Inscription engraved on an inaccessible rock face on the main road between Babylon and Ecbatana. The text of this piece of propaganda was also distributed in copies throughout the empire. The inscription was written in Akkadian, Elamite, and a newly invented written form of Old Persian. Cambyses died (either accidentally or by suicide) while returning to Persia in 522 in order to deal with a revolt led by a figure claiming to be his brother Bardiya (Smerdis in Herodotus). According to Darius, who was the eventual victor in this conflict, the central figure in this uprising was an imposter, a court official named Gaumata, the false Smerdis, who was pretending to be Bardiya. The real Bardiya, according to both Darius and Herodotus, had actually been secretly murdered earlier by Cambyses. The phony Bardiya had claimed the throne while Cambyses was in Egypt. Darius was able to overcome this imposter with the aid of Ahura Mazda. Many modern historians, however, suspect that this Gaumata really was Bardiya, the brother of Cambyses, and that Darius was the actual usurper. Certainly Darius's version of events is self-serving.

Gaumata (Bardiya) was killed by Darius and seven coconspirators in 522 in Media. Darius claimed descent from the Achaemenid dynastic progenitor Achaemenes through his father Hystaspes, who was a great-grandson of Teispes. Moreover, Darius was married to the daughter of Cyrus II, Atossa, which bolstered his claim to the throne. He immediately had to wage civil war against the Persian noble Vahyazdata and also faced rebellions in numerous provinces that had remained loyal to Bardiya. Most seriously, Babylon also rebelled, having elevated a son of Nabonidus to the throne as Nebuchadnezzar III (Nidintu-Bel according to Darius, who also claims that he was an imposter). Darius was finally able to stabilize the situation by the end of 521, demolishing the walls and gates of Babylon and impaling three thousand residents (Herodotus, *Hist.* 3.159). Darius had to fight nineteen battle against nine local pretenders, all of whom he attacks as liars in the Behistun Inscription. The official line was that Ahura Mazda had chosen the Achaemenid family to rule, and Darius's accomplishments demonstrated that he was the god's choice.

Around 520 Darius reorganized the system of satrapies and subordinate provinces. There were twenty at first, but the number later grew.

Each satrap was responsible for producing a fixed amount of tax revenue based on its resources and productivity. Yehud was part of the fifth satrapy, Beyond the River, which encompassed the territory west of the Euphrates formerly part of the Neo-Babylonian Empire (Syria-Palestine, Phoenicia, and Cyprus). At some point, either in the reign of Darius or of his son Xerxes, the administration of Babylonia and Beyond the River were separated. By 502 at least, Tattenu (Tattenai in Ezra 5:3, 6; 6:6, 13) was satrap (meaning "protector of the realm") of Beyond the River. The subordinate provinces within the satrapies had various types of local government. Some (such as Samaria and Yehud) were under native governors appointed by the Persians. Other subunits of the fifth satrapy were Cyprus, Ashdod (that is, Philistia), Ammon, Moab, and Idumea, along with city-states in Syria and Phoenicia. Darius unified his empire by introducing imperial coinage (notably the nearly pure gold daric) and a system of post riders. He visited Egypt in 518, where he piously buried the recently deceased Apis bull, sponsored the search for a new one, and dedicated a temple to Ammon-Re. These public-relations activities in the religious sphere parallel in some ways his sponsorship of temple reconstruction in Jerusalem and support of its cult (Ezra 6:6–12).

Darius continued to use Pasargadae (the site of coronations) and Ecbatana (as a summer residence), but Babylon and Susa served as his main capitals. He built himself a splendid palace at Susa. He also created a ceremonial center at Persepolis to memorialize and celebrate imperial ideology. Darius expanded Persian control into the Indus River Valley in 516–515.

Conflict with the Greeks began around 512, when Darius, campaigning against the Scythians, crossed the Bosporus into Thrace (Herodotus, *Hist.* 4.83–144). He continued north and crossed the Danube, but had to pull back. He did create a satrapy out of Thrace. The Ionian cities rebelled with Athenian support in 499. This insurrection seems to have been instigated by Aristagorus, the tyrant of Miletus. The Greeks captured Sardis in 498 and burned the city. Darius responded with a siege and naval blockade of Miletus. A significant naval victory at the island of Lade off the coast of Miletus permitted Darius's capture of the city. His vengeful and vicious destruction of Miletus and the deportation of half its population (494) became an emotional flash point for the ongoing struggle between the Greeks and Persia (Herodotus, *Hist.* 6.21). Darius vowed to punish Athens and Eretria in Euboea for their support of the revolt. In 492 he sent Mardonius to secure the European side of the Bosporus, but many of his ships were destroyed in a storm and he had to turn back. Finally in 490 a Persian expeditionary force landed near Marathon, where they were confronted by an Athenian army. After a stalemate while the Athenians waited for their Spartan allies to arrive, the Persians started to embark their horses to attack at another place. The resulting absence of Persian cavalry inspired the Athenians to attack and win a decisive victory. Darius planned another campaign, but this was stalled by an Egyptian rebellion just before his death in 486.

5.4.2. Zerubbabel and Joshua

Zerubbabel ("seed of Babylon") is given the title governor in Hag 1:1 but nowhere else. According to Ezra 2:2; 3:2, 8, he had a leadership role with the initial group of returnees and in the first, aborted attempt at temple rebuilding. He played the decisive role, along with the high priest Joshua, in the restart of the temple reconstruction project in 520. Passages in Haggai and Zechariah witness to a high level of eschatological excitement about Zerubbabel's political prospects as scion of the Davidic royal house (Hag 2:20–23; Zech 3:8; 4:1–10; 6:9–15; cf. the messianic language of "my signet ring," "my servant," "branch"). The astonishing coup that brought Darius to the throne produced an atmosphere of uncertainty and expectation in various corners of the empire. Judah was ideologically disposed to be disloyal to an imperial regime that had existed for less than twenty years. Rebellious notions emerged in some quarters that envisioned a potential future for Zerubbabel as king over an independent Judah. The presence of a direct heir of Jehoiachin in high office, dreams that a reconstructed temple would soon arise, and the stimulating oracles of two prophets made for an explosive mix.

How things eventually worked out is a mystery, but it seems significant that Zerubbabel plays no role in the description of the completion of the temple building in Ezra 6:13–18. This contradicts the implications of Zechariah's oracle in Zech 4:4–7 that Zerubbabel would complete the temple. In addition, redactional irregularities about the symbolic crown (or crowns) described in Zech 6:11–15 indicate that Zerubbabel was subsequently censored out of the text and the honor focused solely on the high priest Joshua. The disappearance of Zerubbabel from leadership and the Zech 6 text suggests that the Persian authorities removed him from office as a threat. However, there is no actual evidence of this. In any case, an unprovenanced seal of "Shelomith maidservant of Elnathan the governor," hints at a public role for Zerubbabel's daughter who bore that name (1 Chr 3:19; COS 2.78C:203). That she occupied a public office occupied by her is implied by "maidservant," understood to be equivalent to *'ebed*, "servant," in the sense of minister or official.

The high priest Joshua son of Jehozadak (Jeshua son of Jozadak) appears in Ezra, Haggai, and Zechariah. There was apparently some question among more rigorous parties about his background (Zech 3:1–5). There was an expansion of the status, power, and role of the high priest in the new situation of the restored community. Power in Yehud was shared to some degree by the governors and high priests. This state of affairs, termed a *diarchy* by scholars, is clearest for Zerubbabel and Joshua (e.g., Ezra 3:2, 8; 5:2; Hag 1: 1, 12, 14; 2:2, 4) and later for Bagoas (Bagohi) and Johanan, to whom the Elephantine community sent a petition.

The completion of the temple and its dedication (Ezra 6:15) took place on March 12, 515 (Ezra 6:13–17; the text of 1 Esd 7:5 puts it twenty days later). This would have been very close to the seventy years after the fall of Jerusalem predicted by Jeremiah (Jer 25:11–12; 29:10; cf. Zech 1:12; 7:5). Perhaps this date is suspicious, but it could also have been the result of intentional scheduling. The report of the dedication ceremony is modeled on that of Solomon in 1 Kgs 8. A few weeks later, Passover was celebrated.

The temple became the center of political and economic life in Yehud and the chief reason for Jerusalem's growing prestige. It served as the center of the economic obligations listed in Neh 10: 33–40 [EV vv. 32–39] and 13:12–13. There was probably some level of imperial sponsorship, at least for sacrifices offered for the Persian king and his family (Ezra 6:10). The temple became a focus of piety and affection, as reflected in the Songs of Ascent collection in the book of Psalms (Pss 120–34; also 26:8; 65:5 [EV v. 4]; Ps 84). The evolving patterns of temple worship and the organization of temple personnel are revealed in 1 Chr 23–26 and 2 Chr 29–30. Nevertheless, much religious observance still fell outside what would eventually be considered orthodox Judaism (cf. Isa 65:2–5; the temple at Elephantine; perhaps the Persian-era solar temple at Lachish). It is significant that the Chronicler advances the ideal that Yahwists from northern areas including Galilee played an important part in Jerusalem worship (2 Chr 15:9–15; 30:11, 18). The narrow exclusivism promoted by the author of Ezra-Nehemiah was apparently not the whole story.

5.5. The Later Restoration Period (515–ca. 430)

5.5.1. Xerxes I (485–465)

We know nothing about what may have happened in Yehud between 515 and the arrival of Ezra in 458. Xerxes I (biblical Ahasuerus) was able to succeed his father Darius, even though he was not the eldest, because he was the son of the influential Atossa, Cyrus's daughter. He immediately had to deal with a revolt in Egypt that he inherited from his father. In 482 he destroyed Babylon in response to a rebellion that began with the murder of its satrap Zopyrus and was suppressed by the satrap's son Megabyzus. Possibly it was at this time that Babylon and Beyond the River were made into separate administrative units.

Xerxes then turned his attention to avenging his father's humiliating defeat by the Greeks. In 480 he led a massive army into European Greece, supported by a large fleet. Many city-states submitted, but some, including Athens and Sparta, chose to resist. Xerxes won an initial encounter with a small force at Thermopylae. However, he was defeated by the Greeks in the naval battle at the island of Salamis when his ships were too closely packed into the narrow straits to maneuver effectively. Xerxes himself left for home, but left his commander Mardonius behind. In 479, Mardonius was defeated at Plataea and much of the remaining Persian fleet was destroyed at Mycale. Xerxes broke off his attack on the Greeks in 478. He and his heir apparent were assassinated in a palace coup in 465. A trilingual foundation tablet of Xerxes, reproduced in *ANET*, 316–17, lists the nations under his control and describes his assured relationship with Ahura Mazda.

5.5.2. Artaxerxes (464–424/423)

Artaxerxes I Longimanus was a younger son of Xerxes, installed by the plotters who had killed his father. Starting around 460, he had to deal with a revolt in Egypt by Inaros, son of Psamtik III. This uprising was supported by Athens. In 454 Megabyzus, satrap of Beyond the River, was victorious at the siege of Prosopitis in Egypt against the Athenian-dominated Delian League. In 449 the Peace of Callias supposedly ended Persian moves against the Greeks in Europe. This purported treaty is referenced by several classical authors (e.g., Herodotus, *Hist.* 7.151–152), but many historians doubt the authenticity of this story and describe the treaty as more of a temporary truce. In 448 Artaxerxes had to deal with a revolt of Megabyzus, an event that might provide the context for the correspondence reproduced in Ezra 4:7–23 (see §5.3.2). These geopolitical realities made Yehud strategically significant to the Persians and probably led to the appointment of Ezra in the seventh year of Artaxerxes (458) and of Nehemiah in the king's twentieth year (445). It was only with the internecine and self-destructive Peloponnesian War (431–404) that any serious Greek threat to Persian domination was eliminated. Dating from the reign of Artaxerxes I is the Aswan Dedicatory Inscription (*COS* 2.41:163).

5.5.3. Ezra

There has been a long-standing controversy about whether to date Ezra's appointment to the reign of Artaxerxes I (458) or that of Artaxerxes II (398). The Artaxerxes I date (458) makes much more sense because at that time the Persians needed to secure Yehud as a buffer on the south. A second disputed matter is the order in which Ezra and Nehemiah worked. The traditional order set forth in the book Ezra-Nehemiah seems to be supported by Neh 5:15, in which Nehemiah states his opinion of the generally negative record of former governors. Nehemiah's reforms with regard to mixed marriages are similar to those of Ezra, which suggests that Ezra was not totally successful. The "wall" mentioned by Ezra in Ezra 9:9 is a metaphor, not a reference to Nehemiah's achievement.

The historian must remember that a pro-Persian ideology permeates Ezra-Nehemiah. In fact, the Bible generally endows the Persian Empire with positive theological significance. Second Isaiah is the clearest example. Reasonable suspicion is appropriate when one reads that both Ezra and Nehemiah were situated in and sent out from the very center of the imperial government. This same literary theme—the Jew who holds a position in the royal court and is thus able to help the people—is pivotal to the stories of Joseph and Esther. It is important to remember that the Persians could be as vicious as any other imperial power. Darius destroyed the temple at Didyma in Ionia (Herodotus, *Hist.* 6.19) and deported the inhabitants of Barca in Lydia to Bactria (4.204; for other examples of resettlement see 5.13–16; 6.20). Xerxes I devastated Babylon to punish it for a revolt. Nehemiah's prayer draws a credible picture of the Jews' discontent with their overlords (Neh 9:32, 36–37).

Ezra's mission to promulgate and enforce the traditional law of Yehud is sometimes related to a supposed Egyptian parallel. The royal physician Udjahorresnet (see §5.4.1) was sent back to Egypt by Darius in order to reconstitute the temple college system. Many modern historians, however, judge that this was an isolated measure intended to secure local loyalty or a royal favor to a favored individual, not a matter of general state policy. Yet it is also true that Darius also ordered the satrap of Egypt, Ariandes, to recruit native scholars in order to collect and codify the old pharaonic laws. About a century later, the mid-fourth-century Xanthus (Letoon Trilingual) Inscription evidences Persian approval of cultic initiatives in Lycia, which some take as an indication that it is quite believable that Artaxerxes I might have authorized the promulgation of Jewish law by Ezra.

Ezra's charge was to engage in a fact-finding mission to Yehud to discover the status of "the law of your God that is in your hand" (Ezra 7:14). He was also authorized to bring back gifts of money and donated vessels for the temple (vv. 15–19) and to draw on local treasuries for further funds (vv. 20–24). He was commissioned to appoint judges to uphold both divine law and the king's law (vv. 25–26). As to the content of the law referred to in his commission, one can say little except that his acts and references to this law do not obviously match the Pentateuch (especially Ezra 10:3 and the apparent quotation in Neh 8:15).

To summarize the biblical report of Ezra's career, he was commissioned in 458 to lead back a group of returnees, regularize temple worship, and promulgate and enforce an extensive (Neh 8:3) law code that had originated among elite Jews in Babylonia. He arrived in August 458 and read out the law at the Festival of Booths that same year. He then carried out an investigation of mixed marriages that concluded in the spring of 457. The biblical author sought to create the impression that the missions of Ezra and Nehemiah partially coincided by arranging the sequence of events reported in Ezra 2:2; Neh 8 (cf. v. 9); 12:26, 36. The evidence does not support any such overlap.

5.5.4. Nehemiah

Nehemiah served as governor of Yehud from 445 to 433 and then served a second term of uncertain duration. The Nehemiah Memoir, incorporated into Ezra-Nehemiah, is a first-person account that justifies Nehemiah's public career. It was addressed to God, as was the convention. He boasts about rebuilding the city defenses in the face of opposition and promoting social and religious reforms. This source is reproduced in Neh 1:1–7:73a; 12:31–32, 37–40; 13:4–31. It is similar in genre to Egyptian tomb inscriptions of royal officials, who used them to report on their dedicated careers (*ANET*, 233–34; *COS* 2.1:5–7). Most consider the Nehemiah Memoir to be an authentic autobiography. However, its historical value has also been questioned. There are certainly romantic elements in the narrative that are similar to those in the stories of Joseph or Esther. No doubt, Nehemiah indulged in some poetic license and selective memory in crafting his memoirs. As royal cupbearer in far off Susa, Nehemiah is deeply moved when he hears from a group from Yehud about the sad state of affairs in Jerusalem. He seeks authority to rectify the situation directly from the king himself.

Nehemiah's commission to build a defensive wall is puzzling. It seems odd that the Persians would be interested in fortifying a city so far inland from the usual trade and military route to Egypt (that is, Megiddo to Gezer to Ashkelon to Gaza). However, Nehemiah's tour of inspection (Neh 2:11–16) makes good geographical sense, and the process of rebuilding is described in a detailed and credible way (Neh 3). The wall-building process sounds practicable. Nehemiah made individual Jerusalem family groups responsible for work on individual segments. The Jerusalem groups worked with gangs from rural areas of Judah, who were perhaps employed and paid by the responsible Jerusalem families. The nonelite classes laboring on the wall suffered economic stress from famine and from taxes they had to pay the Persians. In order to alleviate this, Nehemiah was compelled to order a remission of debts in the community and made personal economic sacrifices himself (Neh 5). Outside military threats required that some personnel had to be delegated to provide military protection and that the workers needed to have weapons at hand in order to repel attack (Neh 4:15–20). Opposition from Samaria and other neighbors is a completely believable response to any refortification of Jerusalem (Neh 4; apparently Ezra 4:6–23).

Conflict between Samaria and Yehud as two subprovinces of the fifth satrapy would seem to be inevitable, given the centuries-long history of competition and conflict between the two regions. The presentation of Ezra-Nehemiah is likely accurate on this matter. One flash point would have been the question of participation in the Jerusalem temple cult. Another would have been the restoration of Jerusalem's fortifications.

Opposition from Samaria to refortification is cited somewhat vaguely in Ezra 4:10, 17, but is identified directly with its governor Sanballat in the book of Nehemiah. The Jerusalem exile community's focus on ethnic purity must have been both a cause and a reaction to Samaria's attempts at interference or control. The degree of Yehud's political dependence on Samaria before Nehemiah and just when it became an impendent province with its own governor are matters of controversy. The designation of Sheshbazzar as an independent governor is suspect (Ezra 5:14). Haggai identifies Zerubbabel as governor. Nehemiah speaks of governors before him and calls himself governor in Neh 5:14. He is designated by the Persian honorific title *tirshatha* (something like "His Excellency") in Neh 8:9 and 10:2, texts that are not part of his memoirs.

Nehemiah identifies Sanballat governor of Samaria as his chief opponent. Designating him "the Horonite" seems to indicate he was from Beth-horon. He collaborated with Tobiah "the Ammonite servant" and Geshem the Arab, each apparently provincial leaders of some sort. Tobiah was presumably the progenitor of the later Jewish Tobiad family whose power base was in Ammon. Whether he was ethnically an Ammonite (as hinted by the wording of Neh 2:10; 13:1–3) or a Jew who had achieved power in Ammon is uncertain. He had strong connections to elements in Jerusalem (Neh 6:17–19) to the point of receiving permission from a temple priest related to him to reside in a side room of the temple building (13:4–8). Geshem probably had a leadership role in the region immediately to the south of Yehud. However, if he is the Geshem who appears in either or both of two fifth-century inscriptions (one from Dedan and the other referring the father of a king of Qeder; COS 2.51D:176), then his dispute with Nehemiah must be sought in trade or political matters that went beyond local Palestinian quarrels.

A statement apparently not part of the Nehemiah Memoir reports that Nehemiah increased the population of sparsely occupied Jerusalem by resettling one-tenth of the outlying populace into the city (Neh 11:1–2; cf. 7:4). Nehemiah 13 reports on the other aspects of Nehemiah's reform. He devised a system for a proper distribution of temple resources to its lower-status personnel. He restrained commercial violations of the Sabbath. Unlike Ezra, he did not require that mixed marriages be dissolved, but he did seek to prevent future intermarriage with foreigners. His distress over the inability over the children of these mixed marriages to speak the language of Judah (13:24) clearly indicates his desire to protect the self-identity of the Yehud community and its linguistic distinctiveness.

5.6. Jews in Yehud and Egypt from Darius II to Darius III (424–331)

5.6.1. Governors and High Priests

Yehud as an independent province was eventually able to mint small-value coins. Identified by the inscription "Yehud," these coins date from the early fourth century into the Greek period. They would have been used as small change to supplement larger denominations minted elsewhere. One example is a silver quarter-shekel displaying a bearded god holding a raptor on his arm and sitting on a winged wheel. This is presumably an image of Yahweh (cf. Ezek 1:4–28). The name Yehezqiyah (Hezekiah) the governor is witnessed on one group of these coins.

From such coins, jar-stamp impressions, and seals, one can tentatively reconstruct a roster of Yehud's governors, although the order of succession and dating must remain uncertain. These names are Jewish: Elnathan, Hananiah (?), Yehoezer, Ahzai, Urio, and Yehezqiyah (Hezekiah). Nehemiah and the Persian Bagoas (Bagohi), who is known from Elephantine, must also be included in this roster of governors. This catalog is long enough to undermine the widespread assumption that Judah began under Samaritan authority and only later became an independent province. Some members of this group must have served between Zerubbabel and Nehemiah. Bagoas and Yehezqiyah definitely governed after Nehemiah.

The succession of high priests in the Persian era is also a matter of disputed reconstruction. Evidence comes from the list in Neh 12:10–11 informed by a judicious use of Josephus. There are only six names for a period of about two hundred years, so some names may be missing. Some scholars add additional priests with repeated names (assuming that papponymy [naming a son after his father or grandfather] was practiced). This controversial suggestion is tempting, but not absolutely necessary. These six names are as follows:

- Joshua, who coordinates with Zerubbabel, was son of Jehozadak son of Seraiah, the prominent priest executed by Nebuchadnezzar (2 Kgs 25:18; 1 Chr 5:40–41 [EV 6:14–15]).
- Joiakim, who is perhaps mentioned in Jdt 4:6, 8.
- Eliashib, who coordinates with Nehemiah.
- Joiada (Jehoiada), who also coordinates with Nehemiah. His

son had a marriage connection to Sanballat's daughter (Neh 13:28) and was expelled by Nehemiah
- Johanan, who appears in the Elephantine documents (410) and coordinates with the governor Bagoas (Bagohi). Nehemiah 12:11 probably calls him Jonathan by mistake.
- Jaddua, who apparently served as high priest all the way down to the time of Darius III and Alexander (*Ant.* 11:302–347). It is often suggested that there is a gap in the list during this time or that there was more than one high priest by this name. However, if Johanan was quite young in 410 and Jaddua was old in 330, this is not an impossible duration of tenure.

The governor Bagoas, who must have been a Persian, is also connected to the high priest Johanan by Josephus. *Antiquities* 11.297–301 recounts that Johanan killed his brother Joshua (Jesus) in the temple because the latter was conspiring to seize the high-priestly office. This crime motivated Joshua's supporter Bagoas (Bagoses) to enter the temple and to impose a crippling fine on animal sacrifices for seven years. The high priesthood had already become an object of politics, an ominous foretaste of future developments. Josephus identifies this Bagoas as a general of Artaxerxes II. He should not be confused with the later Bagoas who played the role of kingmaker in the waning days of the empire (see §§5.6.4 and 5.6.5).

A solid reconstruction of a governor list for Samaria is not possible, given the state of the evidence. Sanballat I was succeeded by Delaiah, who with his brother Shelemiah was addressed in the Elephantine correspondence. This brings matters down to near the beginning of the fourth century. The Wadi ed-Daliyeh papyri reveal a Sanballat II, perhaps the son of Delaiah, before the middle of the fourth century. He was perhaps succeeded by his son Isaiah (or Jeshua) and definitely by another son Hananiah (mid-fourth century). If credence can be given to Josephus's story of the foundation of the Samaritan temple (*Ant.* 11.302–311, 321–325, 340–346), then yet another Sanballat, Sanballat III, must be proposed as governing in the time of Darius III and Alexander. Josephus confused him with Sanballat I.

5.6.2. Darius II (423–405)

The son of Artaxerxes I, Xerxes II, was assassinated after a rule of forty-five days by his half-brother Sogdianus, son of a concubine. Sogdianus reigned briefly and was killed in turn by another son of a concubine, his half-brother Ochos, who reigned as Darius II Nothus. The Peloponnesian War (431–404), between Sparta and Athens, gave Darius a chance to regain control of the Ionian cities. After the disastrous reverse suffered by Athens in Syracuse in 413, he began sending financial support to Sparta. Athens ultimately lost the war soon after the death of Darius II.

5.6.3. Elephantine Papyri

The Elephantine papyri offer insight into the life of a garrison of Jews at a military settlement on the island of Yeb (Elephantine). The collection dates from 495 to 399. This community had its own temple for Yahu, referred to as "god in the fortress of Yeb" and "Lord of heaven." At the same other divinities or hypostases of the divine are named in various documents, such as Anat and Bethel (together with Herem-Bethel). The Jedaniah archives show that donations to the temple were given for the service of Yahweh, Eshem-Bethel, and Anat-Bethel. Particularly important documents from this archive are a letter of instructions about observing Passover, two drafts of a petition to rebuild the destroyed temple of Yahu, and the official response to that request (*ANET*, 491–92; *COS* 3.46–53:116–32). In addition, private letters, contracts, conveyances, and two family archives illustrate social and legal situations. The contracts archive of Mibtahiah, a rich Jewish woman who owned substantial real estate and at least four slaves, is especially illuminating. (*COS* 3.59–68:141–67). The archive of the family of the temple official Ananiah contains incidental references to construction that led to the clash between Jews and native Egyptians and the reconstruction of the Jewish temple (*COS* 3.69–81:168–98). In addition, Egyptian Aramaic ostraca letters from the Elephantine area, dated to about 475, are addressed to men and women with Jewish names. These mention Yahweh (Yaho), Passover, Sabbath, a *marzeaḥ* funerary banquet (cf. Jer 16:5), and the Elephantine temple (*COS* 3.87A–K:207–17).

In 419, a certain Hananiah (about whom nothing else is known) wrote to the Jewish leader Jedaniah and the Elephantine garrison to give instructions on how to celebrate Passover. Some of these instructions follow Exod 12:6, 15–20; 13:7, but others find no parallel in biblical texts. The concluding motivation line, "as King Darius commanded," indicates some level of Persian support for or interest in Jewish religious activities. Imperial support may have been intended to suppress native Egyptian opposition to Jewish rites. The Passover sacrifice itself is not mentioned, leaving open the question of whether slaughtering the Passover animal was performed in Egypt or was reserved for the Jerusalem temple. In the latter case, only the unleavened-bread portion of the ceremony could have been observed by Egyptian Jews. An ostracon associated with the Elephantine community implies that Passover was celebrated at home (*COS* 3.87A:208).

Egyptian nativist opposition to Jewish ritual came to a head with the destruction of the Yeb temple in 410 by mob action that involved Egyptian priests and was supported by the local administrator, Vidranga. The satrap Arsames was absent from Egypt at this time, having been recalled to deal with revolts against Darius II in Syria, Media, and Asia Minor. A letter of Arsames that mentions this rebellion has survived (*ANET*, 633). A few years later, in 407, Jedaniah and the Jewish priests petitioned Bagohi (Bagoas), governor of Yehud, for permission to rebuild. The petitioners claim that the Yeb temple had already been in existence when Cambyses came to Egypt and that he had let it continue. They describe an impressive building with stone pillars and gates and a cedar roof. The offering of meal offerings, incense, and burnt offerings have ceased, they say, but if official permission to rebuild is given, these sacrifices will begin again in the name of (for the benefit of?) Bagohi. The authors also refer to an earlier communication they had sent to Bagohi, to Johanan the high priest in Jerusalem, and to Avastana the brother of Anani. Anani is the last Davidic descendent listed in 1 Chr 3:24. This letter was never answered. The petitioners indicate that they are sending a parallel appeal to Delaiah and Shelemiah, the sons of Sanballat.

Delaiah and Bagoas granted permission to rebuild the destroyed temple. This is recorded in a memorandum of their oral agreement, which was apparently reported by a messenger. They authorized incense and meal offerings. However, they remained silent on the topic of the animal sacrifices that had been alluded to in the petition letter. This silence suggests that such offerings were not to be continued, either out of deference to the privileges of the Jerusalem temple or to placate offended native Egyptians. The proscription of animal sacrifices is explicitly confirmed in another Elephantine document (*COS* 3.53:131–32).

Since Delaiah and Bagoas responded jointly, apparently relations between Yehud and Samaria were friendly at this time, at least on the level of their respective governments. It is significant that this Jewish expatriate community looked to Jerusalem for guidance, but also that the guidance of the emerging Torah is never referred to by any of the parties. The divine names or hypostases (Bethel, Anat) mentioned in Elephantine documents indicate an imperfect understanding of monotheism on the part of these Egyptian Jews. Moreover, they are practicing sacrifice at their own temple. Yet Deuteronomy's insistence on strict monotheism and a centralization of sacrifice played absolutely no role in the discussion. Apparently Torah was not considered to be authoritative in the sense that it would later be, at least outside of Babylon. The scope and effectiveness of the mission of Ezra to promulgate divine law must be evaluated in light of this reality. The Elephantine community was continuing concepts and practices characteristic of Yahweh religion in the monarchic period, apparently unimpeded by the reform literature that had been produced by the Deuteronomists and the Priestly writers.

5.6.4. Artaxerxes II to Artaxerxes IV

The eldest son of Darius II, Artaxerxes II Memnon (404–359), immediately faced a civil war with his brother Cyrus the Younger, satrap of Lydia. Cyrus used Greek mercenaries in large numbers, as is famously illustrated by Xenophon's *Anabasis*. Cyrus was killed in 401 at Cunaxa north of Babylon. Ten thousand Greek mercenaries employed by him had to march through hostile territory to reach the Black Sea. Supposedly the dramatic account of this heroic feat by Xenophon would later convince Alexander that Persia was a suitable target for conquest.

Just before or while Artaxerxes II was disputing the throne with Cyrus, Egypt became independent under Amyrtaeus (404–399), the only pharaoh of the Twenty-Eighth Dynasty. The pharaohs of the Twenty-Ninth and Thirtieth Dynasties, the most notable of whom was Hakor (393–380), were hostile to Persian interests. Egypt interfered with Persian domination along the coast of Palestine and Phoenicia and even occupied Tyre and Sidon for a period. The defeat of Athens in the Peloponnesian War in 404 resulted in Persia's supporting Athens against Sparta and adjudicating disputes between Greek cities. In 386 Artaxerxes II was able to dictate the King's Peace with Greece (also called the Peace of Antalkidas after the Spartan diplomat who negotiated it). The Greeks were not to form alliances and were to recognize Persian control of the Ionian cities. This agreement would hold until 376. Artaxerxes had to put down a rebellion by Sardis in 382–381. Successive revolts by several satraps occurred between 372 and in 360.

Artaxerxes III Ochos (358–338) succeeded to the throne after his older brother had been executed for treason by his father and another brother had been tricked into committing suicide. Sidon led a revolt of Phoenician cities from about 350 until 345, inspired by the failure of a Persian offensive against Egypt in 353. Sidon under its king Tennes was brutally sacked, probably in 346, as a preliminary to the reconquest of Egypt by the Persian chief eunuch Bagoas. Artaxerxes III was thus finally able to reconquer Egypt in 343, after sixty years of Egyptian independence and numerous Persian defeats. This brought native Egyptian rule to a decisive end. He, Artaxerxes IV (Arses), and Darius III are considered to be the Thirty-First Dynasty. Nothing is known about what impact this protracted struggle to regain Egypt may have had on Yehud.

Artaxerxes III and all his sons except one were poisoned by this same Bagoas. When the new king Artaxerxes IV (also known as Arses; 337–336) tried to act independently, Bagoas eliminated him as well. About this time Philip II of Macedon (359–336) had succeeded in uniting the Greek city-states through his victory at Chaeronea (338). This laid the groundwork for the triumphs of his son Alexander.

5.6.5. Darius III (335–331)

Darius III Codomanus came to the throne through the scheming of Bagoas. He was a cousin of Artaxerxes IV on his mother's side and descended from Darius II on his father's side through a collateral branch. Bagoas tried to poison him as well. The plot was discovered, and Bagoas had to drink the poison himself.

The Persian central government was slow to react to the threat represented by Alexander of Macedon and expected the satraps of Asia Minor deal with it. It was only after their defeat at the River Granicus in 334 that Darius mobilized all the forces at his command. Darius was defeated by Alexander in 333 in the battle of Issus. After a second defeat in 331 at Gaugamela, Darius was able to escape with a remnant of his force. By 331, however, Alexander had conquered the principal Persian power centers. Darius III was murdered by a nephew, Bessos, satrap of Bactria, who briefly styled himself Artaxerxes V (330–329). He was executed by Alexander.

5.7. Literature of the Period

5.7.1. Persian-Period Prophets

5.7.1.1. Haggai

Haggai records oracles delivered during the initial months of rebuilding the Jerusalem temple, culminating with the day that the foundation of the Lord's temple was laid. Each oracle is dated by the day and month of Darius's year 2 (520). The oracle in chapter 1 calls for the temple project to commence and provides motivation by citing the sorry economic state of the people. The second oracle is dated about a month later and encourages Zerubbabel, Joshua the high priest, and the people. The newly refounded temple will initiate a time of peace and prosperity. The final two oracles were delivered on the festival day when the foundation stone was laid. The first addresses purity concerns about the new ritual. The second speaks of an eschatological future in which Yahweh will rule universally through a Davidic ruler. Hope is directed at Zerubbabel as David's heir, using traditional royal language: "my servant," "signet ring," and "chosen" (2:23).

5.7.1.2. Zechariah 1–8

The oracles in Zech 1–8 are applicable to the time of the reconstruction of the temple and are contemporary with the activity of Haggai. The first six chapters of Zechariah record eight night visions. An angel serves as the prophet's interlocutor, explaining the meaning of what the prophet sees.

- Patrolling riders: God's zeal for the people is certain.
- Horns: The nations will be scattered.
- Measuring line: Jerusalem is protected by a wall of fire.
- Cleansing of the high priest: Any impurity that Joshua has owing to his birth in Babylon is removed, so that the restored sacrificial system can be acceptable and effective.
- Lampstand: Joshua and Zerubbabel are two olive trees that supply oil for a symbolic lamp. Priest and secular ruler are partners in rule and sources for blessing and prosperity.
- Flying scroll: A huge curse document brings doom on wrong-doers.

- Woman in a measuring basket: She is carried to Babylon by two stork-winged women, indicating that the wickedness of the people is removed.
- Chariots: Yahweh controls all nations.

In chapter 6, Zechariah is told to have a symbolic crown prepared for Joshua, who in this fashion points toward Zerubbabel as his partner in rule. This section was redacted to take into account Zerubbabel's eventual disappearance from the scene. Chapters 7 and 8 warn that fasting cannot turn into feasting until the people's behavior changes.

5.7.1.3. Third Isaiah

The collection of prophetic poetry in Isa 56–66 is conventionally termed Third Isaiah, although it is unlikely that all the chapters stem from a single individual. The temple either is under construction or completed (Isa 66:1), so the material should be dated to the years after 520. Jerusalem's society was marred by disagreement about who should make up the temple community and the threat of private cult practices. Much of the community suffered from poverty and economic oppression. Third Isaiah sharply distinguishes the party it represents from those it considers to be in error. The temple community should move past its exclusiveness and welcome any foreigners and eunuchs who are committed to the covenant. The future holds God's promise of prosperity and universal esteem for the audience.

5.7.1.4. Zechariah 9–14

Zechariah 9–11 and 12–14 are often termed Second Zechariah in biblical scholarship and dated to the fifth century. There are no references to specific incidents beyond the enigmatic "shepherds" of chapter 11. However, the two sections, each of which begins with the same heading that introduces Malachi, are late enough to display characteristics of the emerging literature of apocalyptic. The present is a time of tribulation, but the dramatic coming victory of the day of Yahweh will transform the world. Zechariah 9:13 speaks of war between the Greeks and the sons of Zion. Second Zechariah gives evidence of being a late composition, alluding to earlier biblical traditions and texts, including the Pentateuch, Psalms, Hosea, Isaiah, Jeremiah, and Ezekiel. Nevertheless, the redactional shape of Zechariah had been stabilized by the time of the LXX translation. This suggests either a late Persian- or early Ptolemaic-period origin.

5.7.1.5. Malachi

Malachi's concerns over what are considered to be irregularities in the temple ritual and intermarriage with foreign families indicate a date after 515 and before or contemporary with the missions of Ezra and Nehemiah. The book represents the last of three supplements to Zech 1–8, along with Zech 9–11 and 12–14. Each of these units is introduced by the same formula: "an oracle, the word of Yahweh." Blemished animals are being used in sacrifice (1:6–14). There are disorderly offerings and deceptions (3:7–12). Marriages are being contracted with foreign women (2:10–12), while proper matches are being set aside (vv. 13–16). Eschatology provides assurance to the faithful righteous, who will be rewarded on the coming "day" and will rout the wicked. Final references to the contents of Deuteronomy and to Elijah (3:22-23 [EV 4:4–5]) indicate knowledge of and respect for the emerging canon of at least the last book of the Pentateuch and the Former Prophets.

5.7.1.6. Joel

Given its eschatological outlook and its dependence on other biblical texts, Joel should be dated to either the late Persian or Hellenistic periods. Joel uses Hebrew syntax and expressions considered to be late, evidences numerous Aramaisms, refers to the wall of Jerusalem (and is thus later than 445), and speaks of Greeks. Intertextuality with other prophetic texts also suggests a late date. For example, Joel 4:10 (EV 3:10) reverses the imperative of Isa 2:4 and Mic 4:3. Joel cites or alludes to Exod 34:6; Hos 9:2; Amos 1:2; 9:13; and Obad 17–18. The book is a call to repentance in the face of a generic calamity described in terms of an invading army of locusts and drought. "Return to Yahweh your God … who knows whether he will not turn and relent" (Joel 2:13–14).

5.7.2. Fictional Novellas

5.7.2.1. Ruth

Ruth is difficult to date. On the one hand, it reflects the old kinship-based social system in which clan responsibilities for the welfare of its members are prominent and legal matters are in the hands of village elders. On the other hand, Ruth contributes a tolerant view to the controversial issue of the assimilation of foreigners into Judah or the Jewish people. This, along with the book's concern over the continuity of the Davidic dynasty, suggests a date in the Persian period. Unlike the situation in the Hellenistic tales of Esther, Tobit, and Judith, in Ruth Jewish existence or the Jewish way of life is not under threat. Instead Ruth describes an established culture that is being urged to welcome the alien into its social system (cf. §5.7.1.3).

5.7.2.2. Jonah

The date of the composition of the deeply ironic short story about the unwilling prophet Jonah is impossible to determine. Its topic is the place of non-Jews in Yahweh's regard, which was an important issue in both the Persian and Hellenistic periods. The sailors display more religious devotion than Jonah does. Yahweh annuls the word of judgment that Jonah had been given to proclaim and absolves the people of Nineveh after their exemplary repentance. It cannot be later than the second century in light of the reference in Sir 49:10 to the book of the Twelve. The psalm that makes up chapter 2 was borrowed to fit Jonah's dilemma and is similar to canonical laments.

5.7.3. Historiography

5.7.3.1. Ezra-Nehemiah

Ezra-Nehemiah is a single book in the Jewish canonical tradition. It depicts the struggles of the first generations of returned exiles to revive their religious and community life. There are three acts. Sheshbazzar and Zerubbabel rebuild the temple at the instigation of Cyrus (Ezra 1–6). Artaxerxes commissions Ezra to create a purified community through promulgating divine law (Ezra 7–10; Neh 8–10). This same Artaxerxes appoints Nehemiah as governor to rebuild Jerusalem and its wall (Neh 1–7; 11–13). The work's complexity reflects its use of sources, some genuine, some fictional (see §5.3). It was directed about 400 to a Jerusalem community that was characterized by frustrated expectations, poverty, and internal dissension. The community experienced hostility from its neighbors. Ezra-Nehemiah declares a word of legitimacy, divine election, and exclusiveness.

In addition to the question of the genuineness of its sources, Ezra-Nehemiah presents two major challenges as a historical source. The first is a chronological gap of over fifty years between the completion of the temple at the end of Ezra 6 and the start of Ezra's mission in Ezra 7. The second is that the work overlaps the careers of Ezra and Nehemiah, when in fact they did not do so.

5.7.3.2. Chronicles

Chronicles retells the history of the Judahite monarchy from the perspective of the Second Temple community. Based on its ideology, scholars date Chronicles after Ezra-Nehemiah, in the first half or near the middle of the fourth century. Chronicles displays a more open attitude toward northern Yahwists than Ezra-Nehemiah does. The Chronicler used the books of Samuel and Kings as sources, modifying them to present a version of events more in line with the needs and theology of its audience. There are also frequent quotations and allusions to the Pentateuch and prophets. First Chronicles 16 and 2 Chronicles 6 reproduce selections from the book of Psalms when describing the transfer of the ark to Jerusalem and the dedication of the temple. One of these excerpts includes the blessing formula used to round off book 4 in the present canonical shape of Psalms (1 Chr 16:36; cf. Ps 106:36).

Stories of the monarchy period are converted into illustrations of the author's theological principles, and speeches and prayers are added to express these opinions. Themes include joyful and correct worship, God's promise to David, the holiness of the temple, and the distinctive roles of Levites and priests. The so-called doctrine of retribution is applied in an almost robotic fashion. The disobedient suffer, and the pious are rewarded. Chronicles reaches back to Adam to initiate the story of Israel against a universal backdrop and ends on a positive note with Cyrus's permission for the exiles to return home and reconstruct the temple.

5.7.4. Holiness Code

Leviticus 17–26 is a distinct collection of laws within the Pentateuch, closely related to the legal portions of the Priestly writing. The modern designation Holiness Code (H) stems from its repeated directive "You shall be holy, for I the Lord, your God, am holy" (e.g., Lev 19:2; 20:7-8, 26; 21:8, 23; 22:9, 16, 32). Yahweh's demand for holiness not only is about sacred persons, objects, and buildings but also extends to the land and to the whole people. Holiness is achieved by obedience to the laws set forth by God concerning social safeguards, justice, incest, idols, the festival calendar, and Sabbath rest for the land. The date of H in relation to the Priestly writing is disputed, with some scholars considering it earlier than P and others seeing it as a subsequent development. Its strong emphasis on how the people are to act with respect to the land and of how their behavior affects the status of the land (e.g., 18:25, 28; 20:22; 26: 4, 20, 32-33) speaks for a postrestoration, Persian-period date.

5.7.5. Wisdom Literature

5.7.5.1. Proverbs

As a complex work incorporating a number of earlier collections of wisdom material, Proverbs came together over an extended period of time. Nine independent sections are indicated by superscriptions. Like Qoheleth and Wisdom of Solomon, the book was ascribed to Solomon as the conventional patron of wisdom (1 Kgs 4:29–31). The development and transmission of wisdom was a feature of both the governmental establishment and the family and village life of ordinary folk. One of these earlier collections (chapters 25–29) is labeled "These are also proverbs of Solomon that the men of King Hezekiah of Judah copied" (Prov 25:1). Other indications that the collection process began in the Judahite monarchy period are the book's numerous reference to wise behavior with reference to a king and the dependence of 22:17–24:22 on the Instruction of Amenemope. This circumstance points to a time of intellectual interaction with Egypt. The extant textual witnesses to the Egyptian source range in date from the eleventh to the sixth century. The collection process probably came to a close during the Persian period, when chapters 1–9 were added at the beginning.

5.7.5.2. Job

This classic exploration of the issue of theodicy evidences a wide variety of theological perspectives as uttered by its characters, including God. At the end, God declares that those humans who have weighed in on the question in an orthodox fashion "have not spoken about me what is right, as my servant Job has" (Job 42:7, 8). One of Job's dogged convictions is that even if he were permitted to address his complaints directly to God as Job requests (7:7–21; 10:1–17; 13:20–28; 30:20–31; 31:35–37), God would provide no real answers but simply overwhelm him with divine omnipotence and vehemence (9:1–20, 32–33; 13:15; cf. 33:13). In this Job proves correct when God answers him out of the whirlwind (38:1–39:30; 40:6–41:26 [EV 40:6–41:34]).

Job follows a venerable tradition of similar literary works—beginning already in the Sumerian, Old Babylonian, and Egyptian Middle Kingdom eras—that explore the questions of undeserved suffering and the apparent failure of divine justice (e.g., *ANET*, 407–10, 589–91, 596–604; *COS* 1.43:98–104, 1.153:486–92, 1.154:492–95, 1.179:573–75). By its very nature, the book is essentially undatable. It is clearly a composite text, as evidenced by the dissonance between the enveloping prose folktale (1:1–2:13 and 42:7–17), and the core poetic dialogues and by the unexpected appearance of Elihu in chapters 32–37. Most scholars suggest the Babylonian or Persian periods, because the destruction of national life in the events of 597 and 586 set in motion anxious assessments about suffering and God's justice.

5.7.6. Psalms

Conventionally termed "the hymnbook of the Second Temple," the canonical book of Psalms gathers together liturgical and personal songs from the monarchic and exilic period, along with those from the Persian epoch. Its organization into five books took place before the completion of 1 and 2 Chronicles (see §5.7.3.2) and the translation of the LXX. Evidence from Qumran, however, suggests that more than one redactional order of Psalms existed in the first century of the common era and that the shape of books 4 and 5 solidified later than that of books 1–3 did. Psalms shows evidences of earlier collections, such as the Psalms of David (Pss 3–41); the Elohistic Psalter (Pss 42–83, in which the divine name has been replaced by the generic designation God); and the Asaph/Korah collections (Pss 42–50; 73–88). Some psalms originated in the tradition of the northern kingdom, for example Pss 73–83. A few contain archaic-sounding language (e.g., Ps 29). Those that speak of the human king of Judah (2; 45; 72; 110) and the inviolability of Jerusalem (46; 48; 76) must have originated in the monarchy period. The trauma of exile is reflected in Pss 89 and 137. Most psalms simply provide no evidence for dating, and indeed knowing a date of origin would be unlikely to help interpreters in any case.

6. The Hellenistic Period (330–63)

Austin, Michael M. *The Hellenistic World from Alexander to the Roman Conquest: A Selection of Ancient Sources in Translation* (2nd ed.; Cambridge: Cambridge University Press, 2006). **Bagnall** Roger S., and Peter **Derow**, eds. *The Hellenistic Period: Historical Sources in Translation* (2nd ed.; Malden, Mass.: Blackwell, 2004). **Bedford**, Peter R. *Temple Restoration in Early Achaemenid Judah* (JSJSup 65; Leiden: Brill, 2001). **Chaney**, Mark. *The Myth of Gentile Galilee* (SNTSMS 118; Cambridge: Cambridge University Press, 2002). **Cohen**, Getzel M. *The Hellenistic Settlements in Syria, the Red Sea Basin, and North Africa* (Hellenistic Culture and Society 46; Berkeley: University of California Press, 2005). **Cohen**, Shaye J. D. *From the Maccabees to the Mishnah* (2nd ed.; Louisville: Westminster John Knox, 2006). **Collins**, John J. *Between Athens and Jerusalem: Jewish Identity in the Hellenistic Diaspora* (Grand Rapids: Eerdmans, 2000). **Collins**, Nina L. *The Library in Alexandria and the Bible in Greek* (VTSup 82; Leiden: Brill, 2000). **Eshel**, Hanan. *The Dead Sea Scrolls and the Hasmonean State* (Grand Rapids: Eerdmans, 2008). **Grabbe**, Lester L. *The Coming of the Greeks: The Early Hellenistic Period (335–175 BCE)* (vol. 2 of *A History of the Jews and Judaism in the Second Temple Period*; LSTS 68; London: T&T Clark, 2008). **Grainger**, J. D. *The Syrian Wars* (Mnemosyne Supplements 320; Leiden: Brill, 2010). **Heckel**, Waldemar. *The Conquests of Alexander the Great* (Cambridge: Cambridge University Press, 2008). **Heckel**. *Who's Who in the Age of Alexander the Great: Prosopography of Alexander's Empire* (Malden, Mass.: Blackwell, 2006). **Heckel**, Waldemar, and J. C. **Yardley**. *Alexander the Great: Historical Texts in Translation* (Malden, Mass.: Blackwell, 2004). **Hjelm**, Ingrid. *Jerusalem's Rise to Sovereignty: Zion and Gerizim in Competition* (JSOTSup 404; London: T&T Clark, 2004). **Hölbl**, Günther. *A History of the Ptolemaic Empire* (London:

Routledge, 2001). **Magness**, Jodi. *The Archaeology of Qumran and the Dead Sea Scrolls* (Malden, Mass.: Blackwell, 2002). **Nickelsburg**, George W. E. *Jewish Literature between the Bible and the Mishnah: A Historical and Literary Introduction* (2nd ed.; Minneapolis: Fortress, 2005). **Rajak**, Tessa. *Josephus: The Historian and His Society* (2nd ed.; London: Duckworth, 2002). **Sacchi**, Paolo. *The History of the Second Temple Period* (JSOTSup 285; Sheffield: Sheffield Academic, 2000). **VanderKam**, James C. *An Introduction to Early Judaism* (Grand Rapids, Eerdmans, 2001).

6.0. Summary

Alexander conquered the venerable Persian Empire in a series of successful battles. After the death of Darius III, he continued his advance eastward to the verge of India, before returning west. After his premature death, his generals divided the territory under Macedonian control. The bulk of the Asian portion fell under the jurisdiction of the founder of the Seleucid Empire. Egypt and Palestine were ruled by the Ptolemaic line. Control of Palestine shifted from Egypt to Seleucid Syria after the victory of Antiochus III at the battle of Panias about 200. The expansionist ambitions of the Seleucid king Antiochus IV were frustrated, in part by resistance from Rome, which was then emerging as the dominant power in the eastern Mediterranean. For reasons that remain unclear, in 167 Antiochus ordered an unprecedented persecution of the Jewish religion that included bans on Jewish religious practices, attempts to force pagan behaviors on the faithful, and a takeover of the temple ritual.

An insurgency, triggered by the patriarch of a rural priestly family and commanded by three of his sons in turn, eventually succeeded in returning the temple cult to orthodoxy, protecting beleaguered Jews in various corners of the region and expanding independent Jewish control into Galilee, Transjordan, and Idumea. The movement was first led by Judas, whose epithet "the Maccabee" branded the revolt. Seleucid interference in the succession of the high priests had begun with Antiochus IV and continued until Jonathan, a brother of Judas, occupied the office. He was followed by his brother Simon. John Hyrcanus, Simon's son, succeeded to secular and religious leadership and initiated the Hasmonean dynasty. Aristobulus I, one of Hyrcanus's sons, was the first Hasmonean to acquire the title king.

The Maccabees and their Hasmonean descendants negotiated the perilous complexities of the political affairs of the decaying Ptolemaic and Seleucid dynasties with varying levels of success. However, for the most part they were able to preserve Jewish independence. The situation changed decisively when the Roman general Pompey arrived in the eastern Mediterranean to organize matters for Rome. When appealed to by various Jewish factions, Pompey intervened directly in Jewish affairs. He entered Jerusalem and its temple in 63 and arranged the political situation in ways he considered advantageous to Rome. Pompey made the Idumean Antipater, who had played the role of kingmaker in the disputed Hasmonean succession, the effective ruler of Jewish affairs in Palestine. A dependable supporter of Roman interests, Antipater was made procurator by Julius Caesar in 47. His descendants would dominate Palestinian politics for several generations, beginning with his son Herod the Great.

6.1. Alexander the Great (336–323)

Sources for the career of Alexander are abundant (Arrian, Plutarch, Diodorus, Curtius Rufus), but all are written from the perspective of the Hellenistic world. For this reason, the historian must be careful not to read Alexander through a romantic, heroic, or Eurocentric lens. It is obvious today that past interpretations of Alexander were often dominated by a template of triumphant European civilization in conflict with eastern barbarism. Such histories were colored by Orientalism, the European and North American penchant for constructing Arab and Islamic culture as a negative inversion of Western culture. Orientalism can be seen to permeate nineteenth- and twentieth-century art and literature throughout the West. This misperception was classically delineated by Edward Said (*Orientalism* [New York: Vintage, 1979]). The charge that such depictions of Alexander provided an implicit justification for colonialist expansion can hardly be denied.

Under the assertive rule of Alexander's father Philip, Macedon had developed into a centralized territorial state that could support wide-ranging military campaigns. The tactic of the infantry phalanx, maneuverable even in rough terrain and defended on its flanks by the Macedonian cavalry, provided Alexander military superiority over much larger Persian armies.

6.1.1. Alexander's Triumphs

Alexander crossed over into Asia Minor in 334, winning an initial victory at the Granicus River. He then successfully moved against Sardis, Miletus, and Halicarnassus. He progressed along the south coast to Pamphylia, then north inland to Gordium, the capital of Phrygia, and then on to Ancyra. He marched southeast through the pass of the Cilician Gates to Tarsus. Darius III (see §5.6.5) slipped in behind him at Issus in northwestern Syria, but Alexander quickly responded. A cavalry strike from his right flank angled against the Persian center routed the huge Persian army (333). Darius escaped, but Alexander was able to capture the supply train, including Darius's mother, wife, and daughters. Alexander then moved south through Syria and the Phoenician coastal cities in order to secure his seaborne supply lines by capturing the bases used by naval fleets loyal to Darius. Byblos, Sidon, and Acco surrendered. Tyre, located on an island and supported by its North African colonies (notably Carthage), required a seven-month siege and did not fall until July 332. Gaza, the last obstacle to an invasion into Egypt, also offered resistance. After a siege of two months, the city was taken and subjected to memorable atrocities in September. Alexander spent the winter of 332–331 in Egypt, where he established the city of Alexandria and was declared the son of Amun by the oracle at Siwa in the Libyan desert. His coinage sometimes depicted his claim to divinity by way of an image bearing the horns of a ram.

Returning north, Alexander crossed the Euphrates and Tigris and defeated Darius conclusively at Gaugamela near the ruined city of Nineveh (331). Charging Persian chariots were not able to break up the Macedonian phalanxes. These were so well trained that they could open up gaps to let the chariots pass through and then close up again. Once again, Alexander personally led a cavalry charge that broke the center of the Persian line. Darius fled. Alexander secured the Persian capitals in turn: Babylon, Susa, Ecbatana, and Pasargadae. His troops burned Persepolis, the empire's ceremonial capital. As Alexander was closing in on the Persian king south of the Caspian Sea, Darius was killed by one of his satraps. His assassin briefly claimed the kingship as Artaxerxes V (330–329). He was executed by Alexander. After campaigning eastward as far as India, the indefatigable Alexander died in Babylon in June 323 at the age of thirty-two. Perhaps he died of a fever; perhaps he was poisoned.

Alexander repeated the successful Persian policy of promoting native cults and claiming legitimacy through them. Arranging a magnanimous funeral, he buried the body of Darius beside his Achaemenid predecessors, claiming that Darius had named him as his successor. In a public-relations coup, he staged a mass wedding in Susa in 324 during which his senior generals took Persian wives. At this event, in order further to support his claim to the throne, Alexander married both Stateira daughter of Darius III and Parysatis daughter of Artaxerxes III. He was already married to the Bactrian princess Roxana, who after his death would bear his legitimate heir, Alexander IV Aegus.

In addition to Alexandria in Egypt, he founded or repopulated other cities at strategic locations. The coinage of large amounts of specie from captured Persian treasuries led to inflation, but doubtlessly also facilitated an increase in trade and commerce. The assets of the Persian government supposedly totaled 180,000 talents of gold.

6.1.2. Alexander and Palestine

There is hardly any trustworthy information about events in Judea during Alexander's marches south (332) and then north (331) along the coast of Palestine. Although Josephus claims that after the conquest of Gaza Alexander visited Jerusalem and met with the high priest Jaddua, this is clearly legendary (*Ant.* 11.325–339). Alexander had supposedly once dreamed of a man in robes like those of Jaddua and so showed significant honor to the high priest and the God of the Jews, sponsoring a sacrifice in the temple. Shown prophecies in Daniel (presumably 8:21) that were interpreted as predictions of his victory, Alexander granted special favors to Judea and the Jews of Babylon. Equally untrustworthy is the Talmud's anachronistic tale of a meeting with Simon the Just at Antipatris (b. Yoma 69a). Alexander would have had no reason to deviate from his prime objective, Egypt, by leaving the coastal plain to detour inland.

Samaria, in contrast to Judea, was seriously affected by the arrival of Alexander's forces. Josephus says that Sanballat sent troops to aid Alexander at Tyre (*Ant.* 11.321–325). According to Curtius Rufus, Alexander's general Parmenion appointed one Andromachus to be governor of Coele-Syria, which meant a reduction in Samaria's status. When Alexander was in Egypt, Samaria rebelled in reaction to this change and killed Andromachus by burning him alive (331). Alexander put down the rebellion and destroyed Samaria. Either he or his deputy Perdiccas settled it with Macedonian veterans. Skeletons found in a cave at Wadi-ed-Daliyeh north of Jericho along with the Samaria papyri are commonly understood to be those of refugees from this rebellion who were smothered by fire. These Samaria papyri consist of business documents, contracts, and title deeds from 375 to 335, written in Aramaic. One interesting revelation is that slaves could be sold for life, in violation of the Torah. The vast majority of names are Yahwistic, indicating that Yahweh was (at least) the principal deity worshiped.

Because of the destruction of Samaria and its reestablishment as a Greek city, the cultural and religious hub of the northern Yahwists moved to Shechem. It is possible that the Gerizim sanctuary was built at this time. Josephus (*Ant.* 11.302–312, 321–325) tells the story of Manasseh, the brother of the high priest Jaddua. He was reluctant to divorce his wife Nikaso the daughter of Sanballat, and was in danger of losing his priestly office owing to pressure from rigorists who objected to his marriage. His father-in-law Sanballat offered to build a temple for him on Mount Gerizim, where he could serve as high priest. Although Jaddua remained loyal to Darius, Sanballat wisely defected to Alexander's side, providing him with troops for the assault on Tyre. Alexander gave Sanballat permission to build the temple in return for his assistance with the siege of Tyre. Sanballat soon died. This tale is generally discounted by those who point out that the divorce story is a version of Neh 13:28.

The archaeology of Mount Gerizim has been interpreted to date the initial foundation of the Samaritan temple in the middle of the fifth century, with a second and larger building superimposed on it at the start of the second century. In any case, it seems that the erection of a competing temple would not necessarily result in an unbridgeable break between the Yahwists in Judea and those in Samaria. The moderate reaction of the Jerusalem authorities to the temples at Elephantine and (later) Leontopolis and the multiple nonjudgmental references to them in Josephus indicate that there was still a good deal of open-mindedness with respect to sacrificial cults outside Jerusalem. A remarkable level of tolerance to the Leontopolis temple is also indicated in the nuanced judgment of m. Menaḥ. 13:10, which allows the vow of an offering to be made in the house of Onias to be fulfilled by sacrifice there.

6.1.3. Hellenistic High Priests

The succession of high priests in the Hellenistic period is well established. However, it is often suggested that names from the earlier Persian period may have dropped out of the sources because of a supposed practice of papponymy (naming a son after his father or grandfather). Jaddua's father Johanan was active in 410 (as evidenced by the Elephantine letters). It is certainly possible, if Johanan was quite young in 410, that Jaddua could have still been high priest in 332. However, this does require two successive tenures that add up to about eighty years. The Hellenistic-period high priests were as follows:

- Jaddua (contemporary of Alexander)
- Onias I (supposedly contemporary of Areus I of Sparta [309–265])
- Simon I his son (Josephus erroneously calls him Simon the Just)
- Eleazar his brother (contemporary of Ptolemy II [283–246])
- Manasseh, uncle of Eleazar
- Onias II, son of Simon I (contemporary of Ptolemy III [246–221])
- Simon II, son of Onias II (contemporary of Ptolemy IV [221–204]; probably Simon the Just)
- Onias III, son of Simon II (deposed in 175)
- Jason (175–172), brother of Onias III, who bribed Antiochus IV to buy his office
- Menelaus (172–162) who outbid Jason in bribing Antiochus IV
- [Onias IV, perhaps the legitimate heir of Onias III, claimed the office after his father's death in 170]
- Alcimus (162–160/159)
- Jonathan (152–142), son of Mattathias
- Simon III (142–134), last surviving brother of Jonathan
- John Hyrcanus I (134–104), son of Simon
- Aristobulus I (104–103), son of John Hyrcanus
- Alexander Jannaeus (103–76), brother of Aristobulus
- Hyrcanus II (76–67 and 63–40)
- Aristobulus II (67–63)

6.2. The Successors of Alexander

The convoluted history of this period rests on numerous classical sources, including Diodorus, Appaianus, Plutarch, Justin, and Polybius, as well as Josephus.

Alexander's potential heirs were a posthumous son and a mentally deficient brother. Therefore, his senior generals, termed the Diodochi (Greek via Latin: "successors"), maneuvered to divide his empire. After a complex sequence of battles and conspiracies, their rivalry reached a point of relative equilibrium around 275. The former territory of Alexander was distributed among three competing dynastic kingdoms: the Antigonids (Macedonia and Greece), the Seleucids (Syria, Mesopotamia, and farther east), and the Ptolemies (Egypt and, until 198, Palestine).

For the first two decades after Alexander's death, Palestine was often the site of struggles between Alexander's successors. Ptolemy I occupied Palestine in a coordinated land and sea operation in 320. About 317, Antigonus Monophthalmus invaded southward and captured the coastal cities. A complex back-and-forth struggle ensued from 315 to 301. Antigonus handed over command to his son Demetrius Poliorketes ("the city digger"). He was defeated in battle by Ptolemy I and Seleucus I, fighting together at Gaza in 312. Josephus (*Ag. Ap.* 1.186–189, following Hecataeus of Abdera) says that many Jews left Palestine for Egypt in this period, including the priest (but not high priest) Hezekiah, whose name may appear on a series of early Hellenistic Yehud coins. The Seleucid-era chronology (used in 1 and 2 Maccabees) begins with the recapture of Babylon by Seleucus I in 312.

6.2.1. Ptolemy I Soter (323–283)

In 301 Antigonus and Demetrius were decisively defeated by Ptolemy I and Seleucus I acting in concert at Ipsus in Phrygia. Although in the subsequent division of spoils, Palestine had been assigned to Seleucus, Ptolemy continued to hold on to it. In so doing, he was imitating the age-old Egyptian policy of controlling Palestine in order to use it as a military buffer and to exploit its trade routes. Even after Ipsus, Ptolemy had to consolidate his power in Palestine. Eusebius says Demetrius Poliorketes again devastated Samaria for a second time in 296, but this claim is widely doubted. According to Josephus (*Ant.* 12.4–7, following Letter of Aristeas

12–13), perhaps in 301 (but possibly in 312 after his victory at Gaza), Ptolemy moved into Jerusalem on a Sabbath. The Jews refused to fight on the holy day, and he took prisoners to Egypt, where they settled. The Ptolemies were able to hold Palestine until 200.

During the early stages of the struggles that led to Ptolemaic domination of Palestine, Onias I (Hebrew: Johanan) son of Jaddua became high priest (*Ant.* 11.347). First Maccabees and Josephus reproduce a fictive letter to Onias I from the Areus I the Spartan king (1 Macc 12:19–23; *Ant.* 12.226–227), although Josephus mistakenly connects it to Onias III. Onias I was succeeded by his son Simon I, whom Josephus confused with Simon the Just (*Ant.* 12.43, 157–158).

Ptolemy I founded a state that lasted almost three centuries. Its capital was Alexandria. Politically and as a matter of public relations, the Ptolemies legitimized themselves as successors of the pharaohs. They exercised centralized economic control over Egypt's rich agricultural production and thus created great wealth for themselves. A deep economic and class division separated the native Egyptians from the Greeks. In addition, the capital Alexandria was also home to a large Jewish population living in its own quarter.

In the Hellenistic period, Greek merchants and soldiers settled in cities along the Mediterranean coast of Palestine and east of the Jordan. Unsurprisingly, local elites adopted elements of prestigious Greek culture. Josephus reports that Jewish units served in the Ptolemaic army (*Ant.* 12.8). There were some changes in city names in this period: Acco became Ptolemais; Beth-shean, Scythopolis; and Rabbah in Ammon, Philadelphia (after Ptolemy II Philadelphus). Philoteria was founded somewhere southwest of the Sea of Galilee and named after a sister of Ptolemy II. Pella for a time was called Berenice after a Ptolemaic queen. The Seleucids would establish Antiochia near Panias and Seleucia in the Golan. Perhaps Greek colonists were a feature of these acts of foundation and refoundation. The Ptolemies administered Palestine through four hyparchies: Galilee, Samaria, Judea, and Idumea.

Jews lived scattered into both the Ptolemaic and Seleucid realms. In Egypt Jews were concentrated in Alexandria and in the Fayum oasis area. They staffed military colonies at Pelusium and Daphne at the northeastern border and Elephantine and Syene upriver to the south. Other Jews lived in Thebes, and large numbers of papyri witness to the presence of Jews throughout the country. In the Seleucid realm, the long-standing Jewish presence in Babylonia continued. There were also government-sponsored settlements of Jews in Caria, Pamphylia, and Phrygia, and other communities in Asia Minor and mainland Greece (see *Ant.* 12.148–153 and the list in 1 Macc 15:22–23).

6.2.2. The Six Syrian Wars

The course of the complex back-and-forth contest between the Ptolemies of Egypt and the Seleucids is summarized by scholarship into a succession of six so-called Syrian Wars:

- First Syrian War (274–271): Ptolemy I versus Antiochus I
- Second Syrian War (260–253): Ptolemy II versus Antiochus II
- Third Syrian War (246–241): Ptolemy III versus Seleucus II
- Fourth Syrian War (219–217): Ptolemy IV versus Antiochus III
- Fifth Syrian War (201–195): regents of Ptolemy V versus Antiochus III
- Sixth Syrian War (170–168): regents of Ptolemy VI versus Antiochus IV

Three military events are critical for understanding the history of the Jews in Palestine. First is the major Ptolemaic victory at the battle of Raphia (217). Second is the Syrian victory at Panias (200 or 198) that led to the transfer of Palestine to Seleucid control. Third is the conclusion of the Sixth Syrian War (168), the consequences of which eventually led to the start of the Maccabean revolt.

The incidents of the Syrian Wars are summarized in Dan 11:

- 11:5, Ptolemy I
- 11:6, Ptolemy II and Berenice
- 11:7–9, Ptolemy III and the Third Syrian War
- 11:10–12, the Fourth Syrian War
- 11:13–16, the Fifth Syrian War
- 11:17–19, further events involving Antiochus III
- 11:20 Seleucus IV
- 11:21–39, 40–45, Antiochus IV

6. THE HELLENISTIC PERIOD (330–63)

6.3. Palestine under the Ptolemies

6.3.1. Ptolemy II Philadelphus (283–246)

Ptolemy II contended with the Seleucids over control of Syria-Palestine in the First Syrian War (274–271) and Second Syrian War (260–246). The First Syrian War was a victory for Ptolemy. Antiochus I Soter (281–261) had captured areas in coastal Syria and southern Asia Minor, but Ptolemy reconquered these regions by 271 and then further extended his territorial control in Asia Minor. The Second Syrian War was begun by Antiochus II Theos (261–246), who had just succeeded his father. It was fought largely in Asia Minor. Hostilities were concluded around 253 with the diplomatic marriage of Antiochus to Ptolemy's daughter Berenice. To make this possible, Antiochus repudiated his first wife, Laodice. This act would lead later to problems in the Seleucid succession. Antiochus II died in Ephesus in 246, apparently poisoned by Laodice, who is also credited with the later murder of Berenice. Ptolemy's earlier defeat of the Nabateans (about 278) forced the trade routes from Arabia to pass through Gaza, where he could tax and control them. Ptolemy II and Antiochus II both died in the same year, 246, a circumstance that triggered the Third Syrian War.

The Zenon papyri represent the archives of a governmental official who toured Palestine about 259–258 on business connected with Ptolemaic taxing authority. These documents provide important insights into the Ptolemaic political and economic administration of Palestine. Zenon included Jerusalem, Jericho, the Transjordan, and Galilee in his itinerary. He left Palestine through Ptolemais. Significantly, he mentions one Tobias, who lived at the fortress of Ammonitis and who sent gifts to Zenon and his superior. This Tobias most likely had family connections to the much earlier Tobiah "the Ammonite servant," who was an opponent of Nehemiah. In any case, this Tobias represented a politically and economically powerful family (the Tobiads) that would support the Ptolemaic cause over the next century.

The Letter of Aristeas is another important source for this period. It reports that Ptolemy II released thousands of Jews who had been forcibly deported and enslaved by his father. He is also credited with sponsoring the translation of the Hebrew Bible into Greek. Although this legendary account is intended to demonstrate that the resulting Septuagint was inspired and authoritative, such an enterprise does not seem out of character with what we know of this king. It is reasonable to date the onset of the long translation process, which began with the books of the Torah, to about 250.

Eleazar the brother of Simon I succeeded him as high priest. He was contemporary to Ptolemy II and is referred to in the Letter of Aristeas. Perhaps Simon's son Onias was still too young to serve as high priest when his father died. Eleazar was succeeded first by his uncle Manasseh and only after the latter's death by Simon's son Onias II.

6.3.2. Ptolemy III Euergetes (246–221)

The first half of his reign was consumed by the Third Syrian War (246–241), which he began to avenge the murder of his sister Berenice, wife of Antiochus II. On the death of Antiochus II, Berenice had been deposed from her position in favor of the first wife of Antiochus II, Laodice. Laodice was the mother of the new Syrian king Seleucus II Callinicus (246–226). Laodice claimed that Antiochus had named her son as his heir while on his deathbed. Berenice asked her brother Ptolemy III, the new Ptolemaic king, to support the claims of her recently born son as the legitimate heir. By the time Ptolemy arrived in Syria, however, Berenice and her child had both been liquidated. Antioch and its port city Seleucia surrendered to Ptolemy. He then struck into Babylonia as far as the Euphrates but seems to have turned back at first, perhaps because of rumors of a rebellion at home. Nevertheless, Ptolemy regrouped and reached Babylon, according to the cuneiform Ptolemy III Chronicle. He laid siege to the city in early 245. However, he suffered a naval defeat at the hands of Antigonus II king of Macedon (319–239) in that same year. In the end, Seleucus II returned to power in Antioch. The peace treaty of 241 confirmed Ptolemy's possession of Syria-Palestine and awarded him Antioch's port city of Seleucia, which would be held by Egypt until 219. Josephus (*Ag. Ap.* 2.48) briefly recounts a legend that Ptolemy III visited the Jerusalem temple at this time and offered sacrifice.

The high priest Onias II is a major character in the tendentious Tobiad Romance. This work is reproduced by Josephus, but situated by him into the wrong period (*Ant.* 12.160–236). The beginning of this novelistic story is properly placed in the reign of Ptolemy III, not Ptolemy V as Josephus would have it. The high priest Onias II suspended tribute payments to Ptolemy, apparently in the context of the Third Syrian War, and the king sent a delegation to Jerusalem to coerce payment. By his move, Onias had sided with the Seleucids, and so his position was weakened when Ptolemy was able to retain control of Palestine. Onias was opposed by the pro-Ptolemaic Joseph son of Tobias, who gained political control and was able to marginalize the high priest and his party. This Joseph was a son of the Tobias mentioned in the Zenon papyri, and thus had his power base east of the Jordan. Joseph took advantage of the situation to become a successful (but harsh and murderous) tax farmer. The presence of this Transjordanian entrepreneur in Jerusalem shows that the city had by then become an important economic center. From this point on, there would be ongoing rivalry between the Tobiads, favorable to Hellenism, and the priestly Oniad family, headed in turn by Onias II, Simon II, Onias III, and Onias IV. The pro-Ptolemaic Tobiad family was able to navigate successfully the change from Ptolemaic to Seleucid rule after 198.

6.3.3. Ptolemy IV Philopator (221–204)

A Fourth Syrian War was fought between 219 and 217 between two youthful new kings who came to their respective thrones at almost the same time. Antiochus III Megas (223–187) had occupied the Seleucid throne at age twenty, after the brief reign of his brother Seleucus III Ceraunus (226–223) who had been poisoned. Antiochus III sought to recover territory previously held by the Seleucids. By 221 he had reestablished control over Media and Persia. His adversary Ptolemy IV became king at age seventeen. He began his reign by instigating the death of his mother, Berenice II. After an initial setback in 221, Antiochus initiated the Fourth Syrian War in 219. He advanced on Syria, seizing Seleucia, Tyre, and Ptolemais. Leaving an army besieging Dor, he then marched inland from Tyre to the Sea of Galilee, Scythopolis, and Pella, east of the Jordan. With aid from the Nabateans, he captured Philadelphia (Amman) by way of its water system.

Ptolemy's minister Sosibius recruited an army that for the first time supplemented Greek troops with native Egyptians. In summer 217, Ptolemy defeated Antiochus at Raphia on the Egyptian frontier. The two armies were reportedly immense. Ptolemy commanded 70,000 troops, 5,000 cavalry, and 73 elephants. Antiochus fielded 62,000 troops, 6,000 cavalry, and 102 elephants. This important victory preserved Ptolemaic control over Syria and Palestine. Ptolemy made triumphal visits to Joppa (according to preserved inscriptions) and perhaps Jerusalem (3 Macc 1:6–2:24). Subsequently, Ptolemaic Egypt suffered economic problems, and the well-trained native Egyptian troops who had fought at Raphia rebelled. These rebels established an independent kingdom in Upper Egypt.

Third Maccabees recounts legendary stories about Ptolemy IV's attempts to wreak vengeance on the Jews of Alexandria after he was miraculously barred from entering the Jerusalem temple after the battle of Raphia. He shut them into the stadium and turned elephants loose upon them. Two angels protected the Jews, and the enraged elephants turned on the king's soldiers.

6.4. Palestine under the Seleucids

6.4.1. Antiochus III Megas (222–187)

Ptolemy V Epiphanes (204–181) became king of Egypt at age five. Conflicts about control during the regency began with the murder of Ptolemy IV's wife and sister Arsinoë by Agothocles and Sosibius. Agothocles became regent until he was lynched by a mob in Alexandria. For a time the situation in Egypt descended into anarchy as regency passed from one official to another.

The Fifth Syrian War (201–195) began when the Seleucid Antiochus III (the Great) took advantage of chaos in the Ptolemaic government to invade Syria and Palestine in 201. He allied himself with Philip V of Macedon. The two kings sought to divide the Ptolemaic territories outside Egypt between them. Antiochus moved down the coast to Gaza, where he was held up by a protracted but ultimately successful siege. However, Antiochus had to pull back when the Ptolemaic general Scopas marched up through Palestine. Scopas occupied Jerusalem. In the winter of 201–200, he moved to the sources of the Jordan. The two armies met at Panias (Paneion, Banyas; later, Caesarea Philippi) in 200. The Ptolemaic forces were soundly defeated, and Scopas fled to Sidon. Antiochus then spent the next two years until 198 consolidating his gains in Coele-Syria. This concluded with the capture of Sidon after the siege described in Dan 11:15. The date of the decisive battle of Panias sometimes appears in the literature as 198, based on a different interpretation of the order of events derived from the primary sources.

Antiochus moved southward and was received warmly in Jerusalem, where the Tobiads had now become Seleucid supporters (Dan 11:14; *Ant.* 12.136). He renewed the privileges of Jerusalem and its temple in a decree (or two decrees) preserved (and creatively edited) by Josephus (*Ant.* 12.138–144). These benefits to Jerusalem included remissions and reductions in taxes, freedom to its citizens who had been enslaved, and support for the temple ritual and for some sort of temple construction project. Another decree prohibited foreigners from entering the temple (*Ant.* 12.145–146). The battle of Panias brought to an end a century of Ptolemaic control of Palestine and initiated thirty years of relatively uneventful Seleucid rule.

Rome, victorious in the Second Punic War, which ended in 201, was now able to turn its attention to the east. In 200, emissaries from Rome had demanded that Philip V of Macedon and Antiochus III not invade Egypt. Roman policy was directed at protecting the vital export of grain from Egypt on which Rome was increasingly dependent. Philip and Antiochus complied. In the Second Macedonian War, Rome defeated Philip in 197 at Cynoscephalae and confined him to his Macedonian kingdom. These circumstances forced Philip to become a Roman ally. Antiochus responded to this shift in power dynamics by subjugating parts of Asia Minor and then crossing into Europe in 196. This move presented a direct threat to Roman interests.

Ptolemy V, troubled by economic difficulties and the native Egyptian rebellion inherited from his father, signed an unfavorable treaty with Antiochus in 195, leaving the Seleucid king in possession of Syria-Palestine. Ptolemy agreed to marry Antiochus's daughter Cleopatra I (Dan 11:17). Nevertheless, when hostilities finally broke out between Antiochus and Rome, Ptolemy chose to side with the Romans. Warfare between Antiochus and Rome (dubbed the Roman-Syrian War) began in 192. Antiochus invaded mainland Greece (accompanied by Rome's old nemesis Hannibal), but was defeated at Thermopylae in 191. After another defeat in 190 in Magnesia, Antiochus pulled out of Asia Minor. He was forced to submit to the very disadvantageous peace of Apamea (188). Antiochus had to pay the Romans the huge sum of fifteen thousand silver talents and abandon his claims in Asia Minor. To ensure good behavior, his son (later to be Antiochus IV) was held hostage in Rome. Antiochus himself was killed while robbing a temple in Elam in an attempt to raise funds for this tribute (187; Dan 11:19).

Around 185 Ptolemy V was able to recapture the areas of Egypt held by native rebels. The Rosetta Stone (196), proclaiming a tax exemption to the Egyptian priesthood, seems to be connected to measures taken to put down this rebellion.

The degree of control exercised by the Seleucid administration in Palestine is illustrated by the Hefzibah Inscription, consisting of decrees and correspondence of Antiochus III (dated 201–195). These documents concern the economic situation of areas near Scythopolis (Beth-shean) that had been granted to high officials. Apparently the whole Jezreel Valley was held as a royal estate by the Seleucid crown and was later made over to the Hasmoneans (*Ant.* 14.207).

The son of Onias II succeeded to the high priesthood as Simon II (ca. 220–190). He was undoubtedly the Simon designated the Just (Sir 50:1–21; m. 'Abot 1:1). Ben Sira remembers him as one who fortified Jerusalem and repaired the temple. Simon is linked with Ptolemy IV in 3 Macc 1:8–2:24. The story there goes that after his victory at Raphia, the king sought to enter the temple. Simon prayed to prevent this, and Ptolemy was punished by God. Simon's good relations with Antiochus III are evidenced by the favorable decrees issued by Antiochus when he visited Jerusalem after the battle of Panias.

A feud broke out within the Tobiad family between Hyrcanus son of Joseph and his pro-Seleucid older brothers. Hyrcanus supported the Ptolemies and established an independent enclave east of the Jordan at the old family center in the region of Ammonitis. His reconstructed fortress palace, described by Josephus (*Ant.* 12.230–233), may be seen today at Iraq al-Amir, ten miles west of Amman. Each side had its supporters among the Jews of Palestine (*Ant.* 12.228–229). The high priest Simon II sided with the brothers of Hyrcanus, since he and they both championed Antiochus. Simon was succeeded as high priest by his son Onias III (ca. 190–174).

6.4.2. Seleucus IV Philopater (187–175)

Seleucus IV was faced with the need to pay the huge tribute owed to Rome. Second Maccabees 3:1–40 recounts that a dispute developed over administration of the Jerusalem city market between Onias III and one Simon, a pro-Seleucid captain of the temple. This Simon was a brother of Menelaus, who would eventually become high priest. The text of 2 Macc 3:4 is not to be trusted, and this Simon was unlikely to have had a Benjaminite background. Presumably he was a member of the Bilgah priestly division. His brother Menelaus, the future high priest, was thus from a priestly family, but not of the proper Zadokite line.

Onias came out ahead in the dispute, but Simon had revealed to Apollonius, the governor of Coele-Syria and Phoenicia, the existence of money available in the Jerusalem temple. When Seleucus IV heard about this, he sent a government minister named Heliodorus to confiscate these funds. Some of this money belonged to the pro-Ptolemaic Hyrcanus, son of Tobias. Reportedly, Heliodorus suffered supernatural divine retribution, but Onias III offered sacrifice to atone for him and he recovered. These events are described in 2 Macc 3. The Heliodorus Stela, an inscription dated to 178, contains the text of a letter from Seleucus IV to Heliodorus regarding the appointment of an administrator to oversee sanctuaries in Coele-Syria and Phoenicia. Although technically without provenance, fragments of its base were uncovered at Tell Maresha, from where the stela had apparently been looted.

Onias III then went to Antioch to explain the situation and denunciate Simon. However, by that point Heliodorus had assassinated Seleucus. The former king's brother Antiochus IV then succeeded to the throne after defeating Heliodorus (see *ANET*, 567, for the Seleucid King List). Held captive in Syria, Onias III lost his high priesthood in 175 to his brother Jason. Jason had offered the newly enthroned Antiochus IV an enormous bribe of 440 silver talents. Josephus, in contrast to the bribery story told in 2 Macc 4:7-9, reports instead a peaceful and normal transfer of the high-priestly office. Supposedly when Onias III died, his son (the later Onias IV) was considered too young to be high priest (*Ant* 12.237). Presumably the 2 Maccabees version that reports a bribe is correct. Jason's Hebrew name was Joshua.

6.4.3. Antiochus IV Epiphanes (175–164)

Ptolemy VI Philometor (180–145) came to the throne of Egypt as a boy. His mother, Cleopatra I, served as his coregent until 176. In 175, Antiochus IV seized the Seleucid throne after the murder of his brother Seleucus IV. The legitimate claimant was actually Demetrius, elder son of Seleucus IV, but he had been held hostage in Rome since 178. Like Ptolemy V (and two later Seleucid kings) the usurper Antiochus took the epithet Epiphanes ("illustrious, one manifesting [divine] power"). On some of his coins he styled himself more explicitly as "King Antiochus, God Manifest."

Second Maccabees 4 describes the hellenizing policies of Jason the high priest and the subsequent appropriation of the high-priestly office by

Menelaus. Jason had sought and was granted permission from Antiochus to increase the level of Hellenism in Jerusalem. As evidence of the growing prestige of Hellenistic culture, Jason asked to be allowed to establish a gymnasium and a youth training center (*ephebeia*), along with other privileges for Jerusalem's citizens. He attempted to support the Tyrian quadrennial games. Some favored inhabitants of Jerusalem apparently received the privilege of becoming citizens of a special polity termed "Antioch in Jerusalem" (2 Macc 4:9, 19). Josephus, in his use of 1 Macc 1:11–15, attributes these Hellenization moves to Menelaus instead (*Ant.* 12.239–241). Josephus, *Ant.* 12.240–13.214 is mostly a paraphrase of 1 Macc 1:11—13:42, with a few supplements from other sources.

In 171, Jason sent this Menelaus, a brother of the Simon who was the nemesis of Onias III (following 2 Macc 4:23 and not *Ant.* 12.238, 383), to deliver a tribute payment. Menelaus seized this as an opportunity to promise a larger bribe to Antiochus—outbidding Jason by three hundred talents—in order to be appointed as high priest in place of Onias. Josephus was confused and thought that Menelaus was another brother of Onias III, and that he was also sometimes known as Onias. Josephus also fails to mention any bribe and merely reports that Antiochus was angry with Jason (*Ant.* 12.238). The grave scandal in this arrangement was that Menelaus, though a priest, was not of the Zadokite priestly family, for whom the high priesthood was thought to be reserved. Reaction to this outrage against tradition, a practice that would be continued by the non-Zadokite Hasmonean high priests, is evidenced in compositions such as the Aramaic Levi Document (from Qumran and elsewhere); Jubilees 30, 32; and 1 Enoch 12–16. Jason fled to Transjordan.

Menelaus (ca. 172–162) was supported by the Tobiads. Onias III, still in exile near Antioch, accused Menelaus of stealing from the temple. By bribing him with appropriated temple vessels, Menelaus was able to induce Antiochus's deputy Andronicus to kill Onias, who had sought asylum at the holy site of Daphne near Antioch. His death occurred about three years after he had been deposed (171). This significant event is referred to in Dan 9:26; 11:22b, where he is called "anointed prince" and "prince of the covenant" (also see 1 Enoch 90:8). Daniel uses this assassination to begin its calculation of the final seven years of the events of the end time. The death of Onias III is also reported in Josephus (*Ant.* 12.237), but he does not record that Onias was murdered. Later, while Menelaus was visiting Antiochus to explain why he had not paid the promised bribe, his brother Lysimachus sought to rob the temple treasury and was killed by a mob.

Jewish envoys from the council of elders were sent to the king in Tyre in order to explain the situation and bring charges against Menelaus. However, Menelaus bribed the royal official Ptolemy son of Dorymenes, who succeeded in getting the Jewish representative executed instead. These incidents are reported in 1 Macc 4:27–50.

6.5. The Maccabees

6.5.1. The Fiasco of Antiochus IV in Egypt and Its Result

The Sixth Syrian War (170–168) involved two invasions of Egypt by Antiochus IV and two withdrawals from there, one in 169 and one in 168–167. The war was launched when the regents of the young Ptolemy VI declared war on Antiochus. First Maccabees and 2 Maccabees differ in their portrayal of the Egyptian campaigns of Antiochus and events leading up to his desecration of the temple and persecution of the Jewish religion. First Maccabees 1:20-23 refers only to the king's 169 campaign and withdrawal from Egypt and describes his entrance into and plundering of the temple as he returned. A second move against Jerusalem and the imposition of foreign religious practices is reported in 167, but this is not related to a withdrawal from Egypt. Second Maccabees 5 places a rebellion by Jason during the time of Antiochus's second invasion of Egypt in 168 and describes the plundering of the temple after Antiochus's withdrawal as a reaction to this. It says nothing about a despoliation of the temple in 169. Perhaps the best solution to this difficulty is to conjecture that Antiochus plundered the temple twice, first after his 169 campaign and later after his second, forced withdrawal from Egypt. Two visits to Jerusalem are suggested in Dan 11:28-31 and *Ant.* 12.246–250.

The probable course of affairs was this. After his initial victory at the border of Egypt and his drive to Memphis in 169, Antiochus withdrew from his siege of Alexandria at the end of that year. This pullback may have been performed in order to deal with news that Jason the deposed high priest had attempted to capture Jerusalem (unless Jason actually took this action during Antiochus's second invasion). While Antiochus was campaigning in Egypt, Jason heard a false rumor that Antiochus had died. He sought to take advantage of the unpopularity of Menelaus by leading an armed attack on Jerusalem in order to regain the high priesthood. Josephus indicates that Jason enjoyed the support of the pro-Ptolemaic Oniads against the pro-Seleucid Tobiads (*Ant.* 12.229, 239–240). Jason fled to Ammon and then Egypt, eventually dying in Sparta.

Antiochus's moderately successful invasion of Egypt in 169 led to a peace treaty that was disadvantageous to the Egyptians. This situation caused ongoing disarray in the Egyptian royal government. Between 169 and 164, Ptolemy VI had to share rule as part of a triumvirate, along with his obese younger brother nicknamed Physcon, "Sausage" (eventually Ptolemy VIII Euergetes II [145–116]) and their sister Cleopatra II (who was also the wife of Ptolemy VI). Fleeing this intolerable situation in 164, Ptolemy VI went to Rome to seek their support. He was restored to the throne the next year and spent the rest of his reign putting down rebellions. From this point on, the Ptolemaic kingship would be characterized by instability, intrigue, and rapid turnover, until the Romans took control.

To return to the main story, Antiochus invaded Egypt again in 168. This time his way was blocked outside Alexandria by Gaius Popilius Laenas, an envoy from the Roman Senate. Rome was naturally alarmed by the notion of the Seleucids gaining control of Egypt's grain production. Antiochus was told to leave Egypt immediately or face war with Rome. When Antiochus asked for time to consider, the Roman envoy drew a circle round him in the sand and told him to decide before moving outside it. Antiochus pulled back. He then sent a military commander Apollonius to Jerusalem. With Menelaus guiding him, Antiochus plundered the temple (a second time?) in response this humiliation by the Romans (and perhaps in response to Jason's revolt).

The failure of his Egyptian adventure meant that Antiochus now needed a stronger buffer to his south. This strategic consideration seems to have been his real motive for his attacks on Judaism, which he likely distrusted as a potential focus for nativist resistance. The king's religious persecution is difficult to understand otherwise, because Hellenistic rulers were almost universally tolerant of local religious practices. Some historians advance the view that the Seleucid king was trying to promote a common empire-wide culture in order to unite his subjects, a theory that seems to depend on anachronistic notions of the modern nation-state. Perhaps Antiochus felt a need to demonstrate his authority and ruthlessness in order to counteract the public-relations debacle of his humiliation by Rome.

His introduction of alien cult practices in 167 and attempts to curtail traditional Jewish religious observances were certainly performed with the connivance of Menelaus and his party. These are described in 1 Macc

1:41–64 and 2 Macc 6:1–11. Some of these measures affected the public ritual by halting the daily sacrifices (Dan 11:31; 12:11) and imposing the practice of sacrifice to Zeus Olympius. These sacrifices were offered on a supplementary altar constructed over the temple altar. This infamous "desolating sacrilege" (Dan 8:13; 11:31; 12:11) was erected on 15 Kislev 167, and on 25 Kislev sacrifices were first offered on it. Josephus goes beyond his source, 1 Maccabees, to claim that pigs were sacrificed in the temple itself (*Ant.* 12.253). Sacrificing swine did at least take place at local altars (1 Macc 1:47). This must have been intended as a direct attack on traditional Jewish sensibilities. Other measures affected the personal lives of faithful Jews by restricting Torah study, Sabbath observance, and circumcision. Altars for sacrifice were set up outside Jerusalem and became the means for forcing Jews to participate in unlawful sacrifice. Antiochus had the Acra fortress built to dominate temple activities and garrisoned it with his supporters. The location of the Acra is a matter of scholarly dispute, but a good deal of literary and archaeological evidence points to a site somewhere south of the temple. The fortress would be a regular point of contention in the Maccabean revolt and was finally destroyed by Simon after 141.

The violent martyrdom legends of 2 Maccabees (6:12–7:42; 14:37–46) certainly exaggerate the level of persecution in order to legitimate the Hasmoneans, who were not members of the proper high-priestly family. These stories would have a decisive impact on later Jewish and then Christian piety. The decree cited in 1 Macc 1:41 ("his whole kingdom") is presumably an exaggeration. Antiochus's measures were undoubtedly limited to Judea only. The situation in Samaria was very different. A group there petitioned Antiochus (*Ant.* 12.258–263) asking to be defined as non-Jews, to receive a taxation exemption, and to be permitted to associate their temple on Gerizim with Zeus Hellenios (or Xenious, "Friend of Strangers," 2 Macc 6:2). Even if one discounts the story of Josephus that the Gerizim temple was established in the time of Alexander (§6.1.2), it clearly was in existence by 167.

6.5.2. The Maccabean Insurrection

First and Second Maccabees are the chief sources describing the nativist revolt that began in 167. Because these two works differ in the events they report and the order in which these are presented, historians must weigh probabilities in presenting the story.

Perhaps it is not surprising that rebellion should begin with a priestly family in rural Modein. Traditionalist farmers bearing a heavy tax burden might be expected to be at odds with elite Hellenists from Jerusalem. Moreover, peasants are likely to be religiously conservative. Priests like the Maccabee family saw themselves as faithful custodians of religious law (Ezra 7:6; Jer 18:18; Mal 2:7) and could be motivated to violent resistance by the classic legend of Baal Peor as recounted in Num 25:7-8. According to 1 Macc 2:15-28, the trigger for rebellion was a violent reaction on the part of the priest Mattathias. He killed a Jew who agreed to offer a (pagan?) sacrifice outside the Jerusalem temple and the royal representative who had organized it. Mattathias fled to the mountains and began a series of raids, dismantling altars, killing renegades, and circumcising. Royal troops from Jerusalem massacred some Hasidim on a Sabbath, resulting in a decision to fight on the Sabbath if necessary. Mattathias and his sons were joined by a group of Torah loyalists called the Hasidim (Hasideans). This group supported the Maccabee movement, but only until their own religious goals were met (1 Macc 2:42; 7:13; 2 Macc 14:6).

Mattathias died soon after this (perhaps in 166), and three of his five sons took up leadership of the rebellion in turn: Judas, Jonathan, and Simon. From this point on, readers of the two books of Maccabees are confronted by a confusing succession of numerous battles with a bewildering cast of characters. In attempt to achieve clarity, the unfolding events of the Maccabean period are organized into five stages in the discussion that follows.

6.5.2.1. Judas: Apollonius; Beth-horon, Emmaus, Beth-zur (166–164)

Judas began by securing Jerusalem from a series of retaliatory attacks by a succession of Syrian armies. With the allied Hasidim, the rebels centered their base of operations in the hills near Gophna (Jifnah), between Samaria and Jerusalem. Blocking the first of four Syrian moves to relieve the pressure on the hellenizers, Judas defeated and killed Apollonius, regional governor and commander of a force from Samaria (1 Macc 3:10–12).

Judas won a second victory at the battle of Beth-horon (166). The Seleucid commander Seron, marching up from Lydda, sought to relieve pro-Seleucid elements in Jerusalem who were being threatened. He was ambushed and defeated by Judas as he approached via the Beth-horon pass (1 Macc 3:13–26).

The battle of Emmaus (165) again blocked a relief expedition for the pro-Seleucid party in Jerusalem. At the time, Antiochus was occupied in the east and had assigned control of the western part of his realm to Lysias. Lysias sent a more substantial army under several commanders (including Ptolemy, Nicanor, and Gorgias). Attacking this time from the east, an easier approach than from the north, the enemy camped at Emmaus. Judas mustered at Mizpah to their east. Gorgias tried to surprise the rebel forces by a night march, but Judas took advantage of the resulting division of forces. After a night march of his own, he attacked the main Seleucid camp at dawn, with the sun rising at the back of his troops and blinding their adversaries. The enemy withdrew westward via Gazara (Gezer). Judah then turned back to Emmaus. Gorgias, when he had returned from his unsuccessful raid and discovered his colleagues' defeat, withdrew westward as well (1 Macc 3:38–4:25; 2 Macc 8:8–29).

Second Maccabees dates the battle of Beth-zur after the purification of the temple, but most historians agree with 1 Macc 4:26–35 that it occurred beforehand, in 165. Thus this battle also took place before the death of Antiochus IV in 164 (again following 1 Maccabees and not 2 Maccabees) and the accession of Antiochus V (164–162). This pivotal battle resulted when Lysias took to the field himself. He tried to advance on Jerusalem from the south through Idumea, a route that offered a shorter approach to the city. He progressed south to Marisa, then up-country to Beth-zur, where he was driven back by Judas. As a result, Judas was finally free to move into Jerusalem. Although the Acra fortress remained in enemy hands, the temple itself was recaptured. The recovered temple was rededicated on 25 Kislev 164, initiating the ongoing celebration of Hanukkah (1 Macc 4:36–59; 2 Macc 10:1–9; the letter in 2 Macc 1:10–2:18). Apparently Menelaus still was functioning as high priest (2 Macc 11:29, 32).

Letters preserved in 2 Macc 11:16–32 outline the progress of the settlement with Antiochus and Lysias. These letters are not in proper sequence and should be read in the following order: 11:16–21 (perhaps October/November 163, from Lysias); 11:27–33 (archive date March 164, from Antiochus IV); 11:34–38 (same archive date, from two Roman envoys); 11:22–26 (from Antiochus V).

Stories about the death of Antiochus IV differ. According to 1 Macc 6:1–16, he died after the temple rededication. According to 2 Macc 9:28–29 he died beforehand of a disease after trying unsuccessfully to rob a temple in Persia. This description of the circumstances of his death generally agrees with that of 1 Maccabees and the ancient historians. Second

Maccabees 1:13–16 reports an alternate and more dramatic story that he was killed in the very act of plundering a temple.

6.5.2.2. Judas: Rescuing Jews; Beth-zechariah (163–162)

During the next stage of affairs, Judas and his brother Simon campaigned to defend Jews from hostile forces. These campaigns did not attempt to occupy territories but were intended to shield and sometime relocate Jews who were under pressure. First Maccabees describes these events in chapter 5, while 2 Maccabees recounts them in chapter 12 after the second expedition of Lysias. In 163, Judas moved against the Idumeans in Akrabattenee (Acrabeta, perhaps southeast of Shechem) and against the Beonites in southern Transjordan. This was followed by a major campaign to assist Jews in Gilead. Judas was able to capture Bostra in eastern Gilead. He then scattered the army of Timothy, commander of Gilead, to relieve the siege of Dathema (location uncertain). Judas went on to rescue Jews in other places in northern Gilead. This campaign reached its climax with a second defeat of Timothy at Raphon (er-Rafeh). Judas destroyed a temple of the Syrian goddess Atargatis at Carnaim (Karnaim), demonstrating the religious goals of his activities. Jews from Gilead were evacuated to Jerusalem via Ephron and Scythopolis. A final clash with Timothy led to his death and the capture of Jazer. Meanwhile, Simon was engaged in a similar relief expedition in Galilee, where Jews in the coastal areas had been harassed by the inhabitants of Acco, Tyre, and Sidon. He pushed the enemy back to Ptolemais and brought Jews back to Jerusalem.

After the defeat of a Jewish force by Gorgias in a failed attempt to move against Jamnia, Judas struck against Idumeans at Hebron and Marisa and destroyed a temple at Azotus (Ashdod). He engaged in a reprisal for an atrocity against the Jews of Joppa by destroying the city's port. He then treated Jamnia in the same way. His defeat of Gorgias at Marisa proved inconclusive.

Antiochus V Eupator replaced his father in 163 after the latter's sudden death in the East. He would reign for only about a year. He and his regent Lysias sought to relieve the besieged Acra, approaching Jerusalem from the south. At some point in 163 or 162, Lysias induced the young king to execute Menelaus in a gruesome fashion at Aleppo (2 Macc 13:3–8; *Ant.* 12.383–385 tells a similar story).

Lysias defeated Judas at the battle of Beth-zechariah, north of Beth-zur (162), noted for the heroic death of Judas's youngest brother Eleazar, crushed by the elephant he was stabbing (1 Macc 6:46). Short on food because of the Sabbatical fallow year, the rebels at Beth-zur were forced to surrender. Antiochus and Lysias were able to reach Jerusalem and penetrate the temple defenses (1 Macc 6:18–54; 2 Macc 13:9–17). However, Lysias had to make peace and return to Antioch to deal with Philip, a new claimant to be regent (2 Macc 13:18–26).

6.5.2.3. Judas: Capharsalama, Adasa, Elasa (162–160)

Demetrius I Soter (161–150) son of Seleucus IV left his situation as a Roman hostage (see §6.4.3) in order to regain the throne of his father. The kingship had been usurped by Antiochus IV and then passed to his son Antiochus V. Arriving in Syria in 162 as Rome's candidate for the throne, Demetrius put Lysias and Antiochus V to death. He sent Bacchides to Palestine along with a new Jewish high priest whom he had reconfirmed. This was Alcimus (Eliakim, Yakim; 162–159), who was an opponent of Judas. Alcimus had apparently first been appointed by Lysias. When Bacchides arrived in Judea, the Hasidim sought to make peace because they acknowledged Alcimus as being of legitimate high-priestly descent. However, he betrayed them and murdered sixty of their number (1 Macc 7:12–16).

Although Josephus gives contradictory information on this point, it was apparently at the time of the appointment of Alcimus that Onias IV, son of Onias III, emigrated to Egypt (*Ant.* 12.387) and established a Jewish temple in the Heliopolis region in the Delta at Leontopolis (probably Tell el-Yehudiyeh). It seems to have served as a shrine for a Jewish military force stationed in the area. Onias utilized the ruins of a temple dedicated to the goddess Bubastis (*Ant.* 13.62–71). However, there is some debate about the date of his arrival in Egypt. An Aramaic papyrus from Egypt dated 164 is addressed to an individual whose name has been restored as Onias, likely Onias IV. This would place him in Egypt earlier than Josephus reports. That Onias came to Egypt sometime before 164 also fits with *Ant.* 13.62–65, which asserts that Onias had already served Ptolemy Philopater for several years before requesting to build a temple. Leontopolis was in the *nome* of Heliopolis. Josephus describes the temple in *J.W.* 7.426–430. A textual variant at Isa 19:18 witnessed by LXX honors the temple of Onias by replacing a reference to Heliopolis as "City of the Sun" with "City of Righteousness." The Leontopolis temple would function until it was closed by Roman authorities at the time of First Jewish War (73 CE; Josephus, *J.W.* 7.433–436).

Meanwhile, Judas had returned to his old base in the hills of Gophna. Alcimus appealed to Demetrius I for help against him. In response, Nicanor (one of the generals at the battle of Emmaus) moved north out of Jerusalem to force open the road from Jerusalem to the coast through Beth-horon. After failed attempts at negotiation, Nicanor was defeated and repulsed by Judas in 162 at the battle of Capharsalama (Khirbet Salama; 1 Macc 7:25–32). In 161, Nicanor tried again and successfully reached Beth-horon, where he joined up with a force of Syrian auxiliaries. As he was returning to Jerusalem, however, Judas surprised him at the battle of Adasa (Khirbet ʿAdaseh). Nicanor was killed, and his army was pursued to Gazara. This significant victory on 13 Adar was celebrated as the Day of Nicanor (1 Macc 7:39–50; *Ant.* 12.402–412). Second Maccabees 15:1–36 presents a significantly different account of Nicanor's death and the events leading up to it. Judas was able to engineer an alliance with Rome (1 Macc 8). This friendship would be renewed by Jonathan.

In 160, the battle of Elasa marked the low point of the Maccabean revolt. Demetrius I responded to the defeat of Nicanor and Judas's emerging friendship with Rome by dispatching Bacchides to Judea with a large army. He moved by way of the road from Gilgal to Berea (Beeroth) in order to approach Jerusalem from the north via the central ridge road. To protect Jerusalem, Judas took position at Elasa (near present-day Ramallah). Plagued by desertions, Judas ignored advice and advanced with a numerically inferior force. Judas was both outnumbered and quite possibly tricked by a planned retreat in good order by the Seleucid right wing. The Jewish forces were eventually crushed between two elements of the Seleucid army. Judas was killed (1 Macc 9:1–18). Defections from the Maccabean cause were further encouraged by famine (1 Macc 9:23–27).

6.5.2.4. Jonathan: Beth-basi, Jamnia, Hazor; Trypho (160–142)

Jonathan took over leadership of the movement at the death of Judas. First Maccabees 14:29–43 provides a good summary of the accomplishments of Jonathan and Simon.

Bacchides increased the number of fortified locations around Jerusalem, which was again under the control of the pro-Seleucid party. Jonathan first retreated into the wilderness of Judea, then was pushed by Bacchides eastward across the Jordan (1 Macc 9:28–33, 50). The high priest Alcimus had offended pious sensibilities by tearing down an interior wall in the temple, although the details of what he did remain obscure. The alteration may have been connected with the sensitive question of access to the temple by non-Jews. He died in 160 or 159 (depending on which version of the Seleucid-era chronology is being followed). Following this there seems to have been a seven-year vacancy in the office of high priest until Jonathan assumed the office in 152.

After a two-year hiatus, Jonathan won a significant victory at the siege of Beth-basi. Bacchides had returned from Antioch with an army. In response, Jonathan occupied Beth-basi near the ridge road southeast of Jerusalem. When Bacchides attacked, Simon was left in charge at Beth-basi and sallied out to burn the enemy siege works. Meanwhile Jonathan had left the town to harass the forces of Bacchides in the field. Bacchides was forced to negotiate with Jonathan and withdrew from Judea. The agreement with Bacchides permitted Jonathan to use Michmash (Machmas) as his base of operation, from which he was able to gain control of much of Judea. Jerusalem, however, remained under the control of the Hellenist party (1 Macc 9:58–73).

Civil war broke out in the Seleucid kingdom in 153. Jonathan was able to gain concessions and expand his area of control by cleverly supporting each side at different times. Alexander I Balas (150–145) claimed to be son of Antiochus IV (and indeed may have been). Rome recognized him as legitimate. Alexander Balas invaded Ptolemais, leading Demetrius I to court Jonathan's support in 152. He granted Jonathan control of Jerusalem, except for the Acra (1 Macc 10:1–17). In that same year, however, Jonathan shifted his support to Alexander Balas, who reiterated Demetrius's concessions. In addition Alexander appointed Jonathan as high priest (vv. 15–21). The high priesthood thus continued to be in the hands of a non-Zadokite. Demetrius offered even better privileges to Jonathan, but the Jews were unwilling to trust him (vv. 22-45). Demetrius I was killed in battle with his rival in 150. Jonathan met with a grateful Alexander Balas and his new ally Ptolemy VI at Ptolemais and received further honors and privileges (vv. 59–66)

In 147, the son of Demetrius I (eventually Demetrius II) arrived from Crete to seek his father's throne in opposition to Alexander Balas. Demetrius sent Apollonius to subdue Jonathan, who was still supporting Alexander. This led to the battle of Jamnia. After securing Joppa to their rear, Simon and Jonathan were ambushed by Apollonius south of Jamnia. The Maccabean forces found themselves trapped by a feigned retreat. They were caught between the enemy's army and cavalry. The Jews were able to hold their line for a whole day until finally the Seleucids broke under a renewed assault by Simon. Jonathan then captured Azotus and was welcomed by Ascalon (1 Macc 10:67–87).

Ptolemy VI advanced up the coast to attack Antioch in support of Alexander Balas. Upon reaching Antioch, however, Ptolemy shifted his support from Alexander to Demetrius. The Egyptian king dissolved the marriage of his daughter Cleopatra Thea to Alexander and gave her to Demetrius. Ptolemy defeated Alexander in 145, but died soon after, apparently from wounds suffered in battle (*Ant.* 13.117–119). Alexander Balas was killed by the Nabateans in 145. This permitted Demetrius to succeed to the throne as Demetrius II Nicator (145–138, 129–125). Jonathan was able to finesse this transition and reached an understanding with Demetrius II. A letter setting forth privileges granted by Demetrius II to Jonathan is preserved in 1 Macc 11:30–37.

However, civil war continued. Opposing Demetrius II and his general Apollonius (not the Apollonius of 1 Macc 3:10–12) was Diodotus Tryphon (Trypho), regent for the two-year-old son of Alexander Balas and Cleopatra Thea, who was ruling simultaneously with his rival Demetrius II as Antiochus VI Epiphanes Dionysus (145–142; 1 Macc 11:54–59). Jonathan became a supporter of Antiochus. At the battle of Hazor in 144 (1 Macc 11:63–74), the troops of Demetrius II confronted Jonathan. The same fake-retreat-and-ambush tactic used at Jamnia scattered some of the Jewish fighters, but Jonathan eventually prevailed. In 143, military operations by Jonathan in the Lebanon Valley led to the evacuation of the Jews of Beth-zabdai (2 Macc 12:24–32).

The last challenge facing Jonathan was the campaign into Palestine by Trypho, which was intended to rein in Jonathan's behavior as an ostensible but overly independent ally of Antiochus VI. Trypho marched south from Damascus while Jonathan moved up from Jerusalem. They met at Scythopolis (Beth-shean) in 143. Trypho's deceitful promise granting control of Ptolemais induced Jonathan to send home most of his army and move a small force to Ptolemais. There he was treacherously captured. Trypho was unable to prevent the small contingent that Jonathan had left behind in Galilee from making their way back to Jerusalem.

Trypho had young Antiochus VI killed and claimed the throne for himself. Trypho moved into Judea in 142, with Jonathan as his captive. Unwilling to engage with Simon at Adida, he slipped around southward to try to relieve the Seleucid supporters in the Acra by means of a northward advance up the ridge road. A snowstorm forced him break off and move down into the Jordan Valley. Returning up the east side of the valley, he put Jonathan to death at Baskama (Beth-shikma) east of the Sea of Galilee. Jonathan's body was reburied in Modein (1 Macc 12:39–54; 13:1–30).

6.5.2.5. Simon: The Battle of Kidron (142–137)

The treacherous murder of Jonathan caused his older brother Simon to side unambiguously with Demetrius II, who granted Judea independence in 142. Simon became high priest in that year, but the circumstances of how he secured his office are unclear (1 Macc 13:36–42; *Ant.* 13:213). Later, Demetrius's brother Antiochus VII would confirm these privileges (1 Macc 15:1–9). Simon was given permission to strike coinage, an important concession of independent political status, though apparently only John Hyrcanus would actually mint coins. Simon incorporated Gazara into his domain as a major strong point. He finally was able to overpower the Acra in 141 (1 Macc 13:43–51; *Ant.* 13.215). Demetrius II marched east into Parthia, perhaps in hopes of gaining assistance against Trypho, but was taken prisoner by the Parthians and exiled to the shore of the Caspian Sea.

In 137, Trypho was eventually deposed by a new king, Antiochus VII Sidetes (138–129), brother of Demetrius II. The wife of Demetrius, Cleopatra Thea, married Antiochus VII in 137, providing him with some further basis for claiming the throne. Through her three marriages she became the mother of four kings: Antiochus VI by Alexander Balas, Seleucus V (whom she had murdered) and Antiochus VIII Grypus by Demetrius II, and Antiochus IX Cyzicenus by Antiochus VII Sidetes.

The victory of Antiochus VII over Trypho allowed him to change his conciliatory stance toward Simon. In 137 he ordered his general Cendebeus to fortify a place called Kidron on Judea's southwestern border. Simon's sons John Hyrcanus and Judas advanced via Modein to Kidron. At this battle of Kidron, the two armies faced each other across the Valley of Sorek. Interspersing his horsemen among his foot soldiers, Hyrcanus was able to cross the valley, scatter the enemy, and pursue them to Azotus (1 Macc 15:38–16:10; *Ant.* 13.223–235). Later, Simon and two of his sons were slain by treachery during a banquet in 135 by his son-in-law Ptolemy son of Abubus. John Hyrcanus at Gazara was forewarned and was able to kill the assassins sent by Ptolemy (1 Macc 16:11–24).

6.6. The Hasmonean Period

6.6.1. John Hyrcanus (134–104)

The leadership of John Hyrcanus I, third and only surviving son of Simon and successor to the high priesthood, begins the Hasmonean period. This name is said to derive from the family's dynastic ancestor, Hashmonay. Almost immediately John Hyrcanus faced an invasion by Antiochus VII, who besieged him in Jerusalem (*Ant.* 13.236–248). Hyrcanus had to accept significant concessions in order to achieve a peace agreement. To raise the necessary tribute and to pay mercenaries, Hyrcanus felt compelled to loot the tomb of David (*Ant.* 13.249).

A few years later, Hyrcanus joined Antiochus VII in a campaign against the Parthians, who had been holding the king's brother Demetrius II hostage. Fortunately, Hyrcanus returned home before Antiochus was killed in battle with the Parthians in 129. Demetrius II was released and regained his throne in 129, ruling until 126. These new circumstances gave Hyrcanus freedom to expand. He was able belatedly to move against Ptolemy, the murderer of his father and brothers, who controlled Jericho. However, he failed to capture Ptolemy. The mother of Hyrcanus, who had been Ptolemy's captive and had been tortured by him to keep Hyrcanus from prosecuting the siege, was killed.

In 128 Hyrcanus moved east of the Jordan to capture Medeba and Samaga (location unknown) in order to control the trade route along the King's Highway (*Ant.* 13.255). In 124 he wrote a letter about the celebration of Hanukkah to the Jews of Egypt (2 Macc 1:1–9). At an uncertain date he captured Shechem and evidently destroyed the Samaritan temple on Gerizim (*Ant.* 13.255–258, *J.W.* 1.63; perhaps Megillah Ta'anit 22). The long-simmering differences between Samaritan Yahwists and Jews must have been exacerbated by Samaritan acquiescence to the demands of Antiochus Epiphanes. The destruction of their temple attests that a complete break between the two communities had now taken place. The conquests of Hyrcanus in Idumea in 112 (Hebron, Adora, Marisa) pushed the southern limit of Jewish control down to Beer-sheba and Wadi Besor. Josephus claims that he forcibly converted the Idumeans to Judaism, but this is doubted by modern historians (*Ant.* 13.257–258). Most likely, the local population was gradually assimilated into Jewish life and religion. No doubt, prominent families, such as that of Antipater, founder of the Herodian line, took the lead.

Continuing quarrels over the Syrian throne gave Hyrcanus space for these independent actions. He had opposed Demetrius II when he returned from Parthia to reclaim his throne. Hyrcanus instead was friendly to the pretender Alexander II Zabinas (128–122), who defeated Demetrius II and then was defeated in turn by Antiochus VIII Grypus (125–96) son of Demetrius II. Hyrcanus then worked in opposition to Antiochus VIII, who was in conflict with his stepbrother Antiochus IX Cyzicenus (113–95), the son of Antiochus VII and Cleopatra Thea.

In 108–104, Hyrcanus launched a second campaign against the region of Samaria, this time besieging the city of Samaria, populated by Greeks and probably Hellenizing Samaritans. The city appealed to Antiochus IX (following *Ant.* 13.275–277). The king advanced to Scythopolis, only to be defeated on his way to relieve Samaria by Hyrcanus's sons Aristobulus and Antigonus. A legend says that the news of their victory was miraculously delivered to Hyrcanus while he was burning incense in the temple (*Ant.* 13.282–283; t. Soṭah 13:3). His sons captured (or purchased) Scythopolis and then invaded the area around Mount Carmel. Hyrcanus captured Samaria and now controlled the northern hill country completely.

Near the end of his reign, Hyrcanus faced internal opposition from the Pharisees, apparently over the legitimacy of his high priesthood. He turned to the Sadducee party for support (*Ant.* 13.288–296; cf. b. Qidd. 66a). The Sadducees, made up of important, upper-class priestly families, probably allied with other wealthy and influential groups, are known mostly through hostile sources. Given their support of the Hasmonean high priests, it is unlikely that they were committed to the traditional Zadokite priestly line or that their name derives from Zadok. Supposedly going back to the time of Jonathan (*Ant.* 13.173), the Sadducees were a dominant political force except during the reign of Salome Alexandra (76–67). Supporters of the status quo and stability, they rejected concepts not found in the text of the Torah, such as the oral legal tradition, resurrection, angels, and apocalyptic expectations.

The Pharisees, to whom both Josephus and rabbinic sources are positively biased, also appeared in the time of Jonathan according to *Ant.* 13.171. They were essentially a middle-class movement that valued the tradition of an unwritten oral law delivered to Moses on Sinai (*Ant.* 13.297) and emphasized that free will influences human affairs (*Ant.* 13.172; m. 'Abot 3:19).

The Essenes, presumably associated in some way with the Qumran community, are described by Josephus, Philo, and Pliny the Elder. We are told that they engaged in rites of initiation and purification and the common ownership of property. They kept Sabbath strictly and avoided animal sacrifices. They were interested in angels. Significantly, Pliny places them in Ein Gedi, in the neighborhood of the Dead Sea Qumran community. In addition though, Josephus refers to a Gate of the Essenes in Jerusalem and reports that some Essenes married and remained in community with their fellow Jews. Philo too speaks of their residence in villages and cities. Archaeology suggests that the Qumran sectarian community began about 150. Certitude about the identification of the Teacher of Righteousness and the Wicked Priest would give a more solid date for the origin of the Qumran group. Although scholarship favors Jonathan as the latter, the whole matter remains very much in doubt. The Community Rule (1QS) and Damascus Document indicate that this sect saw itself as the true Israel, followed a solar calendar, and engaged in communal meals and rites of water purification. As sons of Zadok, they rejected the current temple leadership and its supposedly erroneous festival calendar.

The Samaritans were another resilient dissenting force. Considering themselves to be the true heirs of Israel, they claimed their own textual tradition of the five books of the Torah as their Scripture and continued to engage in sacrificial worship on Mount Gerizim.

6.6.2. Aristobulus I (104–103)

Aristobulus I, one of Hyrcanus's sons, was the first Hasmonean to acquire the title of king. He starved his mother to death and supposedly was tricked into having his brother Antigonus killed. He conquered areas in northern Galilee controlled by the Itureans, and allegedly forced them to convert through circumcision (*Ant.* 13.319). These Itureans were an Arab group that had migrated into Galilee from their center farther north in the Lebanon area. Hasmonean influence in or control of Galilee is witnesses to by the presence there of the coinage of Hyrcanus and especially Jannaeus. The details of the progression and scope of the settlement of Jews in Galilee are matters of controversy.

6.6.3. Alexander Jannaeus (103–76)

Alexandra Salome, the widow of Aristobulus, married his brother Alexander Jannaeus and made him king and high priest (103–76). He was also known as Jonathan. His opponents saw this marriage as a violation of Lev 21:14. The Jewish state reached its greatest extent during his reign. The first phase of expansion took place in 103–95. Jannaeus moved against Ptolemais (Acco). The city appealed to Ptolemy IX Lathyrus (116–96), who arrived from Cyprus, invaded Galilee, and defeated a Jewish contingent at Asochis (near Sepphoris). Jannaeus was only saved from disaster by Ptolemy's mother and rival Cleopatra III, who forced Ptolemy to return to Cyprus. Alexander Jannaeus was then able to conquer Gadara, Raphia, and Gaza, along with other locales.

The Pharisees rebelled against Jannaeus, dramatically pelting him with lemons at the Feast of Booths, which led to the slaughter of six thousand opponents (*Ant.* 13.372–373). Several rabbinic sources repeat this story, but offer a somewhat different perspective on the motivation for opposition to Jannaeus (m. Sukkah 4:9; b. Yoma 26b; b. Sukkah 48b). His domestic enemies were further emboldened by his defeat at the hands of Obodas I king of the Nabateans near the Golan in about 93. His Jewish opponents eventually appealed to one of the (now four!) rivals for the Seleucid throne, Demetrius III Eucaerus, who invaded from his headquarters in Damascus. However, he was forced to withdraw after apparent success when many of Jannaeus's opponents switched sides. Alexander Jannaeus ended the revolt with a victory at Bemeselis (or Bethoma) and had eight hundred of his enemies crucified in Jerusalem (*Ant.* 13.380). The commentary text 4Q169 (4QpNah) likely alludes to these events, referring to Jannaeus as the Lion of Wrath. In contrast, another text, 4Q448 (4QPsAp), contains a prayer for him using his Hebrew name Jonathan that casts him in a favorable light.

Beginning around 88, Rome was taken up with civil discord involving Sulla. Three wars between Rome and Mithridates IV of Pontus (89–85, 83–82, 73–63) also kept Rome occupied. About 86, the Seleucid Antiochus XII Dionysius (87–84; claimant to the Syrian throne headquartered in Damascus) marched through Judea in a failed attack on the Nabateans. Aretas III of Nabataea (87–62) invaded Judea, but then agreed to withdraw (*Ant.* 13.392). Alexander Jannaeus was now free to engage in a second period of expansion, from 83 to 76.

Josephus gives lists of towns held by the Jews at this time in *Ant.* 13.395 and 14.18. Jannaeus controlled almost all of Palestine. His territory stretched from Dora (Dor) and Strato's Tower down the coast to Gaza and Raphia, and on the south along the Raphia to Beer-sheba to Zoar line. He also ruled Galilee and Transjordan from the headwaters of the Jordan River south through Moabitis. Only Ptolemais (Acco) and Ascalon

(Ashkelon) on the coast and Philadelphia (Amman) in Transjordan were excluded. He ruled over numerous Greek cities, especially in the Decapolis (*Ant.* 13.393-394). Pella supposedly refused to convert to Judaism so was destroyed (*Ant.* 13.397). In 76, Alexander Jannaeus died in the siege of Ragaba (perhaps biblical Argob) east of the Jordan.

6.6.4. Alexandra Salome (76-67)

His widow then reigned as Alexandra Salome. The Pharisees moved into a position of influence during her reign. Her elder son Hyrcanus II was named high priest (in office 76-67, 63-40). Tigranes II king of Armenia (95-55) threatened her realm when he besieged Ptolemais in 69, but Rome's success against Mithridates IV of Pontus forced Tigranes to return home (*Ant.* 13.419-421). Taking advantage of his mother's illness, her other son, Aristobulus, took possession of a number of fortresses and was proclaimed king. Before her death, Alexandra responded by imprisoning his wife and children.

6.6.5. Aristobulus II (67-63)

At the death of Alexandra, civil war broke out between her sons Hyrcanus II and the pro-Sadducee Aristobulus II (*Ant.* 13.427-428). This conflict was seemingly settled by a truce after a battle near Jericho, with Aristobulus becoming king and (apparently) high priest. Instigated by a prominent Idumean named Antipater, however, Hyrcanus II fled to Nabatea and invited the Nabatean king Aretas III to intervene in the dispute. Aretas defeated Aristobulus and besieged him in the Jerusalem temple (*Ant.* 14.19-21). Aristobulus bribed a deputy of the Roman general Gnaeus Pompeius Magnus (Pompey). In 64, Pompey had turned Syria into a Roman province after the assassination of Antiochus XIII Asiaticus (69-64). Pompey's deputy ordered Aretas to withdraw. He and Hyrcanus were defeated on the return to Petra by Aristobulus (*Ant.* 14.29-33).

Both sides, along with a third delegation from the people, appealed to Pompey in 63 (*Ant.* 14.34-38, 41-45). This set the stage for Roman intervention. In that same year, Pompey marched down from Damascus and besieged Jerusalem. Hyrcanus opened the city gates to him. However, the besieged supporters of Aristobulus, who were holed up in the fortified temple precincts, held out for another three months. The Romans finally captured the temple area on a Sabbath, probably in the summer of 63. At the conclusion of the siege, Pompey entered the holy of holies, but apparently did not plunder its treasures (*Ant.* 14.54–72, *J.W.* 1.145–153). Psalms of Solomon 2; 8; and 17 interpret Pompey's victory as God's punishment for the sins of the Hasmoneans and the Jews in general. Psalms of Solomon 2 characterizes Pompey's ignominious death in 48 as an expected result of his violation of temple sanctity.

Pompey now arranged the political situation in a way he considered advantageous to Rome. He reappointed Hyrcanus II as high priest. He removed Greek and hellenized cities and their surrounding territories from Jewish rule, including Samaria. Cities east of the Jordan, together with Scythopolos, were linked together into the Decapolis league. The Samaritans became an autonomous region, while the Greek city of Samaria regained self-rule. The Jewish state was reduced to Judea itself, Galilee, eastern Idumea, and Perea in Transjordan (*Ant.* 14:74–76, 88; *J.W.* 1.156–166, 169–170). Aristobulus and his family were sent to Rome. The Roman proconsul in Syria supervised the supposedly independent cities and territorial units of Palestine. As client of Pompey who had proven his loyalty to Rome, Antipater functioned as administrator of the territory under Jewish authority. A dependable advocate for Roman interests and a supporter of Julius Caesar after the death of Pompey, Antipater was made procurator by Caesar in 47. Antipater named his son Phasael governor of Jerusalem and Herod governor of Galilee. When Caesar was assassinated, Antipater became an ally of Cassius, one of the assassins. His descendants would dominate Palestinian politics for several generations, beginning with his son Herod the Great, who would rule as king from 37 to 4. Antipater was poisoned by a political rival in 43.

6.7. Literature of the Period

6.7.1. Historiography

6.7.1.1. 1 Maccabees

First Maccabees was probably composed in Hebrew as support for the Hasmoneans in the time of John Hyrcanus I, that is, in the late second or early first century. After some introductory background, 1 Maccabees begins in earnest with Antiochus's Egyptian campaign of 169 (it does not mention a second in 167). It concludes with the transition in rule from the murdered Simon to his son John Hyrcanus I in 134. First Maccabees is essentially a family history that extends over three generations (first Mattathias, then his sons, and finally John Hyrcanus). It recounts the exploits of Judas, Jonathan, and Simon in turn. The book emphasizes the positive relationship that the Jews enjoyed with the Romans as exemplified by the promulgated but unrealized treaty cited in chapter 8 and the Roman support described in 12:1–4 and 15:15–24. Current scholarship supports the authenticity of the basic content at least of the documents 1 Maccabees quotes. It appears to be chronologically accurate, although it is possible that two different dating systems for the Seleucid era are used, one starting the era in spring 311 (the system used inside the Seleucid realm) and the other in autumn 312 (the system used in the Macedonian court). For this reason, the dates cited must be considered approximate.

6.7.1.2. 2 Maccabees

Second Maccabees functions as a festal scroll intended to support the celebration of Hanukkah, as the two introductory letters establish. The theme is God's defense of the temple's sanctity against three successive attacks, first by Heliodorus, then by Antiochus IV, and finally by Nicanor. The work begins in the reign of Seleucus IV about 180 and concludes in 161 with the battle celebrated as the Day of Nicanor. The book abridges a five-volume work by one Jason of Cyrene, now lost. It quotes four archival letters in 11:22–38 that are commonly accepted as authentic. The date of the latest matter cited in the introductory cover letter (1:1–9) is 124, which provides the approximate date of the book's completion. Second Maccabees celebrates a theology of heroic martyrdom and suffering (6:12–7:42; 14:37–46) in order to encourage religious fidelity. Chapter 7 promises a resurrection of the body. Second Maccabees incorporates many supernatural events. Sin offerings for the dead are possible according to 12:39–45.

6.7.2. Fictional novellas

6.7.2.1. Esther

The short stories of Esther, Judith, and Tobit all deal with the question of how a Jew should navigate the temptations of a dominant and prestigious foreign culture. This theme came to the forefront during the Hellenistic period. The threat of ethnic cleansing is clearly something conceivable to the audience of the book of Esther, which suggests that the author is reflecting the policies of Antiochus IV. Esther features an improbable dramatic plot set in the exotic venue of Susa during the reign of Xerxes I (apparently). The foreign king is an object of ridicule. In addition to the version preserved in the Masoretic Text, the book also exists in two Greek recensions. A so-called Alpha Text differs considerably from the Hebrew version. A second Greek version of Esther is presented in the LXX. This includes additions interpolated into the story in the form in which it is presented in the Hebrew Bible. These additions undoubtedly stem from the Hellenistic era, since the colophon to the LXX version (Additions to Esther 11) states that it was brought to Egypt in either 77, if Ptolemy XII is the king alluded to, or 114, if the reference is to Ptolemy IX. The circumstance that three versions have survived provides insight into how complex the history of composition, editing, and transmission of biblical books must have been.

6.7.2.2. Tobit

Tobit reflects the world of Diaspora Judaism. Silence on the crisis triggered by Antiochus IV suggests that it was composed before then, apparently in the early part of the second century. Its optimistic plot rests on the nearly universal folk tales of the dangerous bride and the grateful dead. The figure of Ahiqar, well known in the ancient world from various forms of the book of Ahiqar (*ANET*, 427–30), appears as a minor character who supports Tobit.

6.7.2.3. Judith

Judith saves her threatened people by assassinating an enemy general and in so doing provokes them to courage and faithful obedience. The flavor of the book of Judith is distinctly that of Palestinian Judaism rather than of the Egyptian or Mesopotamian Diaspora. The incorporation of the historical persons Holofernes and Bagoas in a fictional setting imply knowledge of the time of Artaxerxes III (358–338). Judith 3:8 and 4:6 suggest a date after the persecution of Antiochus, perhaps in the Hasmonean era.

6.7.3. Wisdom

6.7.3.1. Qoheleth

A Qumran fragment of Qoheleth suggests that this philosophical essay was written before the beginning of the second century. Sirach 20:6 seems to allude to Qoh 3:7, also suggesting a date before 180. The book is notable for its questioning of received wisdom and openness to outside concepts. There is an atmosphere of uncertainty about the future. These features fit the experience of Jews confronted by and sometimes embracing Hellenism. There are echoes at least of Epicurean and Stoic concepts.

6.7.3.2. Sirach

The Wisdom of Jesus son of Sirach (or Ecclesiasticus) was composed in Palestine around the time of the shift from Ptolemaic to Seleucid rule, originally in Hebrew. Scholars usually date the work to about 180. It is silent about the crisis precipitated by Antiochus IV. Sirach 50:1 gives the impression that Simon II has recently died, again pointing to a date around 200. The hostility between Jews and Samaritans has become intense according to 50:26. Some Jews are abandoning the law (41:8). The author reflects pro-Sadducee attitudes and is a strong supporter of the temple hierarchy and ritual. Ben Sira both praises wisdom and teaches it. He was familiar with the Law and the Prophets portions of the Hebrew Bible and certain of the Writings, but shows no knowledge of Ruth, Ezra-Nehemiah, Esther, or Daniel. The book reflects common Hellenistic values about friendship and proper behavior at banquets, Stoic philosophical concepts, and Egyptian literature such as the Satire on Trades (*ANET*, 432–34; *COS* 1.48:122–25; cf. Sir 38:24–39:11). The grandson of Ben Sira moved to Egypt in 132 and translated the work into Greek as a guide to living according to the emerging canon of "the Law and the Prophets and the other books" (prologue).

6.7.3.3. Wisdom of Solomon

Wisdom of Solomon is written in learned rhetorical Greek and mirrors characteristic Hellenistic viewpoints. The Egyptian capital Alexandria is clearly the context, and the work exhibit strong hostility to Egyptians. The work is often dated between 200 and 100 BCE, but a date as late as 40 CE is possible. The argument for a later, Roman-period date rests on the work's strong condemnation of idolatry. This could reflect either the emergence of the cult of Augustus or the pogroms and riots in Alexandria that resulted from the policies of Caligula. A Roman-period date is also suggested by the work's strong affinities with Philo, who was active sometime around 40 CE. The author is familiar with Platonic and Stoic thought. The theme of the book is resistance to assimilation. Judaism is ethically and philosophically superior to the Hellenistic lifestyle. Readers are urged to take pride in their Jewish background. God will protect them as God did their ancestors. Immortality of the soul is God's gift to the righteous. The presentation of the figure of Wisdom (Sophia) parallels that of Prov 8:22–31 and Sir 24:1–22 and is influenced by ancient mythic concepts.

6.7.4. Apocalyptic

6.7.4.1. Isaiah 24–27

This so-called Isaiah Apocalypse exhibits concepts that are clearly later than its surrounding context in the book of Isaiah. It advances themes popular in apocalyptic literature, including earth's destruction through universal divine judgment. The mysterious "city of chaos" is the target of God's wrath (24:10–13; 25:2). In contrast, Jerusalem will be restored (25:6–12). In the context of iniquitous Hellenistic culture, God's promised future requires that this world must come to an end. On that day, oppressing kings will be imprisoned and the wicked destroyed. God will prepare a feast for all the hungry and wretched. All sorrow will end. Faith's answer to the unbearable present is a resurrection of the dead. Yahweh will swallow up death, which now separates the pious from their God. These chapters were apparently introduced into the book of Isaiah to serve as an interpretive conclusion to the foreign-nation oracles of Isa 13–23.

6.7.4.2. Daniel

Daniel combines the genres of apocalyptic with folktales of resistance to state oppression. It obviously refers to the campaigns and persecution of Antiochus IV and the events of 167. An inaccurate description of the death of the oppressive king in a locale between the Mediterranean and Jerusalem rather than in the East indicates a date of composition just before that event, just before the restoration of the temple cult in Kislev 164. Six tales of fidelity, similar to those in 2 Maccabees, are intended to motivate resistance. The end will be soon and will involve apocalyptic anguish and judgment, an end to oppressive imperialism, and a resurrection of selected persons for reward or punishment. The time of the end is calculated as three and a half years ("a time, two times, and half a time") after the beginning of the persecution. Updating at the end of the book indicates that the passing of this deadline led to recalculations of the time line (12:11–13). Daniel 11:34 suggests that those who produced Daniel were not totally supportive of the Maccabees. The Greek version incorporates a poem and two folktales from the Daniel tradition.

6.7.5. Song of Solomon

The Hebrew title of this love poem is Song of Songs, that is, the greatest of all songs. Comparable examples from Mesopotamia describe erotic love between gods and goddesses (*ANET*, 41–42, 52–57, 106–8, 640–45; *COS* 1.108:381–84, 1.169:540–43, 1.173:554–59). Artistic songs celebrating human love were a feature of fourteenth- to twelfth-century Egyptian culture (*COS* 1.49:126–27, 1.50:127–28, 1.51:128–29). Determining the era of composition for the biblical poem is difficult, but its relatively late language suggests the Hellenistic period. However, Isa 5:1–7 and the heading to Ps 45 bear witness to the performance of love songs in the monarchic period (cf. Ezek 33:32). The poem is shaped as a conversation between lovers—a woman and a man—who celebrate the beauty of their lover's body and display the urgency of their passion. Other voices speak. The woman's brothers are angry and protective (Song 1:6; 8:8–10). The "daughters of Jerusalem" address the woman, praising her and prompting her with questions (5:9; 6:1; 8:5). She holds them off with a reserved refrain (2:7; 3:5; 8:4), but reveals her desire to them (5:8). She searches for her lover (3:1–5; 5:2–8). Imagery is powerful: virginity is a wall, she is a palm tree and a rose of Sharon, he is a gazelle and an apple tree. The atmosphere is permeated by the fecundity of garden, vineyard, flowers, fruits, and trees. Repeated phrases create unity out of a whirl of rich language and emotion: "his left hand" (2:6; 8:3), "my beloved is mine" (2:6; 6:3; 7:10), "my mother's house" (3:4; 8:2), "who is that?" (3:6; 6:10; 8:5).

6.7.6. Baruch and Letter of Jeremiah

Baruch consists of three originally independent units held together by an introduction. It presents itself as a letter by Jeremiah's scribe sent from Babylonian exile to the Jews of Palestine. It seems to have been originally composed in Hebrew. This exploration of the themes of penitence and exile features numerous intertextual allusions to books in the Hebrew Bible and to Sirach and Psalms of Solomon. A close dependence on Dan 9:4–19 indicates a date of composition sometime after 164, thus most likely in the late second or early first century.

The Western Christian practice incorporates the Letter of Jeremiah into Baruch as chapter 6, although this is a separate composition and is treated as such by the Septuagint tradition. Supposedly sent by Jeremiah to the Jewish Diaspora in the East, this work is a passionate attack on idolatry. Second Maccabees 2:1–3 seems to allude to it, and a Greek fragment was discovered at Qumran.

Ancient Sources Index

Old Testament/Hebrew Bible

Genesis
10:14	33
12:6–8	38
13:4	38
13:18	38
14	38
14:17–24	49
16:7–14	38
16:12	38
18:1–15	38
21:33	38
22	38
24:10	18
28:11–22	38, 100
32:1	114
32:25–33	38
33:18–20	38
33:19–20	30
34	24, 31, 49, 60
35:22	31
36:31–39	99
38	27
38:29–30	27
46:13	28
46:14	28
49	29, 30, 38
49:3–4	31
49:24	29

Exodus
1:11	8
4:25	102
12:6	210
12:15–20	210
12:29–30	150
12:40–41	92
13:7	210
15	42
17:8	23
17:15–16	23
20:22	137
20:22–23:33	137
22:25–26	155
22:27	137
23:20–33	137
34:6	216

Leviticus
17–26	219
18:6–8	27
18:25	219
18:29	219
19:2	219
20:7–8	219
20:17–21	27
20:22	219
20:26	219
21:8	219
21:14	219
21:23	219
22:9	219
22:16	219
22:32	219
25:47–49	28
26:4	219
26:20	219
26:32–33	219

Numbers		Joshua	
6:24–26	173	5:10–12	157
20:17	98	7:16–18	20
21:1–3	40	9:17	29, 51, 99
21:14–15	37	10:12–13	38
21:17–18	37	11:1	41
21:27–30	38, 41	12:2–3	105
24:7	53	13–19	29, 31
24:20	53	13:3	40
25:7–8	244	13:15–24	72
26:5–50	27	14:15–21	105
26:23	28, 41	15:6	30
26:26	28	15:9	15, 73
26:31	31	15:9–10	23
26:33	26, 105	15:16–19	27
27:1–11	26	15:21–63	155
27:4	28	15:24	23
32:34	113	15:39	155
32:41	28, 59	15:42	114, 155
		15:60	23
Deuteronomy		15:61–62	155
1–3	139, 175	16:8–9	30
2:23	33, 40	16:9	29
6:4	175	16:10	64
7:3–4	66	17:2	26
7:13	136	17:2–3	68
12:11	95	17:3	105
14:22–29	175	17:9	29, 30
14:24–29	69	17:11	30, 51
15:1–11	175	17:11–13	72
16:5–7	157	17:17–18	20
17:14–15	48	18:5	40
17:14–20	47, 66	18:15	15
24:12–13	155	18:16	73
27:17	28	18:17	30
28:4	136	18:21–24	155
28:18	136	18:21–28	155
28:51	136	18:25–28	99
28:53–57	165	18:26	136, 170, 190
31	175	18:28	49, 50
32	175	19:6	6
32:2	23	19:12	39
33	29, 30, 38, 175	19:15	7
33:18–19	39	19:22	39
33:19	29	19:34	39

19:38	40	9:8–15	47
19:41–46	72	9:20	120
19:44	64, 148	9:30	29
21	55	10:1	28
21:29	8	10:1–5	28, 55
24:30	38	10:18	29
		11:1–2	26
Judges		11:6	29
1:17	40	11:8	29
2–12	59	11:19–21	105
2:18	121	11:31	21
2:22–26	24	12:4	26, 38
3	41	12:5–6	31
3:9	121	12:7	39
3:15	121	12:7–15	28, 55
3:31	41	13:5	52
4	41	13:25	31
4:6	39	15:14–17	41
4:12	39	16:31	39
4:14	39	18:12	31, 40
5	23, 25, 26, 29–31, 39, 40, 178	18:19	29
5:4–5	23, 30, 39	18:29	31
5:5	23	18:30–31	65, 100
5:6	41	19–21	52
5:7	39	20–21	170
5:8–9	24	20:1	170
5:11	23, 30, 39	20:26–28	59
5:13	23, 30, 39	20:33	23
5:13–14	39	21:8–14	51
5:16	31		
5:17	29–31	Ruth	
5:19	19, 24, 39	4:3–6	28
5:20–21	41		
6:11	28	1 Samuel	
6:24	28	1:1	27
6:34	25, 26	2	77
7:15–23	24	4–6	54
8:2	26, 38	4:1–7:2	76, 77
8:14	29	6:8	36
8:27	38	6:11	36
8:32	39	6:15	36
9	31, 59, 60	7–11	77
9:1	26	7:7–14	52
9:5	119	8:1–22	47
9:6	120	8:11–18	47, 76

1 Samuel (cont.)		20:17	77
8:19–20	48	20:29	28
9:1	52	20:42	52
9:2	52	21:11	50, 53, 76
9:16–17	52	22:2	55
10:2	30, 39	22:6	50
10:5	52	23	54
10:11–12	50, 72	23:18	52
10:17–27	47	24	52
10:20–21	26	24:21–23	52
10:23	52	26	52
11	51, 52	26:1	54
11:4	50	26:3	54
11:8	52	27:1–6	54
12:1–25	47	27:2	36
13–14	34, 52	29:1	51
13–15	77	30	55
13:1	51	30:14	33
14	51	30:21–25	53
14:2	50	30:27–31	54, 57
14:4–5	50	31:10	52
14:15	52	31:10–12	51
14:35	50	31:11	51
14:47	52	31:11–13	50
14:47–48	52, 55		
14:49–50	50	2 Samuel	
14:50	53	1:17–27	56
15	52, 53	1:18–27	38
15:4	52	1:19–27	50, 77
15:12	50	1:20–21	52
15:34	50	1:22	77
16:11–2 Sam 25:2	55	2:4	50
16:14–2 Sam 25:12	76, 78	2:4–5	51
16:19	78	2:9	39, 50, 51. 76
17	52	2:11	74
17:5	36	2:12–32	50, 54
17:38	36	3:2	52, 53
18:1	77	3:2–5	53
18:3	77	3:3	53
18:7	50, 53, 76	3:6–11	56
18:10–11	51	3:16	73
18:17–19	51	3:28–34	56
19:24	50, 76	3:32	50
20:6	28	4:1	56
20:14–17	52	4:2–3	51

ANCIENT SOURCES INDEX 269

4:9–12	56	16:5–8	51, 73
4:12	50	16:5–13	79
5:2	78	16:22	101
5:4	73	17:14	65, 79
5:5	74	17:18	73
5:6	54	17:27	98
5:8	54	18:6	30
5:13–15	61	18:18	54
5:17–25	58	19:17–24	79
5:18–21	54	19:25–31	56, 79
6	54	19:38	26
6:1–9	76, 77	20	57, 79
6:6–8	54	20:1	32, 51
6:20–23	56	20:4–10	54
7	54	20:7	57
7:12	65	20:23–26	56, 67
7:14–15	65	20:24	57
8:1–14	55	20:25	57
8:3–5	66	20:26	57
8:15–18	56, 67	21:1–10	51
8:17	57	21:6	50
8:18	57	21:7	52
9	56, 79	21:12	51
9:9–11	127	21:12–14	50, 52
9:10–13	171	21:15–22	55
9–12	77	21:19	53
9–20	79	22:2–51	77
10	55, 56, 61	23:1–7	77
10:1–4	98	23:4	152, 159
10:2	52	23:8–39	55
11	56	23:11–12	41
11:27	79	24	38, 54, 61
12:8	101	24:16	150
12:11	79		
12:11–23	61	1 Kings	
12:20	65	1–2	77, 79
12:24	79	2:8–9	79
12:25	65	2:11	73
12:26–31	56	2:22	101
12:31	57	2:34	56
13:37–38	53	2:36–46	79
14:7	28	2:45	65
14:23	53	3:1	61, 63, 66
15:18	33, 57	3:4–13	62
16:1–4	79	3:16	63

1 Kings (cont.)		6:2	194
3:16–28	62	6:36	194
3:28	62	6:37	65
4:1	66, 70	6:38	65
4:2–6	56, 62, 66	7:1–12	63
4:3	66, 67	7:2–8	88
4:7	67–71	7:8	63
4:7–19	62, 67	7:14	63
4:8	68, 71, 72	7:27–39	132
4:8–10	68	7:44	132
4:8–11	70	8	202
4:8–14	72	8:1–3	63
4:8–19	73	8:2	65
4:9	71, 72	8:12–13	38, 65
4:10	68, 71, 72	8:65	63, 124
4:11	71, 72	9:10–13	68
4:11–12	68	9:10–14	62
4:12	64, 67, 68, 70–72	9:11–14	63
4:13	68, 70–72	9:15	74
4:14	68, 71, 72	9:15–19	62, 63
4:15	64, 71	9:15–23	66
4:15–18	72	9:16	63, 66
4:16	70, 71	9:17–18	64
4:17	71, 72	9:18	64, 72
4:18	70–72	9:23	70
4:19	68, 70–72, 105	9:24	61, 63, 64
4:20	72	9:24–25	87
4:29–31	219	9:26	58, 64
5:1	58, 63	9:26–28	63, 111
5:4	58, 63	10:1–2	63
5:5	65	10:1–10	62
5:7	70, 71	10:4–5	62
5:7–8	68, 70	10:11–12	63
5:9	62	10:14–15	63
5:9–14	62	10:22	63, 111
5:14	62, 63	10:23–24	62
5:15–23	62	10:28	66
5:15–32	62	10:28–29	63
5:17–18	66	11	65
5:20	63	11–12	66, 97
5:27	63, 66	11:7	66, 156
5:28	57	11:14–22	99
5:30	70	11:14–28	66
6–7	64	11:19	101
6:1	65, 92	11:23–25	98

11:27	64	15:29–30	104
11:29–39	59, 138	15:33	87, 102
11:40	66	16	104
11:41	62	16:4	104
11:42	73	16:5	85, 86
12	124	16:8	87
12:15	59	16:9	104
12:16	32, 51	16:11	119
12:18	57	16:12	104
12:21–24	138	16:12–13	104
12:25	88, 100	16:15	87, 104
12:32	97	16:15–16	93, 158
13	88, 138	16:18	104
13:2	155	16:20	85, 86, 101, 104, 116
13:30–32	155	16:22–23	93
13:32	156	16:23	87, 104
14	88	16:23–24	105
14:1	100, 101	16:24	88
14:1–18	138	16:27	85, 86
14:11	104	16:29	87, 93
14:19	86, 99, 100	16:29–22:40	106
14:20	93	16:31	104, 106
14:21	60	16:32	105
14:25	73, 99	16:33	121
14:25–28	88	16:34	88, 106
14:26	87	17–2 Kgs 10	88, 110
14:26–28	65	17:1–2 Kgs 8:15	138
14:29	60	17:10–16	138
14:30	99	18	106
14:31	93	19	106
15:2	101	19:15–17	116, 138
15:7	99	20	89, 94, 106, 109, 110, 121
15:10	101	20:13–43	138
15:13	101	20:16	104
15:17	88	21	106
15:18	87, 101, 121	21:4	26
15:18–20	98, 109	22	65, 70, 110
15:20	101, 103, 131	22:1–28	138
15:21	102	22:1–36	110
15:22	88	22:30–37	160
15:23	86, 101	22:39	85, 86, 106
15:24	93	22:40	93
15:25	87	22:45	85, 86, 109
15:27	104	22:46	110
15:29	104	22:47	111

2 Kings (cont.)		10:13	101
22:48	65, 70, 110	10:17	119
22:51	87, 93	10:32–33	116, 117
		10:34	86, 116
2 Kings		10:36	94
1:2	111	11:1	119
1:9–15	138	11:3	118
1:17	93, 111	11:10	119
2:13–14	138	11:14	119
2:23–24	138	11:17–18	119
2:24	119	11:18	112
3	89, 93, 110, 112, 113	11:19	119
3:1	93, 114	11:20	119
3:4–27	89, 111	12:1	94, 118
3:6	112	12:2	120
3:14	112	12:5	120
5	88	12:7	88
5:10–14	138	12:9–15	156
6	89, 109	12:18	120
6:24–7:20	89, 109, 110, 116, 121	12:18–19	88, 120
6:25–29	165	12:19	87
8	109	12:21	64
8:1–6	138	12:21–22	120
8:4	88	13:1	87
8:7–15	84, 109, 116	13:2–5	121
8:12	129	13:3	109, 121
8:16	93, 114	13:3–5	110
8:17	114	13:6	121
8:18	114, 117	13:7	110
8:20	110	13:8	86
8:20–22	114	13:10	87
8:22	110, 114	13:12	86, 120
8:25	93	13:13	94
8:26	114, 117	13:20–21	39
8:28–29	113, 116	13:22	121, 125
9	106	13:22–23	121
9–10	115	13:22–25	110
9:14–28	113, 115	13:23	124
9:14–10:27	116	13:24–25	109, 121
9:22	106	13:25	121, 124
9:29	93	14	125
9:31	104	14:2	95
10	119	14:5	120
10:6–8	119	14:7	88, 95, 125
10:10	119	14:13	125

14:14	87	17:6	134
14:15	86	17:24	134
14:16	94	17:24–33	189
14:17	125	17:27–28	158
14:22	88, 124	18–19	88, 149
14:23	95	18:1	95
14:25	88, 124	18:1–16	149
14:25–27	121	18:4	38, 87, 121
14:28	86, 124	18:7–8	146
15	125	18:8	144
15:1	95, 125	18:9	135
15:5	95, 125, 132	18:9–10	95, 144
15:8	95	18:9–11	134
15:10	128	19:9–12	88
15:14	88, 129	18:11	134
15:15	86, 88, 116, 128	18:13	144, 145, 149
15:16	128, 129	18:13–15	88, 121
15:17	87	18:13–16	149
15:19–20	88, 129	18:13–20:19	138
15:20	129, 132	18:14–16	144, 149
15:23	87	18:15	87
15:25	88, 129	18:17	149
15:27	87, 95, 130	18:17–19	149
15:29	103, 131, 133	18:17–37	144
15:30	88, 131	18:18	150
15:32	132	18:22	144
15:32–33	132	18:36–37	149
15:35	132	19:1–7	144
15:37	132	19:2	150
16:1	132	19:8	148
16:3	132	19:8–34	144
16:3–4	132	19:9	148, 149
16:5–8	132	19:12	107
16:5–9	103, 133	19:19–35	149
16:6	133	19:21–28	150
16:6–9	88	19:32–34	150
16:8	87, 121	19:35	149
16:9	131	19:35–36	149, 150
16:10–17	132	19:35–37	144
16:18	132	19:37	84, 150
17:1	87, 132	20:1–11	114
17:3	135	20:6	145
17:3–6	134	20:12–19	144, 146
17:4	134	20:20	85, 86, 144, 147
17:5–6	88	20:20–21	149

2 Kings (cont.)			
21:3	106, 121, 151	24:12	163, 168
21:3–7	156	24:13	87
21:5	151	24:14	163
21:13	106	24:14–16	166
21:17	85	24:16	163
21:18	54	25	88
21:23	88	25:1	168
21:23–24	153	25:1–12	165
21:26	54	25:3	165, 167, 168
22	156	25:8	168
22:3	155, 167, 174	25:9	169
22:4–7	120	25:11	166, 168
22:9	120	25:12	166, 171
22:11–12	151	25:14	197
22:12	158, 174	25:18	208
22:14	174	25:25	170
23	156	25:26	166
23:4	121, 158	25:27	163, 168
23:4–12	156		
23:5	157	1 Chronicles	
23:6	121	2:16	53
23:7	111, 157	2:21–23	28
23:11	157	2:54	54
23:13	66, 156	3:17–18	196
23:15	121	3:19	196, 202
23:15–19	155	3:24	211
23:15–20	156	5:40–41	209
23:16–18	138	7:1–2	28
23:17–18	39	7:10	41
23:19	156	8:23	41
23:23	167	8:29–33	51
23:29	160	9:4	28
23:31	155	9:35–39	51
23:33–34	161	11	55
23:34	155	16	218
23:35	161	16:36	218
24:1	162	22:1	54
24:2	162	23–26	202
24:5	163		
24:6	163	2 Chronicles	
24:7	163	3:1	54
24:8	163	6	218
24:10–11	163	8:10	70
24:10–17	88	11:5–12	99
		14	103

14:1–7	103	4:4	190		
15:1–15	103	4:4–5	196		
15:9–15	202	4:5	195		
16:12	102	4:6	194, 196		
17–20	111	4:6–23	194		
20	111	4:7	194		
21:10	114	4:7–23	196, 204		
24:23–24	121	4:8–11	194		
26	125	4:10	153, 207		
27:1–6	132	4:12–16	194		
28	134	4:17	207		
29–30	202	4:17–22	194		
30:11	202	4:23	195		
30:18	202	4:24	195		
32:3–6	147	5:1	198		
32:4–5	64	5:2	202		
32:28	147	5:3	200		
34:3	156	5:3–5	195		
34:3–7	156	5:3–17	196		
35:20–27	160	5:6	200		
35:21–22	160	5:6–17	195		
36:6–7	166	5:11–16	195		
36:10	168	5:12	198		
36:22–23	188	5:14	196, 197, 207		
		5:16	197		
Ezra		6	218		
1–6	217	6:1–12	196		
1:1–5	187	6:3–5	187, 193, 195, 196		
1:2–4	193, 196	6:6	200		
1:6	197	6:10	202		
1:8	196, 197	6:12	195		
1:9–11	193, 197	6:13	200		
1:11	197	6:13–17	202		
2	189	6:13–18	201		
2:1–70	193	6:14	198		
2:1–4:5	194	6:15	202		
2:2	201, 205	7	218		
2:59	170, 190, 191	7–10	218		
2:59–60	193	7:6	244		
3:2	197, 201, 202	7:12	195		
3:2–4	197	7:12–26	195, 196		
3:8	197, 201, 202	7:13	196		
3:8–13	194, 196, 197	7:14	196, 205		
4:1–5	194, 196	7:15–19	205		
4:2	153	7:20–24	205		

Ezra (cont.)		11:4–6	28
7:21–24	196	11:25–26	194
7:22	196	11:35	189
7:24	196	12:1–26	194
7:25–26	205	12:10–11	208
9:9	204	12:11	209
10:3	205	12:12–21	28
		12:26	205
Nehemiah		12:31–32	206
1–7	218	12:36	205
1:1–7:73	206	12:37	53
2:10	207	12:37–40	206
2:11–16	206	13	207
2:19	193	13:1–3	207
3	189, 206	13:4–8	207
3:1–32	194	13:4–31	206
3:7	170	13:12–13	202
3:15	53	13:24	190, 207
3:19	170	13:28	209, 228
4	206		
4:15–20	206	Job	
5	206	1:1–2:13	220
5:14	207	7:7–21	220
5:15	204	9:1–20	220
6:17–18	207	9:32–33	220
7	189	10:1–17	220
7:4	207	13:15	220
7:7–72	194	13:20–28	220
7:61	170	30:20–31	220
8	181, 205, 248	31:35–37	220
8–10	218	32–37	220
8:3	205	33:13	220
8:7–8	190	38:1–39:30	220
8:9	190, 205, 207	40:6–41:26	220
8:11	190	42:7–8	220
8:15	205	42:7–17	220
9:32	204		
9:36–37	204	Psalms	
9:38–10:27	194	2	49, 182, 221
10:2	207	2:8	56
10:33–40	202	3–41	220
11	29	18	182
11–13	218	20	59
11:1–2	207	26:8	202
11:3–24	194	29	182, 221

42–50	221	2:4	216
42–83	220	2:6	263
45	182, 221, 262	2:7	262
46	59, 150, 182, 221	3:1–5	262
48	151, 182, 221	3:4	262
48:3	23	3:5	262
59:6	59	3:6	263
65:5	202	5:2–8	262
68	182	5:8	262
68:9	23, 59	5:9	262
68:36	59	6:1	262
72	182, 221	6:3	263
72:8	56	6:10	262
72:18	59	7:10	263
73–88	221	8:2	262
76	59, 151, 182, 221	8:3	262
77	42	8:4	262
78	182	8:5	262, 263
78:60	37	8:8–10	262
80	42		
81	42	Isaiah	
83:10	41	2:3	59
84	59, 202	5:1–7	262
89	221	5:8–10	125
89:19	59	7:1	132
106:36	218	7:1–17	133
110	49, 182, 221	7:4	133
120–134	202	7:6	133
132	182	7:9	133
132:11	65	8:6	133
137	221	8:14	58
137:7	170, 180	9:4	41
		10:9	130
Proverbs		10:16–19	150
1–9	219	10:26	41, 50
8:22–31	261	10:33	150
22:17–24:22	219	11:11	192
25–29	219	12:6	59
25:1	65, 219	13–23	261
		14:28–32	146
Qoheleth		14:13	23
3:7	260	15:2	113
		17:1–3	134
Song of Songs		18:1–19:15	146
1:6	262	19:18	247

Isaiah (cont.)			
19:21–28	150	47:20	124
19:23–26	155	48:1	124
19:32–34	150		
19:35–36	150	Daniel	
20	146	1:1–4	166
21:10	59	8:13	243
22:8–11	147	8:21	227
22:15–19	150	8:24	227
24–27	261	9:4–19	263
24:10–13	261	9:26	240
25:2	261	11:5	232
25:6–12	261	11:6	232
28:21	54	11:7–9	232
29:23	59	11:10–12	232
30:30–33	150	11:13	262
36–39	144	11:13–16	232
40–55	180	11:14	236
44:28	180, 194	11:15	236
45:1–8	180	11:17	237
45:7	181	11:17–19	232
49:26	181	11:19	237
52:6	181	11:20	232
52:11	197	11:21–39	232
56–66	215	11:22	241
66:1	261	11:28–31	241
		11:31	243
		11:34	262
Lamentations		11:40–45	232
2:20	165	12:11	243
4:3–10	165		
4:21–22	180	Hosea	
		1:4	115
Ezekiel		1:4–5	124
1:4–28	208	5:1	39
3:15	170, 191	6:7	175
17:13–18	165	8:1	175
24:1–2	169, 180	8:4	128
25:15–16	33	9:2	216
29:17	180	10:14	117
29:19–21	172	12:8–9	125
29:21–23	171	13:12	124
33:21	169		
33:21–22	180	Joel	
33:32	262	2:13–14	216
47:15	124	4:10	216

Amos		Haggai	
1:2	216	1:1	201, 202
1:3–5	117	1:12	202
1:5	107	1:14	202
1:13	129	1:14–15	197
3:15	105	2:2	202
5:6	40	2:4	202
5:10–13	125	2:18	197
5:18–20	178	2:20–23	201
6:2	130	2:23	215
6:4–7	125		
6:13–14	124	Zechariah	
7:1–9	124	1–8	214, 216
7:10–17	133	1:12	202
7:13	124	3:1–5	202
8:4–6	125	3:8	201
8:14	158	4:1–10	201
9:2	180	4:4–7	201
9:7	33	4:7	198
9:12	181	4:9–10	198
9:13	216	6	201, 215
		6:9–15	201
Obadiah		6:11–15	201
1–4	180	7:1–7	179
4	180	7:5	202
5–7	180	8:19	179
17–18	216	9–14	215
19	51, 180	9–11	215, 216
		9:1–5	145
Micah		9:13	215
1:10–16	148, 177	11	215
2:2	125	12–14	216
3:12	177		
4:2	59	Malachi	
4:3	216	1:1–14	216
6:16	104	1:3–4	169
		2:7	244
Nahum		2:10–12	216
3:8	178	2:13–16	216
		3:7–12	216
Habakkuk		3:22–23	216
2:6–20	179	4:2	152, 159
3	178		
3:3	23		

Deuterocanonical Books

Judith
- 3:8 — 260
- 4:6 — 260

Additions to Esther
- 11 — 259

Sirach
- 20:6 — 260
- 24:1–22 — 261
- 38:24–39:11 — 260
- 41:8 — 260
- 46:18 — 70
- 49:10 — 217
- 50:1–21 — 238
- 50:1 — 260
- 50:26 — 260

1 Maccabees
- 1:11–15 — 240
- 1:11–13:42 — 240
- 1:20–23 — 241
- 1:41 — 243
- 1:41–64 — 242
- 1:47 — 243
- 2:15–28 — 244
- 2:42 — 244
- 3:10–12 — 244, 250
- 3:13–26 — 244
- 3:38–4:25 — 245
- 4:26–35 — 245
- 4:27–50 — 241
- 4:36–59 — 245
- 5 — 246
- 6:1–16 — 245
- 6:18–54 — 247
- 6:46 — 247
- 7:12–16 — 247
- 7:13 — 244
- 7:25–32 — 248
- 7:39–50 — 248
- 8 — 258
- 9:1–18 — 248
- 9:23–27 — 248
- 9:28–38 — 248
- 9:50 — 248
- 9:58–73 — 249
- 10:1–17 — 249
- 10:15–21 — 249
- 10:22–45 — 249
- 10:59–60 — 249
- 10:67–87 — 250
- 11:30–37 — 250
- 11:54–59 — 250
- 11:63–74 — 250
- 12:1–4 — 258
- 12:19–23 — 231
- 12:39–54 — 251
- 13:1–30 — 251
- 13:36–42 — 251
- 13:43–51 — 251
- 14:29–43 — 248
- 15:1–9 — 251
- 15:15–24 — 258
- 15:22–23 — 232
- 16:11–24 — 251

2 Maccabees
- 1:1–9 — 252, 258
- 2:1–3 — 263
- 3 — 239
- 3:1–40 — 239
- 3:4 — 29, 239
- 4 — 239
- 4:7–9 — 239
- 4:9 — 240
- 4:19 — 240
- 4:23 — 240
- 5 — 241
- 5:1–11 — 243
- 6:2 — 243
- 6:12–7:42 — 243, 258
- 7 — 258
- 8:8–29 — 245
- 9:28–29 — 245
- 10:1–9 — 245
- 11:10–2:18 — 245
- 11:16–21 — 245

11:16–32	245	Psalms of Solomon	
11:22–26	245	2	257
11:22–38	258	8	257
11:27–33	245	17	257
11:29	245		
11:32	245	**Rabbinic Works**	
11:34–38	245		
12	246	b. Qiddušin	
12:24–32	250	66a	253
12:39–45	258		
13:3–8	246	m. 'Abot	
13:9–17	247	1:1	238
13:18–26	247	3:19	253
14:6	244		
14:37–46	243, 258	m. Menaḥot	
15:1–36	248	13:10	228

3 Maccabees
   1:8–2:24   235, 238

Megillah Ta'anit
   22   252

1 Esdras
   6:18   197
   7:5   202

t. Sanhedrin
   2:2   168

New Testament

t. Soṭah
   13:3   253

John
   3:30   78

y. Roš Haššanah
   1:56d   191

Romans
   11:1   29

y. Yebamot
   15:2   11

Pseudepigrapha

Other

1 Enoch
   12–16   240
   90:8   240

4Q169/4QpNah   255

4Q448/4QPsAp   255

Jubilees
   30   240
   32   240

Herodotus, *History*
   1.73–74   90
   1.178–186   162
   1.188–191   186
   2.141   148

Letter of Aristeas
   12   93
   12–13   230

   2.157   153
   2.159   160, 162

Herodotus, History (cont.)		12.136	236
2.161	165	12.138–144	237
3.1–38	198	12.145–146	237
3.7–9	198	12.157–158	231
3.91	32	12.160–236	234
3.159	199	12.226–227	231
4.83–144	200	12.228–229	238
6.19	204	12.229	242
6.21	200	12.230–233	238
7.151–152	203	12.237	239, 240
		12.238	240
Josephus, Against Apion		12.239	240
1.108	62	12.239–240	242
1.112–125	62	12.239–241	240
1.121–125	62	12.240–13.214	240
1.123–124	105	12.253	243
1.137–138	162	12.258–263	243
1.156	172	12.383	240
1.186–189	230	12.383–385	246
2.48	235	12.387	247
		12.402–412	248
Josephus, Jewish Antiquities		13.62–71	241
1.136	32	13.117–119	250
7.66	62	13.172	253
8.62	62	13.173	253
8.144–149	62	13.213	251
8.163	62	13.215	251
8.324	105	13.223–235	251
9.283–287	135	13.236–248	252
10.18–23	149	13.249	252
10.21	149	13.255	252
10.181–182	167	13.255–258	252
10.222	162	13.257–258	252
10.228	171	13.282–282	253
11.297–301	209	13.288–296	253
11.302–311	209	13.297	253
11.302–312	228	13.319	254
11.302–347	209	13.372–373	255
11.321–325	227, 228	13.380	255
11.325–339	227	13.392	255
11.340–346	209	13.393–394	255
11.347	231	13.395	255
12.4–7	230	13.397	256
12.8	231	13.419–421	256
12.43	231	13.427–428	256

14.18	255
14.19–21	256
14.29–33	256
14.34–38	256
14.41–45	256
14.54–72	257
14.74–76	257
14.88	257
14.207	238

Josephus, *Jewish War*
1.63	252
1.145–153	257
1.156–166	257
1.169–170	257
7.426–430	247
7.433–436	247

Strabo, *Geography*
16.2.25

Xenophon, *Cyropaedia*
7.5.7–32	186
7.5.58	186

Modern Authors Index

Albertz Rainer	141, 183	Eshel, Hanan	223
Allen, Lindsay	183	Faust, Avraham	1, 43
Athas, George	81	Finkelstein, Israel	1, 34, 43, 81
Austin, Michael M.	223	Fried, Lisbeth S.	183
Bagnall Roger S.	223	Fritz, Volkmar	1
Banks, Diane	1	Garbani, Giovanni	1
Barr, James	1	Gass, Erasmus	1
Barrick, W. Boyd	141	Gerstenberger, Erhard, S.	183
Becking, Bob	43, 183	Gilmour, Rachelle	43
Bedford, Peter R.	223	Grabbe Lester L.	1, 43, 81, 141, 183, 223
Berquist, Jon L.	183	Grainger, John D.	223
Bishop Moore, Megan	141	Grisanti, M. A.	81
Blenkinsopp, Joseph	141, 183	Gunnar Lehmann	2
Bodner, Keith	43	Hagelia, Hallvard	81
Briant, Pierre	183	Halpern, Baruch	43
Chaney, Mark	223	Heckel, Waldemar	223
Cohen, Getzel M.	223	Hess, Richard S.	
Cohen, Raymond	1	Hjelm, Ingrid	223
Cohen, Shaye J. D.	223	Hölbl, Günther	223
Collins, John J.	223	Howard David M.	81
Collins, Nina L.	223	Japhet, Sarah	183
Cook, Steven L.	43	Kalimi, Isaac	141
Curtis, John	183	Kartreit, Magnar	183
Daviau, P. M. Michèle	81	Kelle ,Brad E.	141
Day, John	1	Killebrew, Ann E.	2, 44
De Souza, Philip	183	Kim, Uriah Y.	141
Derow, Peter	223	King, Philip	2
Dever William G.	1, 81	Klingbeil, Gerald A.	1
Dickenson, Oliver	1	Kofoed, Jens B.	81
Dietrich, Walter	43	Lipinski, Edward	81
Dobbs-Allsopp, F. W.	81	Lipschits, Oded	141, 183
Dubovský, Peter	141	Liverani, Mario	2
Edelman, Diana	183	Lux, Rüdiger	43
Ehrlich, Carl	43	Macchi, Jean-Daniel	82
Eph'al, Israel	141	Magness, Jodi	224

Manassa, Colleen	2	White, Marsha C.	43
Matthews, Victor H.	81	Wildberger, Hans	82
Mazar, Amihai	1	Yamada, Shigeo	82
Mazar, Amihai	81	Yardley, John C.	223
McKenzie, Stephen L.	43	Yasur-Landau, Assaf	2
Middlemas, Jill	141	Zevit, Ziony	142
Miller, Robert D.	2		
Mobley, Gregory	2		
Morkot, Robert G.	141		
Mykytiuk, Lawrence J.	142		
Nahkai, Beth Alpert	2		
Nelson, Richard D.	2		
Nickelsburg, George W. E.	224		
Niemann, Hermann M.	43, 71		
Oeming, Manfred	183		
Oren, Eliezer D.	2		
Parpola, Simo	81		
Pfoh, Emanuel	2		
Porter, Michael	81		
Pury, Albert de	82		
Rajak, Tessa	224		
Rad, Gerhard von	60		
Ray, Paul J.	1		
Richardson, Seth	141		
Robker, Jonathan M.	82		
Römer, Thomas	82		
Routledge, Bruce	82		
Sacchi, Paolo	224		
Said, Edward	225		
Schaper, Joachim	183		
Schniedewind, W. M.	184		
Schoors, Antoon	82		
Shalom Brooks, Simcha	43		
Silberman, Neil A.	43		
Smith, Mark S.	142		
Stager, Lawrence E.	2		
Sweeney, Marvin A.	142		
Tadmor, Hayim	82		
Torijano, Pablo A.	44		
Uehlinger, Christopher	82		
Van De Mieroop, Marc	2		
Van Seters, John	44		
Vanderhooft, David S.	142, 184, 224		
Vaughn, Andrew G.	44		
Westbrook, Raymond	1		

Subject Index

1 and 2 Chronicles, 101, 111, 121, 156, 160, 190, 202, 218, 220
1 and 2 Kings, 53, 56, 61, 62, 64, 66, 77, 85, 89, 92, 93, 95, 99, 101, 106, 109, 110, 120, 124, 137, 138, 156, 163, 176
1 and 2 Samuel, 77, 79, 218
1 Maccabees, 241, **257–58**
2 Maccabees, 245, 258
Aaronic priesthood, 59, 100
Abda, 6, 7
Abdi-Heba, 7
Abdon, 42
Abel-beth-maacah, 103, 131
Abiathar, 57
Abiezer, 26
Abigail, 53
Abihu, 101
Abijah, 100, 101. *See also* Abijam
Abijam, 93, 99, 101. *See also* Abijah
Abimelech, 26, 31, 41, 46
Abishai, 53, 55
Abner, 50, 52, 56, 78
Abraham, 31, 38, 59
Absalom, 32, 54
Abu Simbel, 164
accession year, 91, 95, 168, 169, 194
Acco, 7, 10, 246, 255. *See also* Ptolemais
Achaemenes, 185, 199
Achaemenid dynasty, 185, 199, 227
Achan, 27
Achish, 39, 54
Achsah, 27
Achshaph, 7
Acra, 243, 245, 246, 249–51
Adad-guppi, 172

Adad-idri, 84, 109. *See also* Ben-hadad; Hadad-ezer
Adad-nirari I, 5
Adad-nirari III, 83, 84, 89, 121–23
Adasa, 247, 248
Adida, 250
Adon, 162
Adoniram (Adoram), 57, 67
Adora, 252
Adrammelech, 84, 150
Agag, 53
Agothocles, 236
Ahab (king), 75, 83–85, 93, 94, 103, 104, **105–8**, 109–12, 114, 115, 118, 119, 121, 136, 160
Ahab (prophet), 171
Ahaz, 84, 103, 131, **132–34**, 137, 142, 144, 178
Ahaziah (Israel), 92, 94, 101, 111
Ahaziah (Judah), 92–94, 96, 111, **114–16**, 118, 119
Ahhiyawa, 33, 40
Ahijah, 59, 104, 138
Ahilud, 57, 67, 69
Ahimaaz, 69
Ahimelech, 57
Ahinoam, 52, 53
Ahiqar, 259
Ahishar, 57, 67
Ahmose, 6
Ahura Mazda, 188, 192, 199, 203
Ahzai, 208
Ai, 189
Aijalon Valley, 9, 10, 50, 64
akitu festival, 189

SUBJECT INDEX

Akrabattenee, 246
Al Yahudu, 191
Alalakh, 32, 55
Alashiya, 32
Alcimus, 229, 247, 248. *See also* Eliakim
Aleppo, 5, 246
Alexander I Balas, 249, 250
Alexander II Zabinas, 253
Alexander IV Aegus, 227
Alexander Jannaeus, 229, **254–56**
Alexander the Great, 184, 185, 188, 209, 212, 213, **224–28**, 229, 230, 243
Alexandra Salome, 253, 254, 256
Alexandria, 226, 227, 231, 236, 241, 242, 261
alphabet, 14, 64, 192
Amalekites, 40, 45, 52, 53, 55
Amarna letters, 6–8, 33, 41, 49, 70, 73, 96
Amasis, 187, 198, 199
Amaziah, 83, 95, 120, **122–23**
Amenhotep II, 4, 6, 7
Amenhotep III, 23
Amenhotep IV (Akhenaten), 7
Amesha Spenta, 192
Amman Citadel Inscription. 98
Amminadab, 86
Ammon, 11, 18, 45, 52, 55–57, 60, 61, 86, 98, 99, 148, 164, 167, 170, 174, 193, 200, 207, 231, 233, 242
Ammonitis, 233, 238
Amnon, 53
Amon, 95, 96, 151, 153, 154, 158
Amos, 42, 60, 99, 124, 125, 138, 157
Amun-Re, 6, 18
Amurru, 7, 8
Amyrtaeus, 212
Amytis, 159, 185
Anakim, 40
Anani, 211
Ananiah, 210
Anastasi Papyrus I, 8, 30
Anastasi Papyrus III, 8
Anastasi Papyrus VI, 8
Anat, 23, 40, 41, 210, 212
Anat-Bethel, 210

Anathoth, 23, 40, 55
Anatolia, 13, 32, 33. *See also* Asia Minor
Ancyra, 226
Andromachus, 227
Andronicus, 240
Angra Mainyu, 192
aniconic, 159, 174, 132
Anshan, 185
Antigonus, 253, 254
Antigonus Monophthalmus, 230
Antigonus II, 234
Antioch, 234, 239, 240
Antiochia, 231
Antiochus I Soter, 233
Antiochus II Theos, 232–34
Antiochus III Megas, 232, 235, **236–38**
Antiochus IV Epiphanes, 224, 229, 232, **239–43**, 245, 247, 249, 252, 258–60, 262
Antiochus V Eupator, 245, 246, 247
Antiochus VI Epiphanes Dionysus, 250, 251
Antiochus VII Sidetes, 251–53
Antiochus VIII Grypus, 251, 253
Antiochus IX Cyzicenus, 251, 253
Antiochus XII Dionysius, 255
Antiochus XIII Asiaticus, 256
Antipater, 225, 252, 256, 257
Antipatris, 227
Apamea, Peace of, 237
Aphek, 6, 17, 37, 162
Apiru, 7, 8, 42. *See also* Habiru
Apollonius (commander of Antiochus IV), 244
Apollonius (commander of Demetrius II), 249, 250
Appaianus, 230
Apries, 164, 165
Aqabah, 9, 58, 64
Arabah, 10
Arabs, 127, 130, 145, 152, 153, 162, 172
Arad, 75, 158
Arad ostraca, 90, 137, 169, 173
Aramaeans, 5, 13, 14, 18, 45, 55, 56, 98, 101, 103, 106, 115, 116, 118, 124, 136

Aramaic, 136, 177, 188, 190–92, 195, 210, 228, 247
Aram-naharaim, 18
Arda-Mulissi, 84, 150
Aretas III, 255, 256
Areus I, 229, 231
Argob, 129, 256
Arieh, 129
Aristagorus, 200
Aristobulus I, 224, 229, 253, 254
Aristobulus II, 229, 256, 257
ark, 29, 54, 65, 77, 78, 181, 218
Ark Story, 54, 76, 77
Armenia, 5, 185, 256
Arnon, 11, 37, 98, 112, 117. *See also* Wadi Mujib
Aroer, 11, 98, 113
Arpad, 123, 128
Arrian, 225
Arsames, 211
Arsinoë, 236
Artaxerxes I Longimanus, 194, 195, 196, **203–4**, 205, 209, 217, 218
Artaxerxes II Memnon (404–359), 188, 204, 209, 212
Artaxerxes III Ochos, 188, 213, 227, 260
Artaxerxes IV (Arses), 213
Artaxerxes V (Bessos), 213, 226
Arubboth, 68–70
Asa, 93, **101–3**, 108, 121
Asahel, 53, 55
Asaiah, 174
Ascalon, 250, 255. *See also* Ashkelon
Ashdod, 17, 34, 130, 145, 146, 148, 150, 153, 200, 246. *See also* Azotus
Ashdod ware, 36
Ashdoda figurines, 36
Asher, 30, 40, 51, 68, 71, 72
Asherah, 121, 157, 159
Ashkelon, 7, 15, 16, 34, 146, 148, 150, 162, 189, 206, 256. *See also* Ascalon.
Ashna, 137
Ashtaroth, 11
Ashurites, 39, 51
Asia Minor, 4, 9, 119, 152, 172, 184, 186, 188, 211, 213, 226, 232, 233, 237. *See also* Anatolia
Asochis
assassination, 51, 83, 84, 95, 96, 101, 106, 109, 113, 115, 119, 120, 122, 123, 128, 129, 143, 144, 150, 154, 158, 170, 172, 199, 203, 209, 213, 226, 233, 234, 236, 239, 240, 251, 252, 256–59
Assur (city), 90, 108, 159
Assur (god), 89
Assurbanipal, 84, 143, 150–54, 175
Assur-dan III, 123
Assur-etel-ilani, 143, 154
Assur-nadin-shumi, 151
Assurnasirpal II, 106, 107
Assur-nirari V, 123, 127
Assur-ubalit I, 5
Assur-uballit II, 143, 159, 161
Astyages, 185, 172
Aswan Dedicatory Inscription, 204
Atargatis, 246
Ataroth, 105, 113
Athaliah, 49, 85, 92, 94, 96, 106, 114, **118–20**
Athens, 200, 201, 203, 210, 212
Atossa, 199, 203
Atroth-beth-Joab, 27, 54
Augustus, 261
Avastana, 211
Avvim, 40
Azaliah, 174
Azariah 49, 83, 87, 95, **122–25**, 137. *See also* Uzziah
Azariah (son of Nathan), 57, 71
Azariah (son of Zadok), 56
Azekah, 10, 64, 164, 165
Azekah Inscription, 148
Azotus, 246, 250, 251. *See also* Ashdod
Azriyau, 125
Baal, 23, 38, 50, 105, 120, 127, 134
Baal II, 171
Baal Peor, 244
Baalah, 24
Baalath, 64
Baal-ezer, 105

SUBJECT INDEX

Baalis, 170
Baal-perazim, 54
Baal-tamar, 23
Baana, 69, 70
Baasha, 85, 93, 101–4, 109
Babylonian Chronicle, 90, 135, 154, 159, 160, 164, 167, 168
Bacchides, 247–29
Bactria, 185, 186, 204, 213, 227
Bagoas (Bagohi, governor), 202, 208, 209, 211
Bagoas (chief eunuch), 209, 213, 260
Bahurim, 73
Ba'ilirasi, 117
Banyas, 236. *See also* Panias
Barca, 204
Bardiya, 188, 199. *See also* Gaumata; Smerdis
Bar-hadad, 109, 122. *See also* Ben-hadad
Baruch (book), 263
Baruch (person), 174
Bashan, 10, 11, 41, 129
Baskama, 251
Bathsheba, 56, 61
Bealoth, 23, 71
Beer, 37
Beer-lahai-roi, 38
Beeroth, 51, 99, 248
Beersheba, 9, 11, 38, 55, 58–60, 65, 119, 158, 252, 255
Behistun Inscription, 199
Belshazzar, 172
Bemeselis, 255
Benaiah, 57, 60, 67
Ben-geber, 70
Ben-hadad, 84, 104, 109, 110. *See also* Hadadezer, Adad-idri
Ben-hadad I (son of Tabrimmon), 98, 101, 103, 109
Ben-hadad II (son of Hazael), 109, 110, 115, 118, 121, 122. *See also* Bar-Hadad
Benjamin, 10, 11, 15, 20, 29, 30, 32, 39, 41, 44, 49–52, 55–57, 60, 70, 72, 73, 79, 82, 97, 99, 102, 131, 136, 155, 169, 170, 189, 190, 238

Beonites, 246
Beqa Valley, 98
Berenice (city), 231. *See also* Pella
Berenice (daughter of Ptolemy II), 232, 234
Berenice II, 235
Berossus, 149, 172
Beth-arbel, 117
Beth-basi, 249
Bethel, 23, 24, 29, 38, 58–60, 97, 98, 100, 102, 124, 138, 155, 157, 169, 171, 189
Bethel (Elephantine), 210, 212
Beth-haccherem, 189
Beth-horon, 9, 64, 102, 173, 244, 248
Bethlehem, 10, 41, 53–55, 73
Beth-shean, 3, 6, 8, 17, 51, 52, 72, 131, 231, 248, 260. *See also* Scythopolis
Beth-shemesh, 10, 64, 77, 123, 164
Beth-zabdai, 250
Beth-zechariah, 246
Beth-zur, 189, 244, 245, 247
Beyond the River, 191, 194, 195, 200
Bichrites, 51
Bichrome pottery, 3, 23, 35, 36, 75
Bilgah, 238
Bilhah, 31
Bit-Adini, 18, 106, 107
Bit-Bahyani, 18
Bit-Halupe, 18
Bit-Omri, 104, 108, 118. *See also* House of Omri
Bit-Yakin, 134, 151
Bit-Zamani, 18
Black Obelisk, 118
Bohan, 30
Book of Jashar, 38, 50, 77
Book of the Acts of Solomon, **62–66**, 77, 99, 137
Book of the Chronicles of the Kings of Israel, 85, 104, 116, 122, 135, 137
Book of the Chronicles of the Kings of Judah, 60, 85, 87, 118, 119, 120, 151
Book of the Wars of Yahweh, 37
Borsippa, 192
Borzah, 99

Bosporus, 200
Bostra, 246
Bozez, 50
Broad Wall, 147, 152
bronze, 14, 38, 63, 86, 97
Byblos, 18, 106, 189, 226
Cabul, 63, 68
Calah, 136
Caleb, 27, 30, 53, 73, 82, 96, 99
Caligula, 261
Calneh, 130
Cambyses, 184, 188, 193, 198, 199, 211
Canaanites, 6, 7, 16, 17, **19**, 20, 22–24, 36, 39, 41, 45, 65, 70
Capharsalama, 248
Caphtor, 33. *See also* Crete
Cappadocia, 146, 185
Carchemish, 13, 106, 107, 143, 145, 159, 162
Caria, 119, 226
Carmel (Judah), 232
Carthage, 62, 226
Cassius, 257
Cendebeus, 251
centralization, cult, **157–59**, 175, 212,
Chaeronea, 213
Chaldeans, 18, 145, 146, 151, 178
chariots, 7, 14, 16, 19, 24, 41, 101, 103, 104, 107, 108, 135, 136, 157, 215, 226
Chebar, 143, 170
Chephirah, 99
Cherethites and Pelethites, 33, 57
chief, 26, 30, 46, 47, 53
chiefdom, 25, 44, 45, **46–47**, 49, 53, 99, 137
Chinneroth, 103
Chronicles (books). *See* 1 and 2 Chronicles
chronology, 3, 4, 13, 23, 44, 45, 61, 73–75, 86, **90–95**, 114, 132, 249
Cilician Gates, 246
clan, 3, **26–31**, 41, 46, 49, 51, 57
Cleopatra I, 237, 239
Cleopatra II, 242
Cleopatra III, 255

Cleopatra Thea, 250, 253
clientele state, 59, 73
climate, 9, 13, 69, 73
Coele-Syria, 227, 236, 239
collared rim jars
Community Rule (1QS), 254
compliance policy, 84, 132, 142, 151, 154, 163, 164, 170
coregency, 93–95, 114, 125, 132, 144, 151, 198, 239
corridor house, 36
Court History, 56, 61, 65, 74, 77, 79
Covenant Code, 49, 126, **137**, 155
Creator of the Earth Ostracon, 173
Crete 13, 33, 97, 249. *See also* Caphtor
Croesus, 186–88
Ctesias, 184
Cunaxa, 212
Curtius Rufus, 245, 247
Cyaxares, 159, 185
Cynoscephalae, 237
Cyprus, 3, 13, 14, 18, 36, 147, 200, 255
Cyrus Cylinder, 186, 187
Cyrus the Younger, 212
Cyrus II (the Great), 143, 172, 180, 181, 183, 184, **185–87**, 188, 193–99, 203, 217, 218
Dagon, 36, 77
Damascus, 8, 11, 14, 18, 45, 66, 83, 84, 94, 98, 101, 103, 106, 108, 109, 114, 116, 117, 121, 122, 124, 127–31, 133–35, 250
Damascus Document, 254
Dan (city), 31, 58, 60, 65, 74, 97, 98, 100, 103, 116, 124, 125, 158. *See also* Laish
Dan (tribe), 29, 31, 40
Daniel, 172, 227, 240, 260, 262
Danube, 200
Daphne (Antioch), 240
Daphne (Egypt), 231
daric, 188, 200
Darius I, 62, 184, 188, 191, 195, 196, 198, **199–201**, 203–5, 214
Darius II Nothus (Ochos), 188, 198, 210–13

SUBJECT INDEX

Darius III Codomanus, 188, 209, 213, 224, 226–28
Dathema, 246
David, 32, 38, 44–47, 50–52, **53–57**, 58, 59, 61, 62, 65–67, 73–79, 82, 83, 98, 116, 119, 181, 218, 252
David, City of, 53, 61, 64
Davidic dynasty, 52, 65, 78, 79, 119, 143, 170, 182, 201, 211, 214, 217
Dead Sea, 11, 98, 124, 189, 254
Deborah, 39, 41
Deborah, Song of, 31, **39–40**, 72, 97
Decapolis, 256, 257
Deir ʿAlla, 136
Delaiah, 209, 211
Delian League, 203
Delphi, 186
Delta, 8, 32, 33, 152, 153, 188, 193, 198, 247
Demetrius I Soter, 239, 247–49
Demetrius II Nicator, 249–53
Demetrius III Eucaerus, 255
Demetrius Poliorketes, 230
Denyen, 31, 33, 40
deportation, 107, 131, 133, 134, 136, 143, 145, 148, 163, 165–70, 180, 187, 189, 200
desolating sacrilege, 243
Deuteronomistic History, 52, 54, 59, 61, 62, 65, 66, 85, 87, 92, 104, 108, 111, 121, 124, 156, 175, **176–77**,
Deuteronomy, 49, 126, 137, 153, 155, 157, 158, **175**, 212
diarchy, 202
Dibon, 11, 98, 113
Didyma, 204
Dinah, 31
Diodochi, 230
Diodorus, 225, 230
divine warrior, 23, 24, 39, 178
Diyala, 186
Djehuty, 6
doctrine of retribution, 218
Dor, 6, 18, 33, 72, 125, 131, 174, 189, 255
Dur-Sharrukin, 107

Early Bronze Age, 21
Ebal, 10
Ecbatana, 186, 187, 195, 196, 200, 226
economy, 2, 4, 9, 10, **11–12**, 14, 17–24, 26, 40, 46, 48, 99, 102, 125, 126, 128, 134, 138, 143, 157, 158, 169, 170, 172, 173, 177, 187, 189, 192, 202, 206, 214, 215, 231, 235, 237, 238
Edom, 11, 18, 23, 45, 52, 55, 66, 98, 99, 110, 113, 114, 122, 125, 128, 133, 134, 148, 164, 169, 172, 173, 180. *See also* Idumea
egalitarian society, 20, 22, 26, 28, 47
Ehud, 24, 41
Ein Gedi, 190, 254
Ekron, 34, 36, 54, 64, 130, 146, 148, 150, 162
Ekwesh, 33
El, 38
Elah Valley, 10, 64
Elam, 4, 13, 145, 146, 151–53, 164, 185, 187, 188, 199, 237
Elasa, 248
Elath, 122, 125, 133
elders, 27, 29, 137, 171, 191, 195, 217, 241
Eleazar (high priest), 229, 234
Eleazar (Maccabee hero), 246
Elephantine, 202, 208–12, 231. *See also* Yeb
Elephantine papyri, 190, 193, **210–12**, 229
Elephantine temple, 193, 202, 210, 228
Elhanan, 53
Eliakim (high priest), 247. *See also* Alcimus
Eliakim (servant of Yaukin), 164
Eliakim (son of Hilkiah), 150
Eliashib, 208
Elihoreph, 67
Elijah, 106, 110, 111, 138, 216
Elisha, 106, 111, 122, 138
Elishama, 174
Elnathan, 190, 202, 208
Elohist writer, 60, 139, 181
Elon, 28, 41

Eltekeh, 148
Emmaus, 245, 248
Ephraim, 3, 10, 20, 29, 30, 38, 39, 44, 51, 59, 68, 96, 99, 100, 102, 134
Ephrathah, 27
Ephron, 246
Eponym, 90, 128, 130, 136, 153
eponymous ancestor, 27–29, 38
Eretria, 200
Esagila, 89
Esarhaddon, 84, 151–53
Eshem-Bethel, 210
Eshtaol, 31
Essenes, 253, 254
Esther, 191, 204, 206, 217, 259
Ethbaal, 62, 104, 105
ethnicity, 7, 8, 16, 18, 21, **22–23**, 29, 33, 37, 44, 45, 59, 73, 82, 107, 176, 188, 207, 259
Eusebius, 230
Evil-Merodach, 168, 171, 172
Execration texts, 5, 31
exile(s), 42, 143, 148, 150, 162, 166, 170, 171, 176, 180, 181, 185, 187, 221, 263
exodus tradition, 23, 40, 42, 92, 139, 181
exogamy, 27
Ezekiel, 124, 159, 163, 169, 171, **180**, 191, 215
Ezion-geber, 64
Ezra, 169, 181, 184, 190, 193, 195, 196, **204–5**, 207, 212, 216–18
Ezra-Nehemiah, 191, **193–97**, 204–7, **217–18**
famine, 13, 14, 165, 172, 206, 247, 248
father's house, **26–27**
Fayum, 231
Feast of Booths, 97, 205, 255
folktales, 24, 31, 37–39, 40, 41, 46, 54, 55, 62, 63, 76, 97, 104, 105, 111, 138, 220, 259, 262
forced labor, 56, 57, 63, 64, 66, 67, 107, 126, 151
four-room house, 21, 22, 27, 97
Gaal, 41
Gad, 29, 31, 40, 72, 105, 113

Gadara, 255
Gaius Popilius Laenas, 242
Galilee, 9, 10, 20, 49, 51, 69, 96, 103, 124, 131, 136, 161, 190, 202, 224, 231, 233, 246, 250, 254, 255, 257
Gath, 7, 10, 34, 54, 64, 120, 148
Gaugamela, 213, 226
Gaumata, 199. *See also* Bardiya, Smerdis
Gaza, 6, 34, 130, 145, 146, 150, 160, 162, 206, 226, 227, 230, 231, 233, 236, 255
Gazara, 245, 248, 251. *See also* Gezer
Geba, 102
Geber, 70
geber (nuclear family), 26
Gedaliah (governor), 143, **170**, 174
Gedaliah (son of Pashur), 174
Gemariah, 174
Gerizim, 10, 191, 223, 228, 243, 252, 254
Geshem, 207
Geshur, 45, 53, 98
Gezer, 7, 10, 15, 16, 34, 58, 63, 64, 74–76, 97, 125, 136, 169, 206, 245. *See also* Gazara
Gezer Calendar, 12
Gibbethon, 102, 104
Gibeah, 44, 50, 52, 55
Gibeon, 16, 50, 51, 54, 99, 169
Gibeonites, 50, 51, 99
Gideon, 26, 28, 39, 41, 46, 52
Gilboa, 50–52, 77
Gilead, 11, 20, 27, 28, 30, 31, 39, 44, 50–52, 57, 70, 72, 82, 103, 114, 117, 127, 129–31, 145, 158, 246
Gilgal, 60, 248
Gobryas, 186
Goliath, 36, 53
Gophna, 244, 238
Gordium, 226
Gorgias, 245, 246
Granicus, 213, 226
grave traditions, 30, 38, 39, 50, 76, 87, 138
Gyges, 153
Habakkuk, 178
Habiru, 7, 55. *See also* Apiru
Habur, 18

SUBJECT INDEX

Hachilah, 54
Hadad (person), 66, 99
Hadad (god), 67
Hadadezer (Damascus), 108–10, 113, 114. See also Adad-idri, Ben-Hadad
Hadad-ezer (Zobah), 55
Hadiyani, 124
Haggai, 196, 198, 201, 202, 207, **214**
Hakor, 212
Halicarnassus, 226
Halys, 90, 185, 186
Hamath, 5, 8, 108, 122, 124, 128, 130, 135, 145, 165
Hamutal, 161
Hananiah (Elephantine), 210
Hananiah (governor of Samaria), 209
Hananiah (governor of Yehud), 208
Hananiah (prophet), 171
Hannah, 29
Hannah's Song, 77
Hannathon, 131
Hannibal, 237
Hanukkah, 245, 252, 258
Hanun, 55, 61, 98
Harran, 154, 159, 161, 172
Hasidim, 244, 247
Hasmoneans, 87, 224, 225, 238, 240, 252–54, 257, 260
Hattusa, 32
Hattusili III, 5, 8
Havvoth-jair, 28, 129
Hazael, 83, 84, 108–10, 113–18, 120–22
Hazar-enan, 27
Hazor, 3, 7, 9, 17, 42, 58, 63–65, 74–76, 97, 103, 125, 131, 136, 248, 250
Hebron, 9, 10, 29, 38, 44, 50, 53, 55, 57, 59, 60, 74, 147, 169, 189, 246, 252
Hecataeus of Abdera, 230
Hefzibah Inscription, 238
Heliodorus, 239, 258
Heliodorus Stela, 239
Heliopolis, 247
Hepher, 17, 68
ḥerem, 24, 113
Herem-Bethel, 210

Herod the Great, 225, 257
Herodotus, 149, 160, 162, 184, 192, 199
Heshbon, 11, 98, 105
Hezekiah (governor), 209. See also Yehezqiyah.
Hezekiah (king), 54, 58, 65, 84, 87, 93, 95, 96, 121, 131, 134, 142, **144–49**, 150, 151, 157, 158, 176, 178, 219
Hezekiah (priest), 230
Hezion, 98, 103, 124
Hezron, 27
Hilkiah, 150, 156, 174
hill country of Ephraim, 50, 51, 57, 72, 82, 84, 131
Hiram (artisan), 63
Hiram (eighth century king), 128
Hiram (tenth century king), 61, 62
Hissil-el, 86
Hittite Empire, 4–8, 13
Hittites, 13, 14, 17, 32, 33, 40, 55
Holiness Code, 219
Holofernes, 250
Homer, 33, 36, 40
Hophni, 42
Hophra, 164, 165. See also Apries
Horesh, 54
Hormah, 40
Horonan, 113
Hosea, 42, 89, 124, 125, 128, 136, 138, 175, 215
Hoshea, 84, 85, 92, 93, 95, 130–32, **134–36**, 144
Hoshiah, 164
House of David, 32, 53, 58, 62, 83, 115, 116
House of Omri, 32, 104, 108. See also Bit-Omri
Hurrians, 5, 42
Hyksos, 4, 6
Hyrcanus (Tobiad), 238, 249
Hyrcanus II (high priest), 229, 256, 257
Hystaspes, 199
Ibleam, 51, 125, 128
Ibni-Addu, 42. See also Jabin
Idrimi, 55

Idumea, 189, 200, 224, 225, 231, 245, 246, 252, 256, 257. *See also* Edom
Idumean(s), 189, 225, 246, 252, 256
Ijon, 103, 131
Inaros, 203
Indus, 200
Instruction of Amenemope, 219
Ipsus, 230
Ira, 57
Iraq al-Amir, 238
Irhuleni, 108
Iron, 14, 20
Isaiah
Isaiah (governor of Samaria), 209
Isaiah (prophet), 59, 61, 89, 130, 132, 133, 138, 144, 150, 177, **178**
Isaiah Apocalypse, 261
Ishbaal, 44, 50, 51, 56, 57, 72, 76, 78
Ishmael, 23, 38
Ishmael (seal), 174
Ishmael (son of Nethaniah), 170, 171
Ishmaelites, 45
Isin, Second Dynasty of, 4
Israel King List, 86, 91, 94
Issachar, 28, 30, 39, 72, 102
Issus, 213, 226
Itto-baal III, 171
Itureans, 254
'Izbet Ṣarṭah Abecedary, 14
Jaazaniah, 170
Jabbok, 11. *See also* Wadi Zerqa
Jabin, 41. *See also* Ibni-Addu
Jacob, 26, 29, 31, 38, 59
Jaddua, 209, 227–29, 231
Jael, 24, 41
Jahaz, 105, 113
Jair, 28, 57
Jamnia, 246, 248–50
Janoah, 103, 131
Jarmuth, 8
Jason (high priest) 229, 239–42
Jason of Cyrene, 258
Jaush, 164
Jazer, 246
Jebus, 49

Jebusite, 49, 65, 70
Jedaniah, 210, 211
Jedaniah archive, 210
Jedidiah, 61
Jehoahaz (Israel), 83, 110, 117, 120–22
Jehoahaz (Judah), 49, 85, 143, 155, **161**, 163
Jehoash (Israel), 83, 84, 92, 94, 109, 110, **121–22**, 123, 124, 126, 128
Jehoash (Judah), 83, 92, 96, 118, 119, **120–21**, 123, 125, 156, 173
Jehoiachin, 85, 143, **162–63**, 164, 167–69, 171, 172, 176, 191, 196, 197, 201
Jehoiada (priest)
Jehoiakim, 96, 143, 154, 155, **161–62**, 163, 166, 179
Jehoram (Israel), 92, 83, 85, 92–94, 106, 109, 110, **111–14**, 115–17, 121
Jehoram (Judah), 92–94, 103, 111, **114**, 115, 118
Jehoshaphat (king), 65, 67, 85, 93, 101, 103, 106, **110–11**, 113, 114
Jehoshaphat (son of Ahilud), 57
Jehozarah, 150
Jehu (king), 83, 84, 92, 94, 95, 108, 110, 111, 113–15, **116–18**, 119–22, 128, 136
Jehu (prophet), 104
Jephthah, 21, 26, 39, 41
Jerahme-el (kinship group), 31, 99
Jerahmeel (seal), 174
Jeremiah, 37, 157, 159, 161, 163–67, 171, 174, 177, **179**, 202, 215, 263
Jericho, 10, 106, 165, 189, 227, 233, 252, 256
Jeroboam I, 42, 59, 66, 72, 93, 94, 96, 97, 99, **100–101**, 104, 124, 156
Jeroboam II, 83, 121, **123–24**, 125, 126, 137, 138
Jerusalem Pomegranate, 173
Jezebel, 104, 106, 118
Jezreel (city), 39, 44, 51, 115
Jezreel Valley, 7, 10, 12, 19, 26, 30, 49–51, 75, 102, 131, 134, 238
Joab, 27, 53, 54, 56, 57, 60
Joash, 60

SUBJECT INDEX

Job, 220
Joel, 216
Johanan, 202, 209, 211, 229
John Hyrcanus, 224, 229, 251, **252-54**, 257, 258
Joiada, 208
Joiakim, 208
Jonah, 124, 217
Jonathan (Maccabee), 224, 229, 244, **248-50**, 251, 253, 254, 258
Jonathan (son of Saul), 50-52, 62, 77, 78
Joppa, 6, 9, 146, 148, 189, 235, 246, 249
Jordan Valley, 7, 9, 10, 19, 68, 72, 105, 134, 250
Joseph, 26, 29, 30, 40, 99, 205
Joseph (Tobiad), 235, 238
Josephus, 62, 105, 135, 149, 162, 167, 193, 208, 209, 227-31, 234, 237-40, 243, 247, 252, 253
Joshua (book), 17, 29, 39, 40, 68, 72, 155, 156, 176
Joshua (brother of Johanan), 209
Joshua (hero), 38, 60
Joshua (high priest), 201, 202, 208, 214, 215
Josiah, 49, 65, 93, 95, 120-21, 142-44, 153, **154-61**, 167, 173-74, 176, 178-79
Jotbah, 96, 131
Jotham (king), 95, 125, **132**, 137, 144
Jotham (son of Gideon), 60
Jucal, 174
Judah (region), 11, 12, 15, 20, 30, 31, 45, 50, 57
Judah (tribe), 3, 27, 29, 31, 73, 82, 96, 99
Judah King List, 53, 86, 94, 118
Judas Maccabee, 224, **244-48**, 251, 258
judges, 23, 28, 41, 46, 52, 55, 205
Judith, 217, **259-60**
Julius Caesar, 225
Justin, 230
Kalhu, 107
Kanah, 30
Kandalanu, 154
Karnaim, 124, 130, 246
Karnak battle reliefs, 16

Karnak (Bubastite Portal), 100
Karnak inscription, 13, 33
Kashiari, 108
Kassites, 4, 5, 13
Kedesh, 103, 131
Keilah, 54, 189
Kemosh, 112, 113
Kemosh-yatti, 98, 112
Kenites, 30, 40
Kenizzites, 99
Kennaz, 31
Ketef Hinnom amulets, 173
Khirbet Beit Lei, 166
Khirbet es-Sil, 172
Khirbet Qeiyafa, 10, 64. See also Shaaraim
Khirbet-el-Qôm, 136
Khorsabad, 107, 145
Kidron, 251
king lists, 53, 62, 86, 87, 91, 92, 99, 239
King's Highway, 98, 99, 252
King's Peace (Peace of Antalkidas), 212
Kings (books). See 1 and 2 Kings
kinship, 3, 15, 25-29, 32, 44-47, 49, 53, 82, 96, 126, 217
Kir-hareseth, 11, 98, 113
Kiriath-baal, 23
Kiriath-jearim, 77, 99
Kish, 50
Kishon, 24
Kittim, 173
Kuntillet ʿAjrûd, 136
Labashi-Marduk, 172
Labayu, 7
Lachish, 7, 10, 17, 18, 34, 35, 123, 126, 146-48, 150, 151, 155, 158, 165, 169, 174, 190, 202
Lachish letters, 164
Lade, 200
Laish, 31. See also Dan (city)
Lamentations, 179
Laodice, 233, 234
Large Stone Structure, 76
law, 28, 47, 66, 120, 126, 137, 155, 158, 167, 175, 176, 181, 185, 190, 195, 196, 205, 212, 219, 244, 253, 260

Leah, 30
Lebo-hamath, 124
Lehi, 41
Leiden Papyrus, 42
Leontopolis, 228, 247
Letter of Aristeas, 193, 230, 233, 234
Letter of Jeremiah, 263
levirate custom, 27, 28
Levitical cities, 55
Libnah, 114, 148, 155, 161
Libyans, 8, 13, 15, 16, 33, 198
lists, 23, 29, 30, 39, 48, 50, 55, 56, 62, 66–71, 76, 100, 148, 153, 189, 193
lmlk jar stamps, 146, 147, 159
Lod, 189
Lo-debar, 124
low chronology, 3, 23, **34–35**, 75
Lukka, 32, 33. *See also* Lycia
Lutibu, 107
Lycia, 33, 205. *See also* Lukka
Lydia, 153, 184–86, 188, 204, 212
Lysias, 245–47
Lysimachus, 240
Maacah (person), 101
Maacah (place), 55, 98
Maccabees (books). *See* 1 Maccabees; 2 Maccabees
Machir, 31, 39
Machpelah, 31
Mahanaim, 44, 51, 70, 72
Mahaneh-dan, 31, 40
Makaz, 69
Maktesh, 152
Malachi, 215, 216
Mamre, 29, 38
Manasseh (brother of Jaddua), 228, 234
Manasseh (high priest), 229
Manasseh (king), 84, 96, 121, 142, **151–53**, 154–56, 158, 175, 178
Manasseh (tribe), 13, 20, 26, 28–31, 57, 68, 72, 99, 102, 105
Maoch, 36
Marathon, 301
Mardonius, 200, 203
Marduk, 89, 172, 186, 187

Mari documents, 19, 42
marriage
    diplomatic, 3, 6, 8, 53, 60, 61, 63, 65, 104, 106, 114, 118, 159, 233, 259
    mixed, 33, 189, 204, 295, 207, 209, 216, 228
Marisa, 245, 246, 252
maryannu, 7, 19
marzeaḥ, 210
Matrites, 27
Mattaniah, 163
Mattathias, 229, 244
Medeba, 98, 105, 112, 252
Medes, 152–54, 159–61, 185, 187, 143, 186
Median Empire, 184, 186
Medinet Habu, 33
Megabyzus, 194, 203, 204
Megiddo, 3, 6, 7, 10, 17, 18, 34, 35, 51, 58, 63, 64, 72, 74–76, 97, 100, 125, 127, 130, 131, 137, 158, 160, 206
Melqart, 105
Melqart Stela, 109
Memphis, 152, 153, 193, 198, 241
Menahem, 83, 84, 88, 95, **128–29**, 130, 133, 136
Menander of Ephesus, 105, 135
Menelaus, 229, 238, 240
Merari, 42
Meribbaal, 50, 56, 127
Merneptah, 8, 13–17, 33, 34, 40
Merneptah Stela, 2, 15, 16
Merodach-baladan, 84, 134, 144–46, 151
Mesad Hashavyahu, 155
Mesha, 83, 84, 98, 111–14
Mesha Inscription, 31, 40, 53, 90, 105, **112–13**
Mibtahiah archive, 210
Mica, 51, 56
Micah (prophet), 89, 138, **177**
Micah (seal), 174
Micaiah, 138
Michal, 53, 56
Michmash, 249
Middle Assyrian Empire, 4, 5

Middle Bronze Age, 21
Midgol, 162
Midian, Day of, 24, 41
Midianites, 45, 47
Miletus, 32, 200
Milkom-or, 174
Millo, 64, 120
minor judges, 28, 41, 55
Mishneh, 147, 152
Mitanni, 4–8
Mithridates IV, 255, 256
Mizpah, 74, 102, 169–71, 189, 190, 245
mmsht, 147
Moab, 11, 18, 45, 52, 55, 83, 89, 98, 99, 103–6, 110–14, 117, 128, 148, 164, 167, 200
Moabitis, 255
Modein, 244, 251
Monochrome pottery, 3, 23, 35, 36
Moresheth, 177
Moses, 38, 42, 99, 181, 195, 253
Mount Ephraim, 30. *See also* hill country of Ephraim
Mozah, 136, 170, 190
Murashu archives, 191
Mursili I, 4, 5
Muwatalli II, 5, 8
Mycale, 203
Mycenae(an), 4, 13, 14, 36
Naamah, 60
Nabal, 53
Nabateans, 233, 235, 250, 255, 256
Nabonidus, 143, 172, 186, 187, 196
Nabonidus Chronicle, 185
Nabopolassar, 143, 154, 159–62
Naboth, 28
Nabu-nasir, 90
Nadab (king), 90
Nadab (son of Aaron), 100
Nagasuites, 7
Nahash, 52, 61, 98
Nahum, 159, 160, **178**
Naphath-dor, 72
Naphtali, 29, 39, 64, 71, 72, 103, 131
Nathan, 57, 67, 71

Nebo, 113
Nebo-sarsekim, 166
Nebuchadnezzar I, 5
Nebuchadnezzar II, 66, 143, 159, 161–69, 171, 172, 180, 185, 191
Nebuchadnezzar III, 192
Nebuzaradan, 165, 166, 171
Neco I, 152, 153
Neco II, 42, 143, 154, 155, 159–63, 188
Negev, 11, 20, 31, 33, 100, 125, 180
Nehemiah, 184, 193, 204, **205–7**, 208, 209, 216, 218, 233
Nehemiah Memoir, 205–7
Nehushtan, 144
Nephtoah, Waters of, 15, 40
Nergal-sharzer, 166
Neriglissar, 172
Nicanor, 245, 248, 258
Nicanor, Day of, 248, 258
Nikaso, 228
Nimrud, 108
Nimrud Ivories, 136
Nimshi, 136
Nineveh, 107, 136, 143, 151, 159, 178, 217, 226
Nippur, 143, 170, 191
Nisan, 91, 167, 168, 191
No-Amon, 96, 151, 153. *See also* Thebes
nonaccession year, 91, 93–95, 112
Nubia, 8, 146, 148, 152, 164
Obadiah, 169, **180**
Obodas I, 255
Odysseus, 55
Og, 41
Omri, 32, 60, 63, 75, 83–85, 93, 97, 101–3, **104–5**, 108, 112, 114
Omride dynasty, 62, 75, 83, 103, 116, 117
Oniads, 235, 241
Onias I, 229, 231
Onias II, 229, 234, 235, 238
Onias III, 229, 231, 235, 238–40, 247
Onias IV, 229, 235, 239, 247
Ono, 189
Onomasticon of Amenope, 34
Ophel Inscription, 76

Ophel Ostracon, 173
Ophrah, 28, 39, 155
Opis, 186
Oreb, 41
Orontes, 5, 6, 8, 108, 124
Osorkon IV, 134, 145
Othniel, 27, 31, 73
Oxus, 186
Padi, 146, 148
Pahil, 8. *See also* Pella
Palshtu, 122
Pamphylia, 226, 242
Panamuwa Inscription, 131
Panias (Paneion), 224, 231, 232, 236–38. *See also* Banyas
papponymy, 208, 229
Papyrus Harris I, 33
Parmenion, 227
Parthia, 251–53
Parysatis, 227
Pasargadae, 185–87, 200, 226
Passover, 42, 156, 167, 202, 210, 211
Pastoralists, 7, 8, 16, 17, 19–21, 23, 24, 31, 53, 98
Patros, 193
Pazarcik Stela, 124
Callias, Peace of, 203
Pedaiah, 196
Pediese, 164
Pekah, 84, 95, 128, **129–32**, 133
Pekahiah, 84, 96, 128, 129, 133
Pelaiah, 174
Pelasgoi, 35
Peleset, 32–35. *See also* Philistines
Pelusium, 148, 198, 231
Pella, 18, 231, 235, 256. *See also* Pahil
Peloponnesian War, 204, 210, 212
Peniel (Penuel), 23, 38, 59, 100
people of the land, 49, 126, 132, 154, 158, 161, 165, 190
Perazim, Mount, 54
Perdiccas, 227
Perea, 257
Perez, 27
Perez-uzzah, 64

Periplous of Skylax, 189
Per-Ramses, 8
Persepolis, 200, 226
Pharisees, 253, 255, 256
Phasael, 257
Philadelphia, 231, 235, 256. *See also* Rabbath-ammon
Philip (regent), 247
Philip II, 213, 225
Philip V, 236, 237
Philistines, 3, 17, 18, 22, 23, 31, **32–37**, 40, 41, 47, 50–52, 54, 57, 74, 75, 77, 102, 128, 130, 134, 144–46, 148
Philo, 253, 254, 261
Philoteria, 231
Phineas, 42
Phoenicia, 7, 9, 10, 18, 63, 130, 190, 200, 212, 213, 226, 239
Phrygia, 152, 226, 230, 232
Piankhy, 146
pilgrimage, 30, 38
Pirathon, 55
plastered cisterns, 21, 24
Plataea, 203
Pliny the Elder, 253, 254
Plutarch, 225, 230
Polybius, 230
Pompey, 225, 256, 257
pork avoidance, 22, 37, 64, 97
pottery, 3, 14, 17, 20, 23, 35, 36, 65, 75, 155
poverty, 126, 137, 166, 125–27, 215, 218
Priestly writing, 54, 139, **181**, 212, 219
prophet narratives, 59, 88, 89, 100, 106, 109–16, 122, 133, 138, 144, 146, 149, 150
Prosopitis, 203
Proverbs, 65, 219
Psalms, 42, 59, 178, 181, **182**, 202, 215, 218, **220–21**
Psamtik I, 90, 153, 154, 193
Psamtik II, 164, 193
Psamtik III, 98, 203
Ptolemais, 231, 233, 235, 246, 249, 250, 255, 256. *See also* Acco

Ptolemy (commander), 245
Ptolemy (son of Abubus), 251, 252
Ptolemy (son of Dorymenes), 241
Ptolemy I Soter, **230-32**
Ptolemy II Philadelphus, 229, 231, 232, **233-34**
Ptolemy III Euergetes, 229, 232, **234-35**
Ptolemy IV Philopator, 229, 232, 233, **235-36**
Ptolemy V Epiphanes, 232, 234, 236, 237, 239
Ptolemy VI Philometor, 232, 239, 241, 242, 249, 250
Ptolemy VIII Euergetes II, 242
Ptolemy IX Lathyrus, 255, 259
Ptolemy XII, 259
Puah, 28
purity, 22, 97, 181, 185, 192, 207, 214
Pylos, 13
Qadesh on Orontes, 5, 8, 33, 160
Qarqar, 83, 94, 106, 108, 109, 111-13, 117, 145
qāṣîn, 29
Qatsra-yadi, 30
qĕdēšîm, 111
Qoheleth (Ecclesiastes), 219, 260
queen mother, 86, 101, 118
Queen of Sheba, 63
Qumran, 220, 240, 253, 254, 260, 263
Rabbath-ammon (Rabbah), 11, 56, 98, 231. *See also* Philadelphia
Rabshakeh, 149, 150
Rachel, 26, 30
Ragaba, 256
Ramah, 102
Ramat Rahel, 147, 161, 164, 169, 190
Ramathaim-zophim, 27
Ramesses II, 4, 5, 8, 16, 17, 23, 30, 33, 42, 86, 98
Ramesses III, 13, 17, 18, 33, 34, 45
Ramesses IV, 18
Ramesses VI, 18, 34, 45
Ramoth-gilead, 11, 72, 113-15
Raphia, 232, 235, 236, 238, 255
Raphon, 246

Rehob, 7, 8
Rehoboam, 53, 58-61, 65, 74, 93, 94, 97, 98, **99-100**, 101, 102
Rephaim, 40
resistance policy, 83, 84, 107, 117, 128-30, 142, 145, 146, 151, 158, 164, 179
Rezin, 84, 128-33
Rezon, 66, 98
Riblah, 161, 165
Rimah Stela, 122
Rise of David, 76, 78
Rock of Escape, 54
Rome, 224, 225, 237, 238, 244, 245, 247-49, 255-58
Rosetta Stone, 237
rō'š, 29
Roxana, 227
Royal Road, 188
Royal Steward Epitaph, 150
Rumah, 96, 161
Ruth, 217, 260
sacrifice, 11, 28, 29, 38, 112, 132, 156-58, 195, 202, 209, 211, 212, 216
Sadducees, 253, 256, 260
Sais, 134, 198
Saite Dynasty, 90, 152, 153, 198
Salamis, 203
Samaga, 252
Samaria (city), 63, 83, 84, 87, 90, 95, 97, 105, 110, 125, 128, 130, 131, 134-36, 144, 145, 158, 171, 177, 227, 230, 253, 257
Samaria (region), 10, 19, 127, 135, 136, 145, 156, 158, 185, 189-91, 193, 194, 200, 206, 207, 209, 211, 227, 231, 243, 244, 253, 257
Samaria ostraca, 27, 68, 89, 126, 137
Samaria papyri, 228. *See also* Wadi ed-Daliyeh
Samaritan temple, 191, 209, 228, 252
Samaritans, 253, 254, 257, 260
Samson, 24, 31, 37, 39, 41, 52
Samuel, 27, 52, 77, 78
Samuel (books). *See* 1 and 2 Samuel
Sanballat I, 190, 193, 207, 209, 211

Sanballat II, 209
Sanballat III, 209, 227, 228
sanctuaries, local, 28, 29, 37, 38, 49, 78, 97, 100, 174
sanctuary etiologies, 31, 38, 39, 54, 100
sar, 29, 126
Sarcophagus Inscription of Eshmunazor, 101
Sardis, 186, 200, 212, 226
Sargon II, 61, 84, 107, 127, 135, 136, 145, 146, 152
Satire on Trades, 260
satrap, 184, 187, 188, 194, 200, 203, 205, 211–13, 226
satrapy, 184, 191, 196, 200, 206
Saul, 27, 32, 39, 44–47, **49–53**, 55–57, 61, 72–74, 76–79, 82, 98
Saulide, 50, 56, 78, 79
Sayings, 37, 38, 50, 51, 54, 76
Scopas, 236
Scythians, 152, 200
Scythopolis, 231, 234, 235, 246, 250, 253. *See also* Beth-shean
Sea People, 6, 8, 13, 14, 17, 31–33, 40
Sea-Land, 134, 154
Second Isaiah, **180–81**, 194, 204
sedentarization, 16, 20, 21, 49, 98
Sefire Treaty, 123
segmentary society, **25–26**, 46
Seleucia (Golan), 231
Seleucia (port of Antioch), 234, 235
Seleucus I, 230
Seleucus II Callinicus, 90, 232, 234
Seleucus III Ceraunus, 235
Seleucus IV Philopater, 232, 238, 239, 247, 258
Seleucus V, 251
Seneh, 50
Sennacherib, 84, 87, 107, 131, 142, 144, 146–52, 157, 177
Septuagint, 38, 56, 65, 68, 72, 93, 106, 111, 177, 216, 220, 233, 247, 259, 263
Seraiah (priest), 208
Seraiah (seal), 174
Seraiah (Solomonic official), 56
Seron, 244
Seti I, 4, 8, 17
Shaalbim, 64
Shaaraim, 10, 64. *See also* Khirbet Qeiyafa
Shabaka, 146, 148
Shagar, 136
Shalem, 61
Shallum, 83, 92, 128
Shalmaneser I, 5
Shalmaneser III, 83, 84, 89, 94, 105, 107, 108, 113, 116, 117
Shalmaneser IV, 123, 124, 135, 144, 145, 146
Shalmaneser V, 84, 127, 134
Shamash-shum-ukin, 104, 152, 153
Shamgar, 39, 41, 42
Shammah, 41
Shamshi-adad V, 117
Shaphan, 126, 170, 174
Sharon, 9, 263
Sharuhen, 6
Shasu, 7–9, 15, 16, 23.
Shealtiel, 196
Sheba, 51
Shebnah, 150
Shechem, 6, 7, 9, 10, 16, 17, 19, 24, 26, 27, 29–31, 38, 41, 44, 45, 49, 59, 60, 64, 73, 82, 96, 100, 158, 171, 191, 228, 246, 252
Shekelesh, 33
Shelemiah (seal), 174
Shelemiah (son of Sanballet), 209, 211
Shelomith, 202
Shema, 137
Shemaiah, 138
Shemer, 105
Shenazzar, 197
Shephelah, 9, 31, 114, 123, 142, 147, 152, 155, 161, 166, 169, 177, 189
Sherden, 33, 34
Sheshbazzar, 191, 195–98, 207, 217
Sheva, 56
Shiloh, 19, 29, 37, 59, 60, 77, 78, 104, 171
Shimʿon, 7. *See also* Shimron
Shimei, 51, 79

Shimron, 7, 27, 125. *See also* Shimʿon
Shisha, 56, 66
Shishak, 42, 70, 73, 75, 82, 87, 94, 97, 99, 100
Shobi, 98
Sidon, 18, 101, 106, 146, 147, 150, 152, 164, 165, 189, 212, 213, 226, 236, 246
Sihon, 41, 105
Siloam, 90, 147
Simeon, 6, 29–31, 72, 73, 82, 96, 99
Simon (brother of Menelaus), 238–40
Simon (Maccabee), 224, 229, 243, 244, 246, 248, 250–52, 258
Simon I, 229, 231, 234
Simon II (the Just), 227, 229, 235, 238, 260
Sin, 172
Sinai, 9, 23, 137, 253
Sin-shar-ishkun, 143, 154, 159
Sinuhe, 6
Sippar, 191
Sirach, 191, 238, 260, 263
Sisera, 42
Siwa, 226
Smerdis, 199. *See also* Bardiya, Gaumata
So, 134
Socoh, 10, 64, 68, 70, 147
Sogdianus, 209
Solar Temple (Lachish), 202
Solomon, 44–46, 48, 53, 56, **60–73**, 74–76, 78, 79, 82, 85, 87, 92, 96–100, 106, 111, 116, 124, 156, 202, 219, 257, 261–63
Solomonic polity, 45, 48, 59, 70–72, **73**, 96
Song of Songs, **262–63**
Song of the Bow, 38, 50, 77
songs, 24, 37, 38, 41, 50, 53, 77, 175, 179
Sorek, 10, 251
Sosibius, 235, 236
Sparta, 201, 203, 210, 212, 229, 231, 242
statehood, 25, 44, 45, 47, **48–49**, 74
Stateira, 227
Stepped Stone Structure, 64
Strabo, 198

Strato's Tower, 255
Sua of Gilzanu, 118
subsistence agriculture, **11–12**, 21, 22, 24, 47, 138
Sulla, 255
summary citations, 62, **84–86**, 99, 104, 117, 135
Suppiluliuma I, 5
Susa, 153, 187, 188, 200, 206, 226, 227, 259
Syene, 231
Synchronisms, 58, 88, 91, **92–94**, 95, 104, 114, 116, 120, 123, 124, 132
Synchronistic Chronicle, 86, 92
Synchronistic History, 89
Synchronistic King List, 92
Syracuse, 210
Syrian Wars (monarchy period), 89, 94, 110
Syrian Wars (Hellenistic period), 232–37, 41
Syro-Ephraimite War, 132
Taanach, 51, 72, 158, 159
Tabal, 146
Tabeal, 133
Tabnit, 189
Tabor, 29, 39, 60
Tabrimmon, 98, 101, 103, 109
Taharqa, 148, 152, 153. *See also* Tirhaka
Tahpanhes, 193
Tamar, 64
Tanis, 18, 134
Tantamani, 153
Tarsus, 32
Tarsus
Tattenai, 195, 200
Teiman, 172
Teispes, 185, 199
Tel Abib, 170, 191
Tel Dan inscription, 53, 58, 90, 111, 115, 118
Tel ʿIra Census Ostracon, 173
Tel Masos, 35
Tel Motza, 136
Tel Rehov, 136

Tel-harsha 120, 131, 134, 185, 192, 224, 233, 240, 246, 255–57
Tel-melah, 170, 191
Tell Beit Mirsim, 164
Tell el-Farʿah, 3, 10. See also Tirzah
Tell el-Hesi, 190
Tell el-Yehudyeh, 247
Tell es-Safi, 10. See also Gath
Tell Halaf, 18. See also Bit-Bahyani
Tell Malat, 112. See also Gibbethon
Tell Maresha, 239
Tell Qasile, 35, 173
Tell Qasile ostraca, 173
Tell Siran, 86
Tell Tayinat, 65
Teman, 158
Tennes, 213
terraces, 20, 21, 24, 28
Thebes, 96, 151, 153, 178, 231. See also No-Amon
Thermopylae, 203
Third Isaiah, 215
Thrace, 200
Three Shekel Temple Gift, 173
Thutmose III, 4, 6, 31
Thutmose IV, 4, 6
Tibni, 85, 93, 101, 103, 104
Tiglath-pileser I, 13
Tiglath-pileser III, 61, 83, 84, 103, 123, 127, 128, 130–34, 142, 146
Tigranes II, 256
Timothy, 246
Tirhaka, 148. See also Taharqa
Tirzah, 10, 27, 65, 87, 102, 105, 125, 128, 129. See also Tell el-Farʿah
Tishri, 91, 167, 168, 197
Tjeker, 6, 18, 33, 34
Tobiad Romance, 193, 234
Tobiads, 193, 207, 233–36, 238, 240, 242
Tobiah, 193, 207, 233
Tobit, 217, 259
Tola, 28, 41
trade, 4, 5, 9–12, 14, 18, 20, 24, 25, 40, 47, 63, 98, 105, 122, 125, 126, 146, 172, 190, 206, 207, 227, 230, 233, 252
Transjordan, 9–11, 30, 68, 69, 72, 98, 117,

tribute, 48, 65, 83, 84, 87, 88, 94, 95, 103, 105–8, 111, 116–18, 121, 122, 124, 127–31, 133–35, 143 144, 147, 149, 150, 161, 188, 234, 237, 238, 240, 252
tribe, 3, 26, **29–31**, 32, 39, 41, 49, 82
Troy, 32
Trypho, 248, 250, 251,
Tukulti-ninurta I, 5, 13
Turin Canon, 77
Tursha , 33
Tyre, 18, 62, 104–6, 128, 135, 146, 147, 152, 164, 165, 171, 180, 189, 212, 226, 227, 235, 241, 246
Tyre King List, 62
Udjahorresnet, 198, 205
Ugarit, 13, 18, 32, 39, 70, 87
united kingdom, 47, **58–60**, 67
Urartu, 123, 127, 130, 145, 151, 152, 186
urbanization, 13, 20, 74, 125, 126
Uriah (Hittite), 55, 56, 61
Uriah (prophet), 161
Urio, 208
usurpation, 83, 84, 88, 94, 96, 101, 102, 105, 109, 115, 117–20, 145, 172, 188, 197, 239, 247
Uzza, Garden of, 54
Uzziah, 83, 95, 123, 125. See also Azariah
Vahyazdata, 199
Van, Lake, 5, 13
Vassal Treaties of Esarhaddon, 142, 153, 175
Verse Account of Nabonidus, 172, 186
Vidranga, 199
Wadi Besor, 252
Wadi ed-Daliyeh, 190, 209, 227. See also Samaria papyri
Wadi Farʿah, 10
Wadi Feinan, 98
Wadi Hesa, 11. See also Zered
Wadi Mujib, 11. See also Arnon
Wadi Suweinit, 50
Wadi Zerqa, 11. See also Jabbok
Warka, 170

Way of the Sea, 115
Weidner Chronicle, 89
Wen-Amon, 6, 18, 23
Widows Plea, 173
Wisdom of Solomon, 219, 261
women, status of, 41, 210
Xenophon, 184, 186, 192, 212
Xerxes I, 191, 196, 200, 203, 204, 259
Xerxes II, 209
Yahwist writer, 60, 139, 181
Yam, 101
Yanoam, 15, 16
Yarmuk, 10, 11
Yaubidi, 145
Yeb, 210, 211. *See also* Elephantine
Yehawmilk, 189
Yehezqiyah, 208. *See also* Hezekiah
Yehoezer, 208
Yehud, 185, 189–92, 198, 200, 202–8, 211, 213, 230
Yurza, 34
Zabud, 57, 67
Zadok (priest), 56, 57, 67, 69
Zadok (seal), 184
Zadokites, 238, 240, 249, 253, 254
Zagros, 185
Zakkur Inscription, 109, 122
Zaphon, 23
Zekariah, 174
Zebulun, 28, 39
Zechariah (king), 83, 92, 96, 128
Zechariah (prophet), 191, 196, 198, 201, 202, **214–15**, 216
Zedekiah (king), 85, 92, 143, 161, **163–64**, 165–69, 179, 180
Zedekiah (prophet), 171
Zelah, 50
Zelophehad, 26
Zenon papyri, 193, 233, 235
Zephaniah, 178
Zerah (clan), 27
Zerah (Cushite), 103
Zered, 11, 98. *See also* Wadi Hesa
Zerubbabel, 181, 191, 194, 196–98, **201–2**, 207, 208, 214, 215

Zeus, 243
Ziba, 79, 127
Zibiah, 119
Ziklag, 54, 57
Zimri, 85, 92–94, 96, 101–4
Zion, 54, 59, 178, 181, 182, 215
Ziph, 144
Zoar, 255
Zobah, 45, 52, 55, 56, 66, 98
Zopyrus, 203
Zorah, 31
Zoroastrianism, 192
Zuphite clan, 27

www.ingramcontent.com/pod-product-compliance
Lightning Source LLC
Chambersburg PA
CBHW020056020526
44112CB00031B/199